REVELATION
AND THE
BIBLE

Contemporary Evangelical Thought

REVELATION AND THE BIBLE

Contemporary Evangelical Thought

G. C. BERKOUWER

GEOFFREY W. BROMILEY

F. F. BRUCE

GORDON H. CLARK

R. A. FINLAYSON

FRANK E. GAEBELEIN

J. NORVAL GELDENHUYS

EVERETT F. HARRISON

PAUL K. JEWETT

ERNEST F. KEVAN

PIERRE CH. MARCEL

WILLIAM J. MARTIN

J. THEODORE MUELLER

ROGER NICOLE

JAMES I. PACKER

BERNARD RAMM

HERMAN RIDDERBOS

NIC. H. RIDDERBOS

ALAN M. STIBBS

NED B. STONEHOUSE

MERRILL C. TENNEY

DONALD J. WISEMAN

EDWARD J. YOUNG

G. DOUGLAS YOUNG

Edited by

CARL F. H. HENRY

Baker Book House
Grand Rapids 6, Michigan

LIBRARY OF CONGRESS
CATALOGUE CARD NUMBER: 58-59822

ISBN: 0-8010-4053-1

First printing, February 1959
Second printing, November 1962
Third printing, August 1967
Fourth printing, August 1969
Fifth printing, August 1972

PHOTOLITHOPRINTED BY CUSHING - MALLOY, INC.
ANN ARBOR, MICHIGAN, UNITED STATES OF AMERICA
1972

CONTENTS

PREFACE

AFTER a World Evangelical Fellowship conference a few years ago in Clarens, Switzerland, several participants in this symposium met informally to discuss contemporary Protestant theology. While the conversations included many not sharing in the present volume (among them Professor André Lamorte, then at Aix-en-Provence, and Principal René Pache of Emmaus Bible Institute in Lausanne), the contributions of Dr. Frank E. Gaebelein, Professor Roger Nicole, and Principal Ernest Kevan are clearly recalled. It was these informal discussions in Switzerland that provided the impetus for *Revelation and the Bible*.

In assessing the fortunes of Christianity in our century, we all agreed that authority, particularly the authority of Scripture, is the watershed of theological conviction. We concurred, too, that the Christian impact in our lifetime had suffered immeasurably from liberal Protestant deletion of authority from Biblical religion. Growing rejection of the modernist philosophy of religion seemed a good omen, however. We were gathered, as it were, in the land of neo-orthodox giants, such as Karl Barth and Emil Brunner, who had questioned the Protestant disregard for supernatural revelation and redemption, and the vacillating accommodation of Christian belief and experience to the whims of modern man. We could not evade, nor did we desire to do so, their effective influence in undermining entrenched liberal positions.

At the same time we were burdened by the unsatisfactoriness of the newer alternatives, even though they recognized special divine revelation and the uniqueness of the Biblical witness. Gauged by the Biblical norm, the inadequacy and in fact the objectionable character of the new views were apparent enough. This was especially obvious in the religious epistemology formulated by the so-called "theology of revelation." Indebtedness to Kant and Kierkegaard, as well as additional liability to Ebner and Buber in formulating the divine-human encounter; perpetuation of Schleiermacher's profoundly unbiblical notion that God communicates no truths about himself and his purposes; and above all, injustice to the revelation-status of Scripture were some of the features of neo-orthodoxy that specially troubled us.

7

Equally distressing was the relative inertia of evangelical theology in this
time of cultural crisis. Compared with most liberal schools and churches,
evangelical agencies no doubt were doing impressively well; so-called independent efforts, however despised by inclusivist leaders as "free lance,"
nevertheless displayed wholesome vitality and zeal. While liberalism slowed
to a walk along the highway of modern theological influence these throbbings
of evangelical life provided a measure of comfort to evangelical churchmen.
When liberalism toppled in self-exhaustion, the situation changed, however,
for the thrust that crippled liberalism came not so much from evangelical
as from mediating thinkers. In large part, of course, collapse was forced by
the counter-stroke of history, of archaeology, and of the modern study of
personality. The relative ineffectiveness of the evangelical assault on liberalism was due in part also to historical circumstance. The Western world's
crisis had reached its zenith in the first quarter of our century in Europe,
where liberalism's anguished self-confession of irrelevance simultaneously
forced its adherents to the task of theological replacement. In America,
moreover, ecumenical pride, or whatever else it was, tended to deny intellectual hearing to all whose ecclesiastical identification placed them outside
inclusive Christianity. In those days merely to whisper that the "coming
great church" could prove a colossus of corruption (as Luther had already
discovered in an earlier century) was sufficient to provoke the stigma of
divisiveness, despite the fact that ecumenists like Reinhold Niebuhr themselves had warned of similar perils of decay latent in the secular order.
Evangelical scholars outside the orbit of inclusive ecumenism, notably J.
Gresham Machen, gained little recognition from modernist thinkers (though
many humanists read Machen gladly, and even granted him the edge in his
argument with liberalism). By now, moreover, modernist forces had ag-
grandized for their own speculative purposes many academic centers established by evangelical endowments, and enjoyed the funds and facilities once
available to conservative scholarship. Fundamentalist schools became mainly
anti-intellectual in temper, and as its chief concern the evangelical movement concentrated on the neglected task of world evangelism and missions.

Furthermore, first-rate evangelical scholars were increasingly at a premium; for more than a generation it had been popular to defect to the
modernist forces. While evangelicals took some active part in the theological
debate, they tended to reactionary positions in maintaining the defenses, and
were prone to excessive formulations of convictions. Moreover, convictions
were too often asserted *in vacuo;* they failed to expound the larger implications and consequences of acceptance or rejection. Evangelical polemics
became largely negative, and sought primarily the approbation of its own
conservative constituency rather than the effective penetration of competing
spheres of influence. These were among the tendencies that discouraged outside interest in conservative formulations.

To ascribe reactionary positions to all evangelical expositions of the doctrine of inspiration, however, would be both inaccurate and unfair. The selective bibliography at the end of this volume attests this fact. Unfortunately, the prevailing concept of evangelical conviction about Scripture has been gained rather one-sidedly from remarks of popular evangelists and religious pamphleteers rather than from more serious academic expositions. Accordingly, the contributors to *Revelation and the Bible* avoid many of these reactionary defenses of the past. Rather, they discuss Biblical revelation with full reference to God's saving acts and thereby contemplate revealed ideas in association with redemptive history. They do full justice to the historical and personal elements in special revelation. They avoid borrowing modern scientific canons to defend the accuracy and reliability of the Bible. They recognize the need for correlating the doctrine of inspiration with the phenomena of Scripture. They do not rest the entire case for inspiration on the results of inspiration merely, such as inerrancy, nor do they rest it on the traditional datings of all the sacred books. They affirm that the fact that the Bible is a God-breathed book is the foundation of scriptural trustworthiness and reliability.

The writers of this symposium support the high view as over against the classic liberal repudiation and the neo-orthodox evasion of scriptural inspiration. Anyone familiar with the literature of the doctrine of inspiration senses at once their endorsement of the long-standing confidence of the evangelical tradition in the Bible. They are constrained by the meaning and spirit of Scripture, also by an awareness of serious defects in the newer views of inspiration. Even the casual reader will detect their uneasiness over certain features of the "theology of the Word of God": disparagement of the general divine revelation in nature and conscience; exclusion of the laws of logic from the *imago Dei;* deference to sensory-spatial theories of the origin of language; repudiation of biblically disclosed doctrines; evasion of the Bible's witness to its own revelation-status; reduction of Scripture to merely an instrumental framework for dynamic divine-human encounter.

The primary objective of the contributors to this symposium, however, is a positive presentation of the Christian doctrine of the Scriptures. Only secondarily are they concerned with perversions of that view. These scholars are harbingers of an era in which once again the sacred Scriptures communicate their supernatural message with supernatural power. A recent issue of *Christianity Today* (January 20, 1958) comments that "the most hopeful sign on the theological horizon is the renewal of interest in a theology of the Word of God. If ministers professing such devotion could meet together across America, apart from reference to respective ecumenical orbits, and engage in serious study of the witness of Scripture to the Word of God—the Word incarnate and the Word written—they would not only find themselves fulfilling a divinely enjoined responsibility (cf. John 5:39), but could recapture afresh the note of authority that has evaporated from much of contemporary Protestantism." In *The Christian Century* (April 30, 1958)

Arnold W. Hearn, instructor at Union Theological Seminary in New York City, noted irenically that the nonfundamentalist who listens "to his more orthodox brethren . . . is likely to undergo at least one intellectually constructive experience: he will hear some of his own views subjected to acute and searching criticism from a theological viewpoint whose insights he has perhaps prematurely ignored. Particularly is this true in relation to the complex of problems which cluster around the basic question of religious authority." Were all of us—evangelical, neo-orthodox, and modernist alike—driven to a fresh and earnest study of the timeless realities of divine revelation and inspiration, the cause of Christian theology would indeed move ahead. The longer the neglect of this imperative by the ministry, that much longer will Protestant conscience and confidence suffer impairment.

Aware of the great responsibilities many of the symposium writers bear, I wish to include a personal word of appreciation for their participation. It is a genuine privilege to provide a vehicle to carry forward their contribution to contemporary evangelical thought. I gratefully acknowledge also the work of Philip E. Hughes in translating Dr. Pierre Marcel's chapter from the French, of Peter de Visser in translating several chapters from the Dutch, and of Miss Irma Peterson, my secretary, who has uncomplainingly assumed additional responsibilities of correspondence, typing and proofreading.

                                                    CARL F. H. HENRY

Washington, D.C.

GENERAL AND SPECIAL DIVINE REVELATION

G. C. Berkouwer

G. C. Berkouwer is Professor of Systematic Theology at Free University of Amsterdam, The Netherlands. He is completing Studies in Dogmatics in eighteen volumes, six of which have already been translated into English. Among his other published works is The Triumph of Grace in the Theology of Karl Barth, a constructively critical analysis to which Barth refers in his Kirchliche Dogmatik, in the foreword to Volume IV/2, as a "great" book.

1. G. C. Berkouwer

GENERAL AND SPECIAL DIVINE REVELATION

ANYONE who reflects on divine revelation in the world, and permits himself to review the history of the Church and theology, quite naturally encounters a frequently expressed differentiation between *general* and *special* revelation. This differentiation has played an important role in eras of all kinds, and has even precipitated much discussion and strife. Quite understandably the question has often arisen whether theology, in pressing this distinction, has not gone beyond "what was written," and whether or not this differentiation permits a proper view of the wonder of the one divine revelation.

I. THE PROBLEM

Can we distinguish between various types of revelation? If so, do we do justice to God's revelation in its greatness and indestructible unity? Is this perhaps a subtle differentiation that can be reached only when the revelation of God has become merely an idea, and we are no longer under the overwhelming impression that divine revelation is always special, surprising, new and wonderful? Have we perhaps thereby arrived at that stage of scholastic thought which in every area distinguished between "general" and "special" and that now applies this distinction also to the revelation of God?

To the question of terminology we must add still others. Must we not acknowledge that especially in the last centuries the special revelation of God has been attacked from the viewpoint of a much wider general revelation?

Especially when the so-called "history of religions" school in the second half of the nineteenth century called particular attention to the non-Christian religions, a plea was made for *general* revelation; scholars did not wish to cast aside these religions as false religions, but rather, wished to view them in connection with a general revelation of God. From this vantage point the so-called absolute character of Christianity was called more and more into question. The Christian confession of a special revelation in the history of Israel, in the person of Jesus Christ, and in the witness to Jesus Christ (the Holy Scriptures), was increasingly criticized from the viewpoint of "general" revelation.

Thus the concept of a "general" religion arose, corresponding to a "general" revelation; on this basis the teachings of the Church were subjected to sharp criticism. Christianity, it was argued, set far too many boundaries to God's revelation by calling it "special" and by localizing it. Did not *all* religions contain elements with hidden indications of a revelation of God? Was it still possible to accept the *specific* of God's revelation in Israel and in Jesus Christ?

In this manner—as an attack on the Church—the plea was made for a general, universal revelation of God in the world. Of course, one can say that in speaking of a general revelation, the Church and Christian theology mean something quite different from this universalism. But the fact remains that historical circumstances have brought about a serious and almost hopeless confusion. And so the question has arisen whether or not adequate reason now exists to discontinue speaking longer of a "general" revelation so that the term's meaning will not be misunderstood in the Church and theology.

There is, finally, still a third problem. Is not the danger evident that via the route of general revelation we may find ourselves companion to Roman Catholic theology that has always ascribed such great value to the *natural* knowledge of God? This natural knowledge of God, so it was taught, came forth not from the special revelation of God in Jesus Christ; rather, it preceded this by way of the natural light of reason, through which it was possible to know God. This teaching is found not only in Roman Catholic theology as such; it was also declared an infallible doctrine of the Church at the Vatican Council of 1870, when it was announced that God could be known with certainty from that which had been created *through the natural light of reason*. Over against those currents in the nineteenth century Roman Catholic Church, which taught that God could be known only through and by a special revelation in Christ, the Council maintained the possibility of a *true* even though incomplete knowledge of God apart from the revelation in Christ. Inseparably linked to this teaching was the Roman Catholic doctrine of the proofs for the existence of God. This was apparent from the interpretation of the words of 1870 by the anti-modernistic oath of 1910 to mean that God not only could be *known* but indeed could be *proved* by the natural light of reason.

These three difficulties (the question of terminology, the modern attack on the absoluteness of Christianity, and the natural theology of Rome) furnish good reasons for a closer consideration. Is the present situation in which the Church and theology find themselves perhaps of such a nature that it would be better to ignore the distinction between general and special revelation? Or does this distinction preserve a religious and theological necessity, so that we cannot and may not abandon it, but must explain and clarify it amid and despite the confusion of these days?

II. NECESSARY CLARIFICATIONS

Because of the twentieth century situation, it is certainly not necessary to abandon the doctrine of general revelation; but to clarify and to guard it against misunderstanding is urgent.

First of all, we must insist that "general" revelation does not and cannot mean an attack upon the special revelation in Jesus Christ. The modern interpretation of general revelation had led to such an attack. But in so doing it came into direct conflict with the holy Scriptures which declare the absoluteness of God's revelation. The debate over the absoluteness of Christianity always recalls those words from John's Gospel that Christ is *the* way, *the* truth, and *the* life (14:6) and that no one comes to the Father but *through him.* In the modern view, Christ himself was not *the revelation* of God; rather, Christ invited decision regarding his teaching. But this teaching is inseparably connected with *his person:* "Blessed is he who is not offended in me" (Matt. 11:6).

Therefore, neither the Church nor theology can ever speak of general revelation if in so doing it fails to do justice to the absoluteness of the revelation of God in Jesus Christ, who was "God revealed in the flesh" (I Tim. 3:16). Scripture speaks much too plainly to allow such error, for it points us to the great mystery revealed at the end of the ages, which had previously remained hidden (Rom. 16:25; Heb. 9:26). Whenever the Church and theology speak of general revelation, no shadow whatever must be cast over special revelation. Certainly such shadowing has never been the purpose of the Church's exposition of general revelation.

When the Belgic Confession in Article 2 affirms faith in general revelation, it in no wise opposes the absoluteness of God's revelation in Christ, which this Confession emphatically expresses elsewhere. *In this harmony* of the special and general lies the touchstone for any legitimate discussion of general revelation.

In the second place, it is necessary to clarify the term "general revelation" in order to distinguish it from the Roman Catholic idea of natural theology fixed in 1870. It is clear that the Christian Church, in speaking of general revelation, never intended to assert that *true* knowledge of God is possible through the natural light of reason.

Assuredly, in the time of the Reformation men believed in the general revelation of God, but not with the understanding that through this revelation they could arrive at the idea of a natural, *true* knowledge of God. Moreover, the rupture between God's revelation and the human heart was pointed out.

That Romans 1 is cited in Article 2 of the Belgic Confession is no accident, nor the fact that special reference is made to men's guilt (Rom. 1:20). The purpose of this record was to indicate the existence of a revelation of God in all the works of his hands, but that man, who comes in daily contact with this revelation, in his unrighteousness wards off this truth. This is exactly the import of Romans 1. But this gulf between revelation and true knowledge of God does not come to expression at all in the Vatican pronouncement, although it too cites Romans 1.

Right here we reach a central point in the discussion of general revelation. To speak of the general revelation of God does not in any respect mean doing less than justice to the revelation of God in Jesus Christ. Rather, it emphasizes the guilt and lost condition, the darkness and the blindness, of fallen man, who sees the works of God's hand no more, and no longer can discover God therein.

So also for the Apostle Paul in Romans 1, the idea of the revelation of God "since the creation of the world" does not conflict with what he writes of Christ Jesus. Romans 1 points to the *anger* of God (v. 18): the light of the gospel shines into the darkness of unfaithful human life that holds back the truth in unrighteousness (v. 18), that substitutes the image of a perishable man for the majesty of the eternal God (v. 23), and that honors and worships the creature above the Creator (v. 25). Because the general revelation of God is placed in Romans 1 in this uncontradictable context, it ever remains impossible to speak of the general revelation of God without considering also the anger of God (v. 18), which condemns man's suppression of the truth in unrighteousness.

And herein is established the impossibility of rivalry or competition between the confession of the general revelation of God and the special revelation of God in Jesus Christ. The confession of God's revelation in all the works of his hands does not demean the revelation in Christ to relative or to lesser importance, but, on the contrary, *serves rather to point toward* that revelation in its saving character amid human estrangement from God.

From all this it also becomes clear that confession of the special revelation of God does not make the general revelation superfluous. From Paul's teaching in Romans 1 on the anger of God, and his indication that the heathen will not be held guiltless (v. 20) because they suppress the truth in unrighteousness, it is apparent that human life, even in deepest depravity, *does not stand out of connection with the revelation of God.*

Man is not situated in a silent, purposeless and senseless world in which no voice whatever addresses him. Much rather, over against nihilism it must be asserted that human life bears an *answering* character. Although man is not conscious of it, his whole life *is* a reply, even to the deepest aspects of his religion. This religion is not an automatic instinct rising out of the depths of the human heart, but rather, constitutes the depraved answer to the revelation of God. In innumerable variations it reveals the unrest of the heart, which does not come to rest until it rests in God (St. Augustine).

From this we can illuminate the fact that Reformation theology called attention to the revelation of God in the works of his hands and at the same time confessed the necessity of the knowledge of God in Jesus Christ. The reality of general revelation does not lead to the knowledge of God, but is *misunderstood* and *denied.* It is true that man—sinful and fallen man—is still surrounded by the light, but—to speak in the terms of the Canons of Dort—this same man pollutes the light of nature and holds it back in unrighteousness (Canons of Dort, III, IV, 4). This relationship of holding back and pushing away the truth cannot be denied or abandoned. Bound up in the general revelation of God is a fact that makes plain and certain how seriously man is estranged from the life of God (Eph. 4:18): Man is . . . not to be held *guiltless.*

When Article 2 of the Belgic Confession asserts this general revelation of God, this does not mean a "natural theology" in the sense of Rome. For in this natural theology conclusions are drawn from this revelation to the true knowledge of God, whereas for Article 2 of the Belgic Confession that is precisely where the problem lies. Over against this "true knowledge," Reformation thought understandably posited the corruption of the estrangement, and naturally took a critical stand toward the proofs of the existence of God in Roman Catholic theology. These proofs prompted the impression that isolated human reason must lead to the conclusion of the existence of God. But such isolation is impractical and impossible because man's thinking exists and functions only in relationship to the whole man. In this totality the matter of human decision falls within the realm of the heart and of faith.

It is impossible to deny that the proofs for God's existence in general have wielded but little influence. For they stand—especially in our times—in the shadow of a great many "proofs" *against* the existence of God. That God can be proved as the first cause or prime mover of all things finds less agreement these days among modern men. Even in Roman Catholic circles some voices say that the Roman Catholic proofs mean little or nothing *for those who do not already believe.* And in our times, in opposition to the proofs for the existence of God, a deep agnosticism elaborates the conviction of the absence of God; no longer recognizing the world as purposeful, this agnosticism abandons it to senselessness and absurdity and sees the existence of man in the world as a meaningless and purposeless jest.

The Church of Jesus Christ does not idealize the world. It is aware of the curse of the Fall (Gen. 3:17) and with Paul it knows the creation as subject to vanity and subjugated to the temporal (Rom. 8:20 f.). It hesitates

to fraternize with every convenient theodicy that tries to justify God's direction of the world to the judgment bar of human reason.

But at the same time the Church confesses that God maintains and rules
the world. Thus we confront the fact that it is precisely the believer who
becomes conscious once again of the universality of the acts of God in the
world. It is striking that Article 2 of the Belgic Confession contains no mention of "nature." Often the general revelation of God is called the revelation
in nature. But Article 2 speaks of God's creation, providence and rule "in
which these are before our eyes as a beautiful book, in which all creatures,
small and large, are like letters, which allow us to view the invisible things
of God."

Herein we are not offered an optimistic view of life, in which the curse,
suffering and terrors of life are denied. Rather, we gain an outlook on the
universal dealing of God. In the so-called nature Psalms (e.g., Ps. 8, 19, 65,
104) we are not presented with a natural theology, but we have here Psalms
of Israel, lifted out of the sanctuary. Faith in Israel's God again opens up the
windows to the world, and man once more discovers the works of God's
hands. For this world, for the sun and the moon and the stars—for all that
God has made—there arises renewed interest and importance. Certainly it
is not accidental that the Reformation acted as a stimulus to the development of the study of nature and science. How could "the believing" have no
interest in nature and in history? Yet at the same time we discern that our
eyes are opened for this world *only* through the revelation of God in Jesus
Christ, or, as Calvin has said in a striking simile, that the special revelation
is as a glass through which we are once more in a position to read the book
of the general revelation of God. Through the special revelation we understand again the *purpose* of the creation of God and we discover—in justice
and in grace—the works of God's hands.

In this connection we must note the fact that in our time sharp criticism
has been leveled at the doctrine of the general revelation of God. For instance, Karl Barth especially has aligned himself emphatically against Article
2 of the Belgic Confession because in this he detected a second source of
divine revelation alongside that in Christ Jesus. From the history of the
Church and of theology it can be demonstrated, Barth asserts, that acceptance of a *second* source of the knowledge of God—for example, Scripture
and tradition, Scripture and reason, Scripture and emotion—has always led
to devaluation of the first source. Now indeed, it is undeniable that tradition
(Rome) has often jeopardized Scripture, that reason and emotion (rationalism and subjectivism) also have jeopardized the revelation of God in Jesus
Christ.

But the consideration of general revelation need not involve us in a theory
of sources of equal value existing adjacent to each other. The relationship
between general and special revelation is actually of an entirely different

nature. It is not to be likened to the view of Rome, which puts Scripture and tradition next to each other.

In this relationship between general and special revelation lies the crux of the problem. More and more the fact is clear that the general revelation of God does not stand *next* to the special revelation, but that special revelation opens our eyes to the greatness of God's works and points the way to the Psalmist's song of praise: "O Lord our Lord, how excellent is thy name in all the earth!" (Ps. 8:1).

The Barthian criticism of the idea of general revelation is an impressive reaction against the jeopardizing of special revelation in Jesus Christ by other sources of the knowledge of God. That Barth especially sensed this threat is understandable when we recall that, under the influence of national socialism, Christianity in Germany seemed to identify the voice of God in history with the seizure of power by Hitler in Germany in 1933. This menace was very real and exceedingly dangerous; even in the Church many persons were misled by this correlation.

But the Church doctrine of the general revelation of God moves on an entirely different level. Its level is not that of Trent, nor of rationalism, nor of national socialism, but that of Psalm 8 and Romans 1—the level of the revelation of guilt, and of the discovery of the dealings of God through eyes made to see anew through the power of the Holy Spirit.

Only when it becomes fully clear that the doctrine of the general revelation of God poses no threat to the special revelation of God in Jesus Christ does it become possible for this doctrine to resound throughout the world of our time. General revelation remains a reminder of the guilt of *closed eyes.* Precisely this doctrine, therefore, uncovers for us the absoluteness of the revelation of God in Jesus Christ.

III. MEANING OF GENERAL REVELATION

In the foregoing comments we have laid emphasis upon the fact that the general revelation of God must not be delineated without attention to the connection of guilt and the anger of God (Rom. 1). From this some might infer that general revelation has no significance for life beyond establishing the impossibility of man's guiltlessness. It would then point to the guilt of the closed eye, but have no effect in actual life. Therefore, it is necessary here to penetrate further into its significance.

For it is clear that, while the Word of God points with emphasis to the relationship between general revelation and guilt, it indicates also that fallen man in his practical life is not freed from the revelation of God.

When the Apostle Paul, after pointing out in Romans 1 the guilt of estrangement, is then fascinated in Romans 2 by the life of the heathen, we touch this fact in a clear and unmistakable manner. He has indicated the serious consequences of this estrangement from God in the moral life, and has directed attention to the judgment of God revealed therein (Rom. 1: 26 f.). But he does not shut his eyes to the fact that phenomena other than uncleanness and immorality are ofttimes also to be noticed in the lives of the fallen and the estranged.

He calls attention to the heathen who, while they lack the Law (i.e., the Law of Moses), nonetheless *by nature* do the things that are contained in the Law (Rom. 2:14). Apparently life even in estrangement from God has not passed totally into nihilism and anarchy and lawlessness: "which show the work of the law written in their hearts, their conscience also bearing witness" (Rom. 2:15).

Paul indeed does not say that the *Law* is put in their hearts as we read of this Law in the prophecies of the new covenant (Jer. 31:33; Heb. 10:16). But he does discover a conformity with what God has commanded in his Law, and he sees its reality in their consciousness of norms, namely, in their *conscience* (Rom. 2:15). In connection with his warning (of judgment against proud Jewish self-exaltation above the Gentiles), Paul does not delve deeper into this noteworthy appearance of conformity with the Law, but nevertheless by pointing to it, he emphasizes that even in estrangement some connection remains between man and God.

Men have sought to explain conscience in all kinds of ways—sociologically, or psychoanalytically, or also as the voice of God in man. Paul does not propound any theory of conscience. But he calls attention to it as he sees that even in the heathen world people in one manner or another are preserved or held back from the *full* consequences of estrangement from God.

In Acts 17 also we find a similar estimate of heathendom. Upon the Areopagus Paul calls for repentance (Acts 17:30), but he points out at the same time that, even in his apostasy, man is not loose from God and that this connection is evident in his life. It is one of the heathen poets who himself has said: "For we also are his offspring" (Acts 17:28). Surely this is something other than a confession of creation after God's image, and likely the heathen poet had intended "his offspring" in a pantheistic way. But Paul seized upon this word to remind them of the dealings of God, that it had been established that men should seek God, if haply they should find him, though he was not far from every one of us (Acts 17:27). Man—also heathen man—is in all circumstances and thoughts of his life not freed from God. He is involved with God, and this fact is apparent also in his religion and his morality. He cannot be freed from the revelation of God, even less from the command of God—from the (for him) not *entirely* hidden goodness of God's command and ordinances.

Certainly everywhere and often we see manifold evidences of departure from God's Law (Rom. 1), but defection from God does not always mean radical nihilism. Life on this earth does not yet disclose the full consequences of sin. Calvin speaks of "common grace" and, in this connection, he discusses virtues to be seen also in the lives of unbelievers. He did not wish to ascribe these phenomena to a left-over goodness in nature—as if the apostasy from God were not so serious—but rather he discerned here the power of God in revelation and in grace preserving life from total self-destruction.

While this "morality" does not justify man, it must not on that account be denied. There is a working of conscience that has significance in the tensions of human life. This conscience, however, is not an unchanging content, an unthreatened morality. A man can become what we may call a "conscienceless" being, consciously trampling God's Law under foot. And in the latter days, we are told, there will be people without natural affection, turning away from the good, with more love for self-satisfaction than for God (II Tim. 3:1 f.). One cannot build upon this type of conformity with the Law!

But this does not diminish the fact that life is not yet wholly fragmented in chaos. A relationship to God remains even in man's estrangement from him, a *work* of the Law that is written in the hearts of men. There is still *contact* with the works of God's hand even though men do not look to the *Father*hand of God. That does not mean that human corruption is not serious, but it does mean that man never is fully severed from connection with God and that—even though he does not recognize the Lawgiver—in many respects he still comes under the influence of the Law and the ordinances of God.

In sin itself lies a driving power that estranges man from God and from his neighbor. But in the preservation of human life there is still community, marriage, love, justice, mercy. *Because of the existence of sin,* because of apostasy, these are wonderful phenomena in the fallen world. Here God still holds fast the world and human life, even *in* the Fall. He does not abandon it, because he has loved the world—in Christ (John 3:16). Over against sin, he still holds life in being, and makes room for the preaching of the gospel. He still allows fallen man his place in the world, and he does not disallow himself a witness, through the goodness of rain and harvest time. He blesses with an overflow of food and happiness (Acts 14:17) and he lets his sun rise over the evil and the good, and allows the rain to refresh the just and the unjust (Matt. 5:45). And all of this does not stand alongside the plan of salvation in Jesus Christ, but is built thereon. His general revelation is not *concurrent* with the special revelation in Christ. This general disclosure puts the world in the middle of the glorious works of God's hand; it does not detach and disengage the world. For God still binds man to his neighbor and preserves human life even in its most extreme individualism.

True, sometimes we see the power of sin carried to the very borders of nihilism. Talk about demonization of life is widespread especially in our time, when one man turns another over to destruction and death without mercy (do we need more evidence than concentration camps and anti-Semitism?). But there *still* arises a protest, and then comes a reaction.

Following nihilism comes the resurgence of humanism. Certainly life is not safe in this haven of humanism, but nonetheless life is still preserved.

Because of man's involvement with the goodness of God's command, it is clear that the Church may not abandon its doctrine of general revelation. It may not proclaim this revelation as a second source of knowledge next to the revelation of God in Jesus Christ, but it may and must use it as a reminder of the God who does not abandon the world and who sets man in the midst of greatness and majesty. The message of the general revelation of God rings out the accusation (not the excuse) of man, yet simultaneously the gospel sounds out to the world (the Areopagus, Acts 17:30), so that life once more may be turned toward the living God who has displayed his love for the world. This God and his message stand forth against all devaluation of the world that he has created.

All nihilism is evidence of the pride of man who forsakes God and surrenders himself to criticism of the works of God's hands. In this tendency we stand before what in many respects is the most dismal image of our times. Man sees his own life in the world as senseless and absurd. But the Church that preaches the gospel refuses to accept this senselessness and absurdity. It cries out against the spirit of the times with the message of repentance.

Upon the path of conversion the light shines again and the promise of restoration comes to view. For this entire creation sighs in birth pangs until it shall be free of the bondage of corruption (Rom. 8:21). Then shall come the new heaven and the new earth (II Pet. 3:13). These form the contents of God's promise. Upon this new earth justice shall dwell. Then the glory of God shall be manifested, when God himself is the Light (Rev. 22:5) and the Lamb is the Lamp (Rev. 21:23).

Then the distinction between general and special revelation shall be removed: when God *dwells* "with men" (Rev. 21:3), when night is banished (Rev. 22:5), when God himself shall wipe all tears from our eyes.

For us humans this future is beyond imagination. But it remains the object of the promise. It consists not only in the salvation of the *soul,* but in the renewing of all of life. Before this future there still hangs the curtain of God's last revelation: "It is not yet revealed what we shall be" (I John 3:2). But "we shall see him as he is" (I John 3:2) when the veils of secrecy shall be taken away, and the windows are open to all the works of God's hands. Then the full meaning of Psalm 8 will be revealed in the resurrection from the dead and in the new presence of the King of the ages: "O Lord our Lord, how excellent is thy name in all the earth!"

IV. HUMAN LIFE AND THE GENERAL REVELATION OF GOD

We have seen that the distinction between general and special revelation does not concern a subtle or scholastic difference. Neither is a rivalry intended between general revelation and the revelation of God in Jesus Christ, like that of modern theology, which attacks and perverts the absoluteness of the revelation in Christ. The meaning of the distinction is otherwise.

It is all too evident, however, that in exhibiting this distinction, we must express ourselves in faulty language. The words "general" and "special" are borrowed from earthly human relationships and do not appear in Scripture. Still, it is good to call attention to the fact that many attempts to arrive at a new terminology have fallen short of expressing the underlying reality. In most cases either the general *or* the special revelation was not done full justice. And in view of this, we must emphasize that the decision involves not merely a matter of terminology, but rather, of the basic issues designated by the terms employed.

The distinction between general and special revelation does not posit a rupture in the unity of God's revelation, but points out rather the revealing acts of God in history in the way of creation, fall and redemption.

In the revelation of God in Christ Jesus—saving and propitiating—the Light rises once more *over the world.* Jesus Christ is Saviour of men, but he is also Light of the *world* (John 8:12) and he has come as a Light in the world (John 12:46). The world has come into existence through Christ (John 1:10) and without the Word, without him, was nothing made that was made (John 1:3). But the world knew him not (John 1:10), even though the Light shone in the darkness. Because of this Light, however, the world and human life are still possible.

Despite nihilistic tendencies, modern man still evidences continuously a violent interest in the world. In many respects this interest is not an interest in the Creator of heaven and earth. The cosmos is isolated and abstracted from the Creator. But neither in scholarship nor art has man ever yet done away with what faith sees as the work of God's hands. And if the revelation of God in Jesus Christ opens the eyes, then the abstraction is broken, and life in the world becomes the *service* of God and of one's neighbor. Then the *meaning* of life and the world is revealed once more, and supplies the believer with the power of the promise that one day shall be fulfilled.

Then at last the shortcomings of human language are to fall away in *worship* and a *song of praise.* And then we shall understand also how firmly the distinction between general and special revelation is connected with *guilt* and *estrangement.*

Consequently, in all our considerations of this distinction we must be careful that the guilt is not denied. The special revelation of God in Jesus Christ is the divine answer to this guilt as the surprise of God's love, as the new spring of God's mercy. Therefore the way to the works of God's hands leads always by the way of the *Cross.* Here the windows are opened and the Light shines forth. Here sympathy is awakened for the world and here the world is seen in God's light. Here all egocentric piety is broken and man once again finds his proper place as the image of God.

And because the way to the works of God's hands leads by the Cross, we are taught lifelong by the Word of the Cross. This very *special* instruction teaches us our place in the *world:* in order to *serve* every day, we are to give all our thoughts over as captive to the obedience of Christ (II Cor. 10:5). And in that full life in the world we are warned to pay attention to the light of the Word: "We have also a more sure word of prophecy, whereunto ye do well that ye take heed, as unto a light that shineth in a dark place, until the day dawn, and the day star arise in your hearts" (II Pet. 1:19).

SPECIAL DIVINE
REVELATION AS
RATIONAL

Gordon H. Clark

Gordon H. Clark is Chairman of the Philosophy Department in Butler University, Indiana. He holds the A.B. and Ph.D. degrees from University of Pennsylvania, where he taught philosophy from 1924–36. After teaching in Wheaton College, Illinois, from 1936–43, he went to his present post. His published writings include Readings in Ethics, Selections from Hellenistic Philosophy, A Christian Philosophy of Education, A Christian View of Men and Things, *and* Thales to Dewey.

2. *Gordon H. Clark*

SPECIAL DIVINE REVELATION AS RATIONAL

THE HANDIWORK and the glory of God displayed by the heavens and the firmament have been called General Divine Revelation. In this category one may also include the constitution of human personality, for man himself is a creation of God and in some sense bears the marks of his Creator. This "light of nature and the works of creation and providence do so far manifest the goodness, wisdom, and power of God, as to leave men inexcusable; yet they are not sufficient to give that knowledge of God and of his will, which is necessary unto salvation." It is thus that the Westminster Confession briefly warns us that general revelation is inadequate. This inadequacy is partly a result of the noetic effects of sin, but there is a prior and inherent inadequacy as well.

I. INADEQUACY OF GENERAL REVELATION

The beclouding effects of sin upon the mind as it tries to discover God and salvation in nature may best be seen in the divergent results obtained among the pagan religions. The ancient Babylonians, Egyptians, and Romans looked on the same nature that is seen by the modern Moslem, Hindu, and Buddhist. But the messages that they purport to receive are considerably different. This, which is so evident when these far away religions are mentioned, holds true also within Western civilization. What the humanist and logical positivist see in nature is entirely different from what the orthodox

Christian believes about nature. Even if the humanist professes to discover in experience certain moral ideals and spiritual values that are at least superficially similar to those of the Bible, it can well be supposed that he actually learned them from his Christian heritage and not from an independent study of nature and man. The kindly atmosphere of humanitarianism is notably absent from societies to which the Christian message has not been taken.

The existence of divergent concepts of God, of moral ideals, and above all of schemes of salvation show the power of sin in the mind of man; but they also show the inherent inadequacy of general revelation. It is not because of sin alone that man fails to get God's message. The truth is that nature has less of a message than some people, particularly some Christian people, think.

The planets above and the plants below show some of the wisdom and power of God; that is to say, they show it to those who already believe that God has created them. Even to a devout Christian, however, the universe does not show the full power and wisdom of God, for God has not exhausted himself in his creation. No doubt the stellar systems display a vast and unimaginable power, yet a greater number of stars with more complicated motions is conceivable. Therefore omnipotence is not a necessary conclusion from the stars.

Neither is righteousness. The moral attributes that the Bible ascribes to God are still less deducible from an observation of nature. Indeed, the problem of evil—physical calamities like earthquakes and tragedies caused by wicked men—has led some philosophers to deny God altogether or to posit a finite god. John Stuart Mill thought that the universe tended imperfectly toward the production of good; modern humanists are more likely to say that the universe is neutral with respect to the hopes and aspirations of man; while Bertrand Russell and Joseph Wood Krutch counsel bravery in the face of inevitable defeat. These various opinions, though partly due to human sinfulness, depend as much, I believe, on the inadequacy of general revelation in itself. God's message in the heavens is simply not extensive enough to cover these questions.

Again, the Hebrew-Christian view that "the heavens declare the glory of God" does not, in my opinion, mean that the existence of God can be formally deduced from an empirical examination of the universe. If on some other grounds we believe in the God of Abraham, Isaac, and Jacob, we can see that the heavens declare his glory; but this is not to say that a person who did not believe in this God could demonstrate his existence from nature. Further reference to this point will be made a little later.

Now, finally, the inadequacy of general revelation is most obvious in the case of ideals or ethical norms. And this inadequacy is not solely the result of sin, but it is an inherent inadequacy. The exposure of infants in Greece, temple prostitution in Babylonia, human sacrifice in Canaan and elsewhere, were not practices which those societies condemned; they had full social sanction. These were their norms, these were their moral ideals. Similarly, contemporary humanism, though some of its values are superficially similar to Christian precepts, diverges more and more from the Biblical identification of right and wrong. Jesus is no longer regarded as sinless, but is accused of minimizing the values of scientific intelligence, of holding inferior sociological views on labor and property, and even of insisting on too rigid a sexual standard.

If, now, someone wishes to argue that this ethical divergence does not indicate the inadequacy of general revelation, but merely the darkness of the sinful mind, the clinching reply, for a Christian, is that God spoke to Adam *before the fall* and gave him commands that he could not have otherwise known.

When Adam was created and placed in the Garden of Eden, he did not know what to do. Nor would a study of the Garden have led to any necessary conclusion. His duty was imposed upon him by a special divine revelation. God told him to be fruitful and multiply, to subdue nature, to make use of the animals, to eat of the fruit of the trees, with one fateful exception. Thus moral norms, commands and prohibitions were established by a special and not a general revelation. Only so could man know God's requirements, and only so later could he learn the plan of salvation.

Such is the Christian viewpoint. Secular philosophers today assert that the story of Adam is a myth and that the idea of special revelation is irrational. Dependence is placed in reason, not in revelation. All truth is to be obtained by one method, the method of science. The Bible is alleged to be self-contradictory and historically inaccurate; its morals are those of a bygone age; and evolution is credited with disproving creation. These themes have been well publicized and widely accepted. Can the Christian therefore face the charge of intellectual dishonesty, frequently brought against him, and meet the objection that revelation is unreasonable?

II. DEFENSE OF REVELATION AS RATIONAL

In the history of Christian thought the antithesis between faith and reason has been approached by several different methods. The debate, whether among Christians or between Christians and secularists, sometimes generates confusion because the terms are not always clearly defined. Not only do Augustine and Kant differ as to the nature of faith, but the term reason itself has borne different meanings. After providing a minimum of historical background, the writer hopes to avoid such confusion by suggesting a definition of reason that may help in the defense of revelation as rational.

The Medieval Scholastic Attempt

In this brief historical survey the first method of relating faith and reason to be discussed will be *the Thomistic philosophy* of the Roman Catholic Church. Aside from the personal assent of the believer, faith in this system means the revealed information contained in the Bible, tradition, and presumably the living voice of the Church. Faith then is revealed truth. Reason means the information that can be obtained by a sensory observation of nature as interpreted by intellection. Whereas the rationalists of the seventeenth century contrasted reason with sensation, Thomas contrasts reason with revelation. Truths of reason are those truths which may be obtained by man's natural sensory and intellectual equipment without the aid of supernatural grace.

These definitions of faith and reason make revelation "unreasonable" only in a verbal manner; revelation cannot be called unreasonable or irrational in any pejorative sense. Sometimes one suspects that the secularists seize upon the verbalism to suggest something more sinister.

Thomism indeed insists on an incompatibility between faith and reason, but it is a psychological incompatibility. If the Bible reveals that God exists, and if we believe the Bible, we have this truth of faith. It is possible, however, according to Thomism, to demonstrate the existence of God from ordinary observation of nature. Aristotle did it. But when a person has rationally demonstrated this proposition, he no longer "believes" it, he no longer accepts it on authority; he "knows" it. It is psychologically impossible to "believe" and to "know" the same proposition. A teacher may tell a student that a triangle contains 180 degrees, and the student may believe the teacher; but if the student learns the proof, he no longer accepts the theorem on the word of the teacher: he knows it for himself. Not all the propositions of revelation may be demonstrated in rational philosophy; but on the other hand some truths capable of demonstration have also been revealed to man, for God well knew that not all men have the intellectual capacity of Aristotle; therefore God revealed some truths, even though demonstrable, for the sake of the greater part of mankind.

The non-demonstrable contents of revelation (such as the doctrines of the Trinity and the Sacraments), though outside the range of reason as defined, are not irrational or nonsensical. Medieval Mohammedans and modern humanists may claim that the Trinity is irrational; but reason is quite competent to show that this doctrine does not contain any self-contradiction and that the objections to it are fallacious. The higher truths of faith do not violate any of the conclusions of reason; on the contrary, the doctrines of revelation complete what reason could not finish. The two sets of truths, or, better, the truths obtained by these two different methods are complementary. Far from being a hindrance to reason, faith can warn a thinker that he is blundering. One should not picture the believer as a prisoner to his faith who should be liberated; faith restricts only from error. Thus faith and reason are in harmony.

Only one criticism of this construction will be made, but it is one which

Thomists and objectors alike will concede to be crucial. If the cosmological argument for the existence of God is a logical fallacy, Thomism and its view of the relation between faith and reason cannot stand.[1]

The difficulties with the cosmological argument recall the earlier comments on the inadequacy of general revelation. If it is assumed that all knowledge begins in sensory experience and that therefore one looks out on nature in ignorance of God, the manifest calamities of men and the finitude and change of nature, vast though the galaxies may be, preclude any necessary conclusion to the existence of an omnipotent God who is good as well.

To these objections which Hume stated so forcefully may be added specific criticisms of Thomas's Aristotelian formulation. Three will be mentioned. First, Thomism cannot survive without the concepts of potentiality and actuality, yet Aristotle never succeeded in defining them. Instead he illustrated them by the change of phenomena and then defined change or motion in terms of actuality and potentiality. To justify this objection would require too much technical apparatus for the present purpose; and if the reader wish, he need put no stress on this first point.

Second, Thomas argues that if we trace back the causes of motions, still this regress cannot go on to infinity. The reason explicitly given in the *Summa Theologica* for denying an infinite regress is that in such a case there could not be a first mover. But this reason, which is used as a premise to conclude for the denial, is precisely the conclusion that Thomas puts at the end of the complete argument. The argument is supposed to prove the existence of a first mover, but this first mover is assumed in order to deny an infinite regress. Obviously therefore the argument is a fallacy.

There is a third and still more complicated criticism. Inasmuch as this involves material that has recently become a subject of widespread debate, it is worthy of more detailed attention.

For Thomas Aquinas there are two ways of knowing God; first, the way of negative theology, which we shall not discuss; and second, the method of analogy. Since God is pure being, without parts, whose essence is identical with his existence, the terms applied to him cannot be used in precisely the sense in which they applied to created things. If it is said that a man is wise and that God is wise, it must be remembered that the wisdom of man is an acquired wisdom, while God has never learned. The human mind is subject to the truth; truth is its superior. But God's mind is the cause of the truth by thinking it, or, perhaps, God is the truth. Hence the term "mind" does not mean precisely the same thing in the case of God and man. Not only these terms, but the notion of existence, also, is not the same. Since God's existence is his essence, an identity unduplicated in any other instance, even

---

[1] Some Romanists take the cosmological argument, not as logically demonstrative, but as a method of directing the attention to certain features of finite beings from which the existence of God can be seen without a discursive process. Cf. E. L. Mascall, *Words and Images,* p. 84. But, I judge, this is not standard Thomism.

the word "existence" does not apply univocally to God and the world of creation.

At the same time Thomas does not wish to admit that the terms are equivocal. When it is said that playboys lead *fast* lives, while ascetics *fast*, the word has no meaning in common. Though the letters and pronunciation are the same, the intellectual contents in the two instances are utterly diverse. Between such equivocation and strict univocity, Thomas asserts that words may have an analogical use; and that in the case of God and man, the predicates are applied analogically.

If, now, the analogical meanings of "wise" or of "existence" had a common area of meaning, that common area could be designated by a univocal term. This term then could be applied univocally to God and man. But Thomas insists that no term can be so applied. This in effect removes all trace of identical meaning in the two instances. But if this be so, how can an argument, the cosmological argument, be formally valid, when its premises use terms in one sense and the conclusion uses those terms in a completely different sense? The premises of the cosmological argument speak of the *existence* of *movers* within the range of human experience; the conclusion concerns the *existence* of a first *mover*. But if these terms are not taken univocally, the argument is a fallacy.

Therefore the Thomistic attempt to relate faith and reason—more because of its view of reason than its view of faith—must be adjudged a failure, and another attempt must be made to defend the rationality of revelation.

The Renaissance Attack

The dominance of the medieval scholastic viewpoint, of which Thomas was the most brilliant example, ceased with the Reformation and Renaissance. Since this chapter aims to defend the Reformation position, *the Renaissance* will be discussed first. The discussion must be extremely brief: for, since the Renaissance gave rise to modern secular philosophy, the subject is too vast; modern philosophy, moreover, is not a method of harmonizing faith and reason, but of denying faith in favor of reason. Nevertheless, something ought to be said to indicate that this modern attack on revelation has not been completely successful.

Certain details of the attack, such as the allegations that Moses could not have written the Pentateuch because writing had not yet been invented in his day, and that the Hittites never existed, are more appropriately treated under the topic of higher criticism. Here only the guiding principles of its philosophy can be kept in view.

These guiding principles were those employed in the crucial problem of knowledge. Epistemology is the attempt to show that knowledge is possible; and modern philosophy is heavily epistemological. Did these schools succeed in establishing rational knowledge apart from faith or revelation?

The first main school was the seventeenth century school of rationalism.

Their basic belief was that all knowledge is derived from logic alone. One should note that by reason these men meant logic as opposed to sensation. Experience, in their opinion, was the source of error. Only that which could be demonstrated as theorems of geometry are demonstrated, i.e., without appeal to experimentation, is trustworthy.

In general these thinkers, of whom Descartes, Spinoza, and Leibniz were by far the greatest, relied on the ontological argument to prove the existence of God. The ontological argument contends that God has the attribute of existence just as a triangle has the attribute of containing 180 degrees. To deny that God exists is as much a self-contradiction as to deny the geometrical theorem. Thus the existence of God is proved by reason alone, that is by pure logic, without an appeal to sensory experience. Then from the existence of God the rationalists attempt to deduce the laws of science.

Not many contemporary philosophers think that the ontological argument is valid; no contemporary thinker admits that Descartes or Spinoza succeeded in deducing the contents of science in the manner indicated. However stimulating the rationalists may be, however informative on some points, they are universally judged to have failed in the main matter of showing that knowledge is possible. Therefore a Christian can legitimately claim that their attack on revelation collapses with their system as a whole. This is a brief and summary treatment of rationalism indeed, but no one will expect a complete history of modern philosophy in these pages.

Empiricism remains today as a living philosophy. Therefore it may not be said that Locke, Berkeley, and Hume are universally regarded as complete failures. Yet today's empiricism is noticeably different from the eighteenth century variety; and in some cases where it shows greater similarity, one wonders what answers the empiricist would give to the standard objections against Hume.

There are three chief objections to empiricism. First, the impossibility of discovering any "necessary connection" between events or ideas (i.e., the denial of causality) makes historical and scientific investigation futile. At best, knowledge could not extend beyond one's own present impressions and their traces in memory. Second, the disintegration of "the self" results in a world of perceptions that no percipient perceives. This in effect annihilates memory. Third and fundamental, empiricism makes use of space and time surreptitiously at the beginning of the learning process, while explicitly these concepts are learned only at the end.

Thus empirical objections to revelation, and in particular Hume's argument against miracles, are deprived of all foundation.

Immanuel Kant tried bravely to remedy the defects of empiricism by assigning to the mind certain a priori forms. Space and time were supposed to preserve meaning for sensory experience, and the a priori categories were to make thinking possible. Kant's works stand as a monument to his genius, but hardly had the later volumes been published than Jacobi put his finger on a very sore spot. To enter Kant's system it is necessary to assume "things-in-themselves," but the full theory of categories makes the assumption impossible. This conflict between the a priori *forms* of the mind and the *matter* given in sensation started the advance to Hegel.

During his lifetime Hegel attained the acme of professional recognition. And for seventy-five years more his thought was extremely influential. Yet today we see that two of his students, who completely rejected his absolute idealism, Karl Marx and Soren Kierkegaard, have won the decisive battle against him. There are still idealists, of course; and Hegel may still count a few followers. But the assertion of Hegelian bankruptcy cannot be dismissed as a prejudiced Christian device to maintain a theory of revelation.

However, as long as Hegel has some disciples, and as long as remnants of empiricism remain, one might insist that these philosophies have not been conclusively refuted. Therefore, although these viewpoints are not in my opinion the characteristic position of the twentieth century, a Christian defense of revelation is probably under some obligation to show how they should be treated. Unfortunately, not more than one example can be included.

The late Edgar Sheffield Brightman worked out a philosophy of religion along mainly empirical lines, though retaining some ideas from Kant. Values and religious ideals were to be discovered in experience; revelation either plays no part, or, if it is theoretically possible, still it must be judged on the basis of reason. Revelation, he says, must be tested by reason, not reason by revelation. By the term reason, Brightman does not mean the processes of logic as did the rationalists; for him reason is a set of empirically derived principles by which we organize the universe of our experience. He speaks of concrete empirical reason as opposed to bare formal logic. Revelation, he asserts, cannot be used as the basic principle by which to organize experience.

Historically, or course, revelation has been so used; and Brightman never shows why, if there is a living God, revelation could not possibly furnish us with information that would enable us to understand the world and organize our lives. Serious flaws in Brightman's conception of God I have discussed elsewhere (cf. *A Christian View of Men and Things,* Eerdmans, 1952).

What is perhaps the basic difficulty is one that Brightman shares with the humanists, though generally he and they are in radical disagreement. Their concurrence on this point therefore gives it considerable importance, for it furnishes a test that extends beyond the views of one man.

The vulnerable point of Brightman's empirical method, and of all contemporary empiricism, is the professed derivation of genuine values from experience. That there are factors in experience which people actually enjoy is not to be denied. But the problem is to go from the actual and diverse enjoyments to values that have a legitimate claim upon all people. One man enjoys prayer; another whiskey. One man enjoys the life of a retired scholar;

another enjoys being a brutal dictator. Can experience show that these are anything more than personal preferences? Can experience furnish a ground for a universal moral obligation? It is my conclusion, supported by detailed argument in the volume just cited, that this is impossible. For such reasons, then, these remnant philosophies fail to undermine Biblical revelation.

Post-Hegelian philosophy is an important factor in arriving at this negative judgment on the "reason" of Spinoza, Hume, and Hegel. The criticisms of Marx, Nietzsche, and the contemporary instrumentalists have damaged this reason beyond repair. Insofar as these men have signalized the failure of modern philosophy to solve the epistemological problem, their conclusions seem incontrovertible. But since they are violently opposed to revelation, they have been forced to adopt a skepticism so deep that not even reason in the sense of the laws of logic is exempt.

In anticipation of Freud, Nietzsche tells us that all thinking is controlled by biological functions. The distinction between truth and falsity as such is unimportant: a false opinion that sustains life is better than a truth that does not. In fact, truth might well be defined as the kind of error without which a species cannot live. Logic with its law of contradiction is the result of a blind evolution which might have been different. At any rate, logic falsifies nature; it puts different things into the same category by ignoring their differences; and the coarser the organ, the more similarities it sees. The fact that we use logic merely signifies our inability to examine more closely; and the result is that logic holds good only for assumed existences which we have created and not for the real world.

F. C. S. Schiller, A. J. Ayer, Jean Paul Sartre, each in his own way attacks the necessity of logic. Thus the typical philosophic position of the twentieth century is not so much to be designated skepticism as outright irrationalism.

The Neo-orthodox Compromise

Although these men are openly anti-Christian, there is also a twentieth century form of irrationalism, derived directly from Hegel's student Kierkegaard, that clothes itself with Christian terminology and tries to avoid the excesses of Nietzsche by an appeal to revelation. It sometimes claims to be a return to the Reformation point of view. One must ask not only whether this claim can be historically justified, but more particularly whether this philosophy provides an adequate validation of the Christian concept of revelation.

This so-called neo-orthodox or existential movement willingly admits that reason has come to grief. Even inanimate nature is beyond intellectual understanding because there is no motion in logic and no logic in motion. Becoming is open and reality is chance. If logic founders on physical motion, it is all the more impotent in the issues of life. What is needed is not conclusions but decisions. We must therefore make a leap of faith and accept a revelation from God.

To many devout people, disturbed by the popularity of secular scientism, oppressed by the deadening influence of modernism, and (unjustifiably) frightened by the negations of higher criticism, neo-orthodoxy seemed like manna from on high. Revelation had now been saved; reason had been defeated!

However, before the heirs of Luther and Calvin can properly rejoice, they must know precisely what this revelation is, what sort of faith is meant, and whether anything of worth remains after reason's defeat. The failure of seventeenth century rationalism causes no alarm; the fate of Hume and Hegel can be taken in stride; Brightman's concrete and empirical reason can well be dispensed with; but what remains if reason in the sense of the laws of logic has to be abandoned? Of what value would be an irrational or illogical revelation?

The chief law of logic is the law of contradiction, and it is this law that maintains the distinction between truth and falsity. If this distinction cannot be maintained, then as the ancient Sophists showed, all opinions are true and all opinions are false. Any proposition is as credible as any other. If therefore Nietzsche or Freud have used reasoning in coming to their position, and if reasoning distorts reality, and if one theory is no more true than another, it follows that these men have no good ground for asserting their theories. To deny reason, in the sense of the laws of logic, is to empty conversation or argument of all meaning.

Now, this is what neo-orthodoxy as well as Nietzsche does. In his *Concluding Unscientific Postscript* Kierkegaard had said that it makes no difference whether a man prays to God or to an idol, provided he prays passionately. Truth, he said, lies in the inward How, not in the external What. If only the How of the individual's relation is "true," then the individual is in truth, even though he is thus related to untruth.

Brunner also abolishes the distinction between truth and falsity. First, he refers to a kind of "truth" that cannot be expressed in words or grasped in intellectual concepts. What this truth is, no one can say. Second, the words, sentences, and intellectual content that "point to" this hidden truth may or may not be true. God can reveal himself (*Wahrheit als Begegnung*, p. 88) through false propositions as well as through true ones. We can never be sure, therefore, that what God tells us is true. Falsehood and truth have equal value.

Surely such value must be very little. For one thing, it relieves us of the responsibility of being consistent. Our creed can contain contradictory articles. Brunner argues that "straight line inference" must be curbed. We dare not follow out our principles to their logical conclusions. Not always, at any rate. Brunner, indeed, points out Schleiermacher's contradiction in insisting both on the absoluteness of Christianity and the discovery of a common element in all religions. He is also consistent when he argues that man must have been created righteous, for otherwise there could have been no Fall. But when Brunner comes to Romans 9 and finds its obvious meaning distasteful, he declares that election is illogical and that if we drew inferences from it, we would conclude that God is not love. One cannot have love and logic both. Hence the Bible is consistently illogical.[2]

But if the Bible is illogical and if Brunner is illogical, do we not have a logical right to ignore them, for there is no illogical necessity that our faith should leap in their direction?

The purpose of the whole argument to this juncture has been to make three points: neo-orthodoxy's irrational defense of revelation is self-destructive; modern philosophy's rational attack on revelation left itself without an epistemological foundation; and the kind of reason Thomism used to defend revelation was beset with fallacies. But now to continue the argument, the general procedure of Reformation thought provides another possibility for a rational revelation.

The Reformation Way

In this case a *rational* revelation is one that preserves the distinction between truth and falsity. It is in its entirety self-consistent. In other words, reason is identified as the laws of logic. Christianity is under no obligation to justify itself as rational in any other sense, for the history of philosophy has shown that all the other senses result in skepticism. Therefore to claim that election, or the atonement, or any other doctrine is "irrational" is nothing more than to assert that these doctrines are distasteful to the objector. The accusation is not a substantiated intellectual conclusion, but an emotional antipathy. If the Biblical doctrines are self-consistent, they have met the only legitimate test of reason. This test of logic is precisely the requirement that a set of propositions be meaningful, whether spoken by God or man. And if propositions have no meaning, obviously they reveal nothing.

It is now fair to ask whether this construction is historically the Reformation viewpoint. Did Luther and Calvin accept the Bible as self-consistent, and did they recognize the sole tests of logic?

The first of these two questions is the easier to answer. That the Bible presents a self-consistent intellectual system, and that Calvin was convinced of it, has been made sufficiently clear in his *Institutes* and *Commentaries*. The Westminster Confession is additional testimony. The Calvinistic love of logic is well known; and, as has been seen, it was a distaste for Calvinism that led Brunner to reject logic. This point, therefore, is characteristic of the Reformed faith.

The second of these two questions is more complicated because the Reformers did not explicitly discuss logic as the sole test of a rational revelation. Their silence is understandable, however, for irrationalism is mainly a twentieth century phenomenon that they did not anticipate. Nevertheless, that the preceding construction is implicit in their views may be plausibly

[2] For a thorough analysis of Brunner's thought, see the excellent volume, *Brunner's Concept of Revelation,* by Paul King Jewett, James Clarke & Co., 1954.

inferred from their methods. They abandoned the scholastic philosophy; they spent no time attempting to prove the existence of God, much less the sensory origin of knowledge; the contrast between the *Institutes* and the Summae of Thomas is unmistakable. Hence they could not have used any "concrete and empirical reason." Then, too, the principle that the Scriptures are their own infallible interpreter, and that what is unclear in one passage can be understood by a comparison with other passages, is nothing other than the application of the law of contradiction. Logic therefore must have been the only test that the Reformers could have used.

I freely admit that some passages in Calvin seem to allow for a less skeptical reaction to the course of philosophy than this chapter presents. They must, however, be understood in the light of other very definite statements found in the same contexts.

One of Calvin's most generous acknowledgments of pagan learning is made in the *Institutes*, II, ii, 14 ff. The following summary and interpretation can easily be compared with the original. After rejecting the Platonic pre-existence of the soul, Calvin asserts that human ingenuity constrains us to acknowledge an innate intellectual principle in the human mind. Since this could not possibly be Brightman's concrete empirical reason, is it not more likely that Calvin had the laws of logic in mind? With this innate equipment Roman lawyers delivered just principles of civil order; philosophers described nature with an exquisite science; those who by the art of logic have taught us to speak rationally cannot have been destitute of understanding; pagan mathematics could not have been the raving of madmen. No, the writings of the ancients are excellent because they proceeded from God.

This is indeed high praise. In fact, it is such high praise that its object can hardly be the absolute theoretical truth of pagan philosophies. Admittedly, Calvin was unaware of how mistaken the ancient learning was; nor can it be supposed that he had elaborated an instrumental theory of science. Yet his admiration of the physics, logic, mathematics, and other arts and sciences of antiquity can comfortably and more plausibly be divided between the intellectual brilliance displayed and the practical applications made possible. It is the energy, the ingenuity, the exquisiteness of the ancients that he admires, rather than the truth of their systems.

In the immediate sequel Calvin corrects some misapprehensions of his intention. With respect to the kingdom of God and spiritual wisdom the most sagacious of mankind are blinder than moles. The most apposite of their observations betray confusion. They saw the objects presented to their view in such a manner that by the sight they were not even directed to the truth, much less did they arrive at it. Fortuitously, by accident, some isolated sentences may be true; but human reason neither approaches, nor tends, nor directs its views towards the truth of God.

That Calvin did not base the truth and rationality of Scripture on external supports is better seen in an earlier chapter (I, viii,). The title is:

Rational Proof to Establish the Belief of the Scripture. In a twentieth century setting this title is misleading. Today such a title would suggest an
appeal to the superior authority of, perhaps, religious experience. This was
not Calvin's intention.

Without a prior certainty of revelation, he says, a certainty stronger than
any judgment of experience, the authority of the Scripture is defended in
vain by arguments, by the consent of the church, or by any other support.
Faith is founded, not in the wisdom of men, but by the power of God. For
the truth is vindicated from every doubt, when, unassisted by foreign aid, it
is sufficient for its own support. The thought of this significant sentence is
repeated at the end of the same chapter. While there are many subsidiary
reasons by which the native dignity of the Scripture may be vindicated, he
says, such alone are not sufficient to produce firm faith in it, till the heavenly
Father, discovering his own power therein (i.e., in the Scripture itself),
places its authority beyond all controversy.

To these words of Calvin I should like to add only that the law of contradiction, or reason, is not an external test of Scripture. Logical consistency is
exemplified in the Scripture; and thus the Scripture can be a meaningful
revelation to the rational mind of man. Self-contradictory propositions would
be meaningless, irrational, and could not constitute a revelation.

III. SOME CONTEMPORARY PROBLEMS

If now Calvin could not have addressed himself explicitly to twentieth
century problems, the obligation lies the more heavily on us. Of course, there
are many, but there is one immediate attack on the possibility of a rational
revelation that ought not to be ignored.

Theories of the origin, nature, and purpose of language have been recently
developed that would prevent God from speaking the truth to man on the
ground that language cannot convey literal truth. Some writers say that all
language is symbolic or metaphorical. For example, Wilbur Marshall Urban
(*Language and Reality*, pp. 383, 433) asserts that "There are no strictly
literal sentences . . . there is no such thing as literal truth . . . any expression in language contains some symbolic element." Other writers make more
restricted claims and say only that all religious language is metaphorical.
From which it follows that if God uses language, he cannot tell the literal
truth, but must speak in symbolism or mythology.

Those who defend the Bible as a true revelation must insist that it conveys
literal truth. This does not mean that God cannot sometimes use symbolism
and metaphor. Of course there is symbolism in Ezekiel, there are parables in
the Gospels, and there are metaphors scattered throughout. God might have
used even mythology and fable. But unless there are literal statements along
with these figures of speech, or at the very least, unless figures of speech can
be translated into literal truth, a book conveys no definite meaning.

Suppose the cross be selected as a Christian symbol, and suppose some flowery speaker should say, Let us live in the shadow of the cross. What can he mean? What does the cross symbolize? Does it symbolize the love of God? Or does it symbolize the wrath of God? Does it symbolize human suffering? Or does it symbolize the influence of the church? If there are no literal statements to give information as to what the cross symbolizes, these questions are unanswerable.

Let a person say that the cross symbolizes the love of God. However, if all language or all religious language is symbolical, the statement that the cross symbolizes the love of God is itself a symbol. A symbol of what? When this last question is answered, we shall find that this answer is again a symbol. Then another symbol will be needed, and another. And the whole process will be meaningless.

This contemporary theory of language is open to the same objections that were raised against the Thomistic notion of analogical knowledge. In order to have meaning, an analogy, a metaphor, or a symbol must be supported by some literal truth. If Samson was as strong as an ox, then an ox must literally be strong. If Christ is the lion of the tribe of Judah, then something must be literally true about lions and about Christ also. No matter with what literary embellishment the comparison be made, there must be a strictly true statement that has given rise to it. And a theory that says all language is symbolic is a theory that cannot be taken as literally true. Its own statements are metaphorical, and meaningless.

Furthermore, a theory of language has to be taken as a part of a more general philosophic system. While some linguists may study a few minute details, a theory that concerns the origin, the nature, and the purpose of language presupposes some over-all view of human nature and of the world in which mankind exists. The contemporary theories are often based on an evolutionary philosophy in which human language is supposed to have originated in the squeals and grunts of animals. These evolutionary theories of language, and some that are not explicitly evolutionary, reveal their connection with epistemology by making sensory impressions the immediate source of language. The first words ever spoken were supposedly nouns or names produced by imitating the sound that an animal or a waterfall made; or if the object made no noise, some more arbitrary method was used to attach a noun to it.

When this view is accepted by Thomists, they inherit the problem of passing from a sensory based language to a proper mode of expressing theological propositions. The logical positivists, on the other hand, conclude with more show of reason that this cannot be done, and that theological language is nonsense. But in any case, a theory of language must be set into a complete system of philosophy. It cannot stand in isolation.

Both the naturalistic evolutionist and the evangelical Christian have their guiding principles. The former has no choice but to develop language from animal cries—no matter what the difficulties may be, and they are insuperable. The latter, by reason of the doctrine of creation, must maintain that language is adequate for all religions and theological expression—no matter what the difficulties may be, but they are not very great. The possibility of rational communication between God and man is easily explained on theistic presuppositions.

If God created man in his own rational image and endowed him with the power of speech, then a purpose of language, in fact, the chief purpose of language, would naturally be the revelation of truth to man and the prayers of man to God. In a theistic philosophy one ought not to say, as a recent Thomist has said, that all language has been devised in order to describe and discuss the finite objects of our sense-experience (E. L. Mascall, *Words and Images,* p. 101). On the contrary, language was devised by God, that is, God created man rational for the purpose of theological expression. Language is, of course, adaptable to sensory description and the daily routine of life, but it is unnecessary to invent the problem of how sensory expressions can be transmuted into a proper method of talking about God.

This immediately overturns the objection to verbal inspiration that is based on the alleged finitude and imperfections of language. If reason, i.e., logic, which makes speech possible, is a God-given faculty, it must be adequate to its divinely appointed task. And its task is the reception of divinely revealed information and the systematization of these propositions in dogmatic theology.

To sum up: language is capable of conveying literal truths because the laws of logic are necessary. There is no substitute for them. Philosophers who deny them reduce their own denials to nonsense syllables. Even where the necessity of logic is not denied, if reason is used in some other sense as a source of truth, the result has been skepticism. Therefore, revelation is not only rational, but it is the only hope of maintaining rationality. And this is corroborated by the actual consistency that we discover when we examine the verbally inspired revelation called the Bible.

SPECIAL REVELATION AS HISTORICAL AND PERSONAL

Paul K. Jewett

Paul K. Jewett is Associate Professor of Systematic and Historical Theology at Fuller Theological Seminary, California. He holds the B. A. degree from Wheaton College, Th.B. and Th.M. from Westminster Theological Seminary, and Ph.D. from Harvard. He studied in Zurich for a year, and is author of Emil Brunner's Concept of Revelation.

3. Paul K. Jewett

SPECIAL REVELATION AS HISTORICAL AND PERSONAL

WHEN THE Christian theologian speaks of revelation as historical, is he
not on a cleft stick? If he talks about history, how can he still talk about
revelation, which has to do with absolute truth? History has always worn the
mean garment of contingency, which makes any claims to absoluteness seem
overweening and presumptuous. In our day this is especially the case. Now
that we know that the eternal hills are not eternal and that the fixed stars
are anything but fixed, now that we can date not only civilizations and cultures but the world itself, what absolute is there left but that of John Dewey's
"Absolutely no absolutes"? Have not the mediating attempts of liberal
theologies proven vain? Is not the end of the way the "History and Psychology of Religion School," in which the divine and the human are finally
and completely identified? History, it is asserted, can never be more than
a documentation of man's religious experience, the record of his quest for
God. Obviously in such a context there can be no admission of a "Thus saith
the Lord." As Karl Barth, while still a young pastor trained in such liberal
theology, once complained, "Both tables of the law slip from the preacher's
hand as he approaches the people" ("Moderne Theologie und Reichsgootes-
arbeit," *Zeitschrift fur Theologie und Kirche,* 1919, p. 317). Is it then
really possible to speak of revelation as historical?

I. REVELATION AS HISTORICAL

To escape this impasse, many religious thinkers have followed the way pioneered by Plato and declared that the realm of time and space is one of flux and change. Revelation for such thinkers is no matter of history at all. It is ridiculous to seek an historical foundation for religious truth. To be sure, one may see in certain events in history the concretion of eternal truths. In the life of Jesus, for example, the idea of sacrificing love is given noble expression; but one could never commit himself to Jesus, for someone will one day surpass him. History knows no absolutes. As Fichte has said, "Only the metaphysical can save, never under any circumstances the historical" (as quoted by Brunner, *Offenbarung und Vernunft*, Zurich, 1941, p. 394).

Need to Escape Relativism and Idealism

So long as we have the mind of the Greeks, we shall never steer the ship of our thought between this Scylla and Charybdis. Historical relativism is that Scylla which makes impossible a *revelation* in history, by denying any realm transcending history. Idealism is that Charybdis which makes impossible a revelation in *history* by its flight from the continuum of time and space into the realm of eternal ideas.

The Biblical View of History as the Medium of Disclosure

All this points up the uniqueness of the Biblical idea of revelation, which is that history is the medium through which the eternal God has revealed himself once for all. The foundation is laid in the Old Testament concept of the history of Israel. Of course the distinctiveness of Israel's history is not in anything that Israel has done. Considered on its own merits, the history of the Jewish people is tied to universal history by the thread of analogy. The wind in Israel goes toward the south and then toward the north and returns again according to his circuits; the rivers run into the sea and thus return to the place whence they came. Not everything is new even under the Hebrew sun. As a segment in the horizontal line of world history, Jewish history is also vanity of vanities (Ecclesiastes 1).

But for prophets and seers of the Old Testament, along with and in this stream of world history there moves a divine history. God is active in Israel's history in a way that he is not in other nations. To be sure, these revelatory acts of God may, by the analogy of history, be explained away. The opening chapters of Genesis may be dismissed as myths of the primitive mind calculated to illumine such naturally intriguing phenomena as why snakes have no legs, why weeds grow, why women have pain in childbirth, why people wear clothes, and the like; the various laws of the Pentateuch may be reduced to species of ancient oriental codes reflecting Palestinian conditions of the time; the Exodus out of Egypt may be viewed as a congeries of singular co-incidences, and the prophecies as instances of shrewd political presentiment.

But for any candid student, this can hardly be the final word. The history of Israel involves more than a miscellany of primitive myths, oriental codes, religious ceremonies, and tracts for the times, interlarded with pious aspiration. Deeply embedded in this history, as an endemic stratum, is the element of teleology, that is the divine purpose. As Dorner has said, "Israel has the idea of teleology as a kind of soul" (*System of Doctrine,* Vol. I, p. 274). Unlike the Greeks, who never made history the object of serious philosophic reflection, for the prophets of the Old Testament, time is (as Kierkegaard would say) "laden with eternity." History is not a series of recurring cycles, as in Stoicism, but it is hastening like an arrow shot from the bow towards its mark. There is real forward movement of the hand on the clock of the universe.[1] This is readily seen when we take a larger view of the Old Testament landscape. The basis is laid in the account of the creation of the world and specifically of man, the lord and heir of all he surveys. When he defects from the path of rectitude, God does not cease to act toward him and to speak with him. He seeks out the guilty pair; he clothes their nakedness and though he pronounces a curse upon their heads, it is a malediction big with benediction (Gen. 3:15). And what is this Protevangelium but the promise that God will not cease to act in history till he has destroyed man's mortal foe and undone the mischief which he wrought?

With the lapse of the nations into heathenism, a new start is made in the call of Abraham and the promise that in his seed all nations of the earth shall be blessed (Gen. 12 ff.). This age of the patriarchs is succeeded by that of Moses and the beginning of Israel's national life according to the terms of the Abrahamic Covenant. With the uprooting of Israel from her place in the family of nations, the divine purpose in history is not frustrated; rather, out of the womb of adversity and seeming defeat, the redemptive purpose of God in history emerges enlarged, clarified, spiritualized, the confidence of all the prophets. But the Old Testament idea of history, as the scene of God's acts as Redeemer of his people, is not an end in itself. Its meaning is Jesus Christ,

---

[1] Cf. E. Brunner, "Das Einmalige und der Existenzcharakte," *Blätter für deutsche Philosophie,* 3:268–70, 1929. Marlowe, in his poem, *The Tragical History of Doctor Faustus,* conveys this mood in a passage unexcelled in English for sheer force:

> *Faustus:*   Ah, Faustus,
> Now hast thou but one bare hour to live;
> And then thou must be damned perpetually!
> Stand still, you ever-moving spheres of heaven,
> That time may cease, and midnight never come;
> Fair Nature's eye, rise, rise again, and make
> Perpetual day; or let this hour be but
> A year, a month, a week, a natural day,
> That Faustus may repent and save his soul!
> *O lente, lente currite, noctis equi!*
> The stars move still, time runs, the clock will strike,
> The devil will come, and Faustus must be damned.

whose name is Emmanuel, God-with-us, who came to "fulfill the law and the prophets." The prophets *had* the Word of God, but Jesus *is* the Word. "And the Word was made flesh and dwelt among us, and we beheld his glory, glory as of the only begotten of the Father, full of grace and truth" (John 1:14). The incarnation is that event in history which gathers up all other revelation into itself. Jesus is the seed of the woman who shall bruise the serpent's head, and when this work shall have been accomplished, then shall the covenant promise be finally fulfilled, then the tabernacle of God shall be with men and he shall be their God and they his people. Thus redemptive history moves from creation to consummation; this is the divine self-disclosure complete.

The Necessity of Divine Interpretation

Having said this much, we must immediately add the obvious, and that is, that this revelation in history, this *Tat-wort* (act-word) of God, as the Germans would say, is no revelation in and of itself. Revelation presupposes someone to whom the revelation is given. In order to have revelation, there must be, as William Temple has said in his Gifford lectures, "the intercourse of mind and event" or "the coincidence of event and appreciation" (*Nature, Man and God*, p. 315 f.) To analyze the character of this "intercourse," whether it is rational or intuitive, whether it involves a communication of general impressions or specific words, is beyond the province of this particular essay. But one thing must be said, and that is, that we cannot, as Christians, speak of historical events *per se*, as revelation, any more than we can speak of revelation apart from historical events. God must, by his grace, disclose the meaning of his acts.

> Blind unbelief is sure to err
> And scan His works in vain;
> God is His own interpreter
> And He will make it plain.

That is what he has done in the minds of the prophets and apostles who wrote the Scriptures. The Bible, from the perspective of our discussion, is simply the sacred record of what God has done in history together with the inspired authoritative interpretation of these saving events. The implications of this position for various questions currently debated in theological circles will be treated more fully in subsequent essays of this volume. We can take the time here to summarize for the reader only the most important phases of the contemporary debate.

Special Problems

First of all, there is the question of the "primal history," that is, Genesis 1-11. The traditional, orthodox view (Augustine was a notable exception) is that this portion of Scripture should be interpreted as a literal piece of history, just as—let us say—the fifteenth chapter of the book of Acts. By contrast, religious liberalism treats the content of these chapters as so many fairy tales, having no more historical value than the fables of Aesop. The neo-orthodox have assayed to straddle the fence,[2] or as they would prefer to say, to rise above this orthodox-liberal antithesis, escaping the guilt on the one hand of "wooden literalism," and on the other, of flippant "enlightenment." Accordingly it is argued that the opening chapters of Genesis are to be understood, not as scientific report, but as revelation. This distinction between science and revelation is, we might almost say, indispensable to one who approaches the Bible with an informed seriousness. The difficulty is, that the neo-orthodox approach involves the abandonment and thus sacrifices the significance of the opening chapters of Genesis as events in time and space. In the writer's opinion, this is to deny the fundamental character of revelation as historical. This is cryptic Idealism in a contemporary form—the shade of Schleiermacher. What the answer is, to certain specific problems posed by present day science, it is neither easy nor imperative for faith to say, but if the Christian view conceives revelation as "mighty acts of God" in history, then, at the very least, it would seem, we must believe (as our Lord and his apostles did believe)[3] that the events reported in the opening chapters of Genesis actually did happen. There was a first man, a first Adam, who was created upright and fell, not *into* history, but *in* history, by a willful act of disobedience bringing

". . . death into the world, and all our woe";

and this event was followed by the assurance of pardon and the promise of deliverance. This "eventness" is not simply the form of revelation, not even the "indispensable" form. It *is* the revelation; and the *prius* of the subsequent revelation of God in Christ, the Word that became flesh.

The other area of the Biblical witness that is most crucial in this debate is the fourfold Gospel tradition. Never has any segment of history sustained such a mass of intense critical probing as the period which we call "the public ministry of our Lord." If, as we have said, revelation, for the Christian, is first of all God's mighty acts in history, and if this revelation culminates in the Incarnation, when God himself entered the scene of temporal life to perform the decisive act of all history, then it is natural enough that this segment of the horizontal line of human affairs should be scrutinized minutely. This critical sifting has established certain facts and raised certain questions about the Gospel tradition that may never be finally answered, such as: just what is the relation of the Synoptics to each other, and of John to the Synoptics; exactly what sources were employed by the several Gospel historians; to what extent do we have a report of the *ipsissima verba* of our

---

[2] Karl Barth, when asked if he believed the serpent really talked, replied, "One should rather ask what he said!" Brunner labeled this an ingenious evasion of a problem that cannot be evaded (*Der Mensch im Widerspruch*, p. 78, footnote).
[3] Cf. Matthew 19:4 f.; 24:38–39; Romans 5:12–21; II Corinthians 13:6; Hebrews 11; I Peter 3:20.

Lord and to what extent a summary in the authors' own words; is it possible, from the Gospels, to construct a chronology of Jesus' life, or are the agglutinative materials in the narratives to be construed loosely as serving a mere literary purpose? If revelation is historical, then the Christian can never shun these and other tensions of critical history, nor can any theory of Biblical inspiration survive if lacking the resilience to adjust to these tensions. But there are dangers even more serious than the obscurantist refusal to enter the strife of history. One is to define the historical basis of our faith in Christ as some "irreducible minimum" far below the requirements of the Gospel tradition (Kierkegaard); another is to declare that the form of the Gospel tradition is "mythological" (Bultmann).

As for the former position, Kierkegaard defined the apostolic witness necessary for faith as follows: ". . . we have believed that in such and such a year, God showed himself in the humble form of a servant, lived and taught among us and thereupon died" (*Philosophische Brocken*, p. 94). This he considered as "more than enough." Emil Brunner, in his massive Christology, *Der Mittler*, the profoundest and most challenging discussion of the problem from a neo-orthodox point of view, elaborates this Kierkegaardian motif. Faith is not interested, as is criticism, in the Biblical history as history, but only as the Word of God. The Eternal cannot be hung as a particularly large pearl in the string of historical events. The eternal as event, as revelation, has as such no historical extension. "The Eternal in history—revelation, that which is absolutely unique, is not perceptible as that which has historical extent." Revelation "is not the extended fact in history which we call the life of Jesus and the historical personality of Jesus . . ." (*Der Mittler*, p. 271). If it were, revelation would be a quantum, and each "piece" of the life of the historical Jesus in its time-space movement a "piece" of revelation (*ibid.*, p. 318.) Such direct identity between the life of Jesus and revelation does not exist. If it did, if God's revelation in Christ is a piece of history, then it is subject to that inexorable law of history according to which one fulfillment overtakes and destroys another, till finally all sinks in that cemetery of world history called the Field of Oblivion. Then the *today* of "Today is this Scripture fulfilled," is shorn of its absolute point of reference. It becomes like the cry of the Germans in 1870, when they won back Alsace. "Today" is our hope fulfilled, said they. But forty years later the last echoes of this "today" died as the French entered Strasbourg ("Der Erfüller," *Zwischen den Zeiten*, 8:273–8, 1930).

Brunner has come to realize, however, that Kierkegaard was guilty of a gross overstatement when he defined the historical basis of faith so narrowly, a mistake which had a fateful effect on his own theology. What Kierkegaard did not clearly see was that the question "What is said to us?" when we read the Gospels cannot be separated from the question "Did that happen?" inasmuch as "it is precisely this that is said, that that *happened*" (*Die christliche Lehre von Gott*, 278). Faith cannot, Brunner says, arise or be sustained apart from the historical picture of Jesus as we have it in the Gospels and the knowledge of the fact that this picture, in its main outlines, corresponds to reality (cf. *ibid.,* p. 281). Without Passion *history,* there can be no message of the Cross! (*Die christliche Lehre von Schöpfung und Erlösung,* p. 289). The Church has always had, he admits, an absolutely central interest in the historical Jesus, only that in the precritical age, this historical Jesus was without question "identified with the sum total of the Gospel tradition" (*ibid.,* p. 289). Brunner rejects the historic Christian disposition to take the tradition without alteration in detail. He feels that this loss is no concern to faith so long as the basic structure, the substance of the tradition, remains unshaken. This insistence on the indispensable character of Passion history is a real advance in the right direction. The evangelical, however, approaches even the details of the Gospel tradition with the greatest possible reverence, for they are the stuff out of which the "substance" of the tradition is made.

As for Bultmann's "demythologizing" of the Gospel history, his fundamental thesis is that the New Testament witness to the Incarnation, as we have it in our Gospels, conceives and states the event in mythological terms which need to be converted into "existential" terms, if modern man is to understand and receive it (cf. D. M. Baillie, *God Was in Christ,* New York, 1948, Appendix, p. 211 f.). He does not mean (and in all fairness to Bultmann the point should be made) that the record of the Gospels is a record of imaginary events and that Jesus is in a class with Zeus or Santa Claus. We pause to make this point since the word "myth," in scientific theological discussion, has often been used in a Hegelian sense. David Friedrich Strauss, for example, when he explained the elements in the Gospel story as mythical, made it plain that he was quite indifferent to the question of historical events. Even if Jesus never existed, Christian faith is unshaken, if it but grasp the eternal truths symbolized by the pictorial language of the myth. This is what Albert Schweitzer has called (with approval) "free-thinking Christianity" which can live "from the insights and energies of an immediate religion, which is independent of all historical foundation" (*Geschichte der Leben-Jesu—Forschung,* Tübingen, 1913, p. 541).

Now Bultmann, by contrast, certainly does believe that the central element in the Gospel narrative—"crucified under Pontius Pilate"—is history in the most obvious terrestrial sense. But it is also true that he shows a lordly indifference to most of the Gospel tradition. The end result of Bultmann's approach reveals that a Gospel, purified from mythology, means a Gospel "purified" from *history;* and when this happens it marks the end of Christianity (cf. N. B. Stonehouse, *Paul Before the Areopagus,* Chapter 5). Bultmann may ask if we believe Christ literally "ascended into heaven." Was he then the first space traveller? And if so, he has yet a long way to go. We would answer that the ascension, to be sure, is not a scientific description of the way in which the glorified Christ entered upon his session at the right hand of the Father. But neither is it a religious myth which must or even may be deleted from our preaching in this age of rockets and Sputniks. The Scriptures say that he was taken up into heaven and that a cloud received him out of the apostles' sight (Acts 1:9, 11). We may not be able to explain how this happened, but the event itself must have happened; he must have been "taken up," or the doctrine of Christ's exaltation is simply an *idea.* Was it not Calvin who said that the Holy Spirit lisps to us in Scripture as a nurse to a child? The theologian must never attempt to speak more plainly than God. If he does, he will end up with a sublimated "Christian Idealism" which dissolves historical revelation into symbols of the Eternal. There is only one objection to such a position and that is that it is not Christianity.

The pith and marrow of what we have said thus far is this: for the Christian, revelation begins with God's disclosure of his purpose in and through our temporality. History is not a God-forsaken stream of meaningless events. We have admitted indeed that no events, *per se,* are revelation. Man can never discover God for himself, in history. " 'Canst thou by searching find out God?' To man's proud 'not yet' the Bible replies, 'nor ever' " (Brunner, *Unser Glaube,* Bern, 1935, p. 11). A truly revelatory situation, then, is one in which God not only *does* something, but interprets what he does; not only *acts,* but *speaks* in, with and through the acts. That is to say, revelation moves in the dimension of personal encounter. The writers of Scripture not only saw what God did and (by faith) what he would do, but they also heard his "still small voice," by which he made known to them his secret. The time has come to develop this phase of our thesis more at length.

II. REVELATION AS PERSONAL

Out of the critical analysis of the fundamental ideas of the past, precipitated by the first World War, there came a little book by Ferdinand Ebner, the thesis of which is that the gift of speech in man is "scientific" evidence that he is made for fellowship. He cannot live alone, apart from his neighbor, but especially apart from God. This idea is briefly summed up in the preface:

> It does not appear entirely superfluous to me, here in the foreword, to reduce the fundamental thought in the *Fragments* to as brief a formula as possible. This fundamental thought is: presupposed that human existence in its kernel has a spiritual significance, that is, a significance which is not exhausted in its natural manifestation in the course of a world event; presupposed that one may speak of something spiritual in man otherwise than in the sense of a fiction of a poetic or metaphoric nature, of a fiction demanded on "social" grounds: then this spiritual entity is essentially defined thereby, that it is fundamentally connected with something *outside* of it, through which and in which it exists. An evidence, and, indeed, an "objectively" tangible evidence, of dependence upon a relation of such a sort and one that is therefore accessible to objective knowledge, is to be found in the fact that man is a speaking being, that he has the "Word." He does not, however, have the word on a natural

or social basis. Society in the human sense, is not the presupposition of speech, but rather itself has as the presupposition of its existence, that the word is lodged in man. If then, in order to have an expression for it, we call this spiritual entity in man, I, and that which is *outside* of him, in relationship to which the "I" exists, thou, we must remember that this I and this thou are given to us precisely *through* the Word and *in* it, in its "inwardness"; not however, as empty words in which dwells no relationship to reality . . . but rather as a word, that "reduplicates" its content and real form in the concreteness and actuality of its being pronounced in and through the situation created by speech. That, in brief, is the fundamental thought (*Das Wort und die geistigen Realitäten, Pneumatologische Fragmente,* Innsbruck, 1921, p. 12).

Ebnerian Personalism

This analysis of man's ultimate involvement through speech in a relationship to a "thou," Ebner sets over against any form of religious thought in which man is involved in a soliloquy, as in the ethical Idealism of Kant, where the transcendental self addresses the empirical self. It was, according to Ebner, Johann George Hamann, "that marvelously profound 'philologist,' " and Wilhelm von Humboldt, who saw the significance of speech in its spiritual roots as of divine origin, something absolutely transcendent. The self which knows no authority outside itself will not allow itself to be spoken to. The autonomous self is the result of the "falling away from God," the refusal to hear God speaking to us, who is "the true Thou of the true I in man. . . ." This absolutizing of the self in its cosmic loneliness, this misunderstanding of the self with itself (Hamann), can mean nothing else than the spiritual death of man, for the true "I" exists only in relation to the divine "Thou" (*ibid.* pp. 17, 21, 26, 113).

A second thinker who came to many of the same conclusions as Ebner, but evidently in an independent way, was Martin Buber. (His views are set forth primarily in his *Ich und Du* [Leipzig, 1923], which appeared two years after Ebner's work; but a notation at the close informs us that a sketch of the work was made in 1916, first written draft in the fall of 1919, and final composition in the spring of 1922.) Buber opens his study with a distinction between two basic word pairs which sum up his fundamental thesis. "The one basic word is the word pair, I-thou; the other basic word is the word pair, I-it" (*Ich und Du,* p. 10). The world of objects is a shallow one, according to Buber, for it does not *change me,* even when I am concerned with "revealing," "secret" experiences. "O secretness without mystery, O heaping up of information—it, it, it!" (*ibid.,* p. 12). The real world for Buber is the world of fellowship. "In the beginning is relationship" (*ibid.,* p. 25).

Brunner's Application to Theology

Though the thought of these personalists has had a general influence on the dialectical school of theology, to Emil Brunner belongs the distinction of having pioneered in working out the implications of this approach for the whole range of theological thinking. A partial explanation of this fact, no doubt, is the interest in "the personal" which he always had as a neo-Kantian. As early as 1919 he wrote, "Only the personal is fruitful . . ." (*Denken und Erleben,* Basel, 1919, p. 27). And in an address before the Kantian Society of Utrecht he argued that the I first realizes itself in the thou-address of the categorical imperative.[4] Brunner testifies that it was the work of Friedrich Gogarten, first of the dialectical theologians to express special appreciation for Ebner, that quickened his own sense of the importance of the personal dimension. His initial major effort in this direction was contained in his Uppsala lectures which appeared under the title, *Wahrheit als Begegnung* (Berlin, 1938), a small but highly stimulating volume and perhaps the most original of any that he has written. In the preface of this work he states his thesis: "The Biblical concept of truth is truth as encounter," encounter, that is, between the Divine Person and the human. He concedes that the implications of such a statement for all spheres of church doctrine and practice are immeasurable and we have in his *Dogmatics,* of which two volumes have now appeared, the first attempt ever made to unfold Christian teaching from the perspective of truth as personal encounter.

The limitations imposed by our subject forbid that we follow the interesting implications (sometimes aberrations) for the various *loci* of theology as drawn by Brunner, the great theologian of personalism. We must content ourselves with the less ambitious assignment of evaluating the contribution of these men to our thought about Christian revelation. The sensitive reader will have perceived that this personalistic emphasis is but a species of the genus, existentialism, and will have anticipated that it has the weakness and the strength of that larger movement. Well, what is the weakness of existentialism? Is it not irrationalism? Ebner once said,

> Either God has a personal existence or He does not exist at all. One cannot, however, comprehend His personality in a speculative way, but only by relating himself personally to him—that is, by making Him the thou of his own I—which indeed is required by man's spiritual life and by God Himself. And when this happens all speculation and every form of theological and metaphysical erudition *eo ipso* ceases (*Das Wort,* p. 168).

How true this is. We rationally analyze things; we meet persons. And God is personal. We cannot discover him at the end of a syllogism. But yet, how untrue it is, if Ebner means to imply that God's self-disclosure to man by-passes his rational facilities. Emil Brunner appears to draw this conclusion

> God and the medium of conceptuality are mutually exclusive. God
> is personal and discloses Himself only in the medium of personality,
> hence in a personal way, not through being thought, but through
> actual address, summons, command. For God is the Lord. What
> does not address us in a way commanding obedience is never God.
> One cannot be related to God by way of thinking, without having
> thereby, at the same time, ceased to be related to God. To know
> God does not mean merely to know about God, but to be personally
> encountered of Him: thou art the man" (*Philosophie und Offen-
> barung,* p. 50).

I can accept the last sentence in this paragraph, but not the first. Surely, to know God means more than to know the *Westminster Shorter Catechism* definition of him. But are we to believe that learning that definition in any way hinders one from coming to a true knowledge of God? Rather, it helps, does it not? In fact, it is an indispensable help. This is not to say that only Presbyterians have a true revelation of God, but it is to say that though revelation involves a personal encounter with God, yet the rational faculty is always supremely active in the encounter. This is evidenced by the very fact that speech is the vehicle of communication between two persons and speech is under all circumstances rational or it is *glossalalia.* It should be remembered that the Spirit who inspired the early Christians to speak in tongues also inspired them to interpret the tongues. (In reacting against this irrationalism, some scholars go so far as to suggest that there is no such thing as "personal revelation.")

A further precaution is in order. One should never, in the interest of a truly existential approach to the question of revelation, so stress the "crisis experience," the "divine-human encounter," the personal confrontation with God on the individual level, as to impugn or obscure the finality of the Biblical witness. We have said that revelation consists of event and inter-pretation. God acts in history and discloses the meaning of his acts. But the disclosure of meaning like the acts themselves is for the Christian a once-for-all disclosure. The interpretation of the prophets and apostles of what God has done in history is itself a part of the revelatory situation. As God acts uniquely within the history of Israel, so he interprets uniquely to the prophets and apostles. Their testimony, their witness, their interpretation is itself revelation. This is the meaning of the doctrine of inspiration and its relation to the larger theme of canonicity. Not that all which the prophets and apostles, as the inspired teachers of the Church, have said is contained in Scripture, but what is contained is sufficient for faith and practice and will never be superseded. The question of canon and Scripture will be treated in its proper place. Here we pause only to underscore the fact that although God continues to reveal himself to men from age to age in an individual way, this revelation is mediated through the once-for-all revelation which we now have in the form of the Sacred Scriptures. It is only in and with the Scriptures that the Spirit convicts of sin, unrighteousness and judgment to come and bears witness with our spirit that we are sons of God. (In the writer's judgment Paul Tillich's discussion of revelation is weak at this point. See, for example, the second chapter of Volume I of his *Systematics,* especially section two on "The Mediums of Revelation.")

Positive Exposition

However, when purged of an unbiblical irrationalism, and guarded from an immediacy that impinges upon the idea of canon, the emphasis on the personal element in Christian revelation is most salutory, and without it an essential dimension would be lacking in our appraisal of the Christian point of view. The God who reveals himself to us is not an idea, He is not even— as Pierre van Paassen would say—"The Great Anonymous" (*Earth Could Be Fair,* p. 49). He has a name. We designate things by universals, but to have a name is the prerogative of a person. This is the heart of Old Testament religion. And because God's name is revelatory, it is sacrilege to take it in vain (Exod. 20:3). The final name of God is Jesus Christ.

Since God is personal, he has not only a name, but a *face.* When man fell, he hid himself, (as Luther translates) from the "face" of God (Gen. 3:8). Cain, feeling the anguish of the curse, complains: "My punishment is greater than I can bear. Behold thou hast driven me out this day from the earth, and from thy face shall I be hid . . ." (Gen. 4:13–14). Throughout the Psalter, like a sigh, we hear the prayer, "Cast me not away from thy presence, hide not thy face from me." Someone has said that man's most ultimate and deepest loss is the lost face of God. By the same token, when God would reveal himself to his people as Redeemer, he instructs Moses to pronounce upon them the following benediction:

> The Lord bless thee and keep thee: The Lord make his face to shine upon thee, And be gracious unto thee: The Lord lift up his countenance upon thee, and give thee peace (Num. 6:23 f.).

In this context, Emil Brunner, in a beautiful figure, compares God in the act of revelation to "a tall man, (who) stoops down to a little child and lowers Himself upon His knee, so that the child may look into His face" (*Offenbarung und Vernunft,* Zurich, 1941, p. 413). For the same reason, he also feels, the Bible, when it would represent the final revelation of God to man, that consummation of personal meeting, speaks of a seeing "face to face" (*ibid.,* p. 185).

This is indeed the end of all revelation, to see the face of God. But this final disclosure, this eschatological revelation, has already broken in upon man in the person of Jesus Christ, ". . . in whom dwelleth all the fulness of the Godhead bodily" (Col. 2:9). God, in himself, is the invisible One, whom no one at anytime has seen or can see; but he has shined in our hearts, Paul tells us, to give the light of the knowledge of his glory in the *face* of Jesus Christ (II Cor. 4:6). "He that hath seen me," said Jesus, "hath seen the Father" (John 14:8, 9). Because God is personal, the final revelation of himself is a person.

One implication of this aspect of our discussion is too obvious to be drawn, but too significant to leave implicit, and that is that the Christian view of revelation as personal, involves decision, response to God. God meets man in the act of revelation not as an Idea, an Unmoved Mover, but as a Person who speaks to us and requires a response from us. The response, whether it be negative or affirmative, is not itself revelation, but it is the necessary corollary of revelation. To say that revelation is historical and personal means, in brief, that God has come into our midst and because he has so come, we can never be the same again.

SPECIAL REVELATION
AS OBJECTIVE

William J. Martin

William James Martin is Rankin Lecturer in Semitic Languages in the Department of Archaeology and Oriental Studies at University of Liverpool, England. A native of Ireland, he holds the B.A. and M.A. degrees from Trinity College, Dublin, the Th.D. from Princeton Theological Seminary, and the Ph.D. from University of Leipzig. As a philologist he has had a long-standing interest in the problem of communication.

4. William J. Martin

SPECIAL REVELATION
AS OBJECTIVE

"OBJECTIVE" is a term applied to outward things, in contrast to "subjective," used to denote those things that belong to the conscious life. Thus whatever is considered as independent of the perceiving and reasoning self is "objective," whereas all that belongs to the conscious life is termed "subjective." We speak of a thing as having "objective reality," that is, it is an object of perception and thought, a "thing" external to the mind, that goes on existing even when we are not thinking about it. The term "subjective" designates the contents of consciousness itself; the term "objective," the raw material or subject matter of the consciousness (the word "matter," of course, here not being restricted to its literal meaning).

I. VERBALIZATION OF REVELATION

The objective aspect of revelation is that embodied in the verbal expression of the message. A great deal of thought has been given by philologists and linguists to the nature of the relationship of the word to its prototype and many attempts have been made to devise a satisfactory terminology. Susan Stebbing suggested the word "referend" for what is signified, and "symbol" for the signifying sign (*A Modern Introduction to Logic*, 1933). French linguists have simplified matters by using *le signifié* for the former, and *le signifiant* for the latter. A. H. Gardiner speaks of the two-sidedness of words, "sound on the one face, and thought on the other" (*Speech and Language*, 1932). He stresses the distinction between meaning and the "thing-meant"; the word "spade" (word as vehicle of meaning)

61

is not a "spade" (the garden implement itself). He would define speech as "the use, between man and man, of articulate sound-signs for the communication of their wishes and their views about things." The definition given by E. Sapir differed little from this: "Language is a purely human and non-instinctive method of communicating ideas, emotions, and desires by means of a system of voluntarily produced symbols" (*Language,* 1921). E. H. Sturtevant defines language "as a system of arbitrary vocal symbols by which members of a social group cooperate and interact" (*An Introduction to Linguistic Science,* 1956).

I am aware that many American linguists in their linguistic analyses eliminate mentalistic terms as far as possible. Thus L. Bloomfield would describe speech merely in terms of stimulus and response, deliberately avoiding all reference to mind or thought (*Language,* 1933). That this approach has proved singularly attractive can be well understood, for, though it is contrary to the facts of experience, it provides what seems to be a scientific reason for avoiding the really complex aspect of language. In this essay I propose to adhere to the traditional terminology, since I am dealing with what might be called "metalinguistics," and since I am fully persuaded that the anti-mentalistic approach is too circumscribed. The fact that a child quickly acquires the facility of using the sound symbol he has learned to associate with a material object even in the absence of that object would justify one in affirming that at least a partial function of languages is to provide a system of sound symbols for the inventory of the mind. It will be objected that the ability to use the symbol in the absence of an external stimulus is not sufficient ground for assuming the existence of a mental concept as the object's counterpart in the mind. It is not, however, the nature of this counterpart that is significant, but the *action* of finding and producing the appropriate symbol at will. In speech two operations take place, that of selection and that of rejection, both equally important, and to measure the first and dismiss the second looks very like saying that it is not the water in the well that counts but only what comes from the pump. In mentioning the process of rejection, it looks as if we are saying in effect that here something is the cause of nothing, but that would imply equating inactivity with nothing. This is very different from acting and speaking as if nothing could be the efficient cause of anything, as is the case when some linguists insist on treating speech as if it were nothing more than a tape-recording. The fact that, in speech, recording and playing-back often seem to take place simultaneously is not a valid reason for either denying or ignoring the dichotomy, and entering into a conspiracy of silence with regard to mentalistic expressions. No scientist would be content to confine himself to the correlation of a series of phenomena and not try to ascertain the circumstances under which they occur. The mentality of a deceased person is beyond scientific investigation, but the products of his mind may persist, and these could be used as evidence of his previous existence. Linguistic research that holds that only the playing-back is its concern may find the "ghost in the machine" becoming recalcitrant.

The verbalization of revelation, as we now possess it, is in written form. Writing was devised for the purpose of giving ephemeral speech a permanent form, and it might aptly be called "substitute" speech. That this was clearly recognized as the function of writing is seen in such expressions as "the scripture (i.e., the writing) says" (cf. Rom. 4:3; 9:17; 10:11; 11:2; James 2:23). That written words have the same validity as the actual words of the speaker is shown by the fact that they are admissible as evidence in a court of law, carrying the same weight as those of a living and present witness, while the legislation concerning inheritance depends almost exclusively on the tacit admission that written testimony is in no way inferior to the spoken word. In fact, nuncupative or oral wills are only admissible in very special circumstances, for instance, the death of the testator in battle. The preference for a documentary will is a matter of plain common sense; one ground among others for this preference is the fact that a written document excludes the necessity of an intermediary, whose *bona fides* in turn would have to be scrutinized. A view of revelation as a kind of nuncupative will is hardly worthy of the concept of an omniscient God.

II. NATURE OF LANGUAGE

The linguistic aspect of the message as its embodiment raises at once the question of the nature of language. Since the days of F. de Saussure it has been customary to distinguish between language (*langue*) and speech (*parole*) (*Cours de linguistique generale,* 1916). Language is considered as that linguistic deposit at the disposal of a community using the same linguistic medium, whereas speech is the use made of this deposit by an individual at any given moment. Thus language is something passive, whereas speech is active. The description of language as a "system of sound symbols for the inventory of the mind" differs from those definitions which start at an earlier stage before the inventory of a given environment had been reduced to mental concepts, and describes language as a code of symbols for things, objective and subjective. Speech, on the other hand, is the act by which the speaker provides with perceptible garments the invisible offspring of his mind. These perceptible garments, in themselves as transitory as the breath that produces them, may be given an ageless counterpart by the process of writing. Speech reduced to writing takes on an independent existence, unaffected by time and distance. The veracity of a letter, for instance, that takes several weeks to come from Hong Kong is as unaffected by the time factor as if it had come only from a neighboring state, and thus the reduction of a message to writing can eliminate in certain respects the effect of the time factor altogether.

In the present context the chief interest of language lies in its mode of action and its function. Language makes the communication of thought possible by providing verbal deputies for the ingredients of many situations. Not only has it evolved deputies for visible objects, but also for mental states, and for time sequence and time phases. By language it is possible also for a speaker to superimpose his will on another, and thus it provides the means by which the indispensable team-work of human society is coordinated. Language makes possible even the communication of inaccessible matter. We might consider as an instance of this, a request by a scientist to a non-scientist to pass on certain technical information to a fellow scientist. The full meaning of the message would probably be intelligibly inaccessible to the intermediary, but he could, nevertheless, accomplish the task with exactitude. Hence, the method by which inaccessible matter may be communicated is by the communication of a communication. It would seem, too, that the linguistic medium is essential to all satisfactory communication; even the mind in communication with itself is, apparently, never completely happy until it has reduced its problems to linguistic terms. The preciseness, accuracy, and range of language in communication point to it unmistakably as the first choice of an intelligent being as a medium for revelation.

Before we proceed to discuss the most significant aspect of language, it would be well perhaps to say a brief word about revelation through nature. That God is revealed to us in nature is freely admitted in the Bible, and the accepted primacy of the written revelation has never led Christians to disparage nature as an expression of the glory of God; while laying the supreme emphasis on the verbal revelation, they acknowledge also the glorious wonders of God in nature. But nature can speak only of power and intelligence and not of character, just as three lines of a letter from, say, Rembrandt might tell us more about his character than the most minute study of his greatest masterpiece. Thus we note the inadequacy of a revelation through nature compared with one in language.

III. LANGUAGE AND PERSONAL ENCOUNTER

Above all, inanimate objects cannot effect the personal encounter, which, as we shall see later, the genius of language alone can accomplish. Compared with the linguistic medium all other forms of communication, such as wordless symbols and rites, or the design of a temple, belong intellectually to the most primitive stage of communication, the pictographic. By such means minds may be juxtaposed but there never can be intelligent communication.

In communication, an act of the highest significance takes place: an encounter between two psychical entities. Our five senses tell us of the physical world and its phenomena, but while in four of them the ratio which the response bears to the stimulus is a modest one, in the fifth, the sense of hearing, it may assume astronomical proportions. Given the right occasion, the unpretentious word "peace" may put a whole nation in a state of ecstasy.

By means of the sense of hearing, as the receiver of linguistic communication, one mind can make contact with the mental world of another and can influence that inaccessible and mysterious realm. With the voluntary cooperation of the recipient, one may learn in turn something about the contents of that other mind. Without such voluntary cooperation it remains true: "For what person knows a man's thought except the spirit of the man which is in him?" (I Cor. 2:11). We now speak of the boundary that separates the "I" from the "thou" as a dimensional boundary (Karl Heim, *Glauben und Denken,* 1934). It is not in any sense of the word a spatial boundary; the terms "near" and "remote" when used in reference to it have no spatial significance. The mind of the man next to you in the railway carriage may be quite inaccessible to you, while at that very moment a friend a thousand miles away may be allowing you by means of a letter to learn something of what is beyond this boundary. The act of crossing this boundary is one of the most remarkable phenomena of our experience; it is only our familiarity with it that prevents us from appreciating the marvel of it. That messages actually cross this mysterious boundary can be seen every time anyone by a form of words produces a desired behavior pattern in his fellow. To describe things beyond the sphere of our sense, language is compelled to resort to analogical transference, as happens when we borrow most terminology for time from that of space, for example, the length of time, and shortness of time, and so forth [1]

We have to do something similar to find linguistic terms to describe matters relating to a dimensional boundary, a term that may also be used with the necessary qualifications to describe the very different boundary between God and man. When, for instance, in this connection we speak of "above," a moment's reflection will tell us that "above" is not here used in a literal, spatial sense. We would still continue to use the word "above" even if we were in Australia. What interests us now, however, is not the nature of this boundary but the possibility of crossing it. If God willed to cross this boundary, he could surely do so by the existing means so extensively used between man and man.

Is not this what is implied by the rhetorical questions in Psalm 94:8 f.? "Understand, O stupid among the people, and you fools, when will you get sense? He who plants the ear, will he not hear? He who forms the eye, will he not look?" This is evidently intended to be only a token list, which no intelligent reader would hold to be exhaustive. The Psalmist may well have

---

[1] Since the theory of analogical transference, now widely held, assumes the primacy of sensory objects, it is repudiated as inimical to the Christian faith by Biblical theists who insist that language is God's gift for the purpose (among other purposes) of communing with him. Professor Martin here speaks only of terminology *for time* by way of example; there is no intimation of a general borrowing of spatial terms, or of the spatial-sensory origin of language. While Adam may have invented names for the animals, the power of using names and words is a divine gift, and its purpose, in part, was to enable man to speak with God.—ED.

felt that, as references to God speaking were so numerous, it would have been stressing the obvious to have added "He who makes the tongue, will he not speak?"

There is no more common phrase in the Old Testament than "and God said." The related phrase "the word of God" occurs also with great frequency. The Bible leaves us in no doubt whatever that the vehicle of revelation is language. In view of the versatility of the linguistic medium and the unique role played by it in the reception and transmission of knowledge, it is the only means that possesses the requisite potentiality.

Mystical communication, in which the intellect is in abeyance and the object of the participant is to merge himself by a non-linguistic process in the Godhead, is excluded by a word often on the lips of the writers and prophets, the verb commonly translated by "to hear." The field of meaning of the Hebrew word is more extensive than the modern sense. The Hebrew signifies not only "to hear," but "to understand" and even "to respond" to what is said. For instance, in Genesis 11:7, we must translate "that a man may not *understand* the tongue of his neighbor," where the Hebrew verb is "to hear." Or again, in II Kings 18:26 "And Eliakim the son of Hilkiah, and Shebna and Joab said to Rabshakey, 'Speak Aramaic, please, to your servants for we understand it [literally, hear] and don't speak with us Judaic [*scil.* Hebrew] in the ears of the people that are on the wall.' " The people on the wall would still hear them in our sense of the word when they spoke Aramaic, but not in the Hebrew sense.

From Genesis to Malachi this word is used in conjunction with divine communications. Thus for the Old Testament writers and prophets the process of communication was supraliminal, although on occasion the deeper import of the matter was beyond their full comprehension. In language the end always justifies the means, and the end is invariably effective communication. Here a coin from any mint may be legal tender and the value assigned to it is quite arbitrary and depends on the legality of usage and not on logic. It often avails itself of material that is beyond the world of normal experience, as, for instance, when we say "It is like living in a palace." Ignorance of the experience does not invalidate the phrase as a coin of communication. Again, a phrase may be factually inaccurate but still the current and legitimate equivalent of a certain situation. A phrase such as "the sun rises" is the normal means of describing that natural phenomenon brought about by the revolution of the earth; and not by the motion of the sun. Taken literally it is scientifically false but it is, nevertheless, semasiologically true, and in effective communication that is all that matters. Grave injustice has been often done to the Bible by people who failed to realize the simple fact that inevitably there is an anthropomorphic element in language (H. Guntert, *Grundfragen der Sprachwissenschaft,* 1925). Usage, too, has the power of making a phrase that is non-scientific or even unscientific, legitimate communication. A phrase such as "electric current" reveals precisely nothing as to Michael Faraday's view of the nature of electricity.

Language is, as we saw, the only conceivable means of communicating inaccessible matter, since it makes practicable the communication of communication. Its ability to cross dimensional limits and to traffic in materials free from all spatial limitations points to it as the medium by which the "relativity" barrier might be overcome. Men have long realized that the universe in which they find themselves cannot provide an absolute unit of measurement. It may seem to some a little odd that man with his multiplicity of measuring units is unable to measure. From ancient times we find him busy with measurements using as units dimensions derived from parts of his own body: the foot, the handbreadth, and the ell (the forearm). What he never stopped to ask himself was: "What is really the actual size of my foot?" If he had, he would have discovered that he had no means of ascertaining whether he was a pygmy or a giant. All sizes are relative; in fact, if all consciousness were suspended for a moment of time and in that moment the universe, including all laws such as the relativity of light, was reduced to a thousandth of its present size, we would have no means of verifying the change. Were this disability restricted to spatial measurement, no great harm would come of it but, alas, it invitiates all human judgments. Man can't, for instance, measure mental entities; he can only state their magnitude in terms of an arbitrary norm, called normality, but no self-respecting psychologist would undertake to define normality. We can easily imagine a society in which intellectual conditions very different from ours obtained, where children in the kindergarten already knew as much as our intellectual giants. Spiritual entities, too, are under the ban; if man can't measure even an earthly city, how could he presume to measure the City of God?

Our position is something like that of spectators watching a film of a puppet show. To discover the real size of the puppets, they would require to know the distance, when filming, of the camera from the puppets, and again, the distance of the projector from the screen. Normally, about the former, all information would be inaccessible. Their only hope of ascertaining the actual size of the puppets would be if, inadvertently, the hand of a manipulator appeared on the screen. Then they would know at once the size of a puppet relative to that of a human being. One appearance would be sufficient to break the deadlock and to disclose the dimensions in terms of their measuring system.

This analogy deals with only one aspect of the problem and is, like all analogies, inadequate. Analogical reasoning, however, is here, as is often the case, the only form of reasoning at our disposal. No problem can escape the deadlock of relativity. As no absolute is available, there can be no absolute judgment. We can count, add, subtract, and multiply, but we can't measure. We know nothing whatever about the actual size of the units that form the basis of our calculations. It is reason itself that has drawn attention to our dilemma, and it is reason that has admitted its own limitations. Reason and revelation are not necessarily in conflict. They are not to be envisaged as intersecting lines, not even as converging lines; they are parallel lines going in opposite directions: reason earthwards (and in that we include the universe), and revelation heavenwards, beyond relativity. We may best understand the implications of all this if we take another analogy.

Man finds himself, as it were, aboard a ship, afloat on a vast and vacant ocean. He has never seen land. He has calculated the size of the ship from that of his own body, but he is as ignorant of real size as if he were looking at "a painted ship upon a painted ocean" without the presence of some object to lend it scale. Such a picture might be of a model floating in a tank, as may happen in the world of films, the producer knowing full well that by excluding everything that might indicate scale, his illusion is fool-proof. The passengers in our ship, it is true, have discovered much about our ingenious home: the design of the hull, the wonderful and invisible waves that surround it, the remarkable nature of the materials from which it is constructed. Nevertheless, much as we admire their discoveries, we should not forget when we read treatises on, say, the molecule, that the wonder is not the treatise but the molecule itself. No book, no lecture, could be half so wonderful as this microcosm, a discovery and not an invention of man. Men, even clever men, often forget that philosophically they have no more to do with the creation of truth than clocks have to do with the creation of time. Their role is merely to record, and their goal is to bring their record more and more into accord with objective truth. Not every part of the ship, however, is accessible to them; as they know nothing of a chart-room, destination to them is meaningless. How this "space-ship" got into its present orbit, what keeps it there, or what is the nature of the remote control, are problems that apparently can't be answered. A knowledge of design is interesting, a knowledge of destination and destiny is imperative. Even the seemingly simple task of measuring the ship, they find, is beyond their powers. All they can say about the size of the ship in which they find themselves by nothing of their own doing, is that it contains a certain number of arbitrary units, that is, they can calculate, but the unit itself they can't measure. They can divide it into smaller and smaller units, but wherever they stop, the last unit can't be measured. All sizes are necessarily stated in terms of the size of some object within the ship, or by means of a measuring-unit obtained by taking a fraction of the perimeter of the ship as, for example, the meter. Until comparatively recent times all measuring systems have been predominantly anthropocentric, the human foot being a great favorite. For the measurement of mental quantities the head, or rather, the contents of the "head" of an average passenger, provides the norm. Man's awareness of all this convinces him there must be a realm where absolute magnitude exists. A message from that realm might enable him to make the necessary deductions, and a messenger from there could break the deadlock of relativity. Even one single footprint of such a being would be sufficient to enable him to ascertain his own magnitude in relation to an absolute standard. The Bible claims to know both, a message transmitted to certain men once passengers on the ship, and the royal visit of the Lord of that realm, who accommodated himself to our human limitations, walking across the impassable ocean and bringing with him part of the message explaining the mystery of our relativity-bound existence, and of our ultimate destiny. No one who has ever read the Gospels thoughtfully could fail to detect that this Messenger is applying to the fabric of human society a measuring-unit radically different from that in common use. Measured by the latter, the activity of society is an end in itself, consisting of grave, sober creatures going about the serious business of real and earnest living; measured by Him, it is the playing of petulant children in the market-place. Often the results of his measuring are much more startling, resulting in a complete reversal of human values.

When some philosophers began to assert the universal applicability of the theory of relativity, and the consequent invalidity of all cosmic standards, they were probably not aware that Paul had a word to say on the matter. It is in II Corinthians 10:13. A fairly literal translation of the passage would read something like this:

> Since we do not dare to reckon ourselves among or compare ourselves with certain who commend themselves, but they in measuring themselves by themselves and comparing themselves with themselves have no discernment. We shall not indeed boast in (regard to) non-measurable things, but according to the measure of the standard (or measuring-rod), which the God of measure has marked off for us, to extend also to you.

Intra-cosmic comparisons at whatever level, science would now tell us, have no ultimate value and in this it has the concurrence of Paul. His use of the word *ametra,* the imponderables, the non-measurable things, is highly significant, as is his claim to possess an extra-cosmic measuring unit.

Paul's emphasis on verbal communication as the vehicle for our knowledge of God, and the absence of a reference to any other channel, permits us to assume that also the knowledge of this absolute standard was conveyed in linguistic terms. When we think of the potentiality of language, we would surely hesitate to say that such a thing was impossible. Language seemingly either possesses or can adapt existing terms to serve as verbal deputies for every kind of reality. In many lyric poems, for example, the poet provides an experience with a verbal deputy of such a nature that when it is read or heard it reproduces in a kindred spirit the impact of that experience. The wording of the poem is an indivisible unity standing for an experience which itself may have no name. Paul believed in the supra-human character of the communications vouchsafed to him, and that a corpus of such communications was also in existence. In Romans 1:2 he refers to them as "the holy scriptures." He believed they originated with God, otherwise in this relativity-bound cosmos they would have been valueless. He says in II Timothy 3:16, "Every scripture is God-breathed." As the sentence is a verbless sentence, the only permissible translation is one in which the "is" is supplied. Peter, writing in his second letter, is more explicit. He says (1:21) "For no

prophecy was ever brought by the will of man, but men led by the Holy
Spirit spoke from God."

The language in which they spoke was human language and it would seem
that the men were providentially prepared for the task they were to perform.
In using language, God accommodated himself to a humanly created instrument. This is the implication of the statement in Genesis 2:19, "And God
brought them [the creatures] to the man to see what he would call them, and
whatever he called a living creature, that was its name." Thus what God
gave to man was more wonderful than the gift of a ready-made language;
it was nothing less than the ability to create language.

The language of the Bible shares all the characteristics of human language; if it had been otherwise it would have been incomprehensible to us.
As we call the Bible the Old and New Testaments, perhaps it would not be
out of place here to quote the words of a president of the English Probate
Court.

> I have been long impressed with the wisdom of the rule, now, I
> believe, universally adopted, at least in Courts of law, that, in con-
> struing all written instruments, the grammatical and ordinary sense
> of the words is to be adhered to, unless that would lead to some
> absurdity, or some repugnance, or inconsistency with the rest of the
> instrument, in which case the grammatical and ordinary sense of the
> words may be modified, so as to avoid that absurdity and inconsist-
> ency, but no further (S. T. Coleridge, *Aids to Reflection*).

There is seldom any doubt as to whether a given phrase in the Bible is to
be taken in a literal or metaphorical sense. It soon becomes apparent when
we read the Gospels that certain statements are not intended to be taken in a
literal sense. When our Lord said to the Jews in John 2:19, "Destroy this
temple, and in three days I will raise it up," he was using metaphorical
language of the type found in Psalm 144:12. Again, there is no evidence that
at the present time any body of Christians interprets in a literal sense the
statement in Matthew 5:29 about the removal of an offending right eye.
Hebrew in particular, a language not rich in abstract nouns, often resorts to
the use of concrete for the abstract. Thus the names of bodily organs are
used to express mental and volitional qualities, for instance, the heart for the
seat of the will and emotions. Physical attitudes are used to describe psychological states; "the face falls" can mean "to be sullen." The cause often
expresses the effect, e.g., "mouth" in the meaning of "speech." Coleridge's
remark on this is worth quoting, for he rightly perceived its wider application: "Of the figures of speech in the sacred volume, that are only figures
of speech, the one of most frequent occurrence is that which describes an
effect by the name of its most usual and best known cause: the passages, for
instance, in which grief, fury, repentance, etc., are attributed to the Deity."
Nevertheless in a preceding remark he had laid down a principle that does
credit to his usual sound linguistic sense: "To retain the literal sense,
wherever the harmony of Scripture permits, and reason does not forbid,

is ever the honester, and, nine times in ten, the more rational and pregnant interpretation" (*ibid.*).

It must ever be borne in mind that the function of language is that of a deputy or surrogate of a fact or reality. The word is the prescription and not the medicine, the sign and not the destination. It is, as it were, the stage-player and not the real character, and thus is, in a sense, unreal. It was perhaps something like this that moved Sir Napier Shaw in a work as scientifically prosaic as his *Manual of Meteorology* to write a passage which W. E. Collinson applied to certain syntactical theories: "Every theory of the course of events in nature is necessarily based on some process of simplification of the phenomena and is to some extent therefore a fairy-tale" (*Lingua*, 1948). The need to make the distinction between the word as a deputy and the reality which it represented formed the substance of a rebuke administered by our Lord to the Jews in John 5:39, "You search the scriptures, because you think that in them ye have eternal life, and *those* are *they* which are bearing witness of me." The words of Scripture were not an end in themselves; their function was to point. They were the testament, not the estate. They contained the prescription for eternal life, but they themselves bore not the leaves of the tree of life. It was the distinction, now recognized by all linguists, between the sign and the thing signified, the vehicle of the meaning and the thing meant. The Authorized Version, with its "they are they," brings out the sense better than some modern translations, which seem to miss the point. He was not rebuking them for searching the Scriptures, but for making the wrong use of their evidential value. It was the subjective side that invested the objective side, the written words, with their real value. It was their purpose to introduce men to God, so that they, too, might by his grace cross the dimensional boundary between them and enter into the "I-thou" relationship, but, alas, they were preoccupied not even with the "I-He" relationship but only the "I-it." Had they but known it, the quintessence of the subjective side of Scripture had become temporarily a personal reality before their eyes. The Jews had failed to distinguish between the signpost and the destination to which it pointed. The signpost had become to them an end in itself;[2] a meaning was sought in every dimension, a mystery in every angle. Reverence had been replaced by superstition and faith by fetishism. The message on the direction board, which was a matter of life and death for lost travellers and could have changed men from indifferent wanderers into dedicated pilgrims, was obscured by a mound of cabalistic fancies. Its unspectacular appearance, perhaps, prevented them from realizing its unique

---

[2] The Pharisees were not, of course, engaged in the modern debate over semantics. They failed to grasp what the words signified, and assigned the verbal symbols an incorrect intellectual content. But the Pharisees were interested in *gennatria* (already used in the Epistle of Barnabas and one of the 32 Middoth). See the many statements in the Talmud about the nature of the Torah: Like the throne of glory, it was created; it was one of the seven things created before the creation of the world; it was written down by God in eternity. To deny this excluded one from the future world.—ED.

and irreplaceable character; it alone could restore the lost sense of direction; even a street plan of the celestial city would not have enabled a prodigal in the far country to start on the homeward journey; for this it was absolutely necessary that he should know the way. Alas, for many now as then a sign-post is too mundane, and they lend a ready ear to every talkative passerby, and hanker after the fortunetelling "gypsy."

It is true that, superficially considered, the Bible has much in common with many mundane books. It contains much that concerns the history of a small nation, part of which could have been known from ordinary historical sources. Where then is the evidence of the extra-cosmic character of this information? It is evident in what was selected and in what was rejected. What person in any period before 500 B.C. was in a position to apply to historical incidents a scale of importance since verified by subsequent history? Who could have surmised that records of one of the smallest nations of the Ancient Semitic East would become a major factor in some of the world's greatest civilizations, and that the descendants of this small nation would never disappear from the pages of history? Why are the historical portions of this Book unique in the field of historical writings? Because of their delineation of character, and their unerring ability to trace a development, however seemingly insignificant, back to its true source. From the historical writings of the great neighbors of Israel we learn much of the military campaigns and civic achievements of their kings, but nothing of their character. What uncanny sense did the Old Testament writers possess to see that David the sovereign was subservient to David the sinner?

The linguistic form of revelation as its objective counterpart differentiates it from all private and esoteric communications, and constitutes it a manifesto of evidential value. The Bible claims to be ultra-human and consequently contains much that is professedly beyond reason, but not thereby contrary to reason. A dispassionate rational investigation will reveal that it lacks nothing essential and contains nothing superfluous to the purpose in hand, namely, the revelation of the will of God for lost humanity. It consistently maintains the principle of non-compulsion, the freedom of resistibility, and the inadequacy of externalism. In the Old Testament it is the person of the coming One, in the New, of him who came and shall come, that supplies the unifying theme.

It would now seem that the early Church Fathers "built better than they knew," when they chose the word "canon" to define the corpus of authoritative writings comprising the divine revelation. The word "canon" is literally a "measuring-rod." It was in all probability a loan-word in Greek from some Semitic cognate of the Hebrew *qaneh*, rod, which was also applied to a certain measuring-unit, as we, too, use "rod" for a standard measure. In our plight we can no longer be content to take our bearings from the light at our own masthead. The alternative to the acceptance of an extraneous standard is to perish. It is the fateful "either-or": either we live by every word that proceeds from the mouth of God or we die (Matt. 4:4).

SPECIAL REVELATION
AS SCRIPTURAL

Ned B. Stonehouse

Ned B. Stonehouse is Professor of New Testament in Westminster Theological Seminary, Pennsylvania, and has served also as Dean of the Faculty since 1955. He holds the A.B. degree from Calvin College, Th.B. from Princeton Theological Seminary, Th.M. from Princeton Seminary, and Th.D. from Free University of Amsterdam. He is editor of The New International Commentary on the New Testament, *and author of* The Witness of Matthew and Mark to Christ, The Witness of Luke to Christ, Paul before the Areopagus and Other New Testament Studies, *and* J. Gresham Machen, A Biographical Memoir.

5. Ned B. Stonehouse

SPECIAL REVELATION
AS SCRIPTURAL

THE SPECIFIC question faced in this essay is whether special divine revelation has received embodiment in Holy Scripture. Are the Old and New Testaments to be acknowledged, not only as containing a record of the history of such revelation, but also as being themselves the very Word of God? Do they constitute divine revelation because of their intrinsic character, altogether apart from the response that they may evoke, whether of faith or unbelief?

In connection with the modern occupation with the concept of revelation it is widely insisted that, as *divine* revelation, it must be viewed as personal. Almost as frequently, perhaps, divine revelation is acknowledged as being historical; revelation consists, it is said, of decisive acts of God in history, in such events especially as the death and resurrection of Jesus Christ. Widely prevalent, moreover, if not dominant, is the attitude that, though divine revelation is personal and may be historical, it assuredly is not embodied in the Sacred Scriptures. To regard revelation as scriptural, it is felt, would absolutize human traditions. To quote Harnack, it would chase the Spirit away into a book.

If, on the other hand, one should maintain that special revelation has found incorporation in Scripture—that to employ a somewhat academic but useful term, it has become *inscripturated*—one would have to make a radically different estimate of the origin and character of the Canon of the Old and New Testaments. One would then recognize not only that God has spoken in Christ to accomplish the salvation of man, but also that in the fulfillment of the grand and comprehensive divine plan of redemption by

the gracious sovereign action of the Holy Spirit God has met the need of his
people by providing them with the inestimable blessing of the written Word.
On this view, the recognition of the personal and historical character of
special revelation—when these qualities are defined in accordance with the
data of this revelation—will open the way to an apprehension of its scriptural manifestation. In brief, as the process of revelation is perceived in
its broadest scope, Holy Scripture may be recognized as constituting an
aspect—the climactic historical aspect—of that history in which God in
Christ and by the Holy Spirit graciously fulfills his redemptive purpose.

In keeping with the foregoing estimate of the issues involved, I shall
consider this topic in the perspective provided by the entire history of the
process of divine self-revelation. The diversity of the revelation of the two
covenants must be taken account of as well as its organic unity. For
reasons that are largely obvious the Old Testament will be treated first,
and this will involve consideration of its own self-witness. Especially for
the Christian, however, even the evaluation of the Old Testament cannot
be carried out satisfactorily in isolation from the testimony of the New
Testament. Even at this initial point, therefore, the consideration of the
revelation of the new covenant is in the foreground. And a preponderant
emphasis upon the revelation of the new covenant comes inevitably to
expression in the later sections where the question, most crucial for Christian
faith, of the inscripturation of this final revelation is under discussion.

I. REVELATION OF THE OLD COVENANT

The Process of Divine Disclosure

Although we shall have to look beyond the Old Testament, and particularly to the New Testament, for evidence of the inscripturation of the
revelation of the old covenant, it remains valuable and significant to reflect upon the process of divine revelation which comes to expression within
the Old Testament itself. An indispensable background for the understanding of the ultimate development is thereby provided.

No feature of this revelation is, in our judgment, more basic and illuminating than its covenantal character. The term "covenant" indeed, as
a rendering for *berith,* is not entirely felicitous, and thus it is of vital importance that our usage of "covenantal" be informed by reflection on the
Biblical point of view. Because of its usage in describing purely human
relationships, as in the Wilsonian "open covenants of peace openly arrived
at," the term readily brings to mind the notion of a bilateral agreement,
and perhaps even that of a contract between two independent parties. While
there is, in truth, an element of mutuality in the theological *berith* in the
sense that the covenantal relationship of personal fellowship between God
and his people is conspicuously in view, it is necessary to insist that even
more fundamentally the covenant between God and his people is primarily

a unilateral arrangement initiated and effected by God himself. The Biblical perspective in this regard comes to accurate expression in Hebrews 8:6 in the reference to the *enactment* of a better covenant. In the foreground, accordingly, is the fact of the sovereign action of God in establishing and bringing to concrete realization an arrangement or administration or "covenant" of grace. This accent upon sovereign grace comes to expression in the words which most simply sum up the approach of the God of the covenant: "I will be your God and ye shall be my people." These same words, indeed, are unspeakably rich in their expression of the privilege of fellowship between God and his people. And they carry with them profound implications with regard to religious and ethical obligation on the part of the men who become members of the covenant. It remains true, nevertheless, that the emphasis falls first of all upon the action of sovereign, efficacious grace. In thus graciously drawing near unto man for his salvation God makes himself known to man, and thus the covenant of grace is at one and the same time redemptive and revelatory.

Another fundamental characteristic of the divine covenant is its manifestation at certain decisive moments in history. The revelation and redemption of the covenant are not repeated from person to person, from family to family, and from generation to generation. This historical character of a covenant appears perhaps most conspicuously in the manner in which God established covenant with Abraham, the father of the faithful. As Paul stresses in Galatians 3, a covenant has been established with Abraham in such a unique and irrevocable fashion that those who are of faith are blessed with faithful Abraham, and those who are Christ's are Abraham's seed, heirs according to promise. Thus one also encounters in the Old Testament, as a kind of refrain, a call to *remember* the covenant made first of all with Abraham.

Nor does the Sinaitic *berith* require an essential modification of this judgment. The redemptive action at the Exodus is described as the result of God's remembrance of his covenant with Abraham, Isaac and Jacob (Ex. 2:24; 6:5). Thus, as Paul also teaches, the law at Sinai was *added to* the covenant established with Abraham and by no means set it aside (Gal. 3:16–22). So significant, indeed, is Moses' role as the representative of God, both as deliverer and prophet, that he occupies a distinctive place in the history of the revelation of the old covenant. He was preeminently the prophet of the old covenant, the prototype of the Great Prophet to come (Deut. 18:15), with whom the Lord spoke face to face (Ex. 33:11; Deut. 34:10–12). The very greatness of Moses, however, as the one by whom the law was given, accentuates the historical character of the Old Testament revelation, for it was through him that God decisively made his will known and wrought redemption for his people. And it is of the greatest possible significance in connection with the consideration of our principal topic to observe that the word of the Lord which came by Moses could be and was, because of its historical character, handed down to the people and this from generation to generation. It is obvious that in the transmission of this special revelation the fact of its being so largely committed to writing was highly significant. The fact of its inscripturation assuredly did nothing to modify its essential character as revelation.

Acknowledged as Scripture

The Old Testament as a whole, as distinguished from its various parts, could hardly be viewed as Scripture within the Old Testament itself. The acknowledgment of the Old Testament as canonical, moreover, is evidently not the consequence of ecclesiastical action but rather developed in an historical process in which the writings of the Old Testament accredited themselves to the people of God as being of divine authority. This point of view is reflected in the word of Paul in Romans 3:1, 2 where he indicates that the advantage of the Jew over the Gentile is to be found first of all in the consideration that "they were intrusted with the oracles of God." It is important to remember in this connection also that the Old Testament did not become canonical as the result of the evaluation of it reflected in the New Testament. In particular it was not the action of the Lord or of his apostles that first gave it the status of Holy Scripture. The Lord and the apostles shared essentially the viewpoint with regard to the Old Testament that had come to expression among the Jewish people. Nevertheless, Christian testimony is highly significant. It not merely enlarges our understanding of the view of the Old Testament which prevailed among Jewish people in that era. Most important of all, nothing shows so unmistakably as our Lord's use of and attitude toward the Old Testament that special divine revelation may be, and as a matter of fact is, scriptural.

In view of the fulness with which other chapters in this volume deal with the New Testament evidence concerning inspiration, it is not necessary to undertake a broad survey of the evidence. Only a few details will be recalled here.

The Epistle to the Hebrews, which begins by recalling the fact that God spoke unto the fathers in the prophets, makes abundantly clear especially by its quotations from the Old Testament that it identifies the written documents with the Word of God. For characteristically, rather than referring to the human authors, it introduces quotations of the Old Testament by referring directly to God or the Holy Spirit as the speaker (cf. 1:5, 13; 3:7; 4:3, 4; 8:8, 13; 10:15).

Paul likewise regards the Old Testament as the written Word of God. His Gospel has been made known by the scriptures of the prophets (Rom. 16:26). The action of Scripture is identified with that of God in preaching the Gospel beforehand to Abraham (Gal. 3:8; cf. 3:22). There is a "reading of the old covenant," and though the glory of this revelation is not to be compared with that of the new, that written revelation remains of divine authority and will accomplish its divine purpose if only the minds of those who read are not hardened (II Cor. 3). All Scripture is God-breathed and is given to accomplish, by way of its communication of divine truth, a complete salvation of the man of God (II Tim. 3:15–17).

Our Lord's use of Scripture is especially crucial for the evaluation of our subject, and so it may not be passed over here in spite of the fact that a special chapter is devoted to it. We need not, however, dwell upon such explicit declarations as Matthew 5:17–19 and John 10:33–36, nor reflect upon the way in which he distinguished qualitatively between the Word of God and the word of man in such passages as Matthew 15:1 ff. But we may not pass over the evidence provided by our Lord's utter commitment to the divine authority of Scripture which comes to expression in his application of its teaching to his own life and ministry. He was not content with insisting that it and it alone was to be acknowledged as the Word of God by the men he addressed. Regardless of what it might cost him in the way of humiliation and suffering, even if obedience to it marked out for him a course of action and submission from which his soul shrank with the utmost intensity of feeling, even if it demanded that he die the accursed death of the cross, he was resolved and determined that the Word of God declared in Scripture should be perfectly fulfilled in him. As the Messianic Servant of the Lord he was obedient to the Father who sent him and faithful in carrying out the divine plan of redemption. This is reflected pervasively and emphatically in the Gospels as Christ dwells upon the necessity of obedience only to God in setting the course of his ministry and in particular in going up to Jerusalem to suffer, to be killed, and the third day to be raised up (cf. Matt. 4:4; 16:21 ff.; 17:22 f.; 20:17 ff. and parallels). Nothing is more significant for our subject than the observation that the divine necessity that controlled Christ's ministry and compelled him to go to Calvary is acknowledged again and again as a necessity to fulfill Scripture (Matt. 26:24; Mark 14:21; cf. also Mark 9:12; 12:10 f., 14:21, 27, 49; Luke 4:17–21; 22:37; 24:25–27, 44–46). In the most unambiguous fashion, therefore, the proposition that special divine revelation is scriptural is demonstrated not only by the teaching of the New Testament as a whole but also particularly by our Lord's own ministry. Only by way of a basic skepticism regarding the witness of the Gospels, which might call forth a radical reconstruction of the life and teaching of Jesus, could this testimony to the scriptural character of divine revelation be set aside.

II. REVELATION OF THE NEW COVENANT

As Eschatological Fulfillment

Christianity as reflected in the New Testament, as we have seen, looks back upon the revelation of the old covenant, but contemplates it also as a present possession in view of its having found embodiment in the sacred

Scriptures. Its view of the history of divine revelation is, however, by no means confined to its evaluation of the Old Testament. For no affirmation that Christianity makes is more clearly or more emphatically made than that in the coming of Christ a new epoch of revelation has dawned. As following upon the older revelation it might be thought of simply as standing alongside of the Old Testament and as being an expansion upon it. As *divine* revelation the new revelation stands in organic connection with the old and necessarily is characterized by unity with the old. Nevertheless, this way of describing the relationship between the new and the old is far from doing justice to the fact that within the new revelation there is the pervasive sense of its being the eschatological fulfillment of the old. This diversity, while coming to expression within a sense of organic unity, recognizes that there is genuine progress in the history of special revelation, so that the new surpasses and transcends the old as fulfillment does promise and reality shadow.

Emphatically indicative of this diversity as well as unity is the consideration that within the revelation of the old covenant there comes to expression an eschatological outlook which, because it possesses the character of divine promise, guarantees that the epoch of fulfillment will come into being. This eschatological outlook within the old revelation comes to expression in remarkably varied forms. The new day in the realization of the divine purpose of redemption is set forth by Jeremiah as the making of a new covenant with the house of Israel. It contains a reiteration of the elemental covenantal promise, "I will be their God and they shall be my people," but carries with it also a divine guarantee that the covenant will be kept and realized in the lives of his people (31:31–34). Another highly significant prophetic strain is that God, whose kingdom ruleth over all (Ps. 103:19), will come as a mighty One and his arm will rule for him (Isa. 40:10). Within this perspective must also be placed the specifically Messianic prophecies of the coming of the great Representative of God, who is depicted as being himself divine, but who also comes as the Servant of the Lord (*cf.* for example Isa. 9:6 f.; 42:1 ff.; 52:13–53:12). This great day of future deliverance is also depicted as a time when in a manner that transcends the divine action under the old covenant God would pour out his Spirit upon all flesh (Joel 2:28 ff.). This eschatological expectation views the saving transformation that is to be effected as being so thoroughgoing and comprehensive that it finds expression in the prophecy of the creation of new heavens and a new earth (Isa. 65:17).

The Old Testament thus prepares the way for the understanding of the new epoch of revelation as one of eschatological fulfillment, and it is precisely this perspective that pervades the new revelation itself. The Epistle to the Hebrews is preeminently the Epistle of the new covenant, presenting its message as it does in terms of the historical realization of Jeremiah's prophecy in Christ. And our Lord himself, at the very eve of his crucifixion, points to the significance of that event for the realization of the new covenant.

In his teaching our Lord, however, more pervasively makes use of the concept of the kingdom of God. This term likewise serves to bring to expression the feature of the expectation of a new order in which the prophecy of the rule of God comes to pass, as God himself supernaturally and redemptively manifests his Lordship in history so as to overcome all evil. The fulfillment of Messianic prophecy in Christ is interwoven with the proclamation of the coming of the kingdom of God as expression is given to the glad tidings that it is *in Christ* that God accomplishes his rule. The ministry of Christ in the days of his flesh, the exercise of Lordship at God's right hand and his coming again on the clouds of heaven with great power and glory constitute, accordingly, decisive divine actions whereby the kingdom of God, in various aspects and stages, manifests itself. In claiming Messiahship, whether by the use of various Messianic titles or by the exercise of Messianic prerogatives and functions, Christ shows that he shared to the full the consciousness that his ministry in its various phases constituted evidence of the manifestation in history of the age to which the prophets had looked forward. From this vantage point one can also understand how that, at one and the same time, he could affirm the authority and validity of the Law and the Prophets and yet create astonishment because he taught as having authority and not as the scribes when he sovereignly declared, "But I say unto you." For he so built upon the foundation of the Law and the Prophets that they were to attain their perfect accomplishment and realization through him (Matt. 5:17-20, 21 ff.; 7:28 f.)

One may conclude with confidence, therefore, that the revelation of the new covenant was not characterized by less glory, truth and grace than that of the old. On the contrary, the saving activity of God in Christ and by the Holy Spirit is even more manifest and recreative in the new. Indeed, the new so transcends the old that when, for the moment, the facts of unity and continuity are not considered, it could be said that "grace and truth came through Jesus Christ" (John 1:17). And if the redemptive purpose of God dictated that the revelation of the old covenant should be embodied in Scripture, can one doubt that same divine purpose, as that came to far richer and glorious expression in the revelation of the new covenant, should contemplate that this revelation should likewise be incorporated in Scripture? Thus it might be present with his people to continue to accomplish his gracious purpose.

As Proclamation and Tradition

The revelation of the new covenant, like that of the old, is as to its very nature, we must now emphasize, a revelation *in history*. As the revelation of eschatological fulfillment it consists basically of acts of redemption and revelation which form aspects of a single divinely initiated and controlled movement. And since, in particular, divine revelation finds actual embodiment in history, in the great event of Christ and in the great events of his life and death and resurrection, it possesses a once-for-all character. As such it was proclaimed and as such it was handed down and received. Because it is at one and the same time proclamation and tradition it possesses, therefore, an objective character which must be reflected in the communication thereof.

In speaking above of the manifestation of the new covenant in the blood of Christ and of the coming of the kingdom of God in and through the ministry of Christ, the *historical* character of the new revelation has already been recognized. Hence it is not necessary to show at length that in his preaching of glad tidings to the poor as in his miracles, and thus by his very presence and action with authority and power, Jesus was conscious of bringing to historical manifestation the great age to which the prophets had looked forward (cf. Matt. 11:2–6; 12:28; 13:16 f.; Luke 4:18–21).

This historical character of the divine message which Jesus expressed in word and deed finds the same emphatic expression in the formulation of the apostolic proclamation. As Paul set it forth in I Corinthians 15 it is presented indeed as being "according to the Scriptures." But it evidently consists primarily of the great affirmations that Christ died, that he was buried, and that he was raised up on the third day, together with the declaration of the significance for our redemption of these events. So powerful, in fact, is the emphasis upon the proclamation as history that Paul takes pains to stress at length that apart from the fact of Christ's resurrection his preaching is empty and their faith is futile.

In stressing the historical character of the gospel we should not neglect the subjective aspect of its radical consequences for our lives any more than in emphasizing the objective character of the divine revelation we may minimize or obscure the absolute indispensability of the subjective working of the Holy Spirit in our hearts if we are to receive the divine revelation in a saving way. Nevertheless, it seems to be especially necessary in our day to stress that the Gospel has no meaning or power except as the cross and resurrection, as God's action in Christ, are recognized as actual historical events, which occurred at particular times and places.

When Paul says that he has been crucified with Christ or made alive together with Christ, there is not the slightest discounting of the cross and resurrection as history; rather by the use of perfect and aorist tenses he is indicating that the meaning for us is bound up with the fact that we were united with Christ in the occurrence of these events. II Corinithians 5:16 is often appealed to as if Paul were giving expression to a basic indifference to "Christ after the flesh," and so to the historicity and historical significance of the actual life of Christ upon earth. This estimate of Paul's meaning is, however, radically at variance with his testimony as a whole, very directly also with the emphatic references to the death and resurrection of Christ in v. 15, and with the language of v. 16a which indicates that the words "after the flesh" must be understood as qualifying "know" rather than "no man" or "Christ." In v. 16, accordingly, rather than undercutting the historical foundation of the gospel, Paul is dwelling upon the transforming power of Christ whereby, as a new creation in Christ, one gains a wonderful new apprehension and discernment of Christ and all things. Paul, like the New Testament generally, knows nothing of historic (*geschichtlich*) significance apart from that which is historical (*historisch*).

It remains in this connection briefly to observe that, as historical in the sense indicated above, the gospel is viewed as that which has been handed down. This is a point which has been emphasized by Oscar Cullmann, who felicitously distinguishes between apostolic tradition and ecclesiastical tradition (*The Early Church,* pp. 59 ff.) And it has been recognized even more satisfactorily by Herman Ridderbos in his little book on the New Testament Canon, of which an early translation into English is promised. Paul's opening words in I Corinthians 15 may serve to characterize the New Testament point of view in this regard:

"Now I made known unto you, brethren, the gospel which I preached unto you, which also you received, wherein also ye stand, by which also ye are saved, if ye hold fast the word which I preached unto you, except ye believed in vain. For I delivered unto you first of all that which also I received."

It is significant, moreover, that the tradition which the apostles received from the Lord and they in turn handed down to men comprehended not only the gospel of salvation (I Cor. 15:3; Gal. 1:9, 12) but other aspects of the Christian message as well (I Cor. 11:2, 23; Rom. 6:17; Phil. 4:9; Col. 2:6; I Thess. 4:1; II Thess. 2:15). Thus not only the facts of the proclamation and their interpretation but also the teaching of the apostles as a whole were understood as that which had been committed to them by the Lord for transmission to the Church.

The Epistle to the Hebrews similarly, after having characterized the revelation of the new age as a revelation "in a Son" to distinguish it qualitatively from the earlier revelation, characterizes it as coming with even more solemn sanctions than the word spoken through angels in that it was "at the first spoken through the Lord and confirmed unto us by them that heard" (Heb. 1:1 f.; 2:2 ff.). It is noteworthy also that Luke, in the prologue which appears to have in view the contents of Acts as well as the Gospel, reflects upon the Christian message in terms of "the things which have been fulfilled among us," and speaks of the knowledge of these things as a tradition communicated by those who from the beginning were eye-witnesses and ministers of the word (cf. my *The Witness of Luke to Christ,* pp. 24 ff.).

The revelation of the new covenant, accordingly, as to its very nature—

because it is concerned with a disclosure in word and deed originating with Christ and centering in him—is a once-for-all communication. And inasmuch as it has been delivered to the apostles by the Lord himself that they in turn might deliver it to the Church, this apostolic tradition would be recognized as possessing the authority of the Lord. There would be from the beginning a concern for faithful transmission and thus, while even oral tradition tended to assume a fixed form to satisfy the needs of the Church, these needs would be more fully and permanently supplied as the tradition was committed to writing. The new revelation because of its very nature, therefore, no less surely than the old, was virtually crying out for inscripturation in order that the Church might be provided with assured knowledge of the fulfillment of the divine purpose of redemption.

Initial Evidences of Inscripturation

When we come now finally to deal with the scriptural character of the revelation of the new covenant we appear to be at a great disadvantage. For clearly with regard to an acknowledgment of that revelation as having found embodiment in Scripture there is nothing comparable to the testimony of the New Testament to the Old. There are, however, several considerations which should be borne in mind in this connection. We should keep in view, first of all, that the divine authority of the Bible as Scripture is an intrinsic authority rather than one superimposed upon it, and that, therefore, possession of the attribute of divine authority does not have to wait upon the recognition thereof to be valid. Moreover, it may be recalled that evidently the Old Testament likewise accredited itself in the historical process in which God entrusted his people with the divine oracles. Consideration of the parallelism of this process of self-accreditation and acknowledgment will also caution us not to suppose that every part of the Scriptures would have given evidence of its divine character and authority in exactly the same way. A distinctively prophetic work would naturally bear upon its very surface the marks of its inspiration in a way that would not likely be true of an historical book, while the authority of the Epistles would appropriately come to expression in another distinctive way. Considering all these factors, it is remarkable that there are so many rather than that there are so few specific claims within the New Testament that the divine revelation of the new covenant was regarded as being scriptural in character.

In turning now to consider the explicit evidence we begin with the testimony of Paul. As one reflects, for example, upon the Apostle's exposition and defense of the gospel in the Epistle to the Galatians, where he insists that gospel as he proclaims it is of absolute divine authority and possesses the character of revelation (Gal. 1:6-12), we can hardly allow for any other possibility than that those who received his gospel as true also accorded his written presentation thereof the authority of divine revelation. Inasmuch as he is conscious, as an apostle, of speaking with the authority of the Lord, it is not surprising that in the Epistle commonly judged to be his earliest he already adjures his readers "by the Lord that this epistle be read unto all the brethren" (I Thess. 5:27). The authority of his written word, according to Paul's own estimate thereof, also finds significant expression a little later when Paul insists that his command, as expressed in an Epistle, determined the character and limits of their Christian fellowship (*cf.* II Thess. 3:14). The authority of his Epistles as written documents was assuredly not less than that of the extraordinary claim which he made—in even regulating the exercise of the gifts of the Spirit—when he declared that what he wrote was to be recognized as constituting the commandment of the Lord (I Cor. 14:37). The concern for the circulation of his letters which comes to expression in Colossians 4:16 provides further evidence of the fact that, though the Epistles were first of all directed to particular situations, their intrinsic character afforded them a wider relevancy and authority. The response that Paul anticipated for his Epistles does not therefore differ qualitatively from that accorded them in II Peter. For according to II Peter 3:2 the commandment of the Lord and Saviour "through your apostles," no less than the holy prophets, was available in such a form that it could be remembered. And in II Peter 3:15 f. there is a specific acknowledgment that the Epistles of Paul were documents "which the ignorant and unstedfast wrest, as they do also the other scriptures, unto their own destruction," a statement in which the Epistles are recognized as possessing the same level of authority as the Old Testament, and appear also to be included by implication under the term "Scripture."

In the case of the Gospels, the personality of the individual evangelists remains wholly or largely in the background. The fact, however, that they are publications of the gospel of Jesus Christ must have confronted the Church with the necessity of making a judgment as to their trustworthiness and authority. Moreover, Luke specifically indicates that he is undertaking the preparation of a written work which can provide certainty regarding the things that the Lord had done. And John, who writes in the consciousness that the Spirit of truth was his guide into all truth (John 15:26 f.; 16:12 ff.), in characterizing his book as a whole uses the very language that he and the New Testament commonly use in introducing Old Testament quotations as being "that which is written" (John 20:30, 31; 2:17; 6:31, 45; 10:34; 12:14; 15:25; *cf.* also 21:24 f.).

Most clearly of all, the scriptural character of the New Testament revelation is reflected in the Revelation of John. At the very beginning its contents are described as a divine revelation or unveiling mediated by Jesus Christ. The contents of the book are therefore understandably spoken of as "the word of God and the testimony of Jesus Christ" (Rev. 1:1 f.; *cf.* 17:17; 19:9; 21:5; 22:6, 9). The book itself is characterized as a work of prophecy (Rev. 1:3; 22:18; *cf.* 10:11; 22:6 f., 9 f., 18 f.), and thus appropriately the Spirit is acknowledged as speaking in the book (Rev. 2:7, 11, 17, 29;

3:6, 13, 22, 19:10; *cf.* 1:10; 4:2; 17:3; 21:10). In view of such claims
it is understandable that this book should have come to be acknowledged as
worthy of a place alongside the prophetic Scriptures of the Old Testament.
Nothing is left to inference, however, so far as the claims of the author are
concerned, for in Revelation 1:3, as he contemplates his Christian readers
gathered for public worship—where one leads in the reading of the sacred
writings and others have come to hear—he most solemnly pronounces a
blessing upon the ones that read and those who hear the words of the
prophecy and keep the things which are written therein. And in the epilogue
the line of division between divine Scripture and merely human teaching is
drawn even more sharply.

"I testify unto every man that heareth the words of the prophecy of this
book, if any man shall add unto them, God shall add unto him the plagues
which are written in this book; and if any man shall take away from the
words of the book of this prophecy, God shall take away his part from the
tree of life, and out of the holy city, which are written in this book" (Rev.
22:18 f.). The claim that a writing constitutes Holy Scripture could hardly
have been made more unambiguously and emphatically. These solemn words
of the epilogue, like those of the prologue, directly apply only to the Book
of Revelation, but they show how even within the New Testament the scriptural character of special divine revelation came to explicit expression. On
this background one may understand how gradually the New Testament as
a whole came to be accorded this status, for the decisive fact was recognition
of its revelatory character. Where that was discerned and acknowledged its
recognition as Scripture was largely a formality. And thus the process in
which the canonicity of the New Testament was recognized, even though
considerable time was to elapse before the Church expressed itself with
complete clarity and unanimity on this point, was deeply rooted in the New
Testament and grew out of the history of special divine revelation contained therein.

CONTEMPORARY VIEWS
OF REVELATION

James I. Packer

James I. Packer is tutor at Tyndale Hall, Bristol, England. He was born at Twyning, Gloucestershire, England, in 1926. A scholar of Corpus Christi College, Oxford, he was graduated in classical studies and philosophy in 1948 and in theology in 1950. He received his D.Phil. degree in 1954 for a thesis on the soteriology of Richard Baxter. Published writings are a new translation of Luther's Bondage of the Will *and a work titled* 'Fundamentalism' and the Word of God.

6. *James I. Packer*

CONTEMPORARY VIEWS
OF REVELATION

"WHAT DO we mean by revelation? It is a question to which much hard thinking and careful writing are being devoted in our time, and there is a general awareness among us that it is being answered in a way that sounds very differently from the traditional formulations." These are the opening words of Dr. John Baillie's book, *The Idea of Revelation in Recent Thought* (London: Oxford University Press, and New York: Columbia University Press, 1956) and they are true. Indeed, the point could be stated much more emphatically than this. The question of revelation is at the very heart of the modern theological debate. And, just because Christianity purports to be a revealed religion, whose content and character must be determined from the revelation on which it rests, this means that the real subject under discussion is the essential nature of Christianity. The modern debate is carried on with a measure of awareness of this fact among all parties, though the depth of the cleavage between the evangelical position and its alternatives within modern Protestantism is not always seen.

The aim of this essay is to survey, from the standpoint of evangelical faith, some influential lines of thought which are being prosecuted today concerning the nature of God's saving revelation of himself to man and the place of the Bible in that revelation. While limitations of space will preclude a full assessment of representative theologians, we hope to clarify the trends of the day in terms of underlying principles. It would not, in any case, be fair to take isolated statements by modern theologians, on this or any other topic, as purporting to be final. Theologians generally write today in hope of furthering discussions rather than of finishing them, for modern theology is well aware of its own fluid and transitional character. The Barthian hopes that a new epoch of Church science is beginning; the liberal has never doubted that the Christian apprehension of God requires constant reassimilation and restatement in terms of shifting cultural forms; and theologians of all sympathies within the ecumenical movement envisage the synthesizing of the scattered insights of a fragmented Christendom as a task that claims urgent attention. None doubts that theology is on the move, however much disagreement there may be as to where it is going. In this situation, it would be risky to regard any particular expressions of view as other than exploratory and provisional. Our aim in this chapter must rather be to understand the tendencies which individual modern views embody, and to ask how far these represent progress along the right lines.

I. HISTORICAL ANTECEDENTS OF THE MODERN DEBATE

We shall best understand the modern debate if we first remind ourselves of its historical antecedents.

From the earliest days of Christianity, the whole Church regarded the Bible as a web of revealed truths, the recorded utterances of God bearing witness to himself. Theologians varied in the significance which they attached to the historical character of Scripture (Irenaeus, for instance, allowed it more than Origen). Nor were they all agreed on the limits of the Canon, or on the value of allegorical modes of exegesis. But these differences concerned only the meaning and content of Scripture, and presupposed a common view of its character. In the Middle Ages, it came to be held that Scripture needed to be authenticated, interpreted and supplemented by the *ecclesia docens,* and that faith (here conceived as *fides*—credence—merely) had as its proper object the teaching of the Church, as such; but this did not mean any change of view as to the nature of Scripture. The Reformers broke with the Roman position at many points. They enthroned the Spirit in place of the Church as the authenticator and interpreter of Scripture; and, since they recognized that the Spirit's testimony to Scripture is given in and through the statements of Scripture itself, they expressed their position by speaking of Scripture as self-authenticating (*autopistos* was Calvin's word) and self-interpreting. As self-interpreting, they held, Scripture must be allowed to fix its own sense from within; arbitrary modes of interpretation, such as were practiced by the medieval allegorists, may not be imposed upon it. Scripture has only one sense: the literal (i.e., natural). This insight made possible for the first time a just appreciation of the literary categories of Scripture, and, guided by it, the Reformers laid the foundations of scientific exegesis. Concern for the literal sense in turn led them to a new understanding of the real contents of Scripture—Law and Gospel, saving history and gracious promise, the love of God revealed in Christ. The self-sufficiency of Scripture was also recognized, and the Bible was set up, according to its own demand, as judge of those traditions which had previously been supposed to supplement it. Faith was now correlated with Scripture, both formally and materially; as a result, the concept of faith was enlarged so as to include, along with credence, *fiducia*—personal trust and reliance upon the Biblical promises and the Biblical Christ; and the task of theology came to be conceived, not as a matter of systematizing the agglomerated contents of the Church's teaching (the medieval view), but as, on the one hand, receiving, studying, and expounding the written Word and, on the other, reforming the belief and practice of the Church by it. These changes of view as to the place and use of Scripture in the Church were radical and far-reaching; but—and this is the point that now concerns us—there was in all this no break with the historic conception of Scripture as a unified web of revealed truths. Witness to this was borne as eloquently by Luther's doubts about the canonicity of James and Hebrews, on the grounds of their teaching, as by the proliferation of confessions in which the new-found Biblical doctrines were set out in creedal form.

From the seventeenth to the nineteenth century, however, the history of Protestant thought was one of steady inroads made into the Reformers' position by the forces of subjectivism. By subjectivism we mean the attitude which posits final authority for faith and life in human reason, conscience or religious sentiment. It is the application to theology of Protagoras' dictum: "Man is the measure of all things"; defined in terms of the Reformers' position, it means failure to recognize the need of submitting oneself to the correcting judgment of Scripture, and betrays an unwarrantable confidence in the power of the unaided human mind to work out religious truth for itself. It perverts the Reformers' principle of the right of private judgment, from a demand for freedom to be subject to Scripture into a demand for freedom from such subjection: freedom, that is, to disagree with Scripture where it does not fit in with our previous ideas. Subjectivism has taken two characteristic forms: *rationalistic* and *mystical*. In the first, final appeal in matters of faith is made to the verdict of speculative reason, informed by extra-biblical principles of judgment; in the second, to the content of the empirical religious consciousness. The first appeared on the circumference of seventeenth-century Protestant orthodoxy, in certain a priori developments and modifications of the doctrine of Scripture and in a widespread reversion to the Scholastic belief in the validity of natural theology. But the great efflorescence of rationalistic subjectivism came in the eighteenth-century Enlightenment. The "age of reason" forced Christianity on to the Procrustes' bed of Deism. The Enlightenment was avowedly naturalistic in temper, being as hostile to the idea of supernatural interruptions of the ordered course of nature as to that of supernatural revelation. Accordingly, it whittled down Christianity, as the English Deists had done earlier, to a mere

republication of the religion of nature. Kant, the greatest philosopher of the
movement, denied the very possibility of factual knowledge concerning a
super-sensible order, and this appeared to seal the fate of the historic doctrine of revelation. The legacy of the Enlightenment to the Church of later
days was the axiom that certainly some Biblical teaching, and perhaps all, is
not revealed truth; Biblical affirmations, therefore, should not be received
except as confirmed by reason. Modern Protestantism has not yet fully rid
itself of the incubus of this rationalistic axiom, as we shall see.

At this point Schleiermacher, the father of modern liberal theology,
introduced the mystical type of subjectivism into Christian thought. He
sought thereby to save Christianity from rationalistic malaise, but, despite all
the skill of his ministrations, the cure was in some ways worse than the
disease. To side-step Kant's critique of the idea of revealed truth, he
abandoned the notion altogether, and argued that Christianity is essentially
not knowledge but a feeling of dependence on God through Christ. The
Christian faith is simply an infectious historical mysticism, "caught" (like
measles) from contact with others who have it. Doctrine does not create
Christian experience, but is created by it. Doctrinal statements are attempts
to express in words borrowed from the culture of the day the contents of the
corporate Christian consciousness, and theology is the systematic examination of this consciousness as thus expressed. The proper study of theologians
is man; theology is an account of certain human feelings, and its method is
that of a psychological science. Man's self-consciousness is the reference-point
of all theological statements; to make them is simply a way of talking about
oneself; they tell us nothing of God, but only what men feel about God.
Theology is thus dogmatically agnostic about God and his world. As a
science, it knows nothing of any events but states of mind. For information
about the nature of the world and the course of history—including the
historical process out of which Christianity came—it looks to other sciences.
It reads the Bible as a classic expression of religious experiences, but is not
concerned with it as anything more. Schleiermacher's position made the idea
of revelation really superfluous, for it actually amounted to a denial that
anything is revealed. On his principles, divine revelation must be simply
equated with human advance into God-consciousness. Thus, his legacy to
the Church can be summed up in the axiom that, whatever else revelation
may be, it is not a communication of truth from God to man. This, too, is
an incubus which the Church has not yet succeeded in throwing off.

The vacuum left by Schleiermacher's denial that Christianity involves any
positive world-view or historical affirmations was swiftly filled by nineteenth-
century science. The devotees of "scientific" history practiced "higher criticism" on the Biblical records and rewrote the story of Hebrew-Christian
religion in terms of the naturalistic principle of unilinear evolution. The
supernaturalism which in fact determines the whole Biblical outlook was
eliminated as a matter of method; that miracles happen was not considered

a permissible hypothesis, and miracle-stories in the Bible, it was held, should be dismissed as superstitious accretions, just as such stories should be if found in any other document. The question-begging character of this procedure was not seriously considered. Meanwhile, the "scientific" concept of evolution was pressed into service to provide a clue to the meaning of history, sacred and secular alike, and a glowing eschatology of inevitable progress. These rationalistic developments had the blessing of Schleiermacher's disciples, for they did not in any way impoverish Christianity as this school conceived it. And the liberal understanding of Christianity grew increasingly dominant throughout the nineteenth century.

II. RISE OF THE "POST-LIBERAL" THEOLOGY

The first World War seemed to explode quite decisively the eschatology of inevitable progress, and led to a deep-seated uncertainty as to the rightness of the anthropocentric view of religion which had so gaily sponsored it. In this situation, two significant theological movements appeared, each stressing from complementary angles of approach the reality of the revealing action whereby God speaks to sinful man in judgment and mercy. The first was the dialectical "crisis-theology" of Karl Barth, which summoned the Church in the name of God to humble herself and listen to his catastrophic Word. The second was the "Biblical theology" movement, which first became articulate in English through the work of Sir Edwyn Hoskyns, calling the Biblical scholar in the name of historical objectivity to recognize that the Bible cannot warrantably be treated as a book of mystical devotion, nor as a hard core of non-supernatural history overlaid with unauthentic theology, but that it must be read as a churchly confession of faith in a God who has spoken and speaks still. These two movements, linked together in all manner of combinations, are the parent stems from which the theology of the past generation has grown. Taking as their own starting-point the reality of divine revelation, they have forced the Church to reconsider this theme with renewed seriousness, and to recognize that the proper task of theology is not reading off the surface level of the mind of man, as subjectivism supposed, but receiving, expounding and obeying the Word of God.

But this raises a crucial and complex problem for the theologian of the "post-liberal" age: how are we to conceive of the Word of God? in what relation does it stand to the Bible, and the Bible to it? The complexity of this issue in the minds of present-day theologians arises from the fact that they suppose themselves to be standing amid the wreckage of two fallen idols. On the one hand, the older orthodoxy, which recognized the reality of revelation and sought to build on it, was founded on belief in verbal inspiration and inerrancy; but these beliefs, it is said, have collapsed before the onslaught of Biblical criticism, and are no longer tenable. On the other hand, nineteenth century liberalism, with all its devotion to Biblical science and the study of the religious consciousness, left no room for revelation at all; and that is seen not to be satisfactory either. A new synthesis is held to be required, incorporating what was right and avoiding what was wrong in both the older views. The problem, therefore, as modern theology conceives it, is this: how can the concept of divine revelation through the Bible be re-introduced without reverting to the old, "unscientific" equation of the Bible with the Word of God? It is admitted that the Biblical idea of revelation must be in some sense normative; and the main strands in the Biblical idea—that revelation is a gracious act of God causing men to know him; that his self-communication has an objective content; that faith and unbelief are correlative to revelation, the former meaning reception of it, the latter, rejection; that the subject matter of revelation concerns Jesus Christ; and that the act of revelation is effected, and its content mediated, through Scripture—are matters of general recognition. It is seen, too, that Schleier-macherian mysticism, which denies the reality of revelation *in toto,* and naturalistic rationalism, which substitutes for faith in what God has said faith in what I think, are both wrong in principle. Yet, it is said, we cannot go back on the liberal view of the Bible. Hence the problem crystallizes itself as follows: how can we do justice to the reality and intelligibility of revelation without recourse to the concept of revealed truth? How can we affirm the accessibility of revelation in Scripture without committing ourselves to belief in the absolute trustworthiness of the Biblical record? How can we assert the divine authority of Biblical revelation without foreclosing the possibility—indeed, it would be said, the proved reality—of human error in Scripture? Or, putting it the other way round, how on the basis of the nineteenth century view of the Bible can we vindicate the objectivity and givenness of revelation, and so keep out of the pitfalls of mysticism and rationalism? Plainly, this is a problem of some difficulty. *Prima facie,* it would seem to be an inquiry after ways and means of having one's cake and eating it. The aim proposed is, not to withdraw the Bible from the acid-bath of rationalistic criticism, but to find something to add to the bath to neutralize its corrosive effects. The problem is, how to enthrone the Bible once more as judge of the errors of man while leaving man enthroned as judge of the errors of the Bible; how to commend the Bible as a true witness while continuing to charge it with falsehood. One cannot help thinking that it would be something of a *tour de force* to give a convincing solution of a problem like this. However, such is the task attempted by modern theology. It is proposed, by drawing certain distinctions and introducing certain new motifs, so to refashion the doctrine of revelation that the orthodox subjection of heart and mind to Biblical authority and the liberal subjection of Scripture to the authority of rationalistic criticism appear, not as contradictory, but as complementary principles, each presupposing and vindicating the other. We are now to examine some of the main ideas about the nature of revelation and its relation to Scripture which have been put forward in recent years for the furtherance of this enterprise.

III. CURRENT VIEWS OF REVELATION AND SCRIPTURE

Before going further, however, it is worth pausing to see on what grounds modern theology bases its rejection of the historic view that Biblical revelation is propositional in character; for, though this rejection has become almost a commonplace of modern discussion, and is, of course, axiomatic for those who accept Schleiermacher's interpretation of Christianity, it is clearly not something that can just be taken for granted by those who profess to reject his view.

J. K. S. Reid recognizes that "there is no a priori reason why the Bible should not have this . . . character" (viz., that of being a corpus of divinely guaranteed truths) (*The Authority of Scripture,* London, Methuen, 1957, pp. 162 f.). But if that is so, the a posteriori arguments brought against this view must be judged very far from decisive.

Archbishop Temple, in his much-quoted discussions of our subject (*Nature, Man and God,* London, Macmillan, 1934, Lectures XII, XIII; essay in *Revelation,* ed. Baillie and Martin, London, Faber, 1937), rejected this conception of Scripture on three counts: first, that little of it seems to consist of formal theological propositions; second, that little or none of it seems to have been produced by mechanical "dictation," or anything like it; third, that if we are to regard the Bible as a body of infallible doctrine we shall need an infallible human interpreter to tell us what it means; and "in whatever degree reliance upon such infallible direction comes in, spirituality goes out" (*Nature, Man and God,* p. 353). But, we reply, the first two points are irrelevant, and the third false. To assert propositional revelation involves no assertions or expectations a priori as to the literary categories to which the parts of Scripture will belong (only study of the text can tell us that); what is asserted is merely that all affirmations which Scripture is found to make, and all other statements which demonstrably embody scriptural teaching, are to be received as truths from God. Nor does this position involve any a priori assertions as to the psychology of inspiration, let alone the mechanical "dictation-theory," which no Protestant theologian seems ever to have held. ("Dictation" in old Protestant thought was a theological metaphor declaring the relation of the written words of Scripture to the divine intention, with no psychological implications whatever.) Temple's third point we deny; we look to Scripture itself to teach us the rules for its own interpretation, and to the Holy Spirit, the Church's only infallible teacher, to guide us into its meaning, and we measure all human pronouncements on Scripture by Scripture's own statements.

Others raise other objections to our view of the nature of Scripture. It is said, for instance, that modern study has proved that Scripture errs. But *proved* is quite the wrong word: the truth is, rather, that modern critical scholarship has allowed itself to assume that the presence of error in Scripture is a valid hypothesis, and to interpret the phenomena of Scripture in line with this assumption. However, the hypothesis has never in any case been shown to be necessary, nor is it clear how it could be; and the Biblical doctrine of Scripture would rule it out as invalid in principle. Again, it is held that to regard the Bible as written revelation is bibliolatry, diverting to Scripture honor due only to God. But the truth is rather that we honor God precisely by honoring Scripture as his written Word. Nor is there more substance in the claim that to assert the normative authority of Scripture is to inhibit the freedom of the Spirit, who is Lord of the Word; for the Spirit exercises his Lordship precisely in causing the Church to hear and reverence Scripture as the Word of God, as Calvin reminded the Anabaptists four centuries ago.

However, despite the inconclusiveness of the arguments for so doing and the Bible's self-testimony on the other side, modern theology finds its starting-point in a denial that Scripture, as such, is revealed truth. The generic character which this common denial imparts to the various modern views is clearly brought out by Daniel Day Williams in the following passage:

> In brief this is the new understanding of what revelation is. . . . Revelation as the "self-disclosure of God" is understood as the actual and personal meeting of man and God on the plane of history. Out of that meeting we develop our formulations of Christian truth in literal propositions. . . . Revelation is disclosure through personal encounter with God's work in his concrete action in history. It is never to be identified with any human words which we utter in response to the revelation. In *Nature, Man and God,* William Temple described revelation as "intercourse of mind and event, not the communication of doctrine distilled from that intercourse."

Doctrines, on this view, are not revelation, though they are formulated on the basis of revelation. As Temple put it elsewhere, "There is no such thing as revealed truth. . . . There are truths of revelation, that is to say, propositions which express the results of correct thinking concerning revelation; but they are not themselves directly revealed" (*Nature, Man and God*, p. 317). What this really means is that the historic Christian idea of revelation has been truncated; the old notion that one part of God's complex activity of giving us knowledge of himself is his teaching us truths about himself is hereby ruled out, and we are forbidden any more to read what is written in Scripture as though it were God who had written it. We are to regard Scripture as a human response and witness to revelation, but not in any sense revelation itself. After observing that nearly all theologians today take this view, Williams goes on, in the passage from which we have already quoted, to explain the significance of this change: "What it means," he writes, "is that Christian thought can be set free from the intolerable dogmatism which results from claiming that God's truth is identical with some human formulation of it" (scriptural no less than later creedal, apparently). "It gives freedom for critical re-examination of every Christian statement in the light of further experience, and in the light of a fresh encounter with the personal and historical act of God in Christ" (*Interpreting Theology* 1918–1952, London, S.C.M., 1953; *What Present-day Theologians are Thinking,* New York, Harper, 1952, p. 64 f., drawing on Temple, *op. cit.,* pp. 316 ff.).

Professor Williams' statement well sums up the modern approach, and its wording suggests at once the basic problem which this approach raises: namely, the problem of objectivity in our knowledge of God. What is the criterion whereby revelation is to be known? If there is no revealed truth, and the Bible is no more than human witness to revelation, fallible and faulty, as all things human are, what guarantee can we have that our apprehensions of revelation correspond to the reality of revelation itself? We are sinful men, and have no reason to doubt that our own thoughts about revelation are as fallible and faulty as any; by what standard, then, are we to test and correct them? Is there a standard, the use of which opens in principle a possibility of conforming our ideas of revelation to the real thing? Historic Christianity said yes: the Biblical presentation of, and pattern of thinking about, revelation-facts is such a standard. Modern theology, however, cannot say this; for the characteristic modern position really boils down to saying that the only standard we have for testing our own fallible judgments is our own fallible judgment. It tells us that what we study in Scripture is not revelation but the witness of faith to revelation; and that what as Christian students we have to do is critically to examine and assess the Biblical witness by the light, not of extra-biblical principles (that, it is agreed, would be illegitimate rationalism), but of the contents of revelation itself, which the Church by faith has some idea of already, and which it seeks to clarify to itself by this very study. Such, we are told, is the existential situation in which, and the basic motive for which, the Church studies Scripture. And the "critical re-examination of every Christian statement in the light of further experience" which is here in view is a reciprocal process of reconsidering and re-interpreting the faith of the Church and the faith of the Bible in terms of each other: not making either universally normative for the other, but evolving a series of working approximations which are offered as attempts to do justice to what seems essential and constitutive in both.

Theology pursued in this fashion is held to be "scientific," and that on two accounts. In the first place, it is said, theology is hereby established as the "science of faith," a strictly empirical discipline of analyzing the contents of Christian faith in its actual manifestations, in order to elucidate the nature of the relationship which faith is, and of the object to which it is a response. (Reference in these terms to the reality of the object of faith is thought to parry the charge that this is just Schleiermacher over again.) Then, in the

second place, this theological method is held to vindicate its scientific character by the fact that, in interpreting and restating the faith of the Bible, it
takes account of the "scientific" critical contention that the Biblical witness
contains errors and untruths, both factual and theological—a contention
which, no doubt, is generally regarded these days as part of the faith of the
Church. But it is clear that theology, so conceived, is no more than a dexter-
ous attempt to play off two brands of subjectivism against each other. On
the one hand, the subject proposed for study is still the Church's witness to
its own experience, as such, and the contents of Scripture are still treated
simply as important material within this category. It is true that (at the
prompting of critical reason) the *prima facie* character of this experience, as
one of objective relationship with a sovereign living God, is now taken
seriously, and that due respect is paid to the Church's conviction that the
Biblically-recorded experience of prophets and apostles marks a limit outside
which valid Christian experience is not found, but this does not affect the
basic continuity between the modern approach and that of Schleiermacher.
On the other hand, autonomous reason still acts as arbiter in the realm of
theological methodology, following out only those principles of judgment
which it can justify to itself as "scientific" on the basis of its own independent
assessment of the real nature of Christianity. It is true that (out of regard
for the distinctive character of Christian experience) this "scientific" method
recognizes the uniqueness of Christianity, and resists all attempts to minimize
it; and to this end it requires us to master the Biblical thought-forms, in
terms of which this unique experience received its classical expression. But
it does not require us to accept the Biblical view of their objective significance except insofar as our reason, judging independently, endorses that
view; and in this respect it simply perpetuates the theological method of the
Enlightenment. The effect of following the modern approach has naturally
been to encourage a kind of Biblical double-talk, in which great play is made
with Biblical terms, and Biblical categories are insisted on as the proper
medium for voicing Christian faith, but these are then subjected to a
rationalistic principle of interpretation which eliminates from them their
basic Biblical meaning (e.g., a story such as that of the Fall is treated as
mythical, significant and true as a symbol revealing the actual state of men
today, but false if treated as the record of an objective historical happening).
Thus theological currency has been debased, and a cloud of ambiguity now
broods over much modern "biblicism." This, at least, is to the credit of
Bultmann that, having pursued this approach so radically as to categorize
the whole New Testament doctrine of redemption as mythical, he has seen,
with a clearheadedness denied to many, that the most sensible thing to do
next is to drop the mythology entirely and preach simply that brand of
existentialism which, in his view, represents the New Testament's real
"meaning."
    It is clear that, "scientific" or not, this nicely balanced synthesis of two

forms of subjectivism is not in any way a transcending of sub
leaves us still to speculate as to what the Biblical symbols and
mean, and what is the revelation which they reflect and to whic.. ..., ,
It leaves us, indeed, in a state of utter uncertainty; for, if it is true (as Scripture says, and modern theology mostly agrees) that men are sinful creatures,
unable to know God without revelation, and prone habitually to pervert
revelation when given, how can we have confidence that the Biblical witness,
and the Church's experience, and our own ideas, are not all wrong? and why
should we think that by a "scientific" amalgam of the three we shall get
nearer to the reality of revelation than we were before? What trust can we
put in our own ability to see behind the Biblical witness to revelation so
surely that we can pick out its mistakes and correct them? Such questions
did not trouble the subjectivist theologians of the eighteenth and nineteenth
centuries, who assumed the infallibility of the human intellect and wholly
overlooked the noetic effects of sin; but the mid-twentieth century, haunted
by memories of shattered philosophies and exploded ideals, and bitterly
aware of the power of propaganda and brain-washing, and the control that
non-rational factors can have over our thinking, is tempted to despair of
gaining objective knowledge of anything, and demands from the Church
reasoned reassurance as to the accessibility of divine revelation to blind,
bedevilled sinners. But such reassurance cannot in principle be given by
those who on scriptural grounds acknowledge the reality of sin in the mind,
and hence the bankruptcy of rationalism, and yet on rationalistic grounds
jettison the notion of inscripturated divine truth. For unless at some point
we have direct access to revelation normatively presented, by which we may
test and correct our own fallible notions, we sinners will be left to drift on a
sea of speculations and doubts forever. And when modern theology tells us
that we can trust neither the Bible nor ourselves, it condemns us to this fate
without hope of reprieve.

Modern theology is, indeed, fully aware of the scriptural and churchly
conviction that revelation is objectively and normatively presented in and by
the Biblical witness to it. In an attempt to do justice to this conviction while
still holding Scripture to be no more than fallible human testimony, theologians focus attention on two "moments" in the divine self-revealing activity
in which, they affirm, revelation does in fact confront us directly and
authoritatively. These are, on the one hand, the sequence of historical events
in which revelation was given, once for all, to its first witnesses; and, on the
other, the repeated "encounter" in which the content of that original revelation is mediated to each successive generation of believers. Both "moments,"
of course, have a proper place in the Biblical concept of revelation; what is
distinctive about the modern view is not its insistence on them, as such, but
its attempt to do justice to them while dispensing with that which in fact
links them together and is integral to the true notion of each—namely, the
concept of infallible Scriptures, given as part of the historical revelatory

process and conveying that which is mediated in the "encounter." Most modern statements make mention of both "moments" in combination (compare Williams' reference to "a fresh encounter with the personal and historical act of God in Christ"), but they vary in the emphasis given to each. Scholars whose main interest is in Biblical history, such as C. H. Dodd and H. Wheeler Robinson, naturally stress the first (cf. Dodd, *History and the Gospel,* London, Nisbet, 1938; and Robinson, *Inspiration and Revelation in the Old Testament,* London, Oxford University Press, 1946). Those chiefly concerned with systematic theology and apologetics, such as (reading from the right wing to the left) Karl Barth, Emil Brunner, H. Richard and Reinhold Niebuhr, Paul Tillich and Rudolph Bultmann, lay more stress on the second (cf. Barth, *Church Dogmatics* I. 1, 2: *The Doctrine of the Word of God,* Edinburgh, T. and T. Clark, 1936, 1956; Brunner, *The Divine-Human Encounter,* London, S.C.M., 1944; *Revelation and Reason,* London, S.C.M. 1947; H. Richard Niebuhr, *The Meaning of Revelation,* New York, 1941; Reinhold Niebuhr, *The Nature and Destiny of Man,* I, London, Nisbet, 1941; *Faith and History* London, Nisbet, 1949; Tillich, *Systematic Theology,* I, London, Nisbet, 1953; Bultmann, "New Testament and Mythology," in *Kerygma and Myth,* ed. Bartsch, London, S.P.C.K., 1953). These theologians all agree that what is communicated in the "encounter" is that which was given once for all in Christ; where they differ is in their views as to the essential content of the primary revelation and the precise nature of the existential "encounter." A third group of more philosophically-minded theologians have devoted themselves to fixing and holding a balance between these two emphases: among them, the late Archbishop Temple, Alan Richardson and John Baillie (cf. Temple, *loc. cit.;* Richardson, *Christian Apologetics,* London, S.C.M., 1947; Baillie, *Our Knowledge of God,* London, Oxford University Press, 1939, and *op. cit.*).

Can the objective accessibility of revelation be vindicated in these terms? We think not. Consider first the idea that revelation, imperfectly mirrored in the Bible, is directly available in the historical events of which the Bible bears witness. Temple expounded this idea very clearly. He thought of revelation as God's disclosure of his mind and character in the "revealing situations" of redemptive history. At no stage does God give a full verbal explanation of what he is doing, but he enlightens prophetic spirits to discern it. (The notion somewhat suggests a divine charade, to be solved by the God-inspired guesswork of human spectators.) The Biblical authors were prophetic men, and made roughly the right deductions from what they observed; though their recounting and explaining of revelation is marred throughout by errors due to human frailty. Our task is critically to work over the records which they left, checking and where necessary correcting their representations; and the facts themselves, thus discerned, will speak their own proper meaning to us.

But (not to dwell on the arbitrary and unbiblical features of this view, and

the fact that, if true, it would create a new authoritarianism, by making the
expert historian final arbiter of the Church's faith) we must insist that, on
this showing, so far from being able to use historical revelation as a norm,
we can only have access to it at all through prior acceptance of another
norm. For, as Alan Richardson points out, commenting on Temple, all our
study of the past is decisively controlled by the principle of interpretation
which we bring to it; that is, by our antecedent ideas as to the limits of
possibility, the criteria of probability and the nature of historical "meaning"
and explanation. In this case, if we do not already share the supernaturalism
of the Biblical writers' faith about God and his work in his world, we shall
be debarred from sharing their convictions as to what happened in redemptive history. So the revealing facts of history are only accessible to those who
are already sure that Christianity is true. And how do we become sure of
this? By faith, says Richardson. But what is faith? Receiving what God has
said, on his authority, is the basic Biblical idea. But Richardson cannot say
this, for he has already told us that until we have faith we are in no position
to gather from the human records of Scripture what it is that God has said.
He wishes (rightly) to correlate faith with spiritual illumination. But he
cannot depict this illumination as an opening of blind eyes to see what
objectively was always the case—that the Bible is God's Word written, and
its teaching is his revealed truth; for to his mind this is not the case. He is
therefore forced back into illuminism. He has to represent faith as a private
revelation, a divine disclosure of new information not objectively accessible
—namely, that what certain human writers said about God is in fact true.
On his assumption that Scripture, as such, is no more than human witness,
there is nothing else he can say. So we see that the idea of an objective
presentation of revelation in history, when divorced from the idea of a
divinely authoritative record, can only in principle be maintained on an
illuministic basis. Before I can find revelation in history, I must first receive
a private communication from God: and by what objective standard can
anyone check this? There is no norm for testing private revelations. We are
back in subjectivism with a vengeance.

At this point, however, appeal will be made to the concept of "personal
encounter." This, as generally expounded, attempts to parry the charge of
illuminism by the contention that God, in sovereign freedom, causes the
Biblical word of man to become his word of personal address in the
moment of revelation. Brunner has, perhaps, made more of this line of
thought than anyone else. Basing it on an axiomatic refusal to equate the
teaching of Scripture, as such, with the Word of God, he treats the concept
of personal encounter as excluding that of propositional communication
absolutely. God's Word in the encounter comes to me, not as information,
but as demand, and faith is not mental assent, but the response of obedience.
Truth becomes mine through the encounter; but this truth consists, not in
any impersonal correspondence of my thoughts with God's facts, but in the

personal correspondence of my decision with God's demand. "Truth" is that
which happens in the response of faith, rather than anything that is said to
evoke that response; "truth" is an event, correlative to the event of revelation which creates it. But this is a very difficult conception. If we are to take
seriously Brunner's Pickwickian use of the word "truth," then his idea is
one of a communion in which nothing is communicated save a command.
God speaks only in the imperative, not at all in the indicative. But is it a
recognizable statement of the Christian view of revelation to say that God
tells us nothing about himself, but only issues orders? And what is the relation between the command given in the encounter and what is written in
Scripture? Never one of identity, according to Brunner; Scripture is human
witness proceeding from and pointing to communication in encounter; but
not embodying its content; for that which is given in the encounter is
ineffable, and no form of words can properly express it. So, where Augustine
said: "What Thy Scripture says, that (only that, but all that) Thou dost
say," Brunner says: "What Thy Scripture says, that is precisely *not* what
Thou dost say." But how, in this case, can Brunner parry the charge of
uncontrolled and uncontrollable mysticism? Nor would he be better off if
he said that what is spoken by God in the encounter is the exact content of
Scripture texts, that and no more; for then he would either have to abandon
the idea that Scripture is throughout nothing but fallible and erring human
testimony, or else to say that God speaks human error as his truth, which is
either nonsense or blasphemy.

Has the objectivity of revelation been vindicated by this appeal to the
"encounter"? Has anything yet been said to make intelligible the claim that,
though we regard Scripture as no more than fallible human witness, we still
have available an objective criterion, external to our own subjective impressions, by which our erring human ideas about revelation can be measured
and tested? It seems not. By deserting Richardson for Brunner, we seem
merely to have exchanged a doctrine of illuminism (private communication
of something expressible) for one of mysticism (private communication of
something inexpressible). The problem of objectivity is still not solved; and,
we think, never can be on these terms.

IV. LESSONS FROM THE CONTEMPORARY SITUATION

From this survey, sketchy as it is, we learn three things.

First, we see the essential kinship of the various modern views of revelation. They differ in detail, but all begin from the same starting-point and
have the same aim: to restore essential Biblical dimensions to the older
liberal position.

Second, we see the dilemmas in which modern theology hereby involves
itself. "Post-liberal" thought turns out to be liberalism trying to assimilate
into itself certain Biblical convictions which, once accepted, actually spell its

doom. The spectacle which it provides is that of liberalism destroying itself by poisoning its own system. For liberalism, as such, rests, as we saw, on a rationalistic approach to the Bible; and the acceptance of these new insights makes it as irrational in terms of rationalism as it always was unwarrantable in terms of Christianity to continue following such an approach. By recognizing the incomprehensibility of God and his sovereign freedom in revelation, while retaining its peculiar view of Scripture—by trying, that is, to find room for supra-rational factors on its own rationalistic basis—liberalism simply lapses from coherent rationalism into incoherent irrationalism. For the axiom of rationalism in all its forms is that man's mind is the measure of all things; what is real is rational, and only what is rational is real, so that in terms of rationalism the supra-rational is equated with the irrational and unreal. By allowing for the reality of God as one who in himself and in his works passes our comprehension, theological rationalism declares its own bankruptcy, and thereby forfeits its quondam claim to interpret and evaluate Scripture, with the rest of God's works, on rationalistic principles—a claim which it could only make on the assumption of its own intellectual solvency. It is simply self-contradictory for modern theology still to cling to the liberal concept of Scripture while professing to have substituted the Biblical for the liberal doctrine of God. And the fact that it continues to do the former cannot but create doubt as to whether it has really done the latter.

Again, by admitting the noetic effects of sin, and the natural incompetence of the human mind in spiritual things, without denying the liberal assumption that reason has both the right and the power to test and explode the Bible's view of its own character as revealed truth, modern theology is in effect telling us that now we know, not merely that we cannot trust Scripture, but also that we cannot trust ourselves; which combination of convictions, if taken seriously, will lead us straight to dogmatic skepticism. Thus, through trying to both have our cake and eat it, we shall be left with nothing to eat at all. Modern theology only obscures this situation, without remedying it, when it talks here of paradox and dialectical tension. The truth is that, by trying to hold these two self-contradictory positions together, modern theology has condemned itself to an endless sequence of arbitrary oscillations between affirming and denying the trustworthiness of human speculations and Biblical assertions respectively. It could only in principle find stability in the skeptical conclusion that we can have no sure knowledge of God at all.

Thirdly, we see that the only way to avoid this conclusion is to return to the historic Christian doctrine of Scripture, the Bible's own view of itself, which this book is concerned to present. Only when we abandon the liberal view that Scripture is no more than fallible human witness, needing correction by us, and put in its place the Biblical conviction that Scripture is in its nature revealed truth in writing, an authoritative norm for human thought about God, can we in principle vindicate the Christian knowledge of God from the charge of being the incorrigibly arbitrary product of our own subjective fancy. Reconstructed liberalism, by calling attention to the reality of sin, has shown very clearly our need of an objective guarantee of the possibility of right and true thinking about God; but its conception of revelation through historical events and personal encounter with the speaking God ends, as we saw, in illuminism or mysticism, and is quite unable to provide us with such a guarantee. No guarantee can, in fact, be provided except by a return to the old paths—that is, by a renewed acknowledgment of, and submission to, the Bible as an infallible written revelation from God.

THE WITNESS OF
SCRIPTURE TO
ITS INSPIRATION

Alan M. Stibbs

Alan M. Stibbs has been Vice Principal of Oak Hill Theological College in London since 1938, after missionary service in West China from 1928–35 under the China Inland Mission. He holds the M.A. from Cambridge. He has written The Church Universal and Local, Understanding God's Word, *and* Obeying God's Word. *He was joint editor of the* New Bible Handbook *and of the* New Bible Commentary.

7. Alan M. Stibbs

THE WITNESS OF SCRIPTURE TO ITS INSPIRATION

THE PURPOSE of this chapter is to consider the witness of Scripture itself to its own inspiration. To begin with there is need to distinguish clearly between two different meanings or possible implications of the word "inspiration" when it is thus used of Holy Scripture. The prevalent ideas associated with this term do not conform to that denotation of the word which has scriptural authority and justification, and which supplies the particular meaning which we have in view in a study of this kind.

I. MEANING OF INSPIRATION

When the word "inspiration" is used of the Bible it is often thought to describe a quality belonging primarily to the writers rather than to the writings; it indicates that the men who produced these documents were inspired men. In contrast to this idea, which indubitably has its place, we find that the Scripture employs the word bearing this meaning primarily to describe not the writers but the sacred writings. II Timothy 3:16 reads *pasa graphē theopneustos*. This the RSV renders "All scripture is inspired by God." Let us here notice three points about this statement. (1) The Greek adjective *theopneustos* (meaning literally "God-breathed") is a compound, which begins with an explicit recognition of God as the author; the inspiration is divine. (2) The human agents in the production of the Scripture are here not even mentioned. (3) The Scripture, or writing thus produced, is here described, and is intended to be thought of, as "divinely inspired," or as the KJV renders it, "given by inspiration of God." What, therefore, we are in this chapter to consider as inspired, or produced by divine inspiration, is not primarily the condition or activity of the Biblical writers, but the Biblical writings themselves, the actual written words of Scripture.

II. PLACE OF SELF-AUTHENTICATION

Some will surely raise the objection that Scripture ought not thus to be appealed to for its own vindication. To quote Scripture in support of Scripture seems, admittedly, from one standpoint, to be arguing in a circle, and to be logically inconclusive. It is important, therefore, to see that in this particular case no occasion exists for such misgiving.

(1) First, let us recognize that every man has surely a right to speak for himself; and that testimony to oneself ought not be ruled out as completely improper. Indeed, if men were not liars and deceivers, or not prejudiced and blind and lacking in full understanding, their own testimony about themselves would be sufficient. Consider the unique example of the perfect Man. Although Jesus recognized that the truth about himself needed confirmation by independent witness to satisfy normal human standards, he nevertheless said "Even if I bear witness of myself, my witness is true" (RV.; cf. John 5:31; 8:13, 14).

(2) Not only so, but some truths about people may never be known, unless the individuals concerned themselves bear witness to them. If what they thus say is unreliable, no other means of discovering the truth may exist. Somewhat similarly, the Bible discloses from God himself truths which cannot otherwise be discovered. For our knowledge of them we are wholly dependent upon divine revelation thus communicated through the Scriptures. Surely no justification exists for thus believing what the Bible teaches about other doctrines, wholly beyond independent human confirmation, if we cannot equally rely completely on what the Bible teaches about itself. Moreover, if we are to accept Scripture as our supreme rule of faith and understanding in the one, we ought similarly to do so in the other. In other words, we cannot rightly turn to the Bible for testimony to the otherwise unknown unless we do accept also its testimony to itself.

(3) In the third place, if we believe that the Bible not only claims to be, but is, a book from God, then behind and beyond all its human writers and contributing agents God himself must be acknowledged as its author; and God cannot lie. His word is always true and always trustworthy. The Bible's witness to itself ought, therefore, to be treated as authoritative and decisive; in a very real sense we need none other.

(4) When men wish to confirm witness given about themselves they appeal to one greater; they take an oath and swear by almighty God. Similarly, when God wished to make men doubly sure of his word of

promise, he confirmed it by an oath. But when he came to swear, since there was none greater by whom he could swear, he swore by himself (cf. Heb. 6:13–18). He thus made himself the guarantor of the truth and trustworthiness of his own word. This supremely illustrates the principle that in any realm of activity the supreme authority must be self-authenticating. It is impossible to get endorsement or confirmation of such utterances by appeal to some greater authority. Similarly, if the Bible is from God, and therefore possesses supreme authority among men in what it says, it cannot be other than self-authenticating. Truth is settled by what it says rather than by what others may say about it, or in criticism of it.

(5) Finally, relief from the possible embarrassment of dependence upon a single witness—and that in this case the witness of Scripture to itself—is provided by the Trinity and the eternity of the Godhead. For God is Three in One; and God still speaks. So the truth and trustworthiness of Scripture, as the authoritative and unbreakable divine word, are confirmed to the Christian believer by the witness during his earthly life of the incarnate Son of God, and by the present continuing witness of the illuminating and indwelling Spirit of God.

III. WHAT SCRIPTURE DECLARES ABOUT ITSELF

Let us now consider in detail some of the statements made in Scripture about itself and its production. Such statements, we shall note, inevitably bear witness also to Scripture's consequent distinctive character and authority.

All Scripture is "God-breathed"

We have noted that in II Timothy 3:16, "All scripture is inspired by God" (RSV), the Greek adjective *theopneustos* means literally "God-breathed," i.e., "inspired of God." The word "inspired," however, is not to be understood as indicating something "extra" superimposed on the writer or writing, to make the writing different from what it would otherwise be. It indicates rather *how* the writing came into being. It asserts that the writing is a product of the creative activity of the divine breath. The word thus goes right back to the beginning or first cause of the emergence of Scripture, and indicates that Scripture has in its origin this distinctive hallmark, that it owes its very existence to the direct creative activity of God himself. Although men wrote it, it is God who brought it into being. Its content and character have all been decisively determined by the originating and controlling activity of the creative Spirit. For this reason the context affirms that Scripture is profitable "for teaching, for reproof, for correction, and for training for righteousness," since its character and quality, and indeed its very existence, are God-determined.

This idea of God "breathing" and of the divine "breath" is familiar to students of the Old Testament. It is a graphic metaphor applied to the activity of God, especially to the Holy Spirit, who is the executor of the Godhead. So we read in Psalm 33:6, "By the word of the Lord were the heavens made; and all the host of them by the breath of his mouth." The breath of God is thus almighty to create. By this breath not only the heavens but also man was created. "And the Lord God formed man of the dust of the ground, and breathed into his nostrils the breath of life; and man became a living soul" (Gen. 2:7). Or again, we read in Job 33:4, "The Spirit of God hath made me, and the breath of the Almighty hath given me life." The breath or breathing of God speaks, therefore, of the activity of the One who is the first and final cause of all things. Scripture is said to be the product of his activity, the work of the Holy Spirit of God himself. Nor should we overlook that what is thus said to be Spirit-produced is the actual written Word. Its emergence and its enduring record were the consummation and intended goal of the Spirit's activity.

Men Spake From God

The ascription to Scripture of this special divine origin and consequent unique character is, either explicitly or implicitly, confirmed as true by many statements made elsewhere in the Bible. For instance, in II Peter 1:19-21 the prophetic word given to us in Scripture is said to be the more sure, and a source of light in our darkness to which we ought to give heed, because of its extraordinary and divine origin. Let us note carefully the sequence of thought in Peter's reasoning. "First of all," he writes, "you must understand this, that no prophecy of scripture is a matter of one's own interpretation, because no prophecy ever came by the impulse of man, but men moved by the Holy Spirit spoke from God" (RSV).

So the primary truth about Scripture, the very first thing we need to recognize about it, is that no prophecy in it was produced, or can be interpreted, through any individual man acting independently and alone. Genuine prophecies and their true interpretation do not just break forth "from man." The Spirit of God brings such prophecies to expression to reveal the mind of God; and the same Spirit alone can make plain, to those who hear and study these prophecies, what that mind is.

This essential dependence of true prophecy upon God and not upon man is primarily shown in the way in which it came to exist at all. For it was not brought into being simply by any man's desire, decision and determination to give it utterance. It is not "from man." Man is not the prime mover in its production. Indeed, man acting independently, and solely on his own will and initiative, cannot produce it. For true prophecy has never emerged, except when men have been taken up into an activity of the Spirit of God, and borne along to the place, or into the circumstances and the conditions, where they gave utterance to words of which God was the primary originating cause. Clearly, therefore, what matters most for us is the actual words they were thus enabled to express. The enduring God-given witness to the truth is contained in, and conveyed by, the writing. These words, therefore, we ought to accept as brought into being by the Spirit of God for our instruction. They have supreme and final authority because they are from God himself. He is their real author.

In any attempt to appreciate the method of inspiration, or the way in which men specially chosen and prepared were moved to speak divinely-intended words, it becomes us, as finite creatures, to recognize, in humility and with reverent awe, that the ways of God are past finding out. Men still cannot fully tell how a human child is brought to birth, and a new independent personality created. In a very real sense a baby has human parents and is "born of woman." Yet in a deeper sense it is "of God." If this is true of ordinary child-birth, how very much more was it true of the birth of him who was "conceived of the Holy Ghost, born of the virgin Mary." Also, it seems in harmony with the revealed truth of God to suggest that a similarity in principle prevails between the manner of the birth of the incarnate Word of God and the method of the composition of the written Word of God. Scripture was, so to speak, "conceived or inspired of the Holy Ghost, and thought and uttered by human prophets." Scripture is obviously the work of human writers; and yet it is still more the product and result of a special and supernormal activity of the Spirit. So we may rightly believe it to possess a corresponding perfection.

In thus considering the divine inspiration of Scripture, the difficulty for the human mind is to reconcile the perfection of the divine determination of the finished product with the true freedom and inevitable imperfections of the human writers. How can these two characteristics both apply to the production of Scripture? In principle this problem is only a particular form of the general difficulty always involved in any attempt to reconcile divine predestination and human freewill.

A significant scriptural illustration of the joint working of human freedom and divine predetermination is provided by the one utterance of Caiaphas which is said to be prophecy. To his fellow-members of the Jewish Sanhedrin he said, "It is expedient for us that one man should die for the people, and that the whole nation perish not" (John 11:50). In their immediate historical setting the meaning of these words is obvious enough. They were a counsel of political expediency. It was better, as Caiaphas saw it, to make Jesus a scapegoat and to sacrifice one life, than to risk a popular messianic uprising. For such an uprising could only call forth a drastic Roman intervention, and then the priestly aristocracy, to which Caiaphas belonged, would be the first to suffer. Such was the meaning intended by human freedom.

These words of Caiaphas were thought worthy of a place in the gospel record for an entirely different reason, however. The evangelist interpreted them prophetically, as words not from Caiaphas but from God. He saw the

meaning intended by the controlling Spirit. To him the words were a revelation—a revelation all the more remarkable because it was so completely
hidden from the mind of the man who uttered the words. "And this spake
he," writes John (11:51), "not of himself" (note the words); "but being the
high priest that year, he prophesied that Jesus should die for that nation."
For the high priest had a yearly office, which only he could fulfill, that is, on
the day of atonement to make a propitiation for the sin of the people with
the blood of sacrifice. And none other than he, fulfilling his own priestly
office in a way far beyond his knowing, gave counsel to the Jews that in this
year, the year when all types were fulfilled, it was expedient that a man, not
an animal victim, die for the people. He designated, as it were, the sacrifice
which was to take away sin and procure salvation. And so his words about
the death of Jesus appear in the Scriptures not as an expression of the
natural mind of Caiaphas, though on the lower level they are expressive of
this, but as an expression of the mind of the Spirit, revealing the purpose of
God thus to provide the sacrificial Lamb to take away the sin of God's
people.

If, therefore, the inspiring Spirit can thus secure the utterance of divinely
intended words from the mouth of an opponent of Christ, and words
actually spoken by him in an entirely different sense from their divinely
intended meaning, is it unreasonable to believe that all words of Scripture—
many of them spoken and written by devout saints and uniquely illumined
souls—are, all of them, to be received not chiefly nor exclusively as from
man, but rather and primarily from God? It behooves us, therefore, sub-
missively to receive them as an expression of the divine mind, and as intended to contribute toward our better understanding of God's ways.

Words of Prophets and Apostles Were God-given

If we are to do full justice to the witness of Scripture concerning its inspiration, another necessary and rewarding study pertains to the Biblical use
of the term "prophet," and the Biblical indication of how true prophets
function.

What distinguishes and characterizes the prophets of Scripture is that they
were men unto whom "the word of God came." As simply stated by a writer
a century ago, the Biblical term "prophet" constantly designates "a man
whose mouth utters the words of God" (L. Gaussen, *Theophneustia; The
Plenary Inspiration of the Holy Scriptures,* p. 62). "A prophet in the Bible
is a man in whose mouth God puts the words which he wishes to be heard
upon earth." To illustrate this meaning on the more human level, let us
notice the description given in Scripture of Aaron's relation to Moses as his
spokesman. It is recorded that God said to Moses, "Thou shalt speak unto
him, and put words in his mouth. . . . And he shall be thy spokesman unto
the people; and he shall be . . . to thee instead of a mouth, and thou shalt

be to him instead of God" (Exod. 4:15, 16). Again later, God said, "See, I have made thee a god to Pharaoh: and Aaron thy brother shall be thy prophet" (Exod. 7:1). Clearly, therefore, a prophet is one who speaks words which God puts into his mouth.

Next, let us observe, from the record in I Samuel 3, how Samuel was "established to be a prophet of the Lord," and how "all Israel from Dan even to Beersheba knew." The chapter dramatically records his first experience of the word of God coming to him. It was not a private message for his own soul, but a word about Eli that had to be publicly uttered. He was thereby called to become a prophet, and to speak forth the word which God had thus given to him. From then on this became his repeated experience. "The Lord revealed himself to Samuel in Shiloh by the word of the Lord. And the word of Samuel came to all Israel."

It was through the burden and constraint of such an experience of being given God's words to proclaim that prophets said with conviction, and unmistakable awareness, "Thus saith the Lord." It was clear that thereby they meant, "These are not my ideas, but words from God himself, which I simply must declare." Such was the irresistible urge, and at times the almost intolerable burden, of being compelled to become the Lord's mouthpiece. "The Lord God hath spoken, who can but prophesy?" (Amos 3:8).

Here we cannot do better than let Scripture provide its own explicit and repeated witness through a selection of quotations. All indicate in different ways that the prophets' spoken and written words were God-given. When they had declared their message, it was characteristic of the prophets, for instance, to add "For the mouth of the Lord hath spoken it" (Isa. 40:5; 58:14; Mic. 4:4). Jeremiah looks for the man "to whom the mouth of the Lord hath spoken, that he may declare it" (Jer. 9:12). Aaron is said to have spoken to the elders of the children of Israel "all the words which the Lord hath spoken unto Moses" (Exod. 4:30). David declares, "The Spirit of the Lord spake by me, and his word was in my tongue" (II Sam. 23:2). The Lord is said to have "put a word in Balaam's mouth" (Num. 23:5). Similarly "the word of God came upon Shemaiah the man of God" (I Kings 12:22). And God said unto Jeremiah, "Behold, I have put my words in thy mouth" (Jer. 1:9); and to Ezekiel, "Thou shalt speak my words unto them" (Ezek. 2:7).

The unmistakable scriptural testimony, therefore, is that in their inspired utterances David and the prophets functioned as the mouth of the Holy Spirit. The Apostle Peter explicitly acknowledged this in the very early days of the Church. He appealed, for instance, to "this scripture . . . which the Holy Ghost by the mouth of David spake before concerning Judas" (Acts 1:16). He prayed to God as himself the author of Psalm 2, "who by the mouth of thy servant David hast said, Why did the heathen rage?" (Acts 4:25). Similarly Zacharias recalled what God "spake by the mouth of his

holy prophets" (Luke 1:70). So according to the language and witness of
the Scriptures its prophecies may be said to be the words of God put into,
or expressed through, the mouth of man.

The evidence about prophetic utterance thus far adduced concerns primarily the period and the production of the Old Testament Scriptures. The
New Testament also, however, contains some explicit witness to similar
activity by the inspiring Spirit, giving to the apostles right utterance in the
things of God for the edification of his Church. When Christ himself had
warned his commissioned witnesses about the opposition they would meet, and
about the ways in which they would need to answer charges brought against
them, he had said, "But when they deliver you up, take no thought how or
what ye shall speak: for it shall be given you in that same hour what ye shall
speak. For it is not ye that speak, but the Spirit of your Father which
speaketh in you" (Matt. 10:19, 20). Christ also promised his apostles similar
divine cooperation in the recording of his own work and teaching when he
said of the Spirit, "He shall teach you all things, and bring all things to your
remembrance, whatsoever I have said unto you" (John 14:26). He similarly
promised that the Spirit would guide them into all truth by speaking to them
words from God and from Christ. For as Christ said, even the Spirit speaks
"not of himself; but whatsoever he shall hear, that shall he speak . . . for
he shall receive of mine, and shall shew it unto you" (John 16:13, 14).

We find, too, in confirmation of this, that Paul later testifies that his
apostolic insight and utterance are wholly Spirit-given. He says that the
purposes of God in Christ toward men, and the things prepared for them,
are wholly beyond the natural perception and imagination of men; but that
God has revealed them to his apostles by his Spirit, and that they are, by the
same Spirit, enabled to give right expression to them "not in the words
which man's wisdom teacheth, but which the Holy Ghost teacheth" (I Cor.
2:9–13). So in New Testament and Old Testament alike, the very words of
apostles and prophets were God-given.

In this connection it is also noteworthy that the men whom the Spirit of
God thus used to utter his messages were conscious at times of the compulsion of both divine constraint and restraint. On the one hand, they had to
declare all the God-given words; on the other, they could not add other
words of their own choosing. This compulsion is particularly noticeable in
the case of the prophets, who would have chosen to speak differently if they
could; but they could not. So Balaam said, and repeated, "If Balak would
give me his house full of silver and gold, I cannot go beyond the commandment of the Lord, to do either good or bad of mine own mind; but what the
Lord saith, that will I speak" (Num. 22:18; 24:13). Similarly Micaiah,
when urged to speak good unto King Ahab and not evil, answered, "As the
Lord liveth, what the Lord saith unto me, that will I speak" (I Kings 22:13,
14).

The prophets' sense of compulsion to speak their God-given words, and these only, is significantly complemented in Scripture by a solemn injunction, and ultimately by a severe warning, to all who read God-given words, not to add to, or take away from, what is written. So in Deuteronomy 4:2 we read, "Ye shall not add unto the word which I command you, neither shall ye diminish ought from it"; and in Revelation 22:18, 19, in the section which by God's providential overruling closes the whole Canon of Scripture, we read, "For I testify unto every man that heareth the words of the prophecy of this book, If any man shall add unto these things, God shall add unto him the plagues that are written in this book: and if any man shall take away from the words of the book of this prophecy, God shall take away his part out of the book of life, and out of the holy city, and from the things which are written in this book."

Scripture Quoted in Scripture as the Word of God Himself

When parts of Scripture already recorded are quoted in Scripture by later writers, it is noteworthy that the words thus quoted are sometimes introduced simply as words spoken by God, or as being the utterance of the Lord given through a human prophet. Significantly, too, this characteristic applies not only to those words which in the Old Testament are explicitly said to be utterances of God, but also to words from other parts of the Scripture as well.

So in the Gospel according to Matthew, for instance, Old Testament quotations are introduced which are said to have been "spoken by the Lord through the prophet" (RV), or "what the Lord had spoken by the prophet" (RSV) (*cf.* Matt. 1:22; 2:15). Also, our Lord himself, in his discussions with the Pharisees about divorce, according to Matthew 19:3–6, not only quoted Genesis 2:24 as an authoritative statement about marriage, but explicitly introduced it as a statement made by the Creator himself at the time of man's creation. "Have ye not read," said Jesus, "that he which made them at the beginning made them male and female, and said, For this cause shall a man leave father and mother, and shall cleave to his wife: and they twain shall be one flesh?" Furthermore, our Lord treated this statement as a decisive authoritative expression of the divine mind and purpose about marriage, sufficient in itself to justify the deduction that for men to separate those joined in marriage by divine appointment is wholly improper. Here, therefore, because divine in origin, words from these ancient Jewish writings are appealed to as determining for all time what is proper in the marriage relationship.

Later in Hebrews 1:7, 8, words about God, spoken in praise by the Psalmist, are quoted as spoken by God himself, and, therefore, as carrying decisive weight and authority. We read, "And of the angels he saith, Who maketh his angels spirits, and his ministers a flame of fire" (a quotation from Psalm

104:4). "But unto the Son he saith, Thy throne, O God, is for ever and ever" (a quotation from Psalm 45:6).

Not only are words from the Old Testament thus introduced as spoken by God himself, but sometimes in the New Testament they are used as words having present application, because the living unchanging God is speaking them now. They are his present words for today. So, II Corinthians 6:16 quotes words from Leviticus 26:12: "I will dwell in them and walk in them, and I will be their God, and they shall be my people," to indicate God's present purpose for his redeemed people, and to justify Paul's appeal to his readers that they separate themselves from idolatry and uncleanness.

Similarly, in Hebrews 3:7, words from Psalm 95:7, "Today if ye will hear his voice," are quoted, not as words spoken by the Psalmist long ago, but as words being spoken in the present by God the Spirit—"as the Holy Ghost saith."

Scripture, therefore—so Scripture itself bears witness—may be used as a means of present living communion between God and the individual soul. For what God has once said he may be regarded as still saying (except, of course, where his own fuller revelation has superseded what was previously given only in part or in figure); and responsive words which believers of old have thus been stirred to utter, believers today may rightly still make their own. For example, in Hebrews 13:5, 6, we read, "Be content with such things as ye have: for he hath said, I will never leave thee, nor forsake thee [a quotation from Joshua 1:5]. So that we may boldly say, The Lord is my helper, and I will not fear what man shall do unto me [a quotation from Psalm 118:6]."

All this rich wealth of meaning and usage still to be found in Scripture is possible only because it can be treated and trusted as divinely provided for the permanent enrichment of God's people. It is, therefore, to be regarded and used as God-given, words issued on his authority, and therefore words of supreme and unchanging worth. Such, then, is Scripture's own witness to the character and consequence of its divine inspiration.

Divinely-Intended Purpose of Scripture

Since the direction of too much attention to the details of the process of the production of Scripture by human writers may only perplex us with questions which we cannot answer, it is well that we should recognize that any workman's activity is to be properly understood and appreciated only in the light of his aim and ultimate achievement. This means that, in seeking to estimate the full significance of the divine inspiration of the Bible, we should not primarily look at the materials, the men, and the method used in its composition, but consider rather the finished product as a whole in the light of its divinely intended purpose. For the completed revelation of Scripture, taken as a whole, is meant to serve ends which cannot be served by its constituent parts or contributing human authors and sources taken independently.

Modern historical and literary criticism, with its excess of devotion to analysis and source criticism, has largely been a movement in the wrong direction, which has often involved a real disregard both of the true source and of the proper purpose of the inspiration of Scripture.

It is important, therefore, that we recognize the twofold end of Scripture as a divinely inspired whole. This is, in the first place, Christological, and, in the second, soteriological. The purpose of Scripture is, first, to testify of Christ, "For the testimony of Jesus is the spirit of prophecy" (Rev. 19:10). In the volume of the book it is written of him (cf. Heb. 10:7). The purpose of Scripture is, second, to make men "wise unto salvation through faith which is in Christ Jesus." (II Tim. 3:15). Scripture has been inspired of God to promote the salvation of the world. The Scripture was written, and Christ died and rose again in fulfillment of its prophetic revelation, that repentance and remission of sins might be preached in Christ's name to all nations (cf. Luke 24:46, 47). The New Testament was added to the Old Testament in fulfillment of the promise that the Holy Spirit would guide the apostles into all the truth about the Christ (cf. John 16:12–15). The full significance of the divine inspiration of Scripture can, therefore, be seen in its proper context only if it is seen as an essential part of the redeeming activity of God for the salvation of mankind.

Scripture serves this divine purpose by providing a true record of what God has done in history for man's salvation, and of those events which, under God's providence, have happened and been recorded for man's instruction. This record is by divine inspiration doubly true. On the one hand, it is historically reliable; it corresponds in its witness to what happened. On the other hand, it is sublime and perfect in its discernment and presentation of spiritual values. These two complementary senses in which the scriptural record is true are explicitly emphasized in John 19:35: "And he that hath seen hath borne witness, and his witness is true: and he knoweth that he saith true" ("he knows that he tells the truth," RSV), "that ye also may believe" (RV). Here John means that what he says is true or factually accurate, for he speaks as an eyewitness; and that his form of presentation is "ideal" (Gk. *alēthinos*), in harmony with, and an adequate expression of, the true meaning and value of the events thus recorded, a presentation intended to lead the reader to faith in the person and work of Christ.

For its proper use Scripture, which bears such witness to its own divine inspiration, demands from those readers who are enlightened by God's Spirit to share in this conviction about it the submission of unquestioning acceptance. For Scripture provides, not data to be critically sorted out for acceptance or rejection before we can know the truth, but data to be treated as true and trustworthy and of supreme worth, data within whose witness all

pursuit of the truth must work, if such pursuit is to progress in proper understanding and enjoyment of all the truth which God has thus been pleased
to reveal.

IV. FINAL PRACTICAL AUTHENTICATION

Scripture itself explicitly mentions two distinguishing characteristics by
which words which claim to be divine in origin may be recognized as
genuine, because corresponding in character to their author.

One test is the test of *fulfillment* (cf. Deuteronomy 18:21, 22; Matt.
5:18). For God does not move indecisively. He never speaks without completing his purpose (cf. Num. 23:19). Fulfillment of Scripture is, therefore,
one of the proofs of its divine inspiration. So, when Scripture witnesses to its
own fulfillment, or declares that what it says must yet find fulfillment, it
confirms its own witness that Scripture is divinely inspired.

The other test of the divine origin of words is the test of unchanging
endurance, in contrast to the words of men which have their day and become
obsolete. For, in the last analysis, all words are like their authors in character.
Since men are like the grass that withers, their words similarly cease to carry
weight, and become a dead letter. But not so with God. He lives and abides.
He never changes. He is the same yesterday and today and forever. So, when
he speaks, his words correspond in character to their author. They, too, have
enduring and abiding worth. Therefore, Scripture's unfailing survival and
strength as a fresh, living, undeniable word of truth in every generation
confirm its divine origin. In a world of transient glory, in the midst of an
insecure and impermanent created order, the scriptural Word, and the
scriptural Word alone, not only continues to confront each generation anew,
but increasingly vindicates its truth in fulfillment. "Heaven and earth shall
pass away," said Jesus, "but my words shall not pass away" (Matt. 24:35).
"For all flesh is as grass, and all the glory of man as the flower of grass. The
grass withereth, and the flower thereof falleth away: but the word of the
Lord endureth for ever" (I Pet. 1:24, 25).

OUR LORD'S USE
OF SCRIPTURE

Pierre Ch. Marcel

Pierre Marcel has ministered since 1942 as Pastor of the Reformed Church of St. Germain-en-Laye, near Paris, France, where he was born in 1910. He received the Diploma of Higher Studies in Theology in 1956. He is Vice President of the International Association for Reformed Faith and Action, and also of the Calvinist Society, which he serves as Director of Publications. His published works include A l'Ecole de Dieu, Le Baptême, Sacrement de l'Alliance de grâce *(English translation,* The Biblical Doctrine of Infant Baptism*), and* L'Actualité de la Prédication *(English translation,* The Timeliness of Preaching*).*

8. Pierre Ch. Marcel

OUR LORD'S USE
OF SCRIPTURE

*O*UR LORD'S *use of Scripture:* what a magnificent subject for reflection and what an example for a Christian! Let us study the way in which, with his intelligence and knowledge, Christ quoted, interpreted, expounded, and made use of the Scriptures of the Old Testament. Since he is our Master, without question the most eminent "exegete" of all times, let us derive from his teaching *practical* ideas and precepts concerning the manner in which a Christian, whether a simple believer or a scholar of the Church, can and should use Scripture in the fight of faith or in his witness before others. In this brief study we shall take into consideration only Christ's *explicit quotations,* and we shall pass over those made by the evangelists and those which are no more than allusions. Where there are parallel passages we shall, in the interest of simplicity, ordinarily cite only from Matthew.

I. FORMULAS USED IN INTRODUCING SCRIPTURE

The formulas with which Christ introduced his quotations are familiar: *Scripture, the Scriptures, the Law, the Prophets, the Law and the Prophets, It is written,* and so forth. These designations are very important, for they refer *always* to the canonical Scriptures. Although they do not describe the limits of the Canon, they suppose the existence of a complete and sacred collection of Jewish writings, which, as separate and fixed, is distinct from all other literature. I leave to others the task of saying more about this, and in particular of explaining why we believe that Christ, in his own quotations, was referring to the same Canon as ours.

Whether taken from the Hebrew or from the Greek (LXX), the quotations of Christ are very often *free* (John 8:17; Matt. 19:5; 22:37–39) and sometimes *interpretative* (Matt. 11:10; Luke 7:27). On other occasions Christ *chooses* from within the prophecy he is citing that which emphasizes his meaning (Matt. 26:31; 15:7–9). He also shows a great *exegetical profundity*, for example, in Matthew 15:9 (Isa. 29:13), where he combines the Hebrew version and that of the Septuagint by saying: "teaching as their doctrines the precepts of men," or in Matthew 13:14–16 (Isa. 6:9–10), where he gives preference to the Greek version because the historic aorists "is waxed gross," "are dull of hearing," "their eyes they have closed," express exactly that which he wishes to emphasize, namely, that there remains but very little to add to what this people have done up to the present in order to fill up the measure.

In the Sermon on the Mount the formulas "it was said" (Matt. 5:27, 31, 38, 43) or "it was said to them of old time" (21, 33) are quite different in form from those which introduce genuine citations of Scripture. Here Christ makes no pretense of quoting Scripture in its proper sense (cf. 5:43), but the precepts of tradition, supposedly founded on Scripture, which restrict or even modify the scriptural teaching. He is speaking quite simply as an expositor, to the end that we may know what the Law is, what is its object, and what the extent of its application. But the position of evangelical Christians on this point is well-known; and so we shall not spend more time over it.

Elsewhere, in order to explain the sense and the force of the Law, Christ really *quotes* Scripture. He does so in connection with the Sabbath, the importance of vows, marriage, and the resurrection.

The Sabbath

The Pharisees regard as a violation of the Sabbath the fact that the disciples had plucked some ears of corn for the purpose of eating the grains (Matt. 12:2), or that Jesus used to heal the sick (John 7:22–24), on that day of the week. But Jesus answers them with Scripture, putting into practice the principle of the analogy of faith: You cannot accuse my disciples without accusing David who, on the Sabbath day, ate the shewbread (I Sam. 21:3–6). That which is forbidden for a particular purpose is therefore rendered lawful by reason of necessity. Do the priests cease from their duties on the Sabbath day? Does not the Law command them to serve in the temple, to offer up animals in sacrifice (Num. 28:9), to circumcise infants (Lev.12:3), and to perform all that the service of God demands? From your argument it follows that the Law contravenes the Law. If the temple service sanctifies the manual tasks required in the worship of God, it is the Law itself which shows that these ceremonial demands are not absolute: whoever makes them so *contradicts* the Law. The ceremonial law is subservient to a higher law: the satisfaction of the spiritual needs of the people, the acts of worship by which God is honored and glorified; and so it proclaims restrictions regarding the work of the people at the same time as it commands a temple ceremonial which necessitates work. Restrictions and prescriptions are by no means ends in themselves.

And what then is circumcision? It is not a *work* performed for God, but a sacrament, and thus a blessing of God. It is the religious purification of the procreative organ; it is the sign of a *partial* healing of the body. Can it be said that on the Sabbath day he who is circumcised does not receive with the sacrament the blessing of which it is the seal? Would not the postponement of its administration because the eighth day falls on a Sabbath be a violation of the Law of Moses? How is it that what is an inviolable law in the case of Moses can, according to you, provide a ground of accusation against me? It is therefore permitted also to heal a man *completely* on the Sabbath day (John 7:23). For Moses, the conferring of a blessing, even a small one (a partial healing), is *so important* that he does not make the Sabbath an obstacle to it; for you, a very great blessing (the complete healing of a man) is *so small a thing* that you make the Sabbath an obstacle to it! How is it that you do not *sanction* a great thing when Moses *commands* a small thing? "Go and learn what this means, I desire mercy and not sacrifice" (Matt. 9:13; Hos. 6:6). For faith and spiritual service, with charity, are of themselves pleasing to God; but sacrifices are nothing when they are despoiled of their truth and reality, and are not related to their purpose.

Christ does not abolish the Sabbath by this exegesis in accordance with the principle of the analogy of faith: the divine works do not violate the Sabbath. He restores it to its true purpose. "The sabbath was made for man, and not man for the sabbath" (Mark 2:27): it is therefore improper and wicked to convert to the injury and ruin of man that which God has ordained for his benefit.

Vows

In Matthew 15:3–7 Jesus attacks the theory of vows so dear to the Jews and so contrary to Scripture. To establish a tradition without openly abolishing the Law of God, but by means of an indirect transgression, is to "make void the word of God." Engrossed as they were in their own service, the Jews no longer had leisure to give thought to the true Word of God. If their exegesis is at fault, it is because they renew the hypocrisy of the generation of Isaiah, who well prophesied *concerning them* in saying that their heart is far from God (Isa. 29:13). Now, *the source of all exegesis is in the heart.*

Marriage

The conflict over the subject of divorce, which set the rigorist school of Shammai and the liberal school of Hillel in opposition to each other, is well known. It is the view of Hillel that the Pharisees present to Jesus (Matt.

19:3–9). They ask whether it is *lawful,* showing that they considered marriage and its dissolution to be a matter of *civil* legislation. For the purpose of
"testing" Jesus (the Gospels emphasize this) the question was indeed well
chosen, for it was to be expected that he would be unable to give an answer
without placing himself at a disadvantage. If he says Yes, the Pharisees,
invoking Shammai, will tax him with laxity; while if he adopts Shammai's
position, how will he justify his leniency towards certain sinners? If he rejects
both Hillel and Shammai, and declares himself against all divorce, they will
be able to accuse him of contradicting Moses.

But Jesus replies that marriage was instituted by God, that it is an ordinance *of creation* and not a *civil* institution. Whoever separates those whom
God has united by his own creation opposes himself to God and his will. He
reproaches them for a reading of Scripture that is both partial and partisan.
Besides, Moses did not *prescribe,* but only *permitted* the dissolving of marriage in a legal manner, and then only because of the "hardness of their
hearts." In no way did the permission of Moses modify the original intention
concerning the permanence of marriage.

The reply of Jesus shows the unsuspected resources of Scripture for him
who knows it and uses it under the guidance of the Holy Spirit and in
accordance with the analogy of faith. It points the Christian to the wisdom
and the profoundness with which he can escape from the dilemmas that
human casuistry and rationalism propound. Let us seek to follow the example
of the Master, and to do so in the same spirit!

The Resurrection

In Matthew 22:23–28 the Sadducees put forward a purely theoretical
and unrealistic question, which envisages an impossible situation, an example
of the kind which those invent who study Scripture *with their own logic,*
"because they know neither the Scriptures nor the power of God." Moreover,
their reasoning is absurd because, according to them, there is no third term;
in the world to come the same conditions of existence would prevail as here
below.

It is probable that the Sadducees refused to acknowledge any canonical
authority other than that of the Pentateuch. If this was the case, we see that
Christ refutes their *false deduction* from Deuteronomy by a *valid deduction*
from Exodus (3:6), that he elucidates one passage *of Moses* by another
passage *of Moses,* and that at the same time he authenticates the truth of the
resurrection of the dead which that patriarch has already made known
(Matt. 22:29–32; Luke 20:27). At the level of the texts or of the method
he confutes his adversaries with their own weapons and on their own ground,
but he causes them to realize that, on the spiritual level, a question of this
sort arises from their blindness and not from the Scriptures.

II. APPEAL TO SCRIPTURE AS A TOTALITY

To each question and to each objection Christ replies with the Scriptures and no one is able to prove him wrong (cf. John 10:32–36). His exegesis—unknown to his interlocutors—reduces them to silence. *By the constant use of the principle of analogy—Scripture interprets Scripture*—he overrules his contradictors, and stands far above the parties from which particular heresies emanate because they see only *a single aspect* of the questions and of the Biblical teaching, devoid of any spirit of synthesis and of any true spirituality. We see it again in the case of the two questions: "Master, what good thing shall I do that I may have eternal life?" (Matt. 19:16) and "Master, which is the great commandment in the law?" (Matt. 22:36).

In challenging the rich young man to sell his goods and to give to the poor, Christ is requiring nothing beyond the commandments of the Law, to which he draws attention. The young man has committed no fault outside the observance of the Law, but in the observance of the Law. But as the simple words of this Law convince insufficiently of his condemnation Christ expresses its *inner* meaning in other words.

In order to understand the importance of the second question we must remember that the rabbis had no less than 613 commandments: 248 that were positive and 365 that were negative. In case of conflict, the more important took precedence over the less. But how was one to judge of their importance? The Sadducees rejected all the commandments of the Pharisees which were not literally written in the Law and did not follow the tradition of the fathers. Was Jesus going to take his stand with them? By his simple and direct reply Jesus avoids any objection that he is overthrowing the Law in its capacity as the permanent standard of justice. The Law, general and particular, negative and positive, material and spiritual, is the perfect and complete expression of the eternal and constant will of God.

The Jews desired to honor and magnify the Law: "Great is the Torah," said the sages, "more than truth, for it contains the Truth, more than justice, for it contains Justice, more than love, more than forgiveness, for the Torah contains Forgiveness, the Torah contains Love." Nevertheless, it is Christ, and Christ alone, who explains and reveals, by the Scriptures alone, the Truth, the Justice, the Forgiveness, and the Love of the Law. That is why when he speaks of "your Law" (John 8:17; 10:34) or "their Law" (John 15:25), and not "mine," far from discrediting the Law, Jesus honors it. His relation to the Law is different from ours: the Law was never *given* to him. No more can Jesus say of Abraham "our father"; he says "your father" (John 8:56), for Abraham is not his father in the same sense that he is the father of the Jews, and in this way Jesus indicates the difference of his human descent.

III. FULFILLMENT IN CHRIST

As exegete, as prophet, and as teacher, Christ expounds the Scriptures. It is equally by them that he proves himself to be the Son of David, the Messiah, and the King. He affirms it at Nazareth by his reading of Isaiah 61:1–2 (Luke 4:16–19, 21). This prophecy refers in the first instance to the return from the captivity and has certainly been fulfilled in this sense. Yet it is remarkable that in this place the prophet speaks in the singular, as though assuming the character of the Christ, so that what he says might be more effective in restoring confidence to the hearts of the faithful. Christ interprets these words as directly concerning himself. He alone, in fact, has received the fullness of the Spirit in order to be the witness and ambassador of our reconciliation with God; he alone, by virtue of his Spirit, performs and fulfills all the blessings promised here. And this word *is fulfilled* in Jesus, the Servant of the Lord and the Messiah, who, at the time when he is speaking, is in the very midst of this fulfillment.

Apart from Malachi 3:1 (Luke 7:27; Matt. 11:10), where Christ confirms the authority of John the Baptist and to his own advantage distinguishes between God, the Messiah, and his messenger, undoubtedly the most categorical assertion of his divinity, confirmed by Scripture, is found in Matthew 22:41–44. According to the Pharisees the Messiah ought to be solely a son of David, a messiah who is merely man, however great his human glory and power may be. Because they read Scripture with blinded eyes, his divinity remained hidden from them. On the eve of Palm Sunday Christ desires to reveal himself plainly as the Messiah, Son of David and King of Israel, at the same time that he is seeking to constrain the Pharisees to trust in him, since certain among them are not far from the kingdom of God (cf. Mark 12:34). But, among the multitude of David's descendants, how is the true Messiah to be distinguished? If the people are not to be left in uncertainty, what is the distinctive mark which would place one of the sons of David above the rest and which would point to him as being beyond doubt the promised Messiah? Scripture must provide the answer to this question! Christ was able to establish his *legal* descent on the one hand (Matt. 1) and his *natural* descent on the other (Luke 3:23); but that was not sufficient.

The text to which Jesus appeals is very remarkable: "The Lord said . . .": *Ne' um Yahweh;* literally, "a declaration of the Lord," a declaration, that is, most secret, of a mystery. "To my Lord": *Adonai.* Christ puts forward the Davidic descent of the Messiah as an incontestable fact. He declares that it is David who wrote Psalm 110, that *Yahweh* can call this son of David nothing less than the *Adon* of David—a distinction which, even for Jewish exegesis, is here a clear revelation of the persons of the Trinity—, and that it is *in the Holy Spirit* (Mark 12:36) that David wrote this, not in terms of contemporary realism, like many other prophecies, but on the basis of an ideal, revealed and realized only in the coming of Christ. If that were not the case, the present line of argument, instead of establishing his deity, would discredit it. In this psalm David distinguishes clearly between himself and the person of the Messiah, his descendant and at the same time his all-powerful Lord; he even announces his glorification and his royalty. To be sure, his divine essence is not expressed explicitly, but it is easy to conclude that it is God himself who is exalted above all creatures.

The Pharisees and the chief priests thought that they were the sole competent judges of the redemption to come, so much so that no one ought to be accepted as the Messiah unless they themselves had accepted him and declared him to be such. They arrogated to themselves the honor of distinguishing, among the sons of David, the authentic Messiah. By the parable of the husbandmen Christ demonstrates to them that the contrary is the case, and cites in support Psalm 118:22 (Matt. 21:33 ff.), a prophecy which he in his turn treats in a prophetic manner: it is not at all by the consent of men, but in spite of them, that the Christ will reign by the power of God.

The Jews believed that when Christ came he would set up an earthly kingdom over which he would reign for ever. In signifying the manner of the death he would die (John 12:32) Jesus arouses the question of the multitude, to which he replies, without any explanation, that he himself is the true light. To Nicodemus Christ describes himself as the antitype of the brazen serpent. The miracle of healing by a simple look at the brazen serpent is so real for Jesus that it is the type of a yet greater miracle: whoever believes in the Son, and in the Son crucified, shall have everlasting life. By the verb "to lift up," without the use of allegory, these two liftings-up are compared in their saving significance.

In contradistinction to the Jewish concept of an exclusively glorious Messiah, Jesus appeals to several passages from the prophets (Mark 9:12; Matt. 26:31; Luke 22:37; Matt. 26:53–54; Mark 14:49). The two words which he uttered on the cross, *crying with a loud voice,* are two quotations from the Psalms which the people were able to hear and recognize as a fulfillment. Only the Spirit of prophecy could have placed at the beginning of this psalm the supreme cry of the agony on the cross: "My God, my God, why hast thou forsaken me?" (Matt. 27:46). It is not because David, who is not here a type of the Messiah, wrote this line that Christ utters such a cry, but it is because Christ was to cry thus that David wrote *as a prophet.* Contrariwise, in Luke 23:46 (Ps. 31:5) Jesus utters this cry like David, but the latter is only the type. Jesus says "Father"; David was not dying and said, "I shall commit," and God *saved* him. But the enemies of Christ are already vanquished; his distress is past; he has gained the victory: "It is finished!" It is with peace and joy that *he himself commits* (note the force of the middle voice: *paratithemai*) his spirit, and it is thus that the Father receives it.

Again, it is by the Scriptures that Christ witnesses to *his kingship.* Reply-

ing to the indignant priests, by the prophecy of Psalm 8:3 (Matt. 21:16),
he affirms that it is indeed as the Son of David, the Messiah-King, that he
has come, and all those who acclaim him do exactly as he desires. In Matthew 26:64 (Ps. 110:1; Dan. 7:13), before the supreme tribunal of his
nation, it is *under the testimony of an oath* that Christ affirms the true
reality of his office and person, and foretells his glory and his future coming.
They will see him henceforth no more until they say: "Blessed is he that
cometh in the name of the Lord!" (Matt. 23:39; Ps. 118:26). Enlightened
by the Holy Spirit, some will see him in this world with the eyes of the
spirit, and in heaven with direct vision; but in the case of those who have
hardened themselves, that which took place in the days of Noah or of Lot
will likewise take place at the coming of the Son of Man (Matt. 24:37–39;
Luke 17:28–30). Here Jesus is stigmatizing that blindness which is wicked,
culpable, and damnable. All the preliminary signs of judgment will be explained "naturally," "reasonably," even "scientifically," if it is necessary,
until the fatal day dawns. Nonetheless, the writings of the prophets will be
fulfilled.

It is by the witness of Scripture again that Christ *refuses miracles and
calls to repentance*. At Nazareth he justifies his attitude by the example of
Elijah and the widow of Sarepta (I Kings 17:9) and of Elisha and Naaman
(II Kings 5:14). On several occasions the Jews request him to confirm his
vocation by a miracle (John 6:30–33; Matt. 12:38–42; Luke 11:29–32).
This is symptomatic of the Judaism of that time! It no longer knows the
blessing of hearing and keeping the Word of God; it turns its back on the
signs of grace and forgiveness brought by Christ, and, like so many in our
own day, desires only a sign "from heaven," nothing more than a prodigy!

Christ replies, in the first place, that *he himself* is the miracle they seek:
the living bread which comes down from heaven, in order that he who eats
of it may live forever. As his questioners have cited Scripture, Christ expounds Scripture and explains what was the bread of Moses and what is the
bread of God. Since the Jews reject this miracle of grace which *is* the
Christ, Christ refuses them any other miracle, for another miracle would be
impossible to God or to himself except by discrediting all the other signs
which Jesus gave *or was*, or by abandoning the plan of grace. The sign of
Jonah is both appropriate and sufficient for them: not his preaching, but his
disappearing into the belly of the great fish, where he was thought to be
dead, but where he was preserved safe and sound, and whence he came out
alive, as from a sepulchre, to go and preach to the Ninevites, according to
the will of God. As a miracle of God's omnipotence, Jonah is the type of the
resurrection of Christ. When Jesus is in the tomb the Jews will think that
his career is at an end, but it will not be so at all: he will come back and his
powerful work will continue according to the divine will. They will hear the
voice of the risen Prophet, though they refuse to receive him now. The
Ninevites and the Queen of Sheba will rise up in the day of judgment,

together with this generation, and will condemn it: "For here is a greater than Jonah, and a greater than Solomon." "Except ye repent, ye shall all likewise perish!" (Luke 13:5). Like every calamity, the collapse of the tower of Siloam (Luke 13:4; Neh. 3:15) is a warning from God to escape from everlasting destruction, a divine appeal to repent *in time.* Anticipate the scourges of God, therefore, by a voluntary repentance! If, like the Samaritans in the time of Hosea (Hos. 10:8), you fail to do this, you will prefer sudden death to the horrors of a long siege (Luke 23:30).

"The Father which sent me, he hath borne witness of me" (John 5:37). In the Scriptures the Father has borne a complete witness, provided long since and which abides for ever. Abraham himself saw the day of Christ and rejoiced at it (John 8:56). Why then do the Jews not receive this witness? Because, says Christ, "you have never heard his voice, you have never seen his face, and his word does not dwell in you at all, since you do not believe in him whom he has sent" (John 5:37-38). The Scriptures praise and magnify Christ throughout their length; for without Christ the Law is empty. Now the Jews were sure that they had eternal life in the Scriptures, but they thought they could have it *without the Christ.* How could the Law confer life without Christ when it is he alone who gives it life? That is why Jesus cries: "Search the scriptures, because ye think that in them ye have eternal life; and these are they which bear witness of me; and ye will not come to me, that ye may have life!" (John 5:39-40). Jesus is trying to overcome their unbelief. He confronts them with the Scriptures in which they put their trust. To turn away from this confrontation is to acquiesce in the judgment of Jesus. But to reject the Christ is to reject Abraham and to reject Moses: "There is one that accuseth you, even Moses, on whom ye have set your hope. For if ye believed Moses, ye would believe me; *for he wrote of me.* But if ye believe not his writings, how shall ye believe my words?" (John 5:45-47). The true Moses—not the image which they had made of him—is the one who will condemn them! These verses are weighted with terrible significance.

But just as the Jews hardened themselves against the preaching of Moses, they harden themselves against the preaching of Christ. Thus the prophecy of Isaiah is fulfilled unto them (Matt. 13:14-15; Isa. 6:8-10), susceptible as it is of repeated applications, in the time of the prophet, in the time of Jesus, and in every age, because of the general principle which it contains. Certain events of the New Testament are, in fact, of the same nature as those of the Old: they are parallels. Thus Jesus applies to himself what David spoke of himself (John 15:24-25; Ps. 35:19; 69:5). For the Jews who have hardened their hearts against the word and the works of Moses and the prophets, harden them equally against *the works* of Christ, though they be such as "none other has done." They are therefore in no sense better than their fathers who had hated David. That is why all the murders which have been committed, from that of Abel unto that of Zachariah, will be

judged in the persons of them all (Luke 11:50–51), for in their wickedness
they are the authentic posterity of Cain.

IV. USE OF SCRIPTURE IN TRIAL AND TEMPTATION

The use which Christ makes of the Scriptures *against temptations and
occasions of stumbling* is very interesting. When he first quotes Scripture it
is in order to overcome temptation: "It is written" (Matt. 4:4, 7, 10). In
defending himself Christ wields the shield of Scripture, "a shield, not of
straw, but truly of brass," says Calvin. This is the one and only way of
waging battle if we wish to win the victory. When Satan misuses Scripture
by mutilating a quotation from Psalm 91:11–12, with a view to making the
life-giving Word of God become mortal to Christ and to changing good food
into poison, it is once again with Scripture that Christ repulses such insinua-
tions. As always, it is the principle of the analogy of faith.

When Jesus quotes Micah 7:6 (Matt. 10:35–36) it is for a *pastoral
purpose.* He warns his disciples of the hostility which they may encounter,
because of their faith, in their own families or in the world, because of the
corruption which is revealed wherever the gospel is present. Let no Christian
be troubled when he finds that his faith and his person are the object of
disparagement or of hatred, and sometimes the cause of distressing separa-
tions.

In a whole series of texts Jesus seeks also to protect those who are his
against every offense resulting from the scorn of which he will be the object,
and particularly his sufferings and crucifixion (Mark 9:12; 14:19; John
13:19; Matt. 21:42; 26:31, 53–54, 55–56; Luke 22:37–38; 24:26). It is
also "even as it is written of him" that John the Baptist, the last Elijah, was
treated (Mark 9:13), where Christ undoubtedly refers to I Kings 19, Elijah
being the type of John the Baptist, as Jezebel is that of Herodias. In this way
Christ instructs his own concerning the *necessities* required for our redemption, concerning his *perfect knowledge* of events, and concerning the *freedom*
with which he goes of his own accord to death—things which we ought to
know in order to be able to glorify God.

Since, however terrible and offensive the spectacle of his humiliation may
be, these things are *written in Scripture,* believers ought not in any way to
be troubled at them, so much the more as they are not distant nor separated
from Christ. *The disciples must accept the Redeemer such as God had
already promised him to be:* the Christ of Isaiah 53. A necessity is enclosed
in every prophecy, however ancient it may be, a necessity which follows its
course across the centuries until the present. No prophecy can fail of fulfillment. But, in fact, this necessity is found *in God alone:* the necessity of his
love, his eternal and free will to save the world by Christ, not at all an
abstract necessity which we can discuss in a philosophical manner, as though
God could not have done otherwise. It is *in this way* that it is found ex-

pressed in the Scriptures. A spirit, a will, a plan are at work in history, where God is accomplishing his purposes, even before they take shape as occurrences. Nothing comes to pass apart from his providence and his free determination. It is for this reason that the Scriptures must be fulfilled. "When some absurdity astonishes us," says Calvin, "there is no more suitable remedy for removing the offence than the recognition that so it was pleasing to God, and that whatever happens as a result of His ordinance does not come about rashly or without a good and just reason, *especially* when the event which we see taking place has been predicted of old." When the will of God is manifest to us we have no other duty than to keep silence and to maintain our obedience to his decrees.

It was needful also that the disciples should be warned of their own feebleness: when the shepherd has been struck down the flock will be dispersed. As this dispersion is made known to them in advance, it will not dishearten them to such an extent that they imagine themselves to be shut out from all faith. They will learn, besides, to rely on their Shepherd, for Zechariah adds the promise that God will stretch out his hand in order to lead his dispersed flock back to himself.

In the prophecy relating to Judas (John 13:18; Ps. 41:9), Christ reveals *his perfect knowledge.* What offense the treachery of Judas, an apostle chosen by Christ, could arouse in the hearts not only of his companions but of believers in every age! They must not believe that Jesus has been commonly betrayed and that he is the powerless victim of a man; from the apparent "success" of the traitor they must not draw conclusions capable of calling into question his deity or his divine power and knowledge. That is why Jesus not only declares that he knows all about Judas, but that he had chosen him *in order that* he might betray him. It *had* to be so, because it had been foretold. Jesus knew that Judas was only a son or a product of eternal damnation, *a son of perdition* (John 17:12), a title which was given him not because of the treachery which he committed (*ex eventu*), but because he was actually going to perdition, "to his own place," according to Acts 1:25. Indeed, if in Psalm 41 David is the type of Christ, Ahithophel is that of Judas. It is not possible that Judas was unaware of this allusion or that he failed to remember the tragic manner in which Ahithophel ended his life by hanging himself (cf. II Sam. 17:23). Oh the kindness of Christ who by this quotation as well as by the dramatic end which it suggests seeks, if possible and before it is too late, to touch the heart of Judas and to call him to repentance! We see the perfect knowledge of Christ who, once again, prophesies by making use of a prophecy of Scripture.

Knowing all this, Jesus shows, finally, the *perfect freedom* with which he goes to the cross. It is Jesus himself who authorizes the success of Judas, for he knows his intentions and is able, if he wishes, at any moment to frustrate his plans. It is Christ himself who ought not at any moment to do anything to escape the death to which he knows the Father is calling him. In the

Garden of Gethsemane he had only to speak for his opponents to be thrown
back to the ground: he therefore commits himself voluntarily into their
hands. Thus the Scriptures are fulfilled *in order that the disciples may
believe*. Christ is not at the mercy of Judas: on the contrary, Judas is in fact
at the mercy of Christ. Christ was not captured by the guards: that was
something they could not do. Let them not have, then, even this opportunity
of pride and this personal satisfaction of boasting of victory gained! The
schemings of wicked men, however, will not succeed in robbing Christ of his
dignity: he will maintain the place which the Father has ordained. "It is
marvellous in our eyes!" the wonder of the love and omnipotence of God.

Acting in this way, Christ reveals the existence of a *continuous* process
throughout the whole of history. The use which he makes of Zechariah 13:7
and of the prophecies relating to his sufferings and death introduces a new
conception of *the meaning* of history. Undoubtedly, these passages are prediction, and the life of Christ is their fulfillment which cannot be found
elsewhere. Undoubtedly, the prophecies of the smitten Shepherd and of the
Servant of the Lord are also a summary of the history of Israel. The connection, however, between a prophecy and its fulfillment is deeper than the
simple foreknowledge of an isolated event and its fulfillment. In a certain
sense we are able to say that the event is foreseen *because it is already in
reality a fact*. God calls things which are not as though they were, for it is
sufficient that he should call them for them to be. The relationship of God
with Israel, moreover, had been established in all its essential factors since
the most remote times. It is in an authentic and true sense that "the Lamb
has been slain from the foundation of the world" (Rev. 13:8). That is why
in this, the profoundest penetration of the meaning of history that we can
conceive, Christ is able to say: "All things concerning me have been fulfilled" (Luke 24:44). These prophecies do not depict the portrait of Christ
such as he *ought* to be, but *such as he was*. An original prophecy and its
quotation by Christ are not found to be *remote* from each other: they prove,
both of them, to be *at the very heart* of the same course of events; they reveal
the visible action of forces operating long since in human history and, at
their point of culmination, leading to the drama of the cross. This is the
sole satisfactory interpretation both of these passages and of the drama of
the cross. "The things which God foreshewed by the mouth of all the
prophets, that his Christ should suffer, he thus fulfilled" (Acts 3:18). "All
this is come to pass, that the scriptures of the prophets might be fulfilled"
(Matt. 26:56).

By the sequence of his admonitions by means of Holy Scripture, by their
growing precision and frequency until the fatal moment, by his vision of
history, we see to what point Christ carried—and still carries—the concern
for strengthening those who are his, his warnings full of instructive meaning,
the delicacy of his love, the care which he takes to prepare the hearts of his

disciples of all times for an authentic glorification of God and his work throughout the world's history. Here, again, is an example for us to follow.

This revelation of the prophetic meaning of the Scriptures and of the purposes of God—a cause of joy, of assurance, and of victory—is fully granted by Christ to the disciples of Emmaus and to the Eleven (Luke 24:25–27, 44–47). "Beginning from Moses and all the prophets, he interpreted to them in all the Scriptures the things concerning himself." *Jesus himself is found in all the prophets.* The whole economy of the Old Testament is centered in Christ. The gospel therefore is found also throughout the Old Testament where nothing can be understood without Christ. In the Law one can, one must, discover Christ, his covenant, his mediation, his kingship, the universality of his reign. We would give a great deal to have a list of the passages which he cited, and much more to know his exegesis. But we must search for them ourselves, ceaselessly claiming the enlightenment of his Spirit. Indeed, "He opened their mind, that they might understand the Scriptures."

Lord, open our mind also, so that we may understand the mysteries of God and of thy salvation, and may search them out as they are contained *in the Scriptures alone,* since thou dost not give us thy Spirit to do away with the use of thy Word, but so that it may be useful and salutary to us!

Conclusion

From the manner in which Christ quotes Scripture we find that he recognizes and accepts the Old Testament in its entirety as possessing a normative authority, as the true Word of God, valid for all time. He believes in inspiration by the Holy Spirit since the time of Adam (Matt. 19:5), in the infallibility of the oracles which he utters to the instruments which he has chosen (Matt. 13:14–15; 15:7–9), in the Davidic authorship of Psalm 110, for example, and in David's full inspiration.

He seals with his authority numerous facts which are related in Scripture, and the historicity of numerous events: we are therefore instructed to believe them *all*. He believes in the creation by God, in the existence of the first couple (Matt. 19:4), of Cain and Abel (Luke 11:51), of Noah, in the reality of the flood and its results, and of the ark and its saving function (Matt. 24:37–39); he attests the destruction of Sodom and the tragic death of Lot's wife (Luke 17:28–30, 32).

Moses, to whom he accords divine inspiration (Matt. 15:3–4), is his prophet (John 5:46). Ever since the creation and all down the ages, in the laws and institutions, the ceremonies and rites, the prophecies and promises, Christ is continually present in the mind of Moses who, in his person and in his office, is a type of the coming Mediator. Thus Christ emphasizes the continuity and the consistency of revelation in its entirety, the unity of the old and the new dispensations of the Covenant. He believes in the miracle of the manna (John 6:31–33, 48–51), in the healing of those who, trusting in the promise of God, simply fixed their eyes on the serpent of brass (John 3:14). He believes in the miracle whereby the widow of Sarepta was sustained in the time of famine, and in the healing of Naaman. He believes in the miracle of Jonah who spent three days and three nights *in the belly* of a great fish, in the repentance of the Ninevites, and in the salvation of a large number of them (Matt. 12:39–41; 16:4; Luke 11:32).

"The Scripture cannot be broken" (John 10:35). It is unalterable, indestructible in its truth, indifferent to every denial, to human ignorance and criticism, to charges of error, and to subjective attacks. Let us then be instructed and convinced! The Holy Spirit prevents us from accepting the opinion of those who say that Christ was governed by the intellectual outlook of his time and country, and who *oppose* his testimony in the name of "modern scientific methods." For us, the thought of the Master is canonical. It is an external authority superior to all the most venerable rabbinical, ecclesiastical, and scientific authorities. The witness of the Holy Spirit in our heart disposes us to prefer the affirmations of Jesus. For us, the authority of Christ is a mystical fact of the first order, for we know the power with which his Word is impressed on our faith. In humility we receive his witness which guarantees to us the formal authority of the Old Testament and its divine inspiration, which is the principle of this authority.

NEW TESTAMENT USE
OF THE
OLD TESTAMENT

Roger Nicole

Roger Nicole has been Professor of Theology at Gordon Divinity School in New England since 1945. He holds the Licence D'enseignement es Lettres Classiques (M.A.) from the Sorbonne (Paris), a Th.D. from Gordon Divinity School, and is a candidate for the Ph.D. at Harvard Divinity School. He served as president of Evangelical Theological Society in 1956. He is engaged in the preparation of a volume on the doctrine of the atonement, on which theme he has delivered lectures at several seminaries.

9. Roger Nicole

NEW TESTAMENT USE
OF THE
OLD TESTAMENT

THE NEW Testament contains an extraordinarily large number of Old Testament quotations. It is difficult to give an accurate figure since the variation in use ranges all the way from a distant allusion to a definite quotation introduced by an explicit formula stating the citation's source. As a result, the figures given by various authors often reflect a startling discrepancy.

I. RANGE OF OLD TESTAMENT REFERENCES

The present writer has counted 224 direct citations introduced by a definite formula indicating the writer purposed to quote. To these must be added seven cases where a second quotation is introduced by the conjunction "and," and 19 cases where a paraphrase or summary rather than a direct quotation follows the introductory formula. We may further note at least 45 instances where the similarity with certain Old Testament passages is so pronounced that, although no explicit indication is given that the New Testament author was referring to Old Testament Scripture, his intention to do so can scarcely be doubted. Thus a very conservative count discloses unquestionably at least 295 separate references to the Old Testament. These occupy some 352 verses of the New Testament, or more than 4.4 per cent. Therefore one verse in 22.5 of the New Testament is a quotation.

If clear allusions are taken into consideration, the figures are much higher: C. H. Toy lists 613 such instances, Wilhelm Dittmar goes as high as 1640, while Eugen Huehn indicates 4105 passages reminiscent of Old Testament Scripture. It can therefore be asserted, without exaggeration, that more than 10 per cent of the New Testament text is made up of citations or direct allusions to the Old Testament. The recorded words of Jesus disclose a similar percentage. Certain books like Revelation, Hebrews, Romans are well nigh saturated with Old Testament forms of language, allusions and quotations. Perusal of Nestle's edition of the Greek New Testament, in which the Old Testament material is printed in bold face type, will reveal at a glance the extent of this practice. These facts appear even more impressive when one remembers that in New Testament times the Old Testament was not as today duplicated by the million but could be obtained only in expensive handwritten copies.

If we limit ourselves to the specific quotations and direct allusions which form the basis of our previous reckoning, we shall note that 278 different Old Testament verses are cited in the New Testament: 94 from the Pentateuch, 99 from the Prophets, and 85 from the Writings. Out of the 22 books in the Hebrew reckoning of the Canon only six (Judges-Ruth, Song of Solomon, Ecclesiastes, Esther, Ezra-Nehemiah, Chronicles) are not explicitly referred to. The more extensive lists of Dittmar and Huehn show passages reminiscent of all Old Testament books without exception.

It is to be noted that the whole New Testament contains not even one explicit citation of any of the Old Testament Apocrypha which are considered as canonical by the Roman Catholic Church. This omission can scarcely be viewed as accidental.

II. AUTHORITY OF OLD TESTAMENT REFERENCES

From beginning to end, the New Testament authors ascribe unqualified authority to Old Testament Scripture. Whenever advanced, a quotation is viewed as normative. Nowhere do we find a tendency to question, argue, or repudiate the truth of any Scripture utterance. Passages sometimes alleged to prove that the Lord and his apostles challenged at times the authority of the Old Testament, when carefully examined, turn out to bolster rather than to impair the evidence for their acceptance of Scripture as the Word of God. In Matthew 5:21-43 and 19:3-9, our Lord, far from setting aside the commandments of the Old Testament, really engages in a searching analysis of the spiritual meaning and original intent of the divine precept, and from this vantage point he applies it in a deeper and broader way than had been done before him. In some passages in which comparison is made between the revelation of the Old Testament and that of the New (John 1:17; II Cor. 3:6; Gal. 3:19 ff.; Heb. 1:1, 2, and so forth), the superior glory of the New Testament is emphasized, not as in conflict with the Old, but as the perfect fulfillment of a revelation still incomplete, yet sanctioned by divine authority.

It is noteworthy that the New Testament writers and the Lord Jesus himself did not hesitate on occasion to base their whole argumentation upon one single word of Old Testament Scripture (Matt. 2:15; 4:10; 13:35; 22:44; Mark 12:36; Luke 4:8; 20:42, 43; John 8:17; 10:34; 19:37; Acts 23:5; Rom. 4:3, 9, 23; 15:9–12; I Cor. 6:16; Gal. 3:8, 10, 13; Heb. 1:7; 2:12; 3:13; 4:7; 12:26), or even on the grammatical form of one word (Gal. 3:16).

Of special interest are the formulas by which the New Testament writers introduce their quotations. In a particularly significant way these formulas reflect their view of the Old Testament Scriptures, since they do not manifest any design to set forth a doctrine of Scripture, but are rather the instinctive expression of their approach to the sacred writings.

The formulas emphasize strongly the divine origin of the Old Testament, and commonly (at least 56 times) refer to God as the author. In a number of passages God is represented as the speaker when the quotation is not a saying of God recorded as such in the Old Testament, but the word of Scripture itself, in fact, at times a word addressed to God by man (Matt. 19:5; Acts 4:25; 13:35; Heb. 1:5–8, 13; 3:7; 4:4). These "can be treated as a declaration of God's only on the hypothesis that all Scripture is a declaration of God's" (B. B. Warfield, *The Inspiration and Authority of the Bible*, p. 143).

Often passages of the Old Testament are simply attributed to the Scripture, which is thus personified as speaking (John 7:38, 42; 15:25; 19:37; Rom. 4:3; 7:7; 9:17; 10:11; 11:2; I Cor. 14:24; II Cor. 6:2; Gal. 3:8; 4:30; I Tim. 5:18; James 2:23; 4:5). In Romans 9:17 and Galatians 3:8 the identification between the text of Scripture and God as speaking is carried so far that the actions of God are actually ascribed to Scripture, which is represented as speaking to Pharaoh and as foreseeing justification by faith. Warfield urges that "These acts could be attributed to Scripture only as the result of such a habitual identification, in the mind of the writer, of the text of Scripture with God as speaking that it became natural to use the term 'Scripture says,' when what was really intended was 'God, as recorded in Scripture, said' " (*ibid.*, pp. 299 f.).

The collaboration of man in the writing of Scripture is also emphasized. The names of Moses, David, Isaiah, Jeremiah, Daniel, Joel and Hosea appear in the formulas of quotation. It is noteworthy that, in the majority of the cases where the human author is named, reference is made not to a personal statement recorded in Scripture but to an utterance of God, which the writer was commissioned to transmit as such. In a number of passages both the divine and the human authorship appear side by side.

". . . which was spoken by the Lord through the prophet . . ." (Matt. 1:22). "David himself said in the Holy Spirit" (Mark 12:36; cf. Matt. 22:43). ". . . the Holy Spirit spake before by the mouth of David" (Acts 1:16; cf. 4:25). "Well spake the Holy

Spirit through Isaiah the prophet . . ." (Acts 28:25). "He saith
also in Hosea . . ." (Rom. 9:25).

These passages supply clear evidence that the divine superintendence was
not viewed as obliterating the human agency and characteristics of the
writers, but rather, that God secured a perfectly adequate presentation of
the truth through the responsible and personal agency of the men he called
and prepared for this sacred task.

"It is written" is one of the frequent formulas of introduction, the one, in
fact, which our Lord used three times in his temptation (Matt. 4:4, 7, 10).
This expression does not connote merely that an appeal is made to the
written text of Scripture but, as Warfield so aptly has said, "The simple
adduction in this solemn and decisive manner of a written authority carries
with it the implication that the appeal is made to the indefectible authority
of the Scriptures of God, which in all their parts and in every one of their
declarations are clothed with the authority of God Himself" (ibid., p. 240).

The use of the terms "law" (John 10:34; 15:25; Rom. 3:19; I Cor.
14:21), or "prophets" (Matt. 13:35), where reference is made to passages
belonging, strictly speaking, to other parts of the Hebrew Canon, indicates
that the New Testament writers viewed the whole Old Testament Scripture
as having legal authority and prophetic character.

In their formulas of quotation the New Testament writers give expression
to their conviction as to the eternal contemporaneity of Scripture. This is
manifest in particular in the many (41) instances where the introductory
verb is in the present: "He says," and not "he said." This is reinforced by
the use of the pronouns "we," "you," in connection with ancient sayings:
"That which was spoken unto you by God" (Matt. 22:31); "The Holy
Spirit also beareth witness to us" (Heb. 10:15; cf. also Matt. 15:7; Mark
7:6; 12:19; Acts 4:11; 13:47; Heb. 12:5). This implication gains explicit
statement in Romans 15:4: "Whatsoever things were written aforetime were
written for our learning" (cf. also Rom. 4:23, 24; I Cor. 9:10; 10:11).

The New Testament writers used quotations in their sermons, in their
histories, in their letters, in their prayers. They used them when addressing
Jews or Gentiles, churches or individuals, friends or antagonists, new converts or seasoned Christians. They used them for argumentation, for illustration, for instruction, for documentation, for prophecy, for reproof. They
used them in times of stress and in hours of mature thinking, in liberty and
in prison, at home and abroad. Everywhere and always they were ready to
refer to the impregnable authority of Scripture.

Jesus Christ himself provides a most arresting example in this respect. At
the very threshold of his public ministry, our Lord, in his dramatic victory
over Satan's threefold onslaught, rested his whole defense on the authority
of three passages of Scripture. He quoted the Old Testament in support of
his teaching to the crowds; he quoted it in his discussions with antagonistic

Jews; he quoted it in answer to questions both captious and sincere; he quoted it in instructing the disciples who would have readily accepted his teaching on his own authority; he referred to it in his prayers, when alone in the presence of the Father; he quoted it on the cross, when his sufferings could easily have drawn his attention elsewhere; he quoted it in his resurrection glory, when any limitation, real or alleged, of the days of his flesh was clearly superseded. Whatever may be the differences between the pictures of Jesus drawn by the four Gospels, they certainly agree in their representation of our Lord's attitude toward the Old Testament: one of constant use and of unquestioning endorsement of its authority.

III. ACCURACY OF OLD TESTAMENT REFERENCES[1]

A difficulty comes to the fore, however, when the New Testament citations are carefully compared with the original Old Testament texts. In their quotations the New Testament writers, it would appear, use considerable freedom, touching both the letter and the meaning of the Old Testament passages.

Opponents of verbal inspiration repeatedly have brought forward this objection mainly in two forms:

1. The New Testament writers, not having taken care to quote in absolute agreement with the original text of the Old Testament, it is urged, cannot have held the doctrine of plenary inspiration. Otherwise they would have shown greater respect for the letter of Scripture.

2. The New Testament writers, in quoting the Old "inaccurately" as to its letter, or "improperly" as to its sense, or both, cannot have been directed to do so by the Spirit of God.

The first argument impugns mainly the inspiration of the Old Testament, the second mainly that of the New. Both will be met if it can be shown that the New Testament method of quotation is entirely proper and consistent with the highest regard for the texts cited. In the present treatment it is possible only to delineate the main principles involved, without showing their application to particular cases. We shall consider first, principles involved in the solution of difficulties arising from the New Testament manner of quoting, after which brief comments will be offered regarding the methods of interpretation exhibited by the New Testament authors in their application of Old Testament passages.

---

[1] The material to be found under this heading has in substance been set forth with more detail in a paper presented to the sixth annual meeting of the Evangelical Theological Society, December 30, 1954, at Ringwood, New Jersey. This paper was published in Volume I of the *Gordon Review*, February and May, 1955. Further detail and discussion of the actual quotations in the New Testament, especially in Matthew, were presented in an S.T.M. thesis submitted by the present writer to the faculty of Gordon Divinity School in 1940 under the title: "The Old Testament Quotations in the New with special reference to the Doctrine of the Plenary Inspiration of the Bible."

Form of Quotation

It must be recognized that each of the following principles does not find application in every case, but the writer is of the opinion that, singly or in combination, as the case may be, they provide a very satisfactory explanation of apparent discrepancies in almost all cases, and a possible solution in all cases.

1. The New Testament writers had to translate their quotations. They wrote in Greek and their source of quotations was in Hebrew. They needed therefore either to translate for themselves or to use existing translations. Now no translation can give a completely adequate and coextensive rendering of the original. A certain measure of change is inevitable, even when one is quoting by divine inspiration.

When the New Testament writers wrote, there was one Greek version of the Old Testament, the LXX. It was widespread, well known, and respected in spite of some obvious defects when appraised from the standpoint of modern scholarship. In most cases, it was a fair translation of the Hebrew text, and possessed distinctive literary qualities. Its position in the ancient world is comparable to that of the Authorized Version before the Revised was published. A conscientious scholar writing nowadays in a certain language will use for his quotations from foreign sources the translations which his readers generally use. He will not attempt to correct or change them unless some mistake bears directly on his point. When slight errors or mistranslations occur, generally he will neither discuss them, for in so doing he would tend to direct the reader's attention away from his point, nor correct them without giving notice, for this might tend to arouse the reader's suspicion. This practice is followed by many preachers and writers who use the Authorized Version in English or Luther's translation in German. They are often well aware that some verses rather inadequately render the Hebrew or the Greek, but no blame can be laid on them as long as they base no argument on what is mistaken in the translation. Similarly, the writers of the New Testament could use the LXX, the only Greek version then existing, in spite of its occasional inaccuracy, and even quote passages which were somewhat inaccurately translated. To take advantage of its errors, however, would have been inadmissible. We do not find any example of a New Testament deduction or application logically inferred from the Septuagint and which cannot be maintained on the basis of the Hebrew text.

Some of the recently discovered Dead Sea scrolls at times provide the Hebrew text which underlay the LXX where it differs from the Massoretic text. This is the case, for instance, in Isaiah 53:11, where the scroll Isaiah A reads "He shall see light," thus supporting the LXX rendering. While great caution is still necessary in any textual emendation of the Massoretic text, the possibility that in some divergent translations the LXX occasionally represents the primitive Hebrew original may be held to have received some support from these discoveries. In such cases, of course, it would not only have been proper for the New Testament writers to quote from the LXX, but this would actually have been preferable.

The use of the LXX in quoting does not indicate that the New Testament writers have thought of this version as inspired in itself. *A fortiori* they did not confer inspiration upon the translation of the passages they have used. Samuel Davidson was laboring under a regrettable confusion when he wrote: "It will ever remain inexplicable by the supporters of verbal inspiration that the words of the LXX became literally inspired as soon as they were taken from that version and transferred to the New Testament pages" (*Sacred Hermeneutics,* Edinburgh, Clark, 1843, p. 515). This statement misconstrues verbal inspiration. When the New Testament authors appealed to Scripture as the Word of God, it is not claimed that they viewed anything but the original communication as vested in full with divine inerrancy. Yet their willingness to make use of the LXX, in spite of its occasional defects, teaches the important lesson that the basic message which God purposed to deliver can be conveyed even through a translation, and that appeal can be made to a version insofar as it agrees with the original. It would be precarious, however, to rest an argument on any part of the LXX quotations which appears not to be conformed to the Hebrew original nor to the point of the New Testament writers, for the mere fact that the quotation was adduced in this fashion was not meant as a divine sanction upon incidental departures from the autographs. In the quotations made from the LXX we have indeed God's seal of approval upon the contents of the Old Testament passage, but the form of the citation is affected by the language and conditions of those to whom the New Testament was first addressed. Such use of the LXX was not a case of objectionable accommodation. That the inspired Word is accommodated to humanity is an obvious fact: it is written in human languages, uses human comparisons, its parts are conditioned by the circumstances of those to whom they were at first destined, and so forth. But we cannot admit of an accommodation in which inspired writers would give formal assent to error. In their use of the LXX, however, the New Testament authors were so far from actual endorsement of error that the best scholars of all times have used similar methods in adducing translated quotations, as noted above.[2]

The frequent use of the LXX, it must also be noted, did not impose upon

---

[2] If it be urged that these scholars were not inspired and that therefore their writings can scarcely be compared to Holy Writ, this point will be freely granted. What is significant here, however, is the fact that methods of quotation similar to those of the New Testament writers were used and are still now being used by men who can hardly be viewed as ignorant of the minor differences between the original text and the translations they adduce, and still less as intending to authenticate by their citation what they know to be divergent. These men's unquestioned competence, integrity and attachment to truth prove, for themselves as well as for the inspired authors, that the methods in question do not connote an endorsement of error.

the New Testament authors the obligation to quote always in accordance
with this version. Whenever they wanted to emphasize an idea which was
insufficiently or inadequately rendered in the LXX, they may have retrans-
lated in whole or in part the passage in question. In certain cases the reason
for their introduction of changes may remain unknown to us, but we are not
on that account in a position to say either that a careful reproduction of the
LXX is illegitimate or that a modification of that text is unjustifiable.

2. *The New Testament writers did not have the same rules for quotations
as are nowadays enforced in works of a scientific character.* In particular,
they did not have any punctuation signs which are so important in modern
usage.

a. They did not have any quotation marks, and thus it is not always
possible to ascertain the exact beginning, or the real extent of quotations.
They were not obliged to start actual citations immediately after an introductory formula, nor have we a right to affirm that their quotations do not end
until every resemblance with the Old Testament text disappears. In certain
cases they may very well have made shorter citations than is generally
believed, and also may have added developments of their own, retaining
some words taken from the original source but not actually intended as part
of a quotation. Criticism of such passages if they were not intended as actual
citations is manifestly unfair.

b. They did not have any ellipsis marks. Thus special attention is not
drawn to the numerous omissions they made. These ellipses, however, are not
to be considered as illegitimate on that account.

c. They did not have any brackets to indicate editorial comments introduced in the quotation. Thus we should not be surprised to find intentional
additions, sometimes merely of one word, sometimes more extended (cf. Eph.
6:2).

d. They did not have any footnote references by which to differentiate
quotations from various sources. Sometimes we find a mixture of passages of
analogous content or wording, but we are not justified on that account in
charging the writers with mishandling or misusing the Old Testament.

We readily recognize that the New Testament writers fell into these
patterns, whose legitimacy is universally granted, much more than a present-
day author would. Modern punctuation rules make such practices tiresome
and awkward. One tries nowadays to omit, insert or modify as little as possible in quotations, in order to avoid the complexity of repeated quotation
marks, ellipsis marks, brackets, and so forth. Yet this common present usage
is by no means a standard by which to judge the ancient writers.

3. *The New Testament writers sometimes paraphrased their quotations.*

a. Under this heading we might first mention certain cases where we find
a free translation of the Hebrew rather than a real paraphrase. Such a
procedure certainly needs no justification, since a free translation sometimes
renders the sense and impression of the original better than a more literal
one.

b. Slight modifications, such as a change of pronouns, a substitution of a noun for a pronoun or vice versa, transformations in the person, the tense, the mood or the voice of verbs, are sometimes introduced in order to better suit the connection in the New Testament. These paraphrases are perhaps the most obviously legitimate of all.

c. There are cases in which the New Testament writers obviously forsake the actual tenor of the Old Testament passage in order to manifest more clearly in what sense they were construing it. In this they are quite in agreement with the best modern usage, as represented, for example, in W. G. Campbell, *A Form Book for Thesis Writing* (New York, Houghton Mifflin 1939): "A careful paraphrase that does complete justice to the source is preferable to a long quotation" (p. 15).

d. In certain cases the New Testament writers do not refer to a single passage, but rather summarize the general teaching of the canonical books on certain subjects in phrasing appropriate to the New Testament, although as to the essential thought they express indebtedness to, or agreement with, the Old Testament. This method of referring to the Old Testament teachings is obviously legitimate. The following passages might be viewed as examples of "quotations of substance," as Franklin Johnson calls them in his able treatise on *The Quotations of the New Testament from the Old Considered in the Light of General Literature* (London, Baptist Tract and Book Society, 1896): Matt. 2:23; 5:31, 33; 12:3, 5; 19:7; 22:24; 24:15; 26:24, 54, 56; Mark 2:25; 9:12, 13; 10:4; 12:19; 14:21, 49; Luke 2:22; 6:3; 11:49; 18:31; 20:28; 21:22; 24:27, 32, 44–46; John 1:45; 5:39, 46; 7:38, 42; 8:17; 17:12; 19:7, 28; 20:9; Acts 1:16; 3:18; 7:51; 13:22, 29; 17:2, 3; Rom. 3:10; I Cor. 2:9; 14:34; 15:3, 4, 25–27; II Cor. 4:6; Gal. 3:22; 4:22; Eph. 5:14; James 4:5; II Pet. 3:12, 13.

e. Finally, we must consider the possibility that the writers of the New Testament, writing or speaking for people well acquainted with the Old, may in certain cases have intended simply to refer their readers or hearers to a well-known passage of Scripture. Then, in order to suggest it to their memory they may have accurately cited therefrom some expressions, which they then placed in a general frame different from that of the original. At times the actual words quoted may have been intended merely or primarily to indicate the location of a passage, as the general context of the Old Testament in which the stipulated truth could be found, rather than as an express citation.

4. The New Testament writers often simply alluded to Old Testament passages without intending to quote them. It was quite natural that people nurtured and steeped in the oracles of God should instinctively use forms of language and turns of thought reminiscent of Old Testament Scripture.

> The speakers or writers, in such cases, do not profess to give forth the precise words and meaning of former revelations; their thoughts and language merely derived from these the form and direction, which by a kind of sacred instinct they took; and it does not matter

for any purpose, for which the inspired oracles were given, whether
the portions thus appropriated might or might not be very closely
followed, and used in connections somewhat different from those in
which they originally stood (Patrick Fairbairn, *Hermeneutical
Manual,* Edinburgh, T. & T. Clark, 1858, p. 355).

Only in cases where the New Testament authors definitely manifest the
intention of citing by the use of a formula of introduction can we require
any strong degree of conformity.

With respect to what might be viewed as formulas of introduction, the
following remarks may be made:

a. Only a quotation which immediately follows such a formula is to be
certainly considered as a formal citation. In cases of successive quotations
"and again" always introduces an actual citation (Rom. 15:11; I Cor. 3:20;
Heb. 1:5; 2:13; 10:30), but in the case of "and" or "but," or of successive
quotations without any intervening link, criticisms are quite precarious, since
no formal quotation may be intended.

b. Even when a definite formula points directly to an Old Testament
passage, we may not expect strict adherence to the letter of the source when
this quotation is recorded in indirect rather than in direct discourse. In such
cases we often find remarkable verbal accuracy, but we cannot criticize
departure from the original when the very form of the sentence so naturally
allows for it.

c. When what may appear to be a citation is introduced by a form of the
verbs "say" or "speak," it is not always certain that the writer actually
intended to quote. Rather, the possibility must at times be taken into consideration that we are facing an informal reference to some saying recorded
in Scripture. Perhaps some of the clearest examples along this line may be
found in the discourse of Stephen in Acts 7, in which free references are
made to sayings of God, of Moses, and of the Jews, woven in the survey of
covenant history presented by the first martyr. In Acts 7:26, a declaration of
Moses is mentioned which is not found at all in the Old Testament and
obviously was not intended as an actual quotation. In all cases of this type
it must certainly be acknowledged that a considerable measure of freedom is
legitimate and that one could scarcely expect here the exactness looked
for in actual citations. The following may belong to this category: Matt.
2:23; 15:4; 22:32; 24:15; Mark 12:26; Acts 3:25; 7:3, 5–7, 26–28, 32–35,
40; 13:22; Rom. 9:15; 11:4; II Cor. 4:6; Gal. 3:8; Heb. 1:5, 13; 6:14;
8:5; 10:30; 12:21, 26; 13:5; James 2:11; I Pet. 3:6; Jude 14.

*5. The New Testament authors sometimes recorded quotations made by
others.* Not all quotations in the New Testament are introduced by the
writers themselves for the purpose of illustrating their narrative or bolstering
their argument. Sometimes they record quotations made by the personalities
who appear in the history, as by Jesus, Paul, Peter, James, Stephen, the Jews,
and Satan. In two cases we have a record of a reading—Luke 4:18, 19 and

Acts 8:32, 33. The New Testament writers had at their disposal at least three legitimate methods of recording such quotations:

a. They could translate them directly from the original text;

b. They could use the existing Septuagint and quote according to this version, as suggested earlier;

c. They could translate directly from the form used by the person quoting, often presumably an Aramaic translation of the Hebrew text. A few words are needed here only with reference to the last possibility. Of course, we expect the persons quoting, at least those who were inspired (Jesus, Paul, Peter, James and probably Stephen), to quote accurately, so that in these cases no divergence from the original can be explained by the mere fact that somebody else's quotation is recorded. Since, however, probably most of these quotations were originally made in Aramaic according to a current oral or written Aramaic translation, certain discrepancies between the Old Testament and the New, which cannot be accounted for on the basis of the Septuagint, may have their true explanation in the use of this probable Aramaic version.

6. *Other principles whose application must be limited.* Under this heading we need to consider briefly three additional principles of explanation of apparent discrepancies between the text of the Old Testament and that of the New. These principles, in the writer's opinion, may well be at times the ground of a legitimate explanation, but they ought to be handled with utmost discrimination, lest the assured present authority of Scripture appear to be placed in jeopardy.

a. The texts may have been altered in the process of transmission. We have ample reasons to be grateful for the marvelous state of conservation of the text of Scripture: the New Testament possesses a degree of certainty no doubt unequalled by any other ancient text transmitted to us by manuscript; the Hebrew Old Testament has been the object of the loving and painstaking watchcare of the Jews and the accuracy of the Massoretic text has been confirmed in a striking way by the Dead Sea scrolls. Nevertheless, it is conceivable that at times an early mistake in copying may have vitiated our texts, thereby introducing a discrepancy which was not present in the autographs. Still, it would be very injudicious to indulge in unrestrained corrections of the texts on the ground of the quotations, and the present writer has not found any instance in the New Testament where such a correction might appear as the only possible legitimate explanation of a quotation difficulty.

b. In the quotations, as well as in other inspired texts, the personality of the writers has been respected. It is an unsearchable mystery that the Holy Spirit could inspire the sacred writings so as to communicate his inerrancy to their very words and, at the same time, respect the freedom and personality of the writers so that we might easily recognize their style and their characteristics. The same thing is true of the quotations, for there also we may discern the individuality of the writers in their use of them, in the sources quoted, and in the method of quoting. There is, however, a dangerous distortion of this principle in the appeal made by some to slips of memory in order to explain certain difficulties in the quotations. Now the very idea of a slip of memory undermines seriously the whole structure of inerrancy and is therefore out of keeping with a consistent upholding of plenary verbal inspiration. In fact, as C. H. Toy himself recognized—and he cannot easily be charged with undue bias in favor of the conservative view of Scripture!— so many quotations show verbal agreement with the LXX "that we must suppose either that they were made from a written text, or, if not, that the memory of the writers was very accurate" (*Quotations in the New Testament,* p. xx).

c. *The Spirit of God was free to modify the expressions that he inspired in the Old Testament.* While this is no doubt true with respect to the interpretation of Old Testament passages and with respect to allusions or distant references, the statement should not be made too glibly with respect to quotations, and some conservative writers may have been too prone to advocate this approach when other less precarious solutions might be advanced. Nevertheless, in this connection, one may well give assent to the judgment of Patrick Fairbairn:

> Even in those cases in which, for anything we can see, a closer translation would have served equally well the purpose of the writer, it may have been worthy of the inspiring Spirit, and perfectly consistent with the fullest inspiration of the original Scriptures, that the sense should have been given in a free current translation; for the principle was thereby sanctioned of a rational freedom in the handling of Scripture, as opposed to the rigid formalism and superstitious regard to the letter, which prevailed among the Rabbinical Jews. . . . The stress occasionally laid in the New Testament upon particular words in passages of the Old . . . sufficiently proves what a value attaches to the very form of the Divine communication, and how necessary it is to connect the element of inspiration with the written record as it stands. It shows that God's words are pure words, and that, if fairly interpreted, they cannot be too closely pressed. But in other cases, when nothing depended upon a rigid adherence to the letter, the practice of the sacred writers, not scrupulously to stickle about this, but to give prominence simply to the substance of the revelation, is fraught also with an important lesson; since it teaches us, that the letter is valuable only for the truth couched in it, and that the one is no further to be prized and contended for, than may be required for the exhibition of the other (*op. cit.,* pp. 413 f.).

Meaning of the Old Testament Passages

It has been urged at times that the New Testament writers have flouted the proper laws of hermeneutics, have been guilty of artificial and rabbinical exegesis, and thus have repeatedly distorted the meaning of the Old Testament passages which they quote.

1. This type of objection may appear at first more weighty than those which affect merely the wording of the quotations, since an alleged discrepancy in meaning is more grievous than a mere divergence of form. Yet the problems raised in this area are probably less embarrassing to the advocates of plenary inspiration, since a verbal comparison is largely a matter of plain fact, while the assessment of the full extent of the meaning of a passage calls for the exercise of human individual judgment and fallible opinion. Few Christians, it is hoped, will have the presumption of setting forth their own interpretation as normative, when it runs directly counter to that of the Lord Jesus or of his apostles.

2. There is obviously a deep underlying relationship between the Old Testament and the New: one purpose pervades the whole Bible and also the various phases of human history, more especially of Israel. Thus the Old Testament can and must be considered, even in its historical narratives, as a source of prefigurements and of prophecies. It has been widely acknowledged that, in spite of certain difficult passages, the New Testament interpretation of the Old manifests a strikingly illuminating understanding of Old Testament Scripture. C. H. Dodd, although not a defender of verbal inspiration, could write: "In general . . . the writers of the New Testament, in making use of passages from the Old Testament, remain true to the main intention of their writers" (*According to the Scriptures,* London, Nisbet, 1952, p. 130). And again: "We have before us a considerable intellectual feat. The various scriptures are acutely interpreted along lines already discernible within the Old Testament canon itself or in pre-Christian Judaism —in many cases, I believe, lines which start from their first, historical, intention—and these lines are carried forward to fresh results" (*ibid.,* p. 109).

3. There are certain Old Testament passages in which the connection with the New Testament is so clear that there can hardly be doubt about their applicability and about the fact that the Old Testament writers foresaw some events or some principles of the new covenant. This is not necessary in every case, however, and the Spirit of God may very well have inspired expressions which potentially transcended the thoughts of the sacred writers and of those to whom they addressed themselves. This certainly occurred in the case of Caiaphas (John 11:49–52), and there is no ground to deny the possibility of such a process in the inspiration of the Old Testament Scripture.

4. While the doctrine of verbal inspiration requires that we should accept any New Testament interpretation of an Old Testament text as legitimate, it does not require that such interpretation be necessarily viewed as exclusive or exhaustive of the full Old Testament meaning. In many cases the New

Testament makes a particular application of principles stated in the Old, whose fulfillment is accomplished in more than a single event. Thus certain Old Testament prophecies may have conveyed to the original hearers a meaning more restricted than the perspective opened in the New Testament pages. The original understanding was a legitimate interpretation of the prophecy, yet one which does not preclude the propriety of the larger vistas, authoritatively revealed in the New Testament.

5. Not all the passages quoted in the New Testament are necessarily to be considered as definite prophecies, but many are cited as simply characterizing in a striking way the New Testament situation. At times the New Testament writers may have simply used Old Testament language without intending to imply that there is a distinct relationship of prophecy to fulfillment, or of antitype to type.

6. Writing about this subject, C. H. Toy makes a remark which he apparently intends only with respect to apostolic times, but which may well be viewed as having more general reference: "The deeper the reverence for the departed Lord and for the divine word, the greater the disposition to find him everywhere" (op. cit., p. xxv). Conservatives hope that, judged by this standard, they will not be found to have less reverence for their Lord and for the divine Word than the New Testament writers!

In conclusion, one could wish to quote at length some remarks of B. B. Warfield (op. cit., pp. 218–220), which for the sake of brevity we shall be constrained to summarize here. The student of Scripture is not bound to provide the solution of all the difficulties which he encounters in the Bible. It is better to leave matters unharmonized than to have recourse to strained or artificial exegesis. Even when no solution of a difficulty is offered, we are not thereby driven to assume that the problem is insoluble.

> Every unharmonized passage remains a case of difficult harmony and does not pass into the category of objections to plenary inspiration. It can pass into the category of objections only if we are prepared to affirm that we clearly see that it is, on any conceivable hypothesis of its meaning, clearly inconsistent with the Biblical doctrine of inspiration. In that case we would no doubt need to give up the Biblical doctrine of inspiration; but with it we must also give up our confidence in the Biblical writers as teachers of doctrine" (ibid., p. 220).

It has been the writer's privilege to devote substantial time to the consideration of all quotations of the Old Testament in the New. This study has led him to the conclusion that the principles mentioned above can provide in every case a possible explanation of the difficulties at hand in perfect harmony with the doctrine of the inerrancy of Scripture. There is no claim here that all the difficulties are readily dispelled, or that we are in possession of the final solution of every problem. Nevertheless, possible if not plausible explanations are at hand in every case known to the present writer. It is therefore with some confidence that this presentation is made. In fact, the quotations, which are often spoken of as raising one of the major difficulties against the view of plenary inspiration, upon examination turn out to be a confirmation of this doctrine rather than an invalidation of it. To this concurs the judgment of men who can surely be quoted as impartial witnesses, in statements such as the following, made precisely with reference to Old Testament quotations in the New:

> We know, from the general tone of the New Testament, that it regards the Old Testament, as all the Jews then did, as the revealed and inspired word of God, and clothed with his authority (C. H. Toy, *op. cit.,* p. xxx).

> Our authors view the words of the Old Testament as *immediate* words of God, and introduce them explicitly as such, even those which are not in the least related as sayings of God. They see nothing in the sacred book, which is merely the word of the human authors and not at the same time the very word of God Himself. In everything that stands "written," God Himself is speaking to them (R. Rothe, *Zur Dogmatik,* Gotha, Perthes, 1869, pp. 177 f.).

> In quoting the Old Testament, the New Testament writers proceed consistently from the presupposition that they have Holy Scripture in hand. . . . The actual author is God or the Holy Spirit, and both, as also frequently the *graphe,* are represented as speaking either directly or through the Old Testament writers (E. Huehn, *Die Alttestamentlichen Citate . . . im Neuen Testament,* Tübingen, Mohr, 1900, p. 272).

Such statements, coming as they are from the pen of men who were not at all inclined to favor the conservative approach to the Scripture, are no doubt more impressive than anything a conservative scholar could say. They may be allowed to stand at the end of this study as expressing in a striking way the writer's own conclusions on the subject.

THE CANON OF
THE OLD TESTAMENT

Edward J. Young

Edward J. Young has been Professor of Old Testament at Westminster Theological Seminary, Pennsylvania, since 1946. He holds the A.B. degree from Leland Stanford Junior University, Th.B. and Th.M. from Westminster Theological Seminary, and Ph.D. from Dropsie College for Hebrew and Cognate Learning. His published writings include Introduction to the Old Testament, Arabic for Beginners, *and* Studies in Isaiah. *He is editor of the Tyndale Old Testament commentaries and of the New International Old Testament commentaries.*

10. Edward J. Young

THE CANON OF
THE OLD TESTAMENT

W HAT is meant by the "Canon of the Old Testament"? The word "canon" itself is derived from the Greek, and in that language originally meant a staff or straight rod. In pre-Christian Greek it also bore the connotation "rule," or "standard," and in this sense also is used in the New Testament (cf. II Cor. 10:13, 15, 16; Gal. 6:16). Clement of Rome uses it of a rule possessing authority (I:7:2) and also in the sense of sphere or province of action (cf. I:1:3). Later the word came to designate the rule of faith.

I. IDEA OF THE CANON

The problem we face, however, cannot be limited to the historical significance of the Greek word *kanon*, although its historical significance is a relevant consideration. We do indeed believe that the Canon of the Old Testament is the rule of faith, the standard for judging all controversies of religion. We are compelled to consider, however, why the Old Testament is the rule of faith, and whether in truth it possesses the authority which the Church has traditionally ascribed to it. How did the books of the Old Testament come to receive this authority? When did the Jews and later the Christian Church begin to ascribe divine authority to them? A proper discussion of the question also involves certain subsidiary issues, namely, What is the compass of the Canon? and what is the proper arrangement and division of the books?

At the outset we affirm that the question of the divine authority of the Old Testament has validity only on the grounds of Christian theism. Only if

Christian theism is true can the idea of canonicity itself have validity and meaning. Since this fundamental postulate underlies the following discussion, it will also be incumbent upon us briefly to point out why the concept of canonicity gains its validity from Christian supernaturalism.

In considering the concept of canonicity we must be in every respect Biblical; that is, the Bible alone must be allowed to define canonicity. According to the Bible, the Scriptures of the Old Testament are "God-breathed," breathed forth from the mouth of God (II Tim. 3:16). This verse expresses no isolated thought, but rather succinctly sums up the entire Old Testament concept of saving revelation, namely that God actually spoke his Word to his servants.

The Scriptures are full and explicit in their teaching about special revelation. Such revelation involved the communication of God's words to man. Despite much that is being written today, it was not confined to great acts of God, but rather consisted of both acts and words. The words were essential in order that the acts might be understood. When God's saving words were written down, this written record was in itself revelation and also an integral element in God's plan of salvation.

When the Word of God was written it became Scripture and, inasmuch as it had been spoken by God, possessed absolute authority. Since it was the Word of God, it was canonical. That which determines the canonicity of a book, therefore, is the fact that the book is inspired of God. Hence a distinction is properly made between the authority which the Old Testament books possess as divinely inspired, and the recognition of that authority on the part of Israel.

We have not yet done full justice, however, to the idea of canonicity. Since more than one book was inspired, we are brought to the questions, "How many books were inspired?" "How large is the list of inspired books?" "What are the precise limits of the rule of faith?" The witness of Jesus Christ is decisive at this point. Without question our Lord believed all the Old Testament books and so the entire Old Testament itself to be the Word of God. Inasmuch as he is the eternal Son of God, his word is final (cf. "The Authority of the Old Testament" in *The Infallible Word*, pp. 54–60). That he regarded the Old Testament as the authoritative Word of God is a fact which cannot successfully be denied. Speaking of this Old Testament, he said, "The scripture cannot be broken" (John 10:31–36). On another occasion he remarked, "These are the words which I spake unto you, while I was yet with you, that all things must be fulfilled, which were written in the law of Moses, and in the prophets, and in the psalms, concerning me" (Luke 24:44).

II. RECEPTION OF THE CANON

If any book was actually revealed by God, it certainly would follow that

that book was authoritative, and that all books so revealed would constitute an authoritative and final rule of faith and practice, in fact, a canon. At this point, however, a further question intrudes. "How can one recognize which books are divinely inspired and consequently canonical and which are not?" In the very nature of the case, because God is the Creator and man the creature, man can only identify the Word of God if God himself enables man so to identify it. One of the blessings of regeneration is that the Spirit of God opens the eyes of man's understanding to clearly perceive these strong marks of the divine origin of Scripture to which marks he formerly had been blind. This inward testimony of the Holy Spirit enables a man to recognize the Scripture as truly from God.

God's people, therefore, recognize his Word. "My sheep hear my voice" (John 10:27a), said our Lord. As soon as the Old Testament made its appearance, it was recognized as the Word of God both in its parts and in its entirety (*ibid.*, pp. 60–70). The evidence which supports this statement has often been adduced, but it may not be out of place briefly to summarize it. The Book of the Law was to be placed beside the ark of the covenant; the priests were to read it to the people; the king was to possess a copy thereof; and the Exile is said to have come as a punishment for infractions and transgressions of the Law.

The words of the prophets were likewise regarded as authoritative. These prophets demanded obedience to their words as to the very Word of God, and they declared that calamity had befallen Israel, not only because she had transgressed the Law, but also because she had disobeyed their words. Thus, from many passages of the Old Testament itself we learn that the revelation of God was accepted by God's people as authoritative as soon as it was received.

It is true that in Old Testament times no general council or synod ever declared expressly that the Old Testament was divinely authoritative. What settles the question for Christians, however, is the positive testimony of Jesus Christ himself. And it is interesting to note that between our Lord and the Pharisees there was no controversy respecting the authority of the Old Testament. The controversy entered in because the Pharisees had supplemented that authority by their own tradition. When our Lord, therefore, was on earth, he placed the *imprimatur* of his infallible authority upon the Old Testament Scriptures in that he recognized them as divine. Thus, in God's providence, the individual books of the Old Testament were recognized as canonical and brought together, so that they formed one organic whole which Jesus Christ accepted as Scripture.

III. ALTERNATE THEORIES OF FORMATION OF THE CANON

Only upon the presuppositions of Christian theism can the above sketch of the nature and formation of the Old Testament Canon be correct. There are alternate views, and some consideration of them will enable us more clearly to understand the implications of the view we believe to be correct. Some of these alternate views seek to explain the Canon as a purely human conception, and are concerned with questions of how and why and under what conditions certain writings "were thought to" possess religious authority. Such an approach unavoidably raises the question why certain books were chosen and others rejected. In other words, what determining principle governed the "formation" of the Canon?

According to H. E. Ryle, the problem we face is how the books of Holy Scripture came to obtain recognition as a sacred and authoritative Canon (Hebert Edward Ryle, *The Canon of the Old Testament*).[1] He maintained that a Hebrew literature existed before there was any Hebrew Canon. Three stages assertedly must be noted, first, that of the literary antecedents of the Old Testament books; second, the stage of the redaction of these books to their present form; and finally, the selection of these books for a position in the national Canon of Holy Scripture. Ryle expounded these three separate stages in the canonization of the Old Testament somewhat in detail. Our Pentateuch, he said, is the result of a long period of growth and is a compilation of documents which originally existed independent of one another. When Ezra read the Pentateuch in the hearing of the assembled people (Neh. 8) that Law was acknowledged as binding and so was canonized. Hence, the first Hebrew Canon of Scripture consisted of the Pentateuch. This first Canon, however, proved to be insufficient. By the time of Nehemiah a particular interest had been aroused in preserving the writings and sayings of the prophets. The actual period of their canonization, however, falls between 300 B.C. and the beginning of the second century B.C. What led to this canonization presumably at this time is not positively asserted. Possibly it was the spread of Hellenic culture and possibly also a reaction against the spirit of Ezra. Greater difficulty is conceded with respect to the third Canon. When the Canon of the Prophets was closed, other writings existed, such as Ecclesiastes, which belonged neither to the Canon of the Prophets nor to that of the Law, and these served practically as an appendix to the two existing Canons. The enthusiasm of the Jewish patriots at the time of the Maccabees, assertedly, may have originated the movement which sought to expand the Canon by the addition of a third group of writings. The orders of Antiochus to destroy the Jewish national writings simply enhanced their value in the eyes of the Jews. Subsequent popular usage brought about a regard for these books as authoritative. The actual official recognition of the books is probably to be placed about 100 A.D., it is said,

---

[1] Essentially the same position is expressed in G. Wildeboer, *The Origin of the Canon of the Old Testament* (translated by Benjamin Wisner Bacon), London, 1895: the Law was canonized by Ezra (444 B.C.), the Prophets sometime about 200 B.C., and the Writings were officially canonized by the time of the redaction of the Mishnah by Rabbi Judah the Holy (200 A.D.). Wellhausen (*Einleitung*, pp. 550 f.) thinks that the Pharisees definitely fixed the extent of the Canon.

and was the work of the Synod held at Jamnia (Jabney) near Jaffa about 90 A.D.

A modification of this view of Ryle appears in the work of Oesterley and Robinson who, under the influence of Holscher, find the idea of a canon in the fact that some books are considered more holy than others. Such an idea, they think, could not have arisen all at once, but rather "it was only gradually, and by general consensus, that certain books came to have a special sanctity attached to them" (W. O. E. Oesterley and Theodore H. Robinson, *An Introduction to the Books of the Old Testament,* London, 1934, p. 2; G. Holscher, *Kanonisch und Apocryph,* Naumberg, 1905). At the same time, these authors reject the idea of a threefold canonization. What forced the idea of a canon to arise, in their opinion, were Greek culture and the growth of Greek literature and particularly the spread of Jewish Apocryphal books. The Jewish scribes had to weed out harmful and erroneous literature, and thus the idea of a canon arose. The fixing of the Canon, however, as we know it now, was not accomplished until about A.D. 100. Some Jewish literature, therefore, on this view, underwent a metamorphosis in its nature. The fixing of the Canon was piecemeal, but when once completed, the books of the Old Testament were regarded by the Jews as canonical.

According to Bentzen we are to regard Nehemiah 8–10 as indicating the introduction of that form of the Law which was current in Babylonian Jewish circles of the time. Even as early as Josiah we find the idea of a normative Law Book, and the belief that God could reveal his will by means of a holy book. The seventh century was of particular importance for the formation of the idea of a holy written law. Even earlier, however, is the ancient idea of law as given by a god, and also the ancient Credo of Israel (Deut. 26:5b–9).

Such ideas, however, did not at once lead to a fixed concept of a canon. In the century after the Exile the different strands of tradition were united, and so the oldest part of the Old Testament Canon (the Pentateuch) became an established fact.

The Canon of the Prophets began when Isaiah put upon his disciples the obligation to be the bearers and preservers of the word (Isa. 8:16), and when Jeremiah had Baruch write down his warnings. The Exile gave to the words of the prophets the confirmation of history, and before 200 B.C. the prophetical Canon was essentially finished. The third part of the Canon, thinks Bentzen, is most vaguely defined, as is shown by the different names attributed unto it. The Synod of Jamnia, moreover, is also considered important for the definite fixing of the Canon. (Aage Bentzen, *Introduction to the Old Testament,* Copenhagen, 1952, pp. 20–41).

In his influential *Introduction to the Old Testament* (second edition, New York, 1946), Robert H. Pfeiffer presents a modification of the classic liberal view of the canonization of the Old Testament, the view essentially espoused by Ryle. The first instance of canonization in human history, thinks Pfeiffer, took place when Deuteronomy, discovered in the temple under the reign of Josiah, was regarded as the word of Jehovah, and its precepts put into practice.

About 650 B.C. other literary works in Israel were combined and edited with the result that a great national epic was formed. About 550 B.C. the canonized Deuteronomy was inserted into the compass of the national epic with the result that the latter also came to be regarded as canonical. At still a later date, around 400 B.C., the so-called priestly document was inserted into this combined work and thus it too achieved canonicity.

Perhaps these views may be regarded as fairly representative of what is held by those who discuss canonicity as though it were merely a human process and nothing more. We cannot hope to subject these theories to exhaustive scrutiny in a brief essay, but a few remarks will be in order.

IV. REFLECTIONS UPON ALTERNATE THEORIES

The Synod of Jamnia

Some of these views appeal to a Synod of Jamnia as though that body had made pronouncements concerning the extent of the Old Testament Canon. H. H. Rowley, however, seems to be correct when he remarks,

> It is, indeed, doubtful, how far it is correct to speak of the Council of Jamnia. We know of discussions that took place there amongst the Rabbis, but we know of no formal or binding decisions that were made, and it is probable that the discussions were informal, though none the less helping to crystallize and to fix more firmly the Jewish tradition (H. H. Rowley, *The Growth of the Old Testament*, London, 1950 p. 170).

We really know very little concerning this supposed Synod. After the destruction of Jerusalem by the armies of Titus (70 A.D.) Rabbi Johanan ben Zakkai obtained permission to settle in Jamnia, there to carry on his literary activity. The place became a center of Scripture study, and discussions were pursued concerning the canonicity of certain books, namely, Ezekiel, Ecclesiastes, Song of Solomon, Proverbs and Esther. It may be seriously questioned, however, whether this Synod (known in Jewish sources as the Great Bet Din, literally, house of judgment) actually engaged in discussions as to whether certain books should be included in the Canon. The discussions rather seemed to be centered in the question whether certain books should be excluded therefrom. It cannot legitimately be maintained that formal pronouncement was made at Jamnia concerning the entire Old Testament as such.

Evidence Concerning Ezra and Nehemiah

Nor can it be maintained that the Scriptures or any portion of them were canonized by Ezra or Nehemiah or by their contemporaries. In Ezra 7:6,

Ezra is described as a "ready" (*māhîr*) scribe in the Law of Moses. From
this it is apparent that the Law of Moses is regarded as already authoritative inasmuch as it had been given by God. With the permission of
Artaxerxes, Ezra went up to Jerusalem with the intention of seeing that the
precepts of the Law were carried out. Everything in the seventh chapter of
Ezra points to the fact that the Law was already in existence and that its
commands were to be obeyed (cf. verses 14, 23, 25, 26). Not a word supports
the position that Ezra was to impart to already existing religious writings an
authority which they previously lacked.

Nor can appeal be made, as is done, for example, by Ryle, to Nehemiah
8–10 as presenting an account of canonization. It is one of the great merits
of Pfeiffer's work that he recognizes this fact and breaks at this point with
what might be called the traditional view of negative criticism. According
to these chapters, at the people's request Ezra brought the "book of the law
of Moses which the Lord had commanded to Israel" (Neh. 8:1) and read
this Law to the people. It was a serious reading, and Ezra sought to explain
the Law as he read (cf. Neh. 8:8). When the people heard the reading they
wept. On the second day the leaders gathered together with Ezra in order
to understand the Law (Neh. 8:13), with the result that they observed the
Feast of Tabernacles.

On the 24th day of the month the people were assembled with fasting and
with the signs of repentance, sackcloth and earth (Neh. 9:1), and again they
read in the Law of their God. The chapter then records the beautiful prayer
of Jeshua and others. The result is that, because of God's goodness, they
make and write a covenant. The remainder of the people enter into a curse
and into an oath to "walk in God's law, which was given by Moses the
servant of God" (Neh. 10:29). The Law is here regarded not as something
new but as something very old, so old in fact that it was believed to have
been revealed by God through Moses. And herein lay its authority and
effectiveness. The people did not say "We now pronounce these writings to
be authoritative." They said rather, "These writings received their authority
centuries ago when God made them known to Moses. For that reason we
must obey them."

In the book known as Fourth Ezra it is claimed that all of the Holy Scriptures had been burned in the destruction of Jerusalem. This explains the
fact that the Law of Moses was not known to the exiles who had just returned from Babylon. To the question, how Ezra happened to have a copy,
the answer given is that by special inspiration God made known to him the
content of the books which had been lost (4 Ezra 14:18 ff.). This account
is, of course, to be rejected as fanciful.

Three points may be noted, however. In the first place, Ezra prays to God
for a restoration of the Law that has been burned. He does not "canonize"
this Law nor any of the other books, but recognizes that they had already
been in existence as authoritative. Secondly, in this account Ezra is said to

have written down 94 books altogether. Twenty-four (i.e., the authoritative Scriptures) are to be published, but 70 are to be kept for the wise. Here a distinction is made between the canonical and non-canonical books, and the assumption of the author is that this distinction was also present in Ezra's time. Lastly, it must be noted that not all of the Old Testament had been written by Ezra's time.

The Talmudic tractate, *Baba Bathra* 14b–15a, asserts that "Ezra wrote his book" and it also mentions the "men of the great synagogue" as the authors of Ezekiel, the Minor Prophets, Daniel and Esther. Whatever be the precise significance of the assertion that the men of the Great Synagogue wrote—possibly it merely means that they arranged the books—it is clear that no warrant exists for the assertion that either this body or Ezra "canonized" the Scriptures.[2]

A tradition is recorded in II Maccabees 2:13 ff. to the effect that Nehemiah founded a library and collected books "concerning the kings and prophets and those of David and letters of kings concerning offerings [*anathematōn*]." The reference to the letters of kings may signify letters from the Persian kings concerning gifts for the temple (cf. G. Ch. Aalders, *Oud-testamentische Kanoniek*, Kampen, 1952, p. 31).

In his comments on this passage Zeitlin asserts explicitly that the Pentateuch and first books of the prophets were canonized by Ezra and Nehemiah. Very wisely, however, he does not draw this conclusion from the present passage (Solomon Zeitlin, *The Second Book of Maccabees*, English translation by Sidney Tedesche, New York, 1954, p. 113). If appeal be made here to support the view that Ezra and Nehemiah canonized the Pentateuch, such appeal proves too much. If it proves that they "canonized" the Pentateuch, it proves that they "canonized" other books also, those concerning kings and prophets as well as the Psalms of David and certain letters of kings.

By way of summary, therefore, it may be asserted confidently that the passages invoked to support the idea that Ezra "canonized" any portion of the Old Testament Scriptures do not yield the desired result. Neither Ezra nor Nehemiah nor the men of the Great Synagogue nor the Council of Jamnia "canonized" the Old Testament nor any part thereof. Rather, all the evidence supports the position that the books of the Old Testament, being of divine inspiration, were consequently authoritative, and were recognized as such from the time of their first appearance. This evidence consists, first of all, in the absence of record of any council or group which made official pronouncements about the canonicity of the Old Testament books, but more specifically in the express statements of the Old Testament books themselves when taken at face value.

---

[2] The term "Great Synagogue" may be regarded as a designation of those Jewish teachers who followed Ezra in his exposition of the Law. This "school" of teachers continued to the time of Hillel or possibly Johanan ben Zakkai. Abraham Kuenen showed that the idea of this "Great Synagogue" as an assembly had been based upon Nehemiah 9 and 10.

Certain Factors Involved in Canonicity

What is involved in the recognition of a book as canonical? Some scholars apparently contend that a writing might exist for many years before being considered canonical. Pfeiffer, for example, holds that the popularity of the Former Prophets (Joshua-Kings), together with their religious and patriotic appeal, and the fact that they were thought to have been written by prophets, led to their canonization about 200 B.C. (R. H. Pfeiffer, *The Books of the Old Testament,* New York, 1957, p. 15).

Such a position, however, involves a very low conception of the meaning of the word "canon." All the evidence supports the view that the books which the Jews regarded as canonical were those which they believed to be divine and consequently authoritative. There is no evidence that these particular books existed among the ancient Jews for many years before they were recognized as canonical. Indeed, if a book was actually revealed by God, is it conceivable that such a book would circulate for many years before anyone recognized its true nature? The very marks of divinity which the book would exhibit together with the work of the inward testimony of the Holy Spirit are sufficient answer to this consideration. At this point it becomes particularly clear that the idea of canonicity can have validity only upon the basis of Christian theism. If a lower connotation be placed upon the concept, justice cannot be done to all the factors involved.

A further consideration arises in connection with certain modern theories of canonization. Some of these theories which we have been considering postulate the position that somewhere along the line in the course of Israelitish history canonical books and non-canonical books were placed together. Thus, to cite an example, Pfeiffer asserts that the book of Deuteronomy, a work containing "canonical" elements, was inserted into another work, a national epic. This theory involves a great psychological difficulty. When people consider a particular writing as possessing divine authority, they treat that writing with a reverence superior to that presupposed by this view. The reason so many Christians today object to the inclusion of the Apocrypha in their copies of the Bible is that they do not want books which they regard (and rightly) as merely human compositions to be placed on a par with writings which are the Word of God. Yet we are asked to believe that canonical writings in Israel were inserted in non-canonical works. But the evidence shows that the Jews actually considered their Scriptures to be God's Word. It is inconceivable that they would have correlated that divine Word with some larger writing, no matter how prominent and popular, which they believed lacking in divine origin and authority.

By way of conclusion we are compelled to assert that attempts to explain "canonization" as simply a human process, as merely the recognition by the Jews of certain books as "canonical," do not square with the evidence. For the most part, these theories are based upon a view of the dating and nature of the Old Testament writings which is not in accord with the witness of the

New Testament.[3] In addition, they do not do justice to the basic question of
the inspiration of the Biblical books. They are, therefore, to be rejected. If
we follow the evidence of the Bible, we shall maintain that the Old Testament books were truly inspired, and that their inspired character was
acknowledged by Israel from the beginning. Finally, the witness of Jesus
Christ has settled once and for all time the question of the canonicity of
these books.

V. DIVISIONS AND EXTENT OF THE CANON

There are two further questions to which some attention must be paid.
First, what were the sections into which the Old Testament was divided, and
what were the arrangements of the books within those sections? Secondly,
what was the extent of the Canon? Why were certain books, such as the
book of Jashar and the Apocryphal books, excluded? These latter questions
will lead us to consider in greater detail than hitherto the question, what
was the determining principle in the formation of the Old Testament Canon?

Attestation of the Threefold Division

In Luke 24:44 Christ divided the Old Testament into three parts, the
Law of Moses, the Prophets and the Psalms. The Hebrew Bible today, as is
well known, also consists of three divisions, the Law, the Prophets and the
Writings. By the Law of Moses, Christ of course had in mind the five books
known as the Pentateuch, and the division known as the "Prophets" would
have included the historical books and those of the great writing prophets.
Does the order of books in the Hebrew Bible, however, represent the arrangement with which Christ was familiar?

In his writing Contra Apionem (I:8) Josephus states that the number of
the books which the Jews receive is 22, and these he distinguishes from other
books. Josephus enumerates five books of Moses, thirteen prophetical books,
and finally, four books of hymns to God and precepts for the conduct of
human life. Here again is evidence of a threefold division. Josephus probably
arrives at the number thirteen by including Ruth with Judges, and Lamentations with Jeremiah, and by counting the twelve minor prophets as one book.

Of importance also is the witness found in the De vita contemplativa of
Philo (around 40 A.D.) wherein reference is made to a threefold division. We
may note particularly the Prologue to Ecclesiasticus (after 117 B.C.) in which
three times mention is made of the Law and the Prophets (or prophecies) and
"the others which follow after them," (the masculine tōn prophētōn
refers to the authors) or "the other paternal books" and "the remainder of
the books." The threefold division is thus attested as early as the Prologue

[3] Arguments which have exposed the weaknesses of the views of Scripture which
negative criticism has advanced have been presented many times. The reader may
consult Oswald T. Allis's The Five Books of Moses (Philadelphia, 1943).

of Ecclesiasticus. Inasmuch as the writer of the Prologue states that his grandfather (i.e., the author of Ecclesiasticus, Jesus ben Sirach, around 190 B.C.) gave himself largely to the reading of "the law and the prophets and the other books of the fathers," we may assume that this threefold division was as old as the beginning of the second century B.C.

Is it, however, possible to determine what books constituted the second and third divisions of the Old Testament Canon? Among recent expositors the view has been rather prevalent that the order of books in the Hebrew Bible is original, and that this order was later changed in accordance with that of Alexandria. This popular view has recently been subjected to searching criticism by Peter Katz ("The Old Testament Canon in Palestine and Alexandria" in *Zeitschrift fur die neutestamentliche Wissenschaft,* 47th Vol., 1956, pp. 191–217). He maintains that the reconstitution of Judaism after the temple's destruction is the earliest attestation of the Hebrew selection of books. As evidence that the present Hebrew order is not original, he claims that the order Ezra, Nehemiah, Chronicles is artificial, and that evidence for the number 24 as comprising the totality of the Old Testament books is scanty. The number 22, rather, is original. This number is of Palestinian origin. In a footnote Katz quotes from a special communication which he received from Otto Eissfeldt in which Eissfeldt says "In the tradition represented equally by *G* and by the Qumran texts there has survived a type of Canon which, considered as the outcome of a stage of development antecedent to the verdict of Jamnia, is less rigid than the other and accordingly does not display one form, but several; in the way that the *G*-MSS display manifold discrepancies both in the number of the O.T. books which they contain and in the arrangement of them, thereby undoubtedly continuing an older Jewish tradition."

Governing Principle which Underlies the Threefold Division

It is apposite to ask whether any basic principle underlay the arrangement of the books in a threefold division. The answer to this question, we believe, must be determined from the Bible itself. The first division consists of books written by Moses. In the Old Testament economy Moses occupied the place of pre-eminence as the faithful servant of the Lord (cf. Num. 12:1–7). In the Epistle to the Hebrews, Moses is faithful in God's economy as a servant, but Christ as a Son. It was therefore, above all else, the position which he occupied in the theocracy which distinguished Moses. The books in the first section are Mosaic. They are *the* Law, the foundation upon which the entire Old Testament economy was based.

The books in the second division are designated by the Jews as "the Prophets." All the evidence would support the accuracy of this designation. The prophets were important men in the Old Testament economy, but they were under Moses. It was right that their writings should be separated from those of Moses. The determining factor in distinguishing between the first and the second divisions of the Old Testament Canon, therefore, was the position which the writers occupied in the economy.

What may be said about the books which belong to the third division? If the writers of these books were also prophets (i.e., in the technical sense, as were the writers of the books in the second division) it is indeed strange that a third division should be added. We may then well ask what position in the theocracy or economy was held by the writers of the books in the third section.

It goes without saying that these writers were acknowledged to be inspired men. But were they prophets? Surely it would be difficult to show that Solomon and David occupied the status of a prophet. The book of Daniel may assist us in providing an answer to this question. In ancient Israel a prophet served as a mediator between God and the nation, representing God as a spokesman to the people (cf. Deut. 18:15–18; Exod. 4:16; 7:1). It is clear that this was not the position which Daniel occupied. His training rather (cf. Daniel 1) prepared him for service as a statesman at a heathen court, and as such he served throughout his life. While he possessed the prophetic gift (his very book is a prophecy), he did not occupy the technical status of a prophet in Israel. It is true that in some lists Daniel was included among the prophets, but that in no way militates against the above consideration. A right view of the book of Daniel finally prevailed, and the book stands in our Hebrew Bible where it rightly belongs, namely, in the third division. Books in the third division, it would seem, belong there because they were written by men who were inspired but who were not prophets in the technical sense of the word.

Disputed Books

It is true that in ancient Judaism questions were raised about the canonicity of certain books. According to statements in the Talmud we learn that the canonical books were said "to defile the hands." This phrase was employed to designate canonical books, although the reason why they were so designated is not clear. Zeitlin may be right when he regards it as a measure directed against the priests so that they could not offer the Terumah (oblation) (Zeitlin, *An Historical Study of the Canonization of the Hebrew Scriptures,* 1933, p. 19).

Differences of opinion were held with respect to Ecclesiastes. Rabbi Judah declared that it did not defile the hands (i.e., was not canonical), whereas others held that there was a difference of opinion. In the Tannaitic literature, however, there is apparently no express statement that Ecclesiastes defiles the hands. Zeitlin asserts that at a gathering in the house of Hananiah ben Hezekiah a few years before the destruction of the temple (70 A.D.), the adherents of Hillel maintained that Ecclesiastes was canonical whereas the Shammaites took the opposite position, and apparently won out.

There are also statements in the Talmud that Esther does not defile the hands. Rabbi Jehuda (Megilla 7a) said that it did not defile the hands. Zeitlin thinks that when the Jews wanted to prove that Purim was a day of rejoicing they inferred that fact from Megillat Taanit,[4] which would not have been necessary had Esther been recognized as canonical.

While there may have been difference of opinion with respect to the Song of Solomon, no explicit statement is preserved that it does not defile the hands.

There is some question, of course, as to the significance of these discussions. They appear to have been merely academic, a view that is supported by Zeitlin's claim that popular demand led to the canonization of Esther. It may be that such discussions had little to do with the practical usage of religious life.

The Apocryphal Books

Why were the books known as Apocryphal not recognized as canonical? (Cf. William Henry Green, *General Introduction to the Old Testament, The Canon.* At this point I follow Green's discussion.) The answer must be that these books were not regarded as divinely inspired.[5] This statement, however, involves certain questions. How can one tell that a book is inspired? Is it always possible to discover a book's quality of inspiration? Wherein, one may ask, may it be discerned that the book of Esther or the Song of Solomon was inspired? The answer to these questions is not easy. Had the book of Esther appeared, for example, in a different cultural milieu, would it have been recognized as God's Word? Probably all that can be said by way of answer is that in his providence God brought it about that this particular book was produced in the midst of his people and became intimately associated with their religious life where they would accept it as canonical.

With the Apocryphal books, however, the case was different. There are no marks in these books which would attest a divine origin. As Green has pointed out, both Judith and Tobit contain historical, chronological and geographical errors. The books justify falsehood and deception and make salvation to depend upon works of merit. Almsgiving, for example, is said to deliver from death (Tobit 12:9; 4:10; 14:10, 11).

Judith lives a life of falsehood and deception in which she is represented as assisted by God (9:10, 13). Ecclesiasticus and the Wisdom of Solomon inculcate a morality based upon expediency. Wisdom teaches the creation

---

[4] Megillat Taanit (Scroll of Fasts) is an Aramaic document from the Roman period which lists days on which fasting was forbidden. See Zeitlin, *Megillat Taanit, as a Source for Jewish Chronology and History in the Hellenistic and Roman Period.*
[5] For an up-to-date discussion of the Apocrypha cf. Bruce Metzger's *An Introduction to the Apocrypha* (New York, 1957). Metzger discusses I-II Esdras, Tobit, Judith, Additions to Esther, The Wisdom of Solomon, Ecclesiasticus, Baruch, The Letter of Jeremiah, The Prayer of Azariah and the Song of the Three Young Men, Susanna, Bel and the Dragon, The Prayer of Manasseh and I-II Maccabees.

of the world out of pre-existent matter (11:17). Ecclesiasticus teaches that
the giving of alms makes atonement for sin (3:30). In Baruch it is said that
God hears the prayers of the dead (3:4), and in I Maccabees there are
historical and geographical errors. This is not to deny many fine and com-
mendable things in the Apocrypha, but the books nonetheless show themselves at points to be at variance with divinely revealed truth. They were
consequently never adopted by the Jews as canonical.

Attempts have been made, of course, to discover some other criterion
which would have guided the Jews in accepting or rejecting books as canonical. It has been claimed that in order to give the post-exilic temple the
advantages of the former one, the national literature of the Hebrews was
collected, and so the Canon was formed. But if this were the case, why were
books such as the book of Jashar omitted? Nor was language the determining
criterion. Nor can it be claimed that the canonical books were chosen because
they represent the religion of Israel in its greatest purity. Who was to decide
the answer to this question? Nor was agreement with the Pentateuch the
necessary criterion. Surely the canonical books do agree with the Pentateuch,
but may not such a work as the *Words of Nathan the Prophet* (II Chron.
9:29) have done the same? Was it the intrinsic worth of the books? Why,
then, did the Jews omit certain books? Was it because the books taught
Christ? Was it because their authors were prophets? If so, why was *The
Visions of Jedo the Seer* excluded? Or, was it, as Koole has suggested,
because the canonical books speak of a covenant between God and man (J.
L. Koole, *Het Probleem Van De Canonisatie van Het Oude Testament,*
Kampen, 1955, p. 21)?

To these and other proposed criteria we must reply with a negative. The
canonical books of the Old Testament were divinely revealed and their
authors were holy men who spoke as they were borne of the Holy Ghost. In
his good providence God brought it about that his people should recognize
and receive his Word. How he planted this conviction in their hearts with
respect to the identity of his Word we may not be able fully to understand
or explain. We may, however, follow our Lord, who placed the *imprimatur*
of his infallible authority upon the books of the Old Testament.

THE APOCRYPHA

G. Douglas Young

G. Douglas Young was born in Korea. He holds the B.Sc. degree from Acadia University, the B.D. and S.T.M. from Faith Theological Seminary and the Ph.D. from Dropsie College for Hebrew and Cognate Learning. Professor of Old Testament and Dean of Trinity Seminary of the Evangelical Free Church of America in Chicago, he has written A Grammar of the Hebrew Language *and* Ugaritic Concordance. *He is Director of the newly-formed Israel-American Institute of Biblical Studies.*

11. G. Douglas Young

THE APOCRYPHA

THE TERM apocrypha means different things to different groups. In this chapter it refers, as in the common non-Roman Catholic use, to 14 or 15 specific documents from antiquity. These were composed during the last two centuries before Christ and in the first century afterwards. Since the most easily accessible English edition of these books is the Revised Standard Version (1957), we shall list the titles as given in that volume:

1. The First Book of Esdras
2. The Second Book of Esdras
3. Tobit
4. Judith
5. The Additions to the book of Esther
6. The Wisdom of Solomon
7. Ecclesiasticus, or The Wisdom of Jesus the Son of Sirach
8. Baruch
9. The letter of Jeremiah (The letter of Jeremiah is in some editions incorporated into the book of Baruch as the last chapter)
10. The Prayer of Azariah and the Song of the Three Young Men
11. Susanna
12. Bel and the Dragon
13. The Prayer of Manasseh
14. The First Book of the Maccabees
15. The Second Book of the Maccabees

I. THE PROBLEM STATED

Since 1546 the Roman Catholic Church has considered certain of these books to be inspired and on a par with the Old Testament. These are, specifically, Tobit, Judith, Wisdom, Ecclesiasticus, Baruch, I and II Maccabees, and some supplements to Esther and Daniel. Inasmuch as no religious

group considers any of the other books to be a part of their Bible, consideration is here given specifically to these. Our main problem is whether these
additions in the Roman Catholic Bible should be honored as Scripture, or
whether they should be omitted in conformity with Protestant conviction.

A volume of literature about two-thirds the size of the New Testament is
involved in this discussion. The usefulness of these volumes is not in debate.
Much has been written about their relative value and reference will be made
to it at the end of this chapter. But the primary consideration here is the
question whether these writings deserve a place in the "Canon" or not. This
forces us to consider the attitude of the Church and of Judaism to these
books, both in antiquity and through the centuries. To this problem we shall
address ourselves first from the negative point of view, and then from positive considerations.

Negative Value of Internal Evidence

Considerations of internal evidence are doubtless interesting and valuable.
One writer says: "Certainly a book that contains what is false in fact,
erroneous in doctrine or unsound in morality, is unworthy of God and cannot
have been inspired by Him. Tried under these criteria the Apocryphal books
stand self-condemned" (Merrill F. Unger, *Introductory Guide to the Old
Testament*, p. 109). Another writer observes:

> The most cogent proof that these books are intrinsically on a dif-
> ferent plane from the books of the New Testament is afforded
> merely by reading them side by side with the books of the New
> Testament and allowing each to make its own impression. Then, in
> the words of M. R. James, "it will very quickly be seen that there is
> no question of anyone's having excluded them from the New Testa-
> ment: they have done that for themselves" (Bruce M. Metzger, *An
> Introduction to the Apocrypha*, pp. 172, 262).

But all writers qualify their objections in their survey of internal evidence.
For example, the Book of I Maccabees is quite generally recognized to be on
a different order of accuracy from such a book as Judith, or even II Maccabees. Historically and theologically some of these books are inestimably
superior to others. But if internal evidence is to be the exclusive criterion
for the reception or rejection of a book as Scripture, one must ask whether,
judged by this standard alone, the inclusion of such books as Esther or
Ecclesiastes in the Scriptures can be justified. But we neither accept nor
reject the Apocryphal volumes from the Bible simply because of internal
evidence, whether of doctrine or type of literature.

Negative Value of Internal Order or Language of Composition

Two other indecisive criteria for the rejection of these books are illustrated
by the case of I Esdras. This Greek book covers the same general material
as is found in Chronicles-Ezra-Nehemiah. It differs in the order of the stories

and in some other particulars. Some scholars suggest that this book was rejected because the Hebrew form of these stories was long known and believed to be purer in form. This circumstance would give priority to books written in Hebrew and more familiar in order of content. It is possible, some scholars point out, that such books as Tobit and Judith existed only in the Greek language at the time when the Hebrew Canon was fixed. The additions to Esther are found only in Greek. That is the case with Wisdom. It is assumed, therefore, that a book had to be composed in the Hebrew language to be in the Canon. But this is a poor criterion to apply to the Apocryphal books inasmuch as the language of the original composition of many of them is unknown. It is a poor criterion for another reason. Some of the Apocryphal books were definitely composed in Hebrew. Notable among these is the book of Ecclesiasticus. This book was rejected despite its composition in Hebrew. Thus the value of the argument from original language is very limited, if not altogether valueless. The argument concerning the purity of the form of the stories is purely an appeal to tradition and gives little objective basis for the reception or rejection of a particular book. Neither the criterion of the language of composition nor of familiarity of order serves as an adequate basis for accepting or rejecting the canonical status of a given document.

Time of Composition Important

Jewish authorities put forward another reason for rejecting a book. To merit a place in the collection of canonical literature a given volume had to be written within what they called the "prophetic period." They understood this period to be between the time of Moses and Artaxerxes. This would rule out, automatically, such volumes as I and II Maccabees which were composed considerably after that time.

In summary, then, the Jewish and general reasons for rejecting the non-canonical volumes have included: (1) content which might be either historically or theologically unacceptable, or not in accepted order; (2) language of composition other than Hebrew; (3) time of composition later than Artaxerxes.

II. HEBREW AND GREEK CANONS

The number of books in the Hebrew Old Testament is 24 by the Hebrew method of counting (though sometimes condensed to 22, the same titles are included). This is exactly equivalent to the 39 books of our English Old Testament. The Septuagint version, the pre-Christian translation of the Hebrew Old Testament into Greek, contains 14 additional books or parts of books. These are the Apocrypha. Thus there appear to be two canons, the Hebrew or shorter one, and the longer so-called "Greek Canon." The first is Palestinian and the second Alexandrian. Some have erroneously believed that there were two separate canons and that today we may choose between them. Others assume that the original was a longer canon and that by the first century of the Christian era the extra books were rejected from the Hebrew Canon and that we should therefore accept the longer one today.

The attitude of the early Christian Church toward the Apocrypha deserves special notice. W. O. E. Oesterley (*An Introduction to the Books of the Apocrypha,* pp. 125–130) sums up the view of some scholars as follows: "There can be no doubt that during the first two centuries all the books of the Greek Canon were regarded as Scripture." Thus we are driven to such questions as: What was the original Hebrew Canon? What was the Hebrew Canon at the time of Christ? What Canon did Christ accept?

III. REASONS ALLEGED FOR INCLUDING THE APOCRYPHA

It is alleged that some New Testament books reflect the thought of the Apocrypha, and even quote them, and that these Biblical writers therefore considered the Apocrypha on a par with the Old Testament Scriptures. It is asserted that the New Testament writers took their quotations of the Old Testament from the Greek translation, the Septuagint, rather than from the Hebrew. Since the scrolls of the Apocrypha were mixed together from the earliest times with the scrolls of the Septuagint, this New Testament use of the Septuagint is alleged to sanction the other books preserved alongside the scriptural writings in the Septuagint collection. Thus it is contended that the writers of the New Testament considered the Apocrypha as Scripture.

It is alleged, moreover, that in the earliest post-Biblical Christian literature some Apocryphal books were definitely quoted as Scripture by leaders of the Church, and these leaders used them in public worship services just as they used the canonical books.

It is alleged, furthermore, that the early Church, as represented by such Church Fathers as Irenaeus, Tertullian, Clement of Alexandria, and Origen, accepted all the books of the Apocrypha as Scripture. Origen quotes from almost every book of the Apocrypha. Additional proof of this ecclesiastical reverence assertedly is supplied by catacomb scenes which picture episodes from many of these books.

It is usually alleged also that the "change of attitude" in the Christian Church during the fourth century certifies the earlier acceptance of these books.

It is alleged that these books belong in the Canon on the basis of the fact that the great Biblical manuscripts (Codex Vaticanus, Codex Alexandrinus and Codex Sinaiticus) interspersed the books of the Apocrypha between the books of the Hebrew Canon. For example, Codex B contains all but I and II Maccabees. The other manuscripts, while incomplete, contain some Apocryphal books. Thus the Church which made and preserved these manuscripts assertedly considered them worthy of a place in the Canon.

It is alleged that the attitude of the Syriac Church shows that it accepted these books. The original Peshitta Old Testament, translated from the Hebrew into Syriac in the second century A.D., did not contain the Apocryphal books. But the Syriac Apocrypha was added in the fourth century.)

The Greek (Eastern) Church reverted to the alleged attitude of the early Church in accepting all the books of the Apocrypha. |

[The attitude of the churches in later times may be summarized briefly. After 1672 most of the books absent from the Hebrew Canon were not accepted by the Eastern Church. The Eastern Church accepted only Tobit, Judith, Ecclesiasticus and Wisdom. The Western Church continued to accept the Apocryphal books, but many notable leaders rejected some or all of them. In 1546, at the Council of Trent, the Roman Catholic Church accepted all of the books listed above as Apocryphal except II Esdras and the Prayer of Manasses. These two were kept in the New Testament as an appendix, to be read for edification, but not as Scripture. Not all in the Roman Catholic Church accepted the conclusion of the Council of Trent. The Protestant churches followed the Hebrew Canon, which did not include the Apocryphal books. While rejecting these books, and not considering them as Scripture, some within the Protestant churches continued to refer to them as books of considerable value in certain areas.]

We shall have to investigate the validity of the foregoing arguments. Then we must consider whether some better basis exists for determining the canonicity of the books of the Old Testament, or whether we rest our case for acceptance only of those books found in our present Old Testament, and for the rejection of all the Apocrypha, on considerations of the kind already adduced.

Let us first look at some of the particular allegations professing to find a precedent in the practice of various branches of Christendom for the inclusion of these books.

New Testament Use of Apocrypha

Does the New Testament quote the Apocrypha? The answer is a categorical no. There is not a single quotation from any of the 14 or 15 books. No doubt the New Testament writers knew of the existence of these books. Not in a single instance, however, is one of them quoted, either as inspired Scripture, or as authority, or in any way. Not in a single case is one of them quoted in any way for any purpose. Professor C. C. Torrey, who, in his *The Apocryphal Literature,* lists a very large number of alleged Apocryphal quotations or allusions, is forced to admit of the New Testament that "in general, the Apocryphal Scriptures were left unnoticed" (p. 18). The alleged quotations are from books outside of those under consideration here, the Apocrypha. An example is the quotation of Enoch in Jude. All that can be said is that the New Testament authors have some acquaintanceship with earlier written materials, to which at most they allude indirectly, or with facts which eventually appear in both Biblical and non-Biblical documents.

Concerning New Testament quotation of the Old by way of the Septuagint, which is considered significant because of the fact that the Septuagint preserved the Apocryphal books, it need only be observed that from this source the writers never quote any but a strictly Biblical book. The fact that the collection of books preserved in Alexandria also contained extra-Biblical books does not necessarily mean that those who preserved them considered all of the books preserved as on the same plane, that is, as Scripture. It merely indicates that they chose to preserve the specified number of books. Before we could conclude that because they are listed together they are all intended to be received as Scripture, we would need such additional information from the pens of those who preserved these books. This information is lacking.

Use of the Apocrypha by the Fathers and the Early Church

The contention that the early Fathers regarded the Apocrypha as Scripture and quoted them this way also is unconvincing. Use by post-Biblical writers does not *per se* indicate that they considered the books on a par with what they held as Scripture. All through the period, Church Fathers may be found who surely did not hold that view (Unger, *op. cit.,* pp. 101–107, contains a summary of this evidence). And it may be questioned whether other Fathers who allegedly held the view actually did so. For example, Augustine is asserted to have regarded these books as Scripture. While the influence of Augustine predominated at the Council of Carthage, and the Council of Carthage included in their Canon all the books that the Roman Catholic Church considers as canonical, including the Apocrypha, it remains true that, in writing on the books of Judith, Augustine said this book was not in the Canon as the Jews received it. On another occasion, when an appeal was made to a passage in II Maccabees to settle an argument, Augustine said that those making the appeal were in a bad way to have to resort to a book not in the same category as those received and accepted by the Jews. The testimony of Augustine, then, like that of Jerome, is clear. It is against the inclusion of the Apocryphal books as Scripture.

Certain writers in the fourth century who did not recognize the books of the Apocrypha as canonical cited them nonetheless by the same formulas used when citing from canonical books (see Oesterley, *op. cit.,* p. 126). Thus the force of the argument which relies on the formula of citation is greatly weakened. The formula does not necessarily imply that the one making the quotation regarded what he was quoting as Scripture. One and the same formula was employed for quoting both scriptural and non-scriptural works, without any implication that both are of equal authority.

Even from the first, in fact, some in the Eastern Church did not recognize these books as canonical. The Western Church was much more unanimous in its acceptance of them as Scripture, but important exceptions must not be overlooked: Hilary of Poictiers, Rufinus and Jerome. Jerome accepted only the books in the Hebrew Canon as *libri canonici.* The excluded Apocryphal books, not found in the Hebrew Canon, he accepted as merely *libri ecclesiastici.* The first were canonical, the others held ecclesiastical value only.

In the Thirty-Ninth letter Athanasius discusses the "particular books and their number, which are accepted by the Church." In paragraph 4, he says, "There are, then, of the Old Testament, twenty-two books in number"; and he enumerates only the books in our Bible, in almost exactly the same order as in our present English Bible. In paragraph 4, also, he enumerates the books of the New Testament: these are identical with those now found in our Bible. In paragraphs 6 and 7, he clearly states his attitude on the extra-Biblical books. These are not "included in the Canon" but merely "appointed to be read."

The catalogues of Old Testament books and the evidence of the first four centuries of the Christian era seem quite generally to agree. They favor the Canon as received by the Jews. For example, the oldest catalogue of canonical books of the Old Testament now available is that of Melito, Bishop of Sardis about 170 A.D. His Canon does not contain any of the Apocryphal books. Origen, who died in the middle of the third century, had a catalogue of 22 books only (cf. his *Ecclesiastical History,* 1:25). The testimony of Athanasius we have already noted.

The testimony of the Western or Latin Church is substantially the same as in the Greek or Eastern Church. The early Fathers followed the Hebrew Canon closely. Tertullian, in the early third century, lists 24 books as being canonical. Hilary of Poictiers in France, fourth century, and Rufinus of Italy, early fifth century, listed 22 books in their Old Testament. The testimony of Jerome in the early fifth century is clear. He rejected the Apocryphal books in forthright language. He has only 22 books in his Canon. We have already noted the testimony of Augustine from the same century.

The Great Manuscripts and the Apocrypha

The presence of the Apocryphal books in the great manuscripts preserved by the Christian Church is alleged to argue for their scriptural status. Until actual citations from the writers themselves definitely establish this claim, we can only say that they considered both Scripture and the extra books worthy of preservation. Because they chose to preserve both does not *per se* mean that they considered all the books on an equal plane.

Summary

The plain fact of the matter is that too many arguments for the inclusion of the Apocrypha as Scripture rest on silence. We do not really know why these books were preserved in the Greek Canon. Was it because they actually thought them to be Scripture, or merely because they considered the books to have value for the Church, and so in their library of good books they chose to preserve these works along with Scripture? In any case, the earliest existing manuscripts of the Septuagint are not older than the fourth century A.D. This is 600 years after the translation of the Septuagint. During this 500 to 600 years the Apocryphal books gradually crept into the collection of books preserved by the Christian Church. They were never admitted into any canon of the Jewish community. This is true both in Palestine and in Alexandria. In attestation of this fact we have the witness of not only Josephus but also Philo. Nor is there any evidence to show that they were in the "Canon" of the Church. There simply is no evidence that in the time of Christ, or earlier, both a long and a short canon existed in either Jewish or Christian circles. If there were such competitive canons, is it not quite incredible that no related controversy arose in ecclesiastical circles?

IV. BASIS FOR REJECTING THE APOCRYPHA

If the usual reasons for accepting or rejecting the Apocryphal books may not be relied upon, on what basis may we determine whether a given book belongs to the Canon? If it is sometimes difficult to discover whether a book originated in the Hebrew language, if problems are raised by considering extraneous material in the books, if the alleged New Testament use of these books is not decisive, if the use made of them by early post-Biblical writers and the Church Fathers is inconclusive, and if their presence in certain collections of sacred writings is not conclusive, how may we know what books are Scripture and what books are not?

Here we are concerned only with the books which may or may not have been dropped from the Old Testament. We are not concerned with New Testament Apocryphal or pseudepigraphic books, since all who wish to include the extra books wish to include them in the Old Testament. Thus we may limit our search to reasons for excluding a book from the Canon at the end of Old Testament times, that is, before the New Testament Canon grew up.

A Jewish Condition—"Prophetical Period"

The Jewish authorities had one primary condition of canonicity, doubt-less among others. The book must have been written within what they con-sidered the "Prophetical Period," that is, between the time of Moses and Artaxerxes. This is clear, for example, in the statement of Josephus (*Contra Apionem*, 1, 38–42):

> For we have not an innumerable multitude of books among us, disagreeing from and contradicting one another, (as the Greeks have,) but only twenty-two books, which contain the records of all the past times which are justly believed in. Of them five belong to Moses, which contain his laws and the traditions of the origin of mankind till his death. This interval of time was little short of three thousand years. But as to the time from the death of Moses till the reign of Artaxerxes king of Persia, who reigned after Xerxes, the

prophets, who were after Moses, wrote down what was done in their times in thirteen books. The remaining books contain hymns to God, and precepts for the conduct of human life. It is true, our history hath been written since Artaxerxes very particularly, but hath not been esteemed of the like authority with the former by our fore-fathers, because there hath not been an exact succession of prophets since that time. And how firmly we have given credit to these books of our own nation is evident by what we do; for during so many ages as have already passed, no one has been so bold as either to add anything to them, to take anything from them, or to make any change in them; but it is become natural to all Jews immediately and from their very birth, to esteem these books to contain Divine doctrines, and to persist in them, and, if occasion be, willingly die for them.

Oesterley in *An Introduction to the Books of the Old Testament* (p. 3) refers to this criterion. He states:

> According to Josephus' belief . . . the canonicity of a book depended upon whether it had been written within a clearly defined period. . . . The artificiality of this test is shown by the fact that, as Ryle has pointed out, "the mention of this particular limit seems to be made expressly with reference to the book of Esther, in which alone the Artaxerxes of Josephus (the Ahasuerus of the Hebrew book of Esther) figures."

This is not a valid criticism of the evidence of Josephus on the Canon. Josephus does not use this time range as a test of canonicity as Oesterley here, and some other scholars elsewhere, imply. It may only be inferred from Josephus that, whatever the tests were, they had to apply within this stipu-lated period of history.

Metzger (*op. cit.,* p. 8) does not refer to this particular evidence. But he does state:

> The Hebrew canon had been approved by long and approved usage of the books, and the Assembly of Jamnia (A.D. 90) merely ratified what the most spiritually sensitive souls in Judaism had been accustomed to regard as holy Scripture. . . . The standards of judgment which led to the approval of some books and the rejec-tion of others are unknown to us today. At a later date the theory was elaborated by the Rabbis that inspiration belonged to the prophetic office, which began with Moses and ended in the time of Alexander the Great. Therefore books which were obviously of later origin could not be regarded as canonical.

Metzger rejects this particular criterion as invalid when he says "The fact that this theory does not fit all of the cases (for example, the present form of the Book of Daniel appears to be later than Ecclesiasticus) does not mean that in general most Jews would not have felt its force. From all that is known or can be inferred, the process of canonization was complex and subtle" (p. 9). [For a refutation of the allegation that certain Old Testa-

ment books were written later than the time of Artaxerxes about 400 B.C.,
see the special introduction sections of such a work as E. J. Young's *An
Introduction to the Old Testament* (Eerdmans, 1949). There is no incontrovertible evidence to prove that any book necessarily comes from a period
later than Artaxerxes.]

Importance of the Jewish Canon

Thus the collection of books in the Jewish Canon grew up gradually over
the period of years during which they were being composed. But all Jews
accepted only 24 books, our 39, as Scripture. Those 24 books include none of
the Apocryphal books. This was the Canon of the Jews at the time of Christ,
the Canon which he accepted, the Canon of the Christian Church. The crux
of this argument is that these books in the Hebrew Canon, 24 in number,
were considered a closed Canon by the end of the prophetic era 400 B.C. by
all Jews, including Alexandrian Jews. This point is in debate between liberal
and evangelical authors. Referring to the extra books preserved by the
Christians in Alexandria, Metzger notes: "It is extremely difficult, therefore,
to believe that the Alexandrian Jews received these books as authoritative in
the same sense as they received the Law and the Prophets" (*op. cit.*, p. 177).

This tradition about their Canon did exist in this form among the Jews in
ancient times. It is a matter of historical evidence. One may not like this
conviction, held by the Jews of Josephus' day (just after Christ), but one
cannot deny its existence. We do not know why certain books were received
by the Jews and others rejected. From Josephus' statement and from others,
it is clear, however, that they knew which ones were received and which
were not. This is the significant and only historical basis upon which a conclusion can be reached. We have seen that all other alleged criteria are inconclusive. There is, however, no question as to the number of books received
by the Jews in the time of Josephus (just after the death of Christ) and the
earliest catalogue of the books by name gives us a list identical in number
with the number given by Josephus and Philo.

Hebrew Threefold Grouping

There is another important consideration. From very early times, at least
as early as the time of the prologue to Ecclesiasticus, the books of the Old
Testament were referred to in a threefold way: the Law; the Prophets; and
a third group variously described as Psalms, writings, the rest of the books,
and perhaps in other ways as well. There were, thus, exactly designated
groups, first Law, second Prophets, and third a miscellaneous collection
(although not all the particular books were rigidly classified into the second
or third group). The prologue to Ecclesiasticus in the second century B.C.
refers to the Old Testament in this way. Josephus and Philo refer to the
books in this manner, and Jesus Christ also in Luke 24:44: "These are the
words which I spake unto you, while I was yet with you, that all things must

be fulfilled, that were written in the law of Moses, and in the prophets, and in the Psalms concerning me." In the third group, Jesus mentions only one book, the Psalms. Probably the reason for singling out this one is that it was the best known book of the third division, and that it contained more material relevant to himself than others in the group. As Edward J. Young observes "This was the Christological book par excellence of the third division of the Old Testament canon. In other places Christ referred to other Messianic and prophetic materials" (*op. cit.,* p. 37).

No reason exists for believing that the collection of books thus referred to by Christ and considered as Scripture by him differed in any particular from the collection of the Jews. There is no evidence of any dispute between him and the Jews on this point. Christ opposed the Pharisees, not over the identity of the canonical books but because their oral tradition made the Canon void. The statements of Josephus and Philo make it clear that they also recognized this threefold distinction. By comparing Josephus and the later Talmud and other sources, such as Melito the Bishop of Sardis (170 A.D.), we may learn the names of all the books of the three groups in the Jewish Canon of the day of Christ. These are 24 in number, the same books numbering 39 in our Old Testament Canon.

Reasons for Origin of Threefold Grouping Not Relevant

The historic existence of this threefold grouping of Old Testament books is therefore obvious. The explanations of how it came into existence are both interesting and important. This importance springs in part from the fact that the threefold division is often interpreted in a manner that diverts attention from the principal test of canonicity to secondary considerations. Some say that this threefold division represents three degrees of inspiration. Others, while making no distinction in the level of inspiration, hold that the authors of the third group had the gift of prophecy whereas the second group were men who had the prophetic office as official prophets. Both explanations are purely philosophical. They rest on no objective foundation. They are of no value in helping us to answer the question why certain books belong in the Canon and others do not. Who, today, is going to be able to distinguish between the Holy Spirit and the "Spirit of prophecy," especially when historical books are found in both the second and third groups, and when prophetic books are found in both groups, and when certain books such as Ruth and Lamentations are found sometimes in one group and sometimes in the other, and, finally, when the early threefold groupings do not agree as to the exact content of any but the first group?

These same objections apply to a widely accepted evangelical assumption that the division is determined by the official position or status of the writers: those by Moses, then those by persons having the prophetic office, and finally those having the prophetic gift or the gift of prophecy. If this is our criterion for accepting a given book as canonical, we have no objective basis for canonicity. The simple consideration that some books are written by un-known authors indicates this. How do we know, when the author is un-named, whether he had the prophetic office or just a gift of prophecy? If we answer by stating that his writing is found in the second or third grouping, then we do not rise above circular reasoning.

Another hypothesis for the existence of these three groups is that they are due to different stages or time-periods of canonization. Exponents of this view state that the first five books were canonized between the seventh and fourth centuries B.C., the Prophets or second group sometime before 250 B.C., the final group sometime before the beginning of the Christian era but after 100 B.C., and that all finally received their ratification with the completed Canon at the Council of Jamnia in 90 A.D. This is purely an hypothesis, how-ever. No historical evidence exists that such a threefold collecting took place. Nothing in the historical references to the Great Synagogue indicates that just five books, the Law, were received as canonical in that time. There is no evidence of any council during the time 300–200 B.C. There is no evidence that another group of persons made a third collection sometime between the time of the Maccabees and the time of Christ, or even shortly thereafter. The only evidence upon which this threefold hypothesis presumes to rest is the fact that there are three groups of writings and that there was a Great Synagogue (what it did in this regard is not known), and that finally in 90 A.D. there was a council at Jamnia. This is very tenuous support for a theory so important. Furthermore, the now accumulating evidence from Qumran indicates positively that the Dead Sea community revered alike the books of the so-called third Canon and the second. This has important implications (cf. R. L. Harris, *Inspiration and Canonicity of the Bible*, Zondervan, 1957, chapter 6).

What then is the basis for rejecting the Apocrypha and receiving only 24 books? This question cannot be answered merely from a consideration of the fact that there was a threefold grouping. Whether that threefold grouping can be explained or not is entirely immaterial in determining an answer to our question about the canonicity of these books. It may have been simply for convenience in finding the books quickly for their liturgical use, or it may be because of some particular attitude about them held by the Jews who used them, or for some other reason. The reason is not important for the problem of Canon and thus for the problem of the inclusion or exclusion of the Apocrypha.

A Matter of History

We must pick up the argument at that point where it had to be left when we digressed to explore the problem of the threefold grouping of the Old Testament books.

We do not know why certain books were received by the Jews and others rejected. We do not know why they rejected the Apocrypha. The writers and recipients, those who under God made these decisions, left us no record that elucidates for us this aspect of our total problem. We might make surmises. None of them makes it possible for us to answer our question with satisfaction. Some account for some books, others for other books, but none for all. We do know, however, what books they did receive and when they closed that collection. The Apocrypha were not in that collection.

It would be subjective for us today, in the absence of recorded evidence, to set up the criteria by which the ancients made their decisions that caused the Apocrypha to be rejected. It is a strictly objective and historical matter as to what the Hebrews did receive and what books they did not receive in their devotion to revealed religion.

A purely historical investigation of their selectivity in handling the ancient writings will prove illuminating. We may begin our consideration of this by referring to Deuteronomy 31:24–26.

"And it came to pass, when Moses had made an end of writing the words of this law in a book, until they were finished, that Moses commanded the Levites, which bare the ark of the covenant of the Lord, saying, Take this book of the law, and put it in the side of the ark of the covenant of the Lord your God, that it may be there for a witness against thee." Joshua added his words to the book of the Law; "And Joshua wrote these words in the book of the law of God, and took a great stone, and set it up there under an oak, that was by the sanctuary of the Lord"(Joshua 24:25). Samuel also added at least a part of his writings, for so it would seem from I Samuel 10:25: "Then Samuel told the people the manner of the kingdom, and wrote it in a book, and laid it up before the Lord. And Samuel sent all the people away, every man to his house."

These passages indicate that there was an immediate reception by the people of God of certain writings. The evidence is admittedly scant. It does set the pattern, however. Certain writings were so treated from the first. The writings so treated and received did not include the Apocrypha.

The available historical evidence indicates that in the Jewish mind a collection of books existed from at least 400 B.C. in three groups, two of them fluid, 22 (24 by another manner of counting) in number, which were considered by the Jews from among the many other existing books as the only ones for which they would die rather than add to or take away from them, books which they considered veritably from God. No other historical material exists pointing to any other conclusion. The subsequent historical references, admittedly few in number, yet valuable for their weight, indicate that the same threefold grouping continued to be the authoritative collection of the Jews through the time of Ecclesiasticus, through the time of Jesus, through the time of Josephus and Philo, down to the time when we receive our first listing of Old Testament books by name. That list gives us the exact number

and names of the books and it conforms to the number of books in the
Hebrew Canon and those in our English Old Testament, 39, no more and
no less. The Apocrypha are not included.

Attitude of Church Fathers Not Determinative

Thus certain other considerations are worthy of note. The attitude of the
Church Fathers is significant even if not decisive in weight. Those Fathers
who received the Apocryphal books unjustifiably departed from the tradition
of Jesus and the Jews. Those Fathers who protested and who held the books
of two orders, one canonical and the other ecclesiastical, were correct. The
attitude of the Church Fathers and eventually of the Council of Trent, while
important, does not change the fact that the Canon of the Jews, which Jesus
accepted, did not include these books.

The fact that the Apocryphal books were preserved in Alexandria and not
in Palestine is also of note, as is the presence of these Apocryphal books in
the great manuscripts of the fourth century A.D. and subsequently. While the
attitude of the Christian Church in Alexandria is of interest, it has no bearing on the question of the canonicity of the Apocryphal books because that
question was settled by the attitude of the Jews, both of Alexandria and
Palestine, which Jesus himself accepted. The testimony of Jesus and of the
Jews excludes from the category of Scripture what the early Christian
Church chose to preserve as books worthy of perpetuation. This argument
is strengthened further by the evidence concerning the New Testament use
of the Apocryphal books. Were it clear that the New Testament actually
quotes these books, or a pseudepigraphical work, the picture might be somewhat different. However, when there is no evidence that it actually quotes
any Apocryphal book, or even alludes to one, it becomes increasingly clear
that the attitude of the New Testament, as well as the attitude of Jesus and
the Jews, is the same. There was no room in the thinking of the New Testament writers for any canonical book other than the 22 (or 24) of the Hebrew
Canon.

This approach to the problem also makes unnecessary the consideration of
the language in which the original books were written, or the consideration
of whether this material or that (doctrinal content) is extraneous or not
extraneous.

Summary

In conclusion, then, the case rests wholly upon objective, historical research
into the question of what the recipients considered to be the Word of God
and what they considered to be other books of value but not Scripture. While
the evidence is scant, it is nevertheless clear. History supplies no evidence to
the contrary. Many interesting *philosophical* considerations might lead to
other conclusions, but the historical evidence is unambiguous; the conclusion
from history is that Apocrypha do not merit a place in the Scripture if we

are to limit the Scripture to those books which Jesus, the Jews, and the early Church used and approved as Scripture.

V. VALUE OF APOCRYPHA

Some reference should be made, in conclusion, to the value and usefulness of the Apocryphal books. Even though they may not be considered Scripture, the attitude of the Church, especially in the Western branch, that they have some value is, of course, correct. For this reason it is imperative that they be preserved. One need not discuss here the value of these works. That has been done excellently in the recent volume by Professor Metzger, *An Introduction to the Apocrypha.* One may merely conclude by noting the items under which he outlines the places and media in which the books of the Apocrypha left their mark: "Not only have they inspired homilies, meditations, and liturgical forms, but poets, dramatists, composers, and artists have drawn freely upon them for subject matter. Common proverbs and familiar names are derived from these books" (p. 205).

THE CANON OF
THE NEW TESTAMENT

Herman Ridderbos

Herman Ridderbos is Professor of New Testament at Kampen Seminary in The Netherlands, a post he has filled since 1942. He received the Dr. Theol. degree from Free University of Amsterdam in 1936, after pursuing undergraduate studies at Kampen. He is Chief Editor of the Gereformeerd Weekblad. Published works include The Sermon on the Mount, Paul and Jesus, When the Time had Fully Come, The Epistle of Paul to the Churches of Galatia, *and a major work,* The Coming of the Kingdom, *not yet translated from the Dutch.*

12. Herman Ridderbos

THE CANON OF
THE NEW TESTAMENT

By THE Canon of the New Testament we mean, formally speaking, the collection of 27 books that appear in our Bible beginning with Matthew and ending with Revelation. This formal use of the term corresponds with the Greek word *kanōn*, which can signify "established list," and in this sense of the term is used in connection with the books of the New Testament. However, the Greek word can mean more than just "list," and when we speak of the Canon of the New Testament we also imply a wider meaning. *Kanōn* can also mean "measure," "rule," or "norm." In this normative sense the Greek word has gained influence in the Western world, and we continue to use it in this manner, for instance, in our confessions of faith and in our confessional standards: "We receive all these books as holy and canonical in order to regulate our faith according to them, to base it upon them and to fasten it with them" (Belgic Confession, Article 5).

I. METHOD OF TREATMENT

We can conduct our study of the Canon as such from two different viewpoints. We can ask: *How* and *when* did the Church come to regard these 27 books of the New Testament as an authoritative collection of peculiar books, separated from all others? That is the question of the *history* of the Canon. The answer to this question can remain purely descriptive. But we can also ask: *Upon what grounds* has the Church accepted these books as canonical and was it warranted in doing so? That is the basic question of general introduction to the New Testament. The answer to this question in-

189

volves not only description but also judgment concerning the formation of
the Canon. It is from this latter point of view that we undertake this brief
study.

II. HISTORICAL POSITIONS CONCERNING THE CANON

The question, to what does the Canon owe its position of authority, can
by the Church be answered in only one way: It derives this from God.
For whatever comes to us with the highest authority in matters of faith
and life can only be dependent upon God himself. Authority comes, not
from below, but from above.

This is a general statement. As soon as we attempt to apply this to the
Canon of the New Testament, and to analyze it closely, we see at once the
great divergence of viewpoints concerning the Canon. In the first place,
a basic difference distinguishes Rome and the Reformation. According to
the Roman Catholic view, the Canon *viewed in itself* (*quoad se*) possesses
undoubted inherent authority. But *as it concerns us* (*quoad nos*), the
recognition of the Canon rests upon the authority of the Church. The
Church, as the supposed infallible doctrinal authority, guarantees for its
members the authority of the Canon of Scripture. It is the Church that has
established and fixed its borders. It is the Church also that stands behind
the Canon and upon which the authority rests for the faith that this Canon
is the Word of God.

The Reformation recognizes no infallible doctrinal authority in the
Church, also not in connection with the Canon. The Reformation accordingly did not make the authority of the Canon dependent upon the Church,
but primarily upon the evidences of Scripture itself and upon the internal
witness of the Holy Spirit in the hearts of the believers (*testimonium Spiritus
Sancti internum*). Calvin says in his *Institutes,* "As to the question, how
shall we be persuaded that it came from God without recurring to a decree
of the church? it is just the same as if it were asked, How shall we learn
to distinguish light from darkness, white from black, sweet from bitter?
Scripture bears upon the faith if it is clear evidence of its truth. . . ." (I,
7, 2). For the recognition of Scripture as the Word of God, the Reformation
called upon no other authority than Scripture itself.

Still, the Reformers differed in certain respects, especially with reference
to the Canon of the New Testament. For Luther the books of the New
Testament had authority according to the measure in which they spoke
clearly of Christ and of justification through faith alone ("was Christum
treibet und prediget"). Luther thus followed more or less the principle of
a "Canon in the Canon." On the one hand, in this manner he placed the
Christocentric character of the authority of Scriptures in the foreground
with great force. On the other hand, in this manner he came to a more
critical position with reference to some books of the Canon which, ac-

cording to him, did not contain the essential content of Scripture, or at best contained it partially. However, the churches of the Reformation have held more closely to the views of Calvin than those of Luther in these matters, and the 27 books of the New Testament maintained their position in the Church as holy and canonical until the days of the Enlightenment.

When rationalism gained more and more influence in the Church and faith lost ground, the authority of the Canon was quickly called into doubt and attacked. It is well known that in the years 1771–1775 Johann Salomo Semler published his large work (*Abhandlung von freier Untersuchung des Kanons*), in which he set aside the a priori of the authority of the Canon. He asserted that the value of the books of the New Testament must be investigated critically, and that the Canon rested upon human decisions which often could not withstand the test of criticism. Only such elements in the Bible, he said, which yield evidence of a true religious knowledge have authority for us. But this authority in no way rests upon the idea of their inclusion in a holy book or in a collection of sacred books. Not the Canon, not the Bible, but the religious consciousness of the enlightened man is the final judge in matters of faith and life.

In Semler's view, the element of authority is transplanted from the Canon to the religious man. The great primary principle of the Reformation, namely, that of the self-evidence of Scripture and of the witness of the Holy Ghost, was now perverted into a thoroughgoing subjectivism. Nevertheless Semler's interpretations became the starting point for later critical positions over against the Canon. Especially his thesis, that the Canon was the result of fallible ecclesiastical decisions and that it was therefore subject to free criticism, made a deep impression upon many. It is true that Semler's rationalism and subjectivism were opposed even by some critical schools, which sponsored a variety of attempts to compromise the authority and the criticism of the Canon.

In recent decades the question of the authority of the Canon has again been brought to the fore in New Testament theology. It is often said now that the authority of the Canon is to be accepted *because* and *in so far as* God speaks to us in the books of the Canon. But in this very criterion "in so far as" lies the difficulty of the problem and the danger of subjectivism. Some wish to return to the essential content of the Gospel as the "Canon in the Canon." They search for an incontestable objective measure within Scripture. Others protest that this is a too static interpretation of the Canon. God speaks—so they say—now here, and then again there, in Scripture. It is the preaching, the *kerygma,* they say, in which Scripture again and again shows itself as Canon. This actualistic concept of the Canon is interpreted by others in a still more subjectivistic manner: Canon is only that which *here and now* (*hic et nunc*) signifies the Word of .God *for me.* For one like Ernst Käsemann, for instance, the Canon, as it lies before us, is not the Word of God nor identical with the gospel, but it is God's Word only in so far as it becomes gospel. The question, what then is the gospel, cannot be decided through exposition of Scripture, but only through the believer who "puts his ear to Scripture to listen" and is convinced by the Spirit (cf. Käsemann, *Evangelische Theologie,* 1951–52, p. 21).

It is clear that on this approach the Canon of the New Testament as a closed collection of 27 books becomes a very problematical matter. Can we still hold fast to the creed of the Reformation: We accept all these books as holy and canonical? What basis remains for the Church to believe that God not only wishes to use the books of the Bible as a medium in which he speaks to us through the Holy Spirit, but that he wishes also to bind the Church to the Canon of the New Testament? Can we continue to call upon the self-evidence of Scripture? Or are additional considerations to be gathered out of Scripture itself whereby the place and significance of the Canon of the New Testament come to stand more plainly before us in the plan of God's salvation? In the measure in which we lay emphasis upon the objectivity of the Canon upon Scripture as absolute authority, this question will have our attention.

III. NEW TESTAMENT PRINCIPLES

For a clearer insight into the meaning of the Canon of the New Testament it is of great importance to notice that the foundation for this Canon lies in the history of redemption itself, i.e., in what God has done in the coming and the redeeming work of Jesus Christ. In other words, the significance of the Canon, as a distinctive and authoritative report of what happened "when the time had fully come" and as an objective and fixed norm for faith and life, is given in the New Testament history of redemption itself. While this thought may not be new in itself, recent studies, especially of such concepts as *apostle, witness,* and *tradition,* have produced a deeper insight of what is here at stake and a better understanding of what the Canon means for the Church. Although it is not feasible to go into full detail, a closer appreciation of some outstanding results is important.

In the first place, we should observe in this connection the significance of the *apostles* for the coming Church. We know that the concept "apostle" is defined especially by the idea of authorization, by the transmission of definite powers. In Jewish jurisprudence there existed what was known as the *sjaliach* (apostle), a man who in the name of others could appear with authority and whose significance was thus described: "the *sjaliach* for a person is as this person himself." It is with this meaning that Christ confronted the apostles when he applied the rule, "He that receiveth you receiveth me, and he that receiveth me receiveth him that sent me" (Matt. 10:40; cf. John 13:20). The apostles are Christ's representatives, those to whom in a very special and exclusive manner he has entrusted the preaching

of the gospel. For this purpose he has not only chosen them through the Holy
Spirit (Acts 1:2), but he has also endowed them with the Holy Spirit—the
Spirit of truth—who will teach them all things and recall to mind what Jesus
had said, will guide them into fullness of truth and will also explain the future
(John 14:26; 15:26; 16:13–15). Therefore, the apostles are given a special
significance in the history of salvation. In Hebrews 2:4 ff. they are compared
to the angels of the Old Testament as transmitters of the revelation. The
salvation that has appeared in Christ Jesus, first proclaimed by the Lord
himself, was *validly attested* to us by the apostles.

This peculiar mandate is always paired in the New Testament with
another important datum, namely, that the apostles were *witnesses* of the
salvation revealed in Christ. This concept of *witness* will also have to be
understood primarily in a forensic way, i.e., the apostles were eyewitnesses of
the things that have once occurred, and they bear this testimony for the
forum of the coming Church and the entire world. Exactly for this reason
they are authorized by Christ to bear this testimony in his name. We see,
therefore, that in the history of salvation Christ himself has made this pro-
vision for the sharing of salvation. This presentation was not left to chance,
nor to the general tradition nor to the preaching of the Church. It belongs
in the first place, as apostolic preaching and witness, to the reality of revelation itself and as such it carries an entirely unique and exclusive character.
This apostolic preaching is the foundation of the Church, to which the
Church is bound (Matt, 16:18; Eph. 2:21; Rev. 21:14); it is the most holy
faith, upon which the Church itself must build (Jude 20); it has been delivered to the Church by the apostles as *depositum custodi* (I Tim. 6:20; II
Tim. 1:14; 2:2), which the Church must above all things preserve.

And what holds concerning the New Testament concept of *witness,* holds
also for the concept of *tradition.* In the New Testament, just as certainly as
in the early Church, this has a connotation entirely different from the modern
Western idea of transmission. The latter has an indefinite character; it is
conveyed through a collectivity; its source and trustworthiness are often uncertain. Opposed to this the New Testament concept of "tradition" stands in
clear and complete agreement with the Jewish concept, i.e., it bears an overwhelming authoritative significance. "Tradition" means: what has been
handed down with authority. And this importance tradition does not owe to
its antiquity, nor to the communion in which it is preserved, but to the persons in whom the source of the tradition lies. These persons in the New
Testament are the apostles. The apostolic *kerygma* and the apostolic witness
form the foundation and the authority of the New Testament tradition. This
is then also the technical significance of "tradition" (*paradosis*) in the New
Testament and of the "preservation" and the "holding fast" of the tradition
(I Cor. 11:2; 15:2; II Thess. 2:15; cf. Mark 7:4, 8!). How important a
place the concept of "tradition" occupies, for instance, in Paul's epistles, is

apparent from I Corinthians 15:1–3: "Now I would remind you, brethren, in what terms I preached to you the gospel, which you received [by tradition: *paralambano*], in which you stand, by which you are saved, if you hold it fast [as authoritative tradition: *katecho*]; for I delivered to you [by tradition: *paradidomi*], what I also received [by tradition: *paralambano*], that Christ died for our sins. . . ." That Paul means by this repeated tradition-concept the authoritative apostolic witness appears from the subsequent verses in I Corinthians 15, in which he sums up the apostolic eyewitness which guarantees the content of the tradition referred to.

We can go a step further: the last authority who guarantees the tradition and who himself also carries forward the tradition is Christ himself. Especially curious in this respect is Cullmann's treatment of the utterance of Paul in I Corinthians 11:23: "For I received by tradition from the Lord what I also delivered to you, that the Lord Jesus on the night when he was betrayed took bread. . . ." Of special importance here are the words: "I received by tradition from the Lord. . . ." Often this has been interpreted that the historical Jesus stood at the beginning of the transmission chain. But in this sense Paul can hardly be said to have "received from the Lord" what was here transmitted. Actually, Paul does not say that he has received from the Lord the establishment of the holy supper; he says, rather, that he has received the *message* of the institution of the holy supper by tradition from him: "I received by tradition *from the Lord . . . that the Lord Jesus,*" and so forth. Paul means by this tradition, without doubt, the message that he had received from the original witnesses. Nevertheless he writes that he has for himself (i.e., as apostle) received the deliverances "from the Lord." He means specifically the ascended Lord. The testimony of the eyewitnesses is for him as apostle the delivered word of the glorified Lord. And as such he himself delivers it to the church of Corinth. The ascended Lord stands behind the testimony of his apostles. Not alone as the earthly Jesus, but also as the ascended Lord, he clothes the testimony of the apostles with his authority. Therefore the delivered word of the apostles can also be spoken of as the word of God: "When you received by tradition from us the preached word of God, you accepted it not as the word of men, but as what it really is, the word of God" (I Thess. 2:13).

Even though the apostolic witness and the apostolic tradition in the early period bore primarily an oral character, the inscripturation of the apostolic word came speedily to the fore. New Testament indications of the increasing significance of the scripturally fixed tradition are not lacking. In I Corinthians 15 the Apostle Paul fixed and established in ample and deliberate scriptural form what he had first transmitted orally regarding the resurrection. His purpose here is not the introduction of something new, but that the congregation of Corinth should hold fast this tradition "in what terms I preached it to you" (I Cor. 15:1). Therefore he repeats this tradition in scriptural form. Here the scriptural fixation of what had happened aims to preserve the statement *for now and for ever.* We find the same motive in the prologue of Luke. The evangelist has followed the apostolic tradition accurately from the beginning and has written it down, in order that Theophilus may know the trustworthiness of the things of which he has been informed. Here we can see the beginning of the demarcation-line between the oral and the scriptural tradition, a process which finds its end finally in the formation of the New Testament Canon.

All this suggests the superficiality of the oft-heard contention that neither the authors nor the readers of the New Testament might have seen originally in the books of the New Testament something holy or canonical, and that the real problem of the history of the Canon is, how the books of the New Testament became holy Scripture (Lietzmann). No doubt it may be true that the scriptural form of the apostolic tradition did not receive, provisionally, the same pregnant and outstanding significance as the books of the Old Testament. Nevertheless it should not be forgotten that any apostolic tradition, either oral or scriptural, *as such* had a special authority that ranked with the prophetical word. The authority of the New Testament books was not something merely attributed to them subsequently by the Church, but was inherent in them from the beginning (J. Gresham Machen). The New Testament letters were destined by the apostles themselves for public reading in the congregation and for that purpose they were exchanged by the churches (cf. I Thess 5:27; Col. 4:16; Rev. 1:3). The concept of a new "Scripture" comes to its expression very clearly in the Gospel of John. The evangelist not only applies the promise of the Holy Spirit (to lead and inspire the apostles in their witness) to his own book (John 14–17), but he also explicitly says that "to bear testimony" consists in "to write" (John 21:24), and that what "has been written" in this way ought to induce the readers to the belief in Jesus Christ (John 20:30–31). He uses the technical term, with which he quotes the Old Testament, for his own work when he calls men to believe.

I can only point out these few data. It would be possible, in addition, to bring to mind other scriptural touchstones, for instance in the well-known sayings of II Peter 3:16 and Revelation 22:18, 19. But it seems to me that what has been said in the above justifies sufficiently the conclusion that the great work of salvation of God in Jesus Christ does not confine itself to his actual words and deeds. It consists also in the preservation and in the authoritative communication of what has happened and what has been said in the tradition and the testimonies of specially indicated and qualified bearers and instruments of this revelation. Already in the New Testament itself, the scriptural tradition, represented by these delegated apostles and witnesses, receives the significance of the foundation and standard, i.e., of the "Canon" in behalf of the coming Church.

IV. THE NEW TESTAMENT IDEA OF THE CANON

Here we are distinguishing the redemptive-historical idea of the Canon, in which we may take note of three main elements:

1. That of exclusive authority, according to the authorization of the apostles by Christ himself;

2. That of a qualitatively closed unity, according to the unrepeatable and unique character of the apostolic witness;

3. That of fixation and stabilization, according to its destination as foundation and *depositum custodi* of the Church.

At the same time, it should be stated that this concept of the Canon cannot be harmonized with the idea that the Canon of the Church can be subjected to the so-called "spiritual criticism" of the Church. It must be emphasized that the Church does not control the Canon, but the Canon controls the Church. For the same reason the Canon cannot be the product of the decision of the Church. The Church cannot "make" or "lay down" its own standard. All that the Church can lay down is this, that it has received the Canon as a standard and rule for faith and life, handed down to it with absolute authority. On historical grounds, it can be stated that the Church has been conscious of this in its decisions concerning the Canon. Analysis of the history of the Canon in the Church throws light upon this fact ever more clearly, and it contradicts the interpretation of the Canon as a product or a measure originated by the Church in the battle against Marcion and Montanism. Threats from these sources no doubt induced the Church to clearer reflection and to explicit statements in regard to what had been received in the Canon of the New Testament. But the Church has referred again and again to that which has been handed down by Christ and his apostles, and the only way in which we can adequately judge the rightness or wrongness of the Church in this respect is to judge the validity of this presupposition.

The far more difficult question, whether the Church has been mistaken in receiving this concrete Canon as the Canon of Christ, ought also to be seen essentially in the light of this redemptive-historical a priori. An absolute a posteriori for the acknowledgment of the Canon does not exist. No voice from heaven has been heard upon the decisions of the Church concerning the Canon; no voice in the heart nor in the Church itself can compensate for a divine reaffirmation. Of course, here the antithesis with the Roman Catholic idea of the authority of the Canon is at stake. For the inherent authority of the Canon (*quoad se*) Roman Catholic theology refers to Christ, as do we. But as for the believer's acknowledgment of the Canon and the grounds for it (*quoad nos*), it refers to the authority of the Church. We cannot discuss here this Roman Catholic idea of Church and church-authority in a full way. But as for acknowledgment of the Canon, we must note that the New Testament idea of Canon does not include this element of the authority of the Church. The New Testament says not only that Christ himself has laid the apostolic foundation for the coming Church, but also that he himself will build the Church on this rock. The Church cannot provide the guarantee of its own foundation, neither for the world nor for its own members. The Church can only point to Christ and to his promise. Therefore the a priori of the faith with regard to the authority of the New Testament Canon cannot be of another nature than *christological,* i.e., it can only be founded in the promise of Christ that he will build the Church upon this foundation.

V. ACCEPTANCE OF THE CANON IN THE EARLY CHURCH

All of this does not release us from the task of investigating the history of the Canon. We cannot and we may not a priori identify the redemptive-historical Canon of Christ with the 27 books of the New Testament. The latter is at once prevented by the fact that the apostolic tradition which Christ has established as a rule for his Church carried an oral as well as a scriptural character. But further, it is precisely the history of the Canon in the Christian Church which poses all kinds of questions and problems in regard to the normativity of the final result. We encounter here variations and divergent lines in ecclesiastical handling. The fallibility of the Church is therefore apparent also in connection with the Canon. For these reasons many still regard this Canon as an uncertain matter, and the "problem of the Canon" is spoken of as a hidden, dragging illness of the Church.

This situation has sometimes been exaggerated. On the other hand, we must not picture things as if *consensus* in the entire Church regarding the Canon has always been so great that the true "finger of God" could be seen as manifested in the history of the Church in connection with the Canon. Not only do I regard it generally a very difficult thing to identify the "finger of God" in history, but as it concerns the Canon, the facts would warrant no such interpretation. Alongside a very great consensus in connection with the Canon as such, and also in connection with the majority of New Testament books (the "corpus" of the Canon), a very great measure of uncertainty concerning some books has been apparent for a long time. This appears clearly from the statistical data which we find, for instance, in writers such as Origen and Hieronymus. They speak of *homologoumena* and *antilegomena* or *amphiballomena*—books universally acknowledged and accepted, and others concerning which there was no universal consensus. The temporary exclusion from the Canon of Hebrews in the Western Church, and of the Revelation in the Eastern, the uncertainty concerning four catholic epistles in the entire Church, and the continuing exclusion of these in the Syrian Church, give us in bold lines the true state of affairs. The noteworthy fact hereby comes to the fore, that specifically *orthodox* dogmatical considerations temporarily stood in the way of the acceptance of some Scriptures later acknowledged as canonical. The Apocalypse (Revelation), first universally accepted, was for a long time set aside in the Eastern Church because millennialism fastened itself upon the Apocalypse. The same thing *mutatis mutandis* happened to Hebrews in the West. On the grounds of the *evangelium veritatis* of Valentinus (codex Jung), recently discovered by Nag-Hammadi, it was ascertained that around 150 A.D. the Epistle to the Hebrews did not have a lesser authority in Rome than, for instance, the Epistles of Paul. The later putting aside of Hebrews in the West apparently depended not only upon doubt of its apostolic source—although this was put in the foreground—but certainly was also connected with the way the Montanists attached themselves to Hebrews 6. In any case, from the study of the history of the Canon, it appears clear enough that alongside the certainties concerning the chief points, uncertainties on secondary matters played a not unimportant role.

On the other hand, this same history certainly also points out with incontestable force that the Canon has done infinitely more to the Church than the Church to the Canon. It is not possible here to go into full detail concerning the history of the Canon. But the general picture and the universal import of this history seem to be unmistakable. One can say that the history of the Canon is *the process of the growing consciousness of the Church concerning its ecumenical foundation.* The ultimate determination of the Canon at the end of the fourth and the beginning of the fifth century can be called the confession of the Church regarding this foundation as far as it was still demonstrable in that time. "As far as still demonstrable": for this foundation had in the beginning by its nature much broader limits and form. The Church is not founded only upon the scriptural, but in the beginning also upon oral apostolic tradition. Also, the *entire* scriptural tradition did not come into the permanent depository of the Church. For instance, various letters of Paul have been lost. The first Christian congregations and writers lived out of an apostolic tradition not yet quantitatively fixed in size. At this time there is still scarcely an established technical terminology for the designation of the New Testament Scriptures. It is a question whether in the well-known places in 2 Clement 2, 4 and in Barnabas 4, 14, mention is already to be found, in a technical sense, of "the Scripture " as a description of New Testament writings. In any case, at that time there was greater reference to what "Jesus," what "the Lord," and what "the apostles" had said, or, inclusively, "the gospel." Along the way, indeed, emphasis is found on the *transmitted* character of the gospel, in the New Testament concept of authoritative, apostolic teaching which was received by the Church and was guaranteed especially by those churches which had been founded by the apostles themselves. This tradition is, however, since the time of Irenaeus and Tertullian, identified with the *scriptural* (literary), apostolic tradition. "They deny most decidedly the existence of extra-scriptural tradition. To appeal to revelatory truth apart from Scripture is heretical gnosticism"

(Flesseman-van Leer). This is not to be explained on the basis of a formal, ecclesiastical decision that had been preceded by deliberate reasoning and consideration. Much more the indication lies herein that the Church had never wished to live by anything other than that which had been delivered to it as Canon by way of Christ, and that the Church, in order to be able to *continue* to do this, as a matter of course returned to and concentrated on a scripturally-fixed tradition. Herein also lies the real significance of the so-called "closing" of the Canon in the fourth and fifth centuries. Therefore, the recognition of a continuing oral tradition alongside the scriptural, as Rome wishes, is totally in conflict with the sense and purpose of the formation of the Canon. By accepting the Canon and setting its limits, the Church has not only distinguished between canonical and noncanonical writings, but it has pointed out the borders wherein for itself the authoritative apostolic tradition lay. This development would have been senseless if at the same time an unlimited oral tradition continued to be canonical.

It is certain that, concerning the vast majority of the 27 books of the New Testament, no shadow of doubt existed concerning their character as tradition (or, in later words, their canonical authority). It is just as certain that differences of opinion concerning the precise boundaries of the body of the Canon remained until the fourth and fifth centuries. Still, these differences must also be seen in the right light. The late Professor de Zwaan of Leiden has expressed himself concerning this as follows: "Actual conflicts over differences in 'canon' are unknown to us and apparently did not occur." He says further: "It is also a fact that those books concerning which there were temporary differences in practice can be counted on the fingers of one hand." If one wishes to get a proper insight into the nature of these different practices, we must compare, on the one hand, the *sine ira et studio* mention of the *homologoumena* and the *antilegomena* by authors such as Origen, and on the other hand, the stormy reactions of the Church to Marcion's efforts for a reduction in the Church's accepted apostolic tradition and to the Montanists' attempt to overthrow the absolute borders of this apostolic tradition. This infringement upon what the Church acknowledged as incontestable apostolic depository was something that made it stagger on its foundations. Compared to this, the differences in regard to *homologoumena* and *antilegomena* were scarcely of significance when the issue arose over the two apostolic traditions, even though at times dogmatic and provincial influences disturbed the proper view of the limits of this tradition.

Therefore it is definitely not a simplification of the true state of affairs if we characterize the formation and the later closing of the Canon in the Christian Church as the self-expression of the Church of having been built upon this and no other foundation. Concerning the formation of the Canon, Harnack in his time formulated a number of questions which he characterized as "chief problems of canon history": What was the reason that not merely one, but four Gospels are included in the Canon? Why is there not

one canonical Gospel harmony? Why does the New Testament contain other
books in addition to the Gospels? and so forth. In our estimation, these
questions have never existed for the Church itself and the answers to these
questions never *could* be a point of consideration. For the Church itself
never decided the matter of one or four Gospels, or that of the inclusion of
an apostolic Canon alongside the Gospel Canon. These Gospels and Epistles
(however different in content and character) did not form the *product* but
the *basis* of the Church's decision. The Church never knew anything different or anything better than that it was *these* Gospels (and not any Gospel
harmony as that of Tatianus) and *these* Epistles that had been delivered to
it by apostolic authority. And if we understand something of Church history,
this knowledge came forth out of this source, that the Church indeed never
had any other foundation than this tradition concerning (and from) Jesus
and the apostles. The Church has dealt in this situation as does one who
knows and points to a certain person as father or mother. Such a knowledge
rests not on demonstration but upon direct experience; it is most closely
connected with one's own identity. In this and no other way must we picture
the knowledge and the "decision" of the Church concerning the Canon.
They have a direct character and flow forth out of the very existence of the
Church itself.

Undoubtedly we find among ecclesiastical writers all kinds of arguments
that are supposed to demonstrate the canonicity of certain books. For instance, we observe that Irenaeus, in the matter of the fourfold Gospel, calls
forth the examples of the four winds, the four beasts in the Apocalypse, and
so forth (in his battle against the production of new gospels by the Gnostics) ;
so also many apologists later tried to ascribe apostolic sources to all kinds
of writings. These arguments all have a certain apparent character of proof-
after-the-fact. This appears at once from their artificiality. Without doubt
these arguments never served as *criteria canonicitatis,* but they are to be
viewed merely as attempts to demonstrate against the arguments of others,
what had been considered by the Church as long established.

And what is true of the acceptance of the chief content of the Canon
will have to hold also, even if in a little more relative sense, for the latest
limitation of the Canon, i.e., of final agreement in reference to certain
antilegomena. Here apparently the ecumenical viewpoints carried decisive
force. That does not mean that formal ecumenical pronouncements or
decisions were made but that the circle of the apostolic tradition bestowed
on the Church, seen from an ecumenical viewpoint, appeared to be wider
than has been evident in various portions of the Church. The acknowledgment of the 27 books, therefore, has no other significance than the acknowledgment of what appeared to belong to the foundation of the Church in
its larger connections.

It is possible that some are under the impression that the evidences for
what was given to the Church as Canon are not nearly so absolute in these

later portions as in the body of the Canon universally accepted from the beginning. It is, however, difficult to deny that these final decisions regarding the Canon carry the same self-evident and self-expressing character of the Church concerning its origin and foundation. It was the definitive constituting of that which the Church in the nature of the case had always known and in various ways had always given expression even though not without falling and rising, and not always without hesitation and not always supported by the conscience of the entire Church.

Conclusion

When we review the entire course of the history of the Canon—even though sketched here only in bare outline—it appears, however, that this history supports a posteriori the New Testament christological a priori of the Canon. It is the apostolic tradition received by the Church which it has proclaimed with increasing clarity and certainty as its Canon; it is the Canon in its qualitative finality and, when the oral tradition had passed and become unclear, also the Canon in its quantitative finality of 27 books; it is the Canon as it was entrusted to the Church by Christ and the apostles as its *depositum custodi,* which for the Church continues as the standard and rule for its faith and life.

That this Canon of the New Testament is indeed the Canon of Christ cannot be guaranteed beyond doubt by way of historical demonstration or exegetical skill. But certainly investigation teaches us two things with great clarity. On the one hand, it teaches us to see Christ, who gives to the Church a firm foundation and promises thereupon to build his Church. On the other hand, it teaches us to see the Church, which, in the formation of the Canon, does nothing else than to point out with great positiveness the foundation upon which it is built. That this foundation of the Church is none other than that which Christ has laid, is basically not a subject for scholarly demonstration. It belongs truly to the evidences of the faith, that in the manner in which the Church has accepted the Canon there is seen the fulfillment of the word of the Lord to his apostle: "Thou art Peter, and upon this rock I will build my church" (Matt. 16:18).

THE CHURCH DOCTRINE
OF INSPIRATION

Geoffrey W. Bromiley

Geoffrey W. Bromiley was Rector of St. Thomas Episcopal Church of Edinburgh, Scotland, from 1951–58. Previously he served as Lecturer and Vice Principal of Tyndale Hall in Bristol. He holds the M.A. (Cantab.), Ph.D. (Edin.) and D.Litt. (Edin.) degrees. Currently he serves as Professor of Church History at Fuller Theological Seminary. His writings include Reasonable Service; Zwingli and Bullinger *(Library of Christian Classics),* Baptism and the Anglican Reformers, Thomas Cranmer, Theologian, *and* Sacramental Teaching and Practice of the Reformation Churches. *He is an editor of the English translation of Karl Barth's Church Dogmatics.*

13. Geoffrey W. Bromiley

THE CHURCH DOCTRINE
OF INSPIRATION

THE starting-point of the Church's doctrine of inspiration is obviously to be found in the self-witness of the Bible itself. This has already been treated in a previous chapter, and no more than a brief summary is required in the present context. As far as the Old Testament is concerned, both the Law and the prophetic writings purport to come from God, and in specific cases the New Testament links the giving of messages through human speakers or writers with the activity of the Holy Spirit. Inspiration thus arises naturally and necessarily from the divine source and authority. Nor does it refer only to an ecstatic upsurge of the human spirit; the reference is plainly to the inworking of the Holy Ghost. In the New Testament it is made clear that divine authority extends to the whole of the Old; for example, our Lord shows his disciples "in all the scriptures the things concerning himself" (Luke 24:27). Again, the activity of the Holy Spirit is given a general reference. We read that the Psalmist speaks in the Spirit in Psalm 110 (Matt. 22:43). And finally the two primary verses in II Timothy 3:16 and II Peter 1:21 tell us that "all scripture is given by inspiration of God," and that "holy men of God spake as they were moved by the Holy Ghost."

It is to be noted that the linking of the Biblical writings with the Holy Spirit means that they are brought into direct relationship with the work of the Spirit, namely, to bear witness to Jesus Christ. This is true of the Old Testament with its prophetic testimony, for we read that Jesus himself said of these writings: "They are they which testify of me" (John 5:39). But it is also true of the New, and gives the backward-looking apostolic testimony an assured place alongside the prophetic. For in John 14:26 we are told that the Holy Spirit would bring all things to the remembrance of the apostles; in Acts (e.g., 2:4, 4:8 and *passim*) we find that the Holy Spirit is their co-worker, and in II Peter 3:16 there is a classification of the epistles of Paul with the Scriptures which certifies the divine authority of this written testimony.

A derivative point specifically developed in II Corinthians 3 (cf. I Corinthians 1 and 2) is that the Holy Spirit who gave the Scriptures is the living Lord whose voice must be heard in and through Scripture if its message is to be understood and received. This continuing work of the Spirit does not seem to be described by the Bible as the proper work of inspiration. But it is an unavoidable implicate. If the message is really from the Holy Spirit, it cannot be received merely by the natural understanding. Without the Holy Ghost it can be read only on the level of the human letter. What is given by the Spirit must be read in the Spirit. To the objective inspiration of Scripture there corresponds the subjective illumination of the understanding which safeguards the doctrine against the constant threat of an "Apollinarian" interpretation, and the consequent notion of an *ex opere operato* efficacy.

I. ALIEN CONCEPTIONS THREATENING THE EARLY CHURCH

It is as well to mention this derivative point at once because one of the alien influences to which the early Church was also exposed tended to press it in the direction of this distorted interpretation. This was the Jewish or Judaistic understanding to which there is an oblique allusion in John 5:39, 40, and to which Paul is specifically referring in II Corinthians 3. To be sure, the Jews stood for a high doctrine of inspiration, particularly in relation to the Law. To the extent that their teaching helped to safeguard the Church against the equation of the Bible with "inspired" religious literature we may describe it as salutary. For after all, it had its roots in the Bible itself. But it carried with it a threefold danger. In the first place, it tended to abstract the divine nature and authority of the Bible from the human authors and situations, i.e., from the whole movement of God's saving work in and through the history of Israel and the persons concerned. Second, it clearly abstracted the Bible from the object of its witness when it failed or refused to see in Jesus Christ the object of its witness, thus being left with a mere textbook of doctrine, ethics and ceremonial. Third, in rejecting Jesus Christ it refused the witness of the Holy Spirit, so that in its reading the Old Testament was deprived of its living power. The result of this threefold abstraction is the contradiction that the human element in the Bible is almost completely subsumed into the divine on the one side, but in practice the divine and authoritative text falls victim to only too human exegesis and schematization on the other.

The Judaistic was not, of course, the only danger threatening the infant

Church. Gentile Christians especially were perhaps even more vulnerable to pagan notions. For the heathen religions also had their inspiration, whether in the ecstatic utterances and movements of devotees, the pronouncements of the oracles, the writings of the Sybillines, or literature generally. A writer like Philo had already succumbed to the temptation to bring together the prophetic inspiration of the Old Testament and these pagan phenomena. After all, had not the early prophets given evidence of this type of ecstatic possession? The statement of Plato: "And for this reason God takes away the mind of these men and uses them as his ministers, just as he does soothsayers and godly seers, in order that we who hear them may know . . . that it is God Himself who speaks and addresses us through them" (*Ion,* 533), thus finds a clear parallel in Philo's interpretation of the Old Testament: "For a prophet has no utterance of his own, but all his utterances come from elsewhere, the echoes of another's voice . . . he is the vocal instrument of God smitten and played by His invisible hand" (*Who is the Heir?,* p. 259). In some sense, this is no less a high view than that of Judaism, and it has the advantage of emphasizing the living movement. But apart from its pagan associations, it has the same twofold and apparently contradictory disadvantage of destroying the human element on the one side, yet in so doing, of reducing inspiration to a familiar and psychologically explicable human phenomenon on the other.

II. THE PATRISTIC PERIOD

When we turn to the patristic period, we are struck at once by the way in which all writers accepted the inspiration and authority of Holy Scripture as self-evident. The actual writings of the Old and New Testaments are seen to derive from the Holy Spirit and therefore carry the divine message. Nor is this merely a general inspiration; it extends to the detailed phraseology of the Bible in accordance with the saying of Christ in Matthew 5:18. Thus Clement of Alexandria tells us that not one jot nor tittle can pass because all has been spoken by the mouth of the Lord (*Protrepticus,* IX, 82, 1); and Gregory Nazianzus writes that even the smallest lines in Scripture are due to the minute care of the Holy Spirit, so that we must pay careful attention to every slightest shade of meaning (*Orat.,* 2, 105). In order to emphasize the perfection and authority of the Bible, Irenaeus can say that they are actually spoken by God himself through his Word and Spirit (*C.O.H.,* II, 28, 2). What the authors say is really said by God himself, and must be received and studied not merely or primarily as the word of man but as the Word of God. This emphasis on the divine inspiration of the Bible is obviously reflected again in the many statements in the Fathers which refer to the supreme authority of the Bible in the Church, as in the dictum of Augustine quoted in Cranmer's *Confutation of Unwritten Verities:* "For I do not account Cyprian's writings as canonical, but weigh them by the canonical scriptures;

and that in them which agreeth with canonical I allow to his praise; but that that agreeth not, by his favour I refuse" (*Parker Society ed.*, II, p. 33).

There can be little doubt that a sound and scriptural doctrine of inspiration was for the most part maintained and developed in the patristic period. The primary fact of inspiration was never in doubt. There was no temptation to restrict its range to favored passages of the Bible. It was not abstracted from the true theme of the Bible in Jesus Christ, the temptation in most writers being to find rather fanciful and extravagant allusions to Christ and his work in the most unlikely ways and places (cf. especially the *Epistle of Barnabas*). And no attempt was made to work out a systematic understanding of inspiration along lines which might replace its true miracle and mystery by a false.

At the same time there are elements in the patristic teaching which show that the pressure of Judaistic and pagan doctrine was not without its effect. The latter is reflected in the typical attempt by the Apologists to commend the Bible by comparing it with the Sibyllines (cf. Theophilus of Antioch, *Ad autol.*, 2, 9), and more seriously perhaps by the doubtful suggestions of Athenogoras that the Holy Spirit uses the prophets as a flute-player blowing on his flute (*Leg. pro Cht.*, 7 and 9) or of Hyppolytus that he plays on them as on a zither or harp (*De Antichristo*, 2). Fortunately, perhaps, the excesses of Montanism served as a decisive check to thinking in terms of pagan ecstaticism. But the impulse to depreciate the human element found no less serious expression in another form. Augustine, for example, approached the thought of a dictation of the Holy Scriptures when he stated that the Christ used the evangelists "as if they were his own hands" (*De consensu evang.*, I, 35),[1] and this was pressed almost unbearably (though not without a real element of truth) by Gregory the Great when he said of Job: "He Himself wrote them, who dictated the things that should be written. He did Himself write them, who both was present in the saint's work, and by the mouth of the writer," the identity of the author being of no consequence (*Moralia praef.*, I, 2). This tendency was the more dangerous because the reaction against Montanism entailed a concentration upon the given letter at the expense of the free movement of the Holy Spirit, not in divorce from the letter as in Montanism, but in his disposal of it.

We must not exaggerate these weaknesses in relation to the real strength of the patristic doctrine and its avoidance of cruder errors especially in relation to pagan ecstaticism. Indeed, even the human element is not altogether lost in the divine, for Augustine can find a place for this side by side with his doctrine of dictation (*De consensu evang.*, II, 12), and it was realized that the unpolished style of some of the authors could not be attributed to the Spirit except by way of condescension. Indeed, some writers like Origen and Theodore of Mopsuestia were prepared to go further and speak of various

---

[1] Although in the context this does not mean more than that the members of Christ's body act in behalf of Christ himself as the Head.

levels of inspiration, although fortunately this opposite extreme did not find general acceptance in the early Church. On the other hand, it has to be conceded that there were dangerous tendencies in this primitive period. The phrase "dictation" can be understood, and was probably intended, in a true sense, but it opens the way to a mechanical view which makes it difficult to appreciate the original setting of the messages, and at the same time eliminates the present work of the Holy Spirit in the illumination of the reader. In addition, there is involved a possible relativization of the Bible which in the long run jeopardizes rather than secures its true authority, placing it side by side with other historically demonstrable phenomena such as extra-Biblical tradition, the Church and at a later date the Papacy.

III. THE MEDIEVAL CHURCH

The incipient dangers in the patristic doctrine come to fruition in the medieval Church, which presents us with the paradox of a high doctrine of inspiration accompanied by a muzzling of its authority and in the later stages a virtual elimination of its living power. In point of fact the Scholastic period is particularly sterile in the matter of inspiration, being far more interested in defining the status of the Bible in relation to that of other authorities in the Church. Abelard, as might be expected, makes a plea for a more human understanding, and expresses doubt as to the inerrancy of Scripture from a historical standpoint. Aquinas has a full and careful discussion of the relation of the human authors and readers to the Holy Spirit as the true Author, and with his usual acuteness he finds a real place for the ordinary element (cf. *S. Theol.* II, 2 qu. 171 ff.). But the whole discussion relates to a Bible Judaistically understood as a textbook of divine truth, divinely given and therefore to be approached with respect, but accessible to human study like any other textbook,[2] and accompanied by other and hardly less important authorities. In these circumstances it is not surprising that over large tracts of medieval life the Bible could not do its vivifying and reforming work, for all that its inspiration was so fully accepted. It is not surprising that the human element excluded in the understanding of the Bible should rise up the more strongly in other spheres and successfully challenge and subjugate the divinely dictated Scriptures. It is not surprising that the Bible should become a mere source-book for dogmatic disputation, ossified in an alien tongue, instead of the living Word of Jesus Christ to the churches. This is not to say that the medieval doctrine was wrong in basic substance. It is not to say that a less high doctrine of inspiration is demanded. It is not to say that the Bible should be understood in terms of religious philosophy or poetry. But it is a warning that even a materially impeccable doctrine may be held and taught and applied in such a way that the true insights of the Bible are suppressed, and the result is a distortion which

---

[2] i.e., in virtual abstraction from the Holy Spirit as its necessary Interpreter.

achieves the very opposite of what is intended, and is almost worse than naked error.

IV. THE REFORMATION

This was the kind of situation which the Reformers had to retrieve in their doctrine of the Bible, and it is against this background that we must try to understand their doctrine of inspiration. In the first place, we can hardly fail to note that it does not play any decisive part in their theology. Their concern is primarily with other matters. Yet this does not mean that it is unimportant, let alone that it is absent. It simply means that they can almost afford to take it for granted. The high inspiration of the Bible; the fact that God himself is the true Author of Scripture; the divine origin of even the detailed wording—these are matters which are not disputed. Luther makes it plain that the whole of the Bible must be accepted as the inspired Word of God (cf. *Weimarer Ausgabe,* 54, 158, 28). Zwingli appeals consistently to the divinely inspired record of the Old and New Testaments in assertion and defense of pure Christian doctrine. Calvin is perhaps the clearest and firmest on this point. He describes the Scriptures as the "only record in which God has been pleased to consign his truth to perpetual remembrance," and says that we cannot have an established faith in doctrine "until we have a perfect conviction that God is its author," i.e., through Scripture (*Institutes,* I, 7, 2 and 4). In his sermon on II Timothy 3:16, he constantly refers to God as the author of the Bible, and in his commentary on this passage he can even speak in terms of "dictation" (*C.R.,* 54, 283 f.). Among the Anglicans, Whitaker has a similar passage in answer to the Romanist contention that the Bible is only mediately the voice of God: "We confess that God hath not spoken of himself, but by others. Yet this does not diminish the authority of scripture. For God inspired the prophets with what they said, and made use of their mouths, tongues, and hands: the scripture, therefore, is even immediately the voice of God. The prophets and apostles were only the organs of God" (*Parker Society ed.,* p. 296). In view of the controversy regarding Reformation teaching, and the suggestion in some quarters that the Reformers more or less abandoned the traditional doctrine of inspiration, it is as well to emphasize this primary element in their thinking. Nowhere, perhaps, is it more authoritatively summed up than in Barth's *Church Dogmatics:* "The Reformers took over unquestioningly and unreservedly the statement on the inspiration, and indeed the verbal inspiration, of the Bible, as it is explicitly and implicitly contained in those Pauline passages which we have taken as our basis, even including the formula that God is the author of the Bible, and occasionally making use of the idea of a dictation through the biblical writers" (I, 2, p. 520).

Yet even a cursory examination of the Reformation literature makes it plain that in three important respects the Reformers moved back from the traditional teaching and its Judaistic basis to a more genuinely scriptural understanding. In the first place, they had a clear realization that Christ is the true theme of the Bible. The Bible is not a mere source-book of Christian teaching to be handled with legalistic rationalism (i.e. for attainment of self-righteousness and self-wisdom) by scholars, ecclesiastics and canonists. It is the book to lead us to Christ, not merely to a mystical Christ, but to Christ prepared and prophesied in the Old Testament, and incarnate, cruci-fied, risen and ascended in the New. Luther makes this point with greatest clarity: "But Holy Scripture refuses to know or put before us anything but Christ. And whoso therefore goes to Scripture or is led by Scripture to Christ, it is well with him and he is on the right path" (*W.A.*, 16, 113, 22). But Zwingli has it too: In the Bible "Christ stands before you with open arms, inviting you and saying, 'Come unto me . . .'" (*Library of Christian Classics*, XXIV, p. 84). And although Calvin does not make it quite so explicitly, it is the theme of his whole understanding of the Biblical story as developed in the main part of the *Institutes* (II, 6 f.).[3]

Secondly, and in consequence, there is a better appreciation of the human aspects of the Bible, not in isolation from the divine work, but in conjunction with it. The Bible tells us the story of God's dealings in salvation and judg-ment. It treats of a people, of the men of this people, and of the One to whom they led and in whom they found fulfillment. The authors have their own place in the development or outworking or recounting of this story. God uses them in their own place and time, and according to their own capacity and endowment. The fact that the Bible is fully inspired does not mean that we have to look for a hidden or allegorical sense, but that the divine message is given in and through the human. It is for this reason that the Reformers dismiss the complicated exegesis of the Middle Ages and insist upon straightforward exposition (cf. Whitaker, *op. cit.*, p. 405 f.), relating the various passages primarily to their human setting. But they are also aware that in this respect the Bible conforms to a christological pattern. As the Word became flesh, and was very man no less than very God, so the written Word is no less fully a human word than a divine. To allow the human word to be minimized or even swallowed up in the divine is not to do true honor to the Bible, but to miss its true miracle and message.

Thirdly, the Reformers all have a vivid sense that, although the meaning of the Bible is for the most part clear and simple in itself, its message cannot be received merely by human reading or scholarship or historical research. There is needed in the reader the work of the same Spirit who gave the writings. This is one of the most widely and firmly attested of all the points made by the Reformers, for it was of crucial importance in their attack on the medieval doctrine and their whole resistance to the traditional view of authority. Luther puts it in this way: "The Bible cannot be mastered by

---

[3] And cf. *Commentary* on John 5:39, "We ought to read the Scriptures with the express design of finding Christ in them."

212 REVELATION AND THE BIBLE

study or talent; you must rely solely on the influx of the Spirit" (*Brief-wechsel*, ed., Enders & Kawerau, I, 141). Zwingli bases his appeal to the nuns of Oetenbach upon it: "Even if you hear the gospel of Jesus Christ from an apostle, you cannot act upon it unless the heavenly Father teach and draw you by the Spirit" (*op. cit.*, p. 79 and cf. the whole contents, pp. 75–95). Calvin gives us the forceful statement: "For as God alone can properly bear witness to his own words, so these words will not obtain full credit in the hearts of men, until they are sealed by the inward testimony of the Spirit. The same Spirit, therefore, who spoke by the mouth of the prophets, must penetrate our hearts, in order to convince us that they faithfully delivered the message with which they were divinely entrusted" (*Institutes*, I, 7, 4).[4] The same emphasis is to be found in Whitaker: "We say that the Holy Spirit is the supreme interpreter of scripture, because we must be illuminated by the Holy Spirit to be certainly persuaded of the true sense of scripture," and again: "For no saving truth can be known without the Holy Ghost" (*op. cit.*, p. 415).

Two subsidiary points are to be noted in passing. The first is that, since Christian understanding rests upon the work of the Spirit, the Bible cannot be treated as a Euclid of Christian faith and conduct to be learned, schematized and applied by the ordinary ways of reason and scholarship. On the basis of a sound doctrine of inspiration, Biblical theology is always a venture of prayer, humility and obedience in the Spirit, and nowhere is this better illustrated than in the works of the Reformers themselves. But second, since the Holy Spirit himself attests the word which he has given, there can be a relative unconcern in relation to its human qualifications. It does not have to be proved that the Bible is the oldest of books, or the best literature, or of superior majesty, though some of these points may well be made by way of confirmation. Again, it need not be *demonstrated with absolute finality* that all the predictions of the Old Testament are fulfilled to the letter, although Christians taught by the Spirit will rejoice as the Reformers did in the fact that this is the case. Finally, the credibility of Scripture does not stand or fall with the *ability to prove* that all the events recorded took place exactly as reported, although for all their freedom in face of apparent contradictions the Reformers have obviously not the slightest doubt that this is the case. As Calvin judiciously points out, these proofs are "not so strong as to produce and rivet a full conviction in our minds," but when the necessary foundation of a higher assurance is laid "they become most appropriate helps" (*Institutes*, I, 8, 1).

V. THE POST-REFORMATION PERIOD

The post-Reformation period presents us with a multiplicity of material on the theme of inspiration which makes it impossible to do more than pick

---

[4] And see esp. *Commentaries* on I Corinthians 20 ff.; II Corinthians 3:6.

out the leading tendencies. As in Reformation doctrine, it was commonly accepted that God is the true Author, not merely of the doctrine of Scripture, but of the writings themselves (Gerhard, *Loci Theologici,* II, 17, Cocceius, S.T., IV, 39). Inspiration applies to the whole Scripture, and not merely to particular parts (Hollaz, *E.T.A.,* p. 90). It does not rule out a concomitant action on the part of the human authors (*ibid.,* p. 91, *Leiden Synopsis,* III, 7). Yet it is more than a mere guidance of the authors in their human action, and is not equivalent to ordinary artistic "inspiration" (Quenstedt, *T.D.P.,* I, 69). It extends to the very words in which the statements are clothed, (*ibid.,* I, 72, Cocceius, *op. cit.,* IV, 41), and includes passages which deal with historical and scientific as well as doctrinal and ethical matters (Hollaz, *op. cit.,* p. 89). It is supported both by the witness of Scripture itself and also by the inner witness of the Holy Spirit through the word (Quenstedt, *op. cit.,* I, 87).

In all these matters it is evident that the Lutheran and Reformed dogmaticians of the seventeenth century are in line with the main teaching of the Reformers themselves. But certain features call for notice which pose the question whether their full and careful codification of doctrine has not involved certain shifts of emphasis, slight in themselves but serious in their historical consequences. In the first place, there is a tendency to return to the patristic overwhelming of the human author by the divine. This must not be exaggerated, for most authors agree that the authors write intelligently and voluntarily, and are certainly not to be regarded as mere machines (H. Heidegger, *S.T.,* II, 36, Scherzer, *Systema Theologiae,* p. 8). But there is a distinct development of the theory of dictation, not merely in the use of the rather ambiguous *dicto* (Calov, *Systema,* I, 555), but in the employment of such phrases as "assistants and amenuenses" (Gerhard, *L.T.,* ii., 26 ff., W. Bucan, *Inst. theol.,* L. IV, 2), and even in the revival by Heidegger of the dubious image of the flute-player (H. Heidegger, *Corp. Theol.,* II, 34). Secondly, there is a tendency to press to an unnecessary extreme the intrinsically true doctrine of verbal inspiration, as in the insistence that even the Hebrew vowel points must be regarded as inspired (Gerhard, *L.T.,* 265). Third, there is a tendency to give a false importance to the doctrine of inerrancy, as if the inspiration of Scripture were finally suspended upon the ability to prove it correct in every detail. To be sure, inspiration is itself the basis of inerrancy, and there is no obligation to prove the latter (Quenstedt, *op. cit.,* I, 77). But in face of attacks upon the inerrancy of the Bible, whether by those who do not regard it as essential to inspiration or by those who deny both, it is only too easy to reverse the true relationship and to come to think of inerrancy as the basis of inspiration (Calov, *op. cit.,* I, 552). Fourth, and in consequence, there is a tendency to subordinate the inner witness of the Holy Spirit, still forcefully maintained, to the external and internal criteria of the authenticity and authority of the Bible. If final assurance comes only with the Holy Spirit, the criteria are of great importance in engendering intellectual conviction and even giving spiritual certainty (Hollaz, *op. cit.,* p. 121), so that even a careful and sympathetic student like Preus is forced to see in the Lutherans "a certain concession to rationalism" at this point (R. Preus, *The Inspiration of Scripture,* p. 114). Finally, and underlying the whole conception, there is a tendency to subject genuinely scriptural material to alien Aristotelian or Cartesian principles and modes of presentation which result in a measure of distortion from the standpoint of true Biblical and Reformation doctrine, which give an ambiguity still reflected in scholarly assessments of the period, and which, contrary to the intentions of the dogmaticians, expose the doctrine of inspiration to the violent reactions of the period of the Enlightenment and theological liberalism.

Whether the post-Reformation orthodox could have contended for the truth of inspiration along other lines is a point worth considering before we rush on to the sweeping and exaggerated condemnations which mark some dogmatic scholars. After all, they were faced by very real difficulties: the demand of the Romanists that they should produce as evident an authority as that of the Church and Papacy (*ibid.,* pp. 93 ff.); the attacks of Socinians upon the historical reliability of Scripture (*ibid.,* pp. 81 f.) and the willingness of Arminians to compromise on this matter (*ibid.,* pp. 83 f.); and the revived Montanism of the sectaries with their appeal to inward illuminations of the Spirit apart from the letter of the Bible (*ibid.,* p. 46). It is also to be recalled that in the matters referred to we are dealing for the most part only with tendencies within a general loyalty, or intention of loyalty, to the Reformation position. Yet the fact can hardly be disputed that a new and non-Biblical rationalism of presupposition, method and approach threatens the Protestant doctrine with these dogmaticians (*ibid.,* pp. 210 f.), that they clearly repeat in some degree the same kind of Judaizing movement as that of the early and medieval Church, and that in so doing they incur a measure of both positive and negative responsibility for the disasters which follow.

VI. EIGHTEENTH CENTURY RATIONALISM

By the inversion characteristic of theological history, the application of inspiration to the minutiae of the Biblical text led to a concentration of interest on the actual documents and history. Hence the eighteenth century saw a rapid and intensive development (e.g., by Michaelis and Semler) of the linguistic and textual studies which had commenced with the Renaissance (cf. K. Aner, *Die Theologie der Lessingzeit,* pp. 202 ff.) Much of this work had no direct bearing upon the doctrine of inspiration. But the case was different when literary and historical questions were raised, for rationalistic attacks upon the reliability and even the authenticity of the records implied a rejection of its inspiration. The calumnies of Voltaire and the Encyclopedists were too outrageous to be seriously effective, but the *Wolffenbüttel Fragmente* constituted a direct challenge with their discussion of the

resurrection narratives, and theologians who had already committed themselves to rationalist presuppositions found it difficult to avoid some kind of
compromise solution. After all, it was argued, "historical truths cannot be
demonstrated," as Lessing maintained (*Werke,* ed., Gosche, VI, p. 241). To
try to defend inspiration in terms of inerrancy is thus to commit it to inevitable relativization. Surely the better course is to intellectualize the concept. Irrespective of its historical reliability, the Bible contains general truths
which are inspired, not in a special or supernatural sense, but insofar as they
conform to the teaching of pure reason. This was the new version of inspiration in neological circles (Aner, *op. cit.,* p. 296), and the tragedy was that
orthodox apologists like Schumann, Riss and Goeze, attempting to meet the
attackers on their own ground, accepted the basic presuppositions instead of
challenging the real enemy in the name of a genuinely Biblical and Reformation understanding.

In its own way, rationalism was no less an evasion of the historical element
than pure supernaturalism. But many forces were making for a study of the
Bible, not merely as an ancient text, nor as a repository of abstract divine
or human truth, but as divine truth in the form of a human product. This
was the contention of Herder, first expressed in his Riga *Sermon on the
Bible,* and then worked out in the *Theological Letters* and *The Spirit of
Hebrew Poetry.* As Herder saw it, the human element in the Bible must be
taken quite seriously. The Bible is a work of literature, written at a particular
time, by a particular people, in particular situations, and conditioned by race,
language, thought-forms, and historical and geographical milieu (*Werke,* ed.
Müller, II, X, p. 257). Its inspiration is not to be denied, but it is not to be
absolutized. It is that of great religious thinkers and poets through whom
God is speaking as he speaks elsewhere through nature, philosophy and the
arts (*ibid.,* p. 271). It is simply a heightened form of true conviction, of
religious enthusiasm in the purer and deeper sense (*ibid.,* XVIII, pp. 53 f.).
As such, it commends itself to the sincere and seeking reader, not by its
outward singularity, but by the direct message which it carries to the soul
(*ibid.,* p. 275). Herder can thus unite a conception of the inward testimony
of the Spirit with his basic reduction of inspiration to the aesthetic level. The
gain in this understanding is that it does take the human element in the
Bible with a sympathetic seriousness hardly attained before in the whole history of the doctrine. But this gain does not offset the failure to see that on its
own terms the Biblical literature and history cannot be classified as merely
one manifestation of the divine Spirit among others, nor its inspiration regarded as one particular species in a common genus. And it is no real compensation that a place is found for the direct speech of the Bible to the heart,
for although this contains an element of truth it is a highly emotionalized
and subjectivized version of the authentic witness of the Holy Spirit, and no
less exposed than the Biblical history to empirical criticism and interpretation in the form of psychological analysis.

With his program of historical Biblical study, Herder initiated the intensive research of the modern period and its more or less sustained polemic against the inerrancy and therefore the special inspiration of the Bible. But theologically his subjectivization of inspiration was no less important, for it combined with Empiricism, Pietism and Kantian Idealism to produce the thoroughgoing subjectivization of Christianity by Schleiermacher which has dominated the whole movement of liberal Protestantism. As Schleiermacher sees it, all religions are relative formulations or descriptions of the basic religious feeling of dependence (*Reden,* p. 21). Of these Christianity is the best because in it this feeling finds perfect expression (p. 212). The doctrines of Christianity are all true and important as the more detailed expressions of emotional states (pp. 84 ff.), the Holy Spirit being the common spirit of the Church (*Der Christliche Glaube,* II, pp. 372 ff.), the Scriptures the first of a series of attempts to express the Christian faith (*ibid.,* pp. 409 ff.), and inspiration the working of the common spirit of believers no less evident in any great doctrinal or devotional work than in the apostolic literature (*loc. cit.*). The almost complete supernaturalizing of the seventeenth century is thus completely reversed and avenged by a no less thorough absorption of the divine element into the human, and the stage is set for the long tragedy of an anthropocentric understanding with all its vanities and vulnerabilities, with its illusory hopes and eventual disillusionment and despair.

Conclusion

Why is it that for all the tenacity displayed and scholarship deployed, orthodoxy has proved so feeble and ineffective in face of this upsurge of the human spirit with its claiming of the Bible and its inspiration for itself? The answer to this question is undoubtedly to be found in the approximation of orthodoxy itself to an abstract, schematized and basically Judaistic understanding of inspiration instead of a genuinely Biblical and Reformed. The attack on the historical reliability of the Bible was damaging just because orthodoxy no longer had full confidence in the witness of the Spirit but must find for it rationalistic support by a reversal of the relationship between inspiration and inerrancy, suspending the former on the latter. The neological compromise was tempting and misleading just because orthodoxy was already finding in the Bible a mere textbook of dogmatic truth rather than a concrete and living attestation of Jesus Christ. The historical program was convincing and dangerous just because orthodoxy found so little place for the human and historical element, and could not contend for the genuinely historical understanding of the Bible in terms of itself to which Biblical scholarship is finding its way after so much debate and confusion. The subjectivization of the Bible and its inspiration was so powerful just because orthodoxy was guilty of all these unfortunate tendencies, suppressing man in his proper place yet exalting him in his rationality, losing sight of Jesus Christ as the true theme and center of the Bible, and showing so little genuine appreciation for the illumination of the Holy Spirit and his work.

In this as in so many matters, the way forward is the way back, namely, to the Reformers, and through them to the Bible and its self-witness by which all our views of inspiration must be tested, corrected, strengthened and empowered. This certainly does not mean that the doctrine of inspiration must be weakened, or a compromise arranged. It means that it must be genuinely asserted, not only in face of error, but also in face of distortions or dilutions of the truth. The prophetic and apostolic word is the word of divine wisdom by which all the rationalism of man is summoned to repentance and renewal. The historical record of the Bible is the account of the divine dealings with man which alone give meaning and direction to all other history. The theme of the Bible is the incarnate Word in whom alone we can find truth, freedom and salvation, and to whom the written Word conforms in divine and human structure. The inspiration of Scripture is genuinely the work of the sovereign Spirit, whose operation cannot finally be subjected to human analysis, repudiation or control, but who remains the internal Master of that which he himself has given, guaranteeing its authenticity, and declaring its message with quickening and compelling power.

CONTEMPORARY IDEAS
OF INSPIRATION

R.A. Finlayson

R. A. Finlayson is Professor of Theology at Free Church College in Edinburgh, Scotland. For many years, until the close of 1957, he served also as Editor of The Monthly Record of the Free Church of Scotland. Born in Ross-shire, Scotland, in 1895, he attended Aberdeen University, where he received the M.A. degree in 1919.

14. *R. A. Finlayson*

CONTEMPORARY IDEAS
OF INSPIRATION

THE CONTEMPORARY mood in theology makes room for super natural revelation but not for supernatural inspiration that gives to the record of revelation its divine authority and validity for us. Despite its advance on the classical liberal position of but a few decades ago, the present theological position still stops short of the historic faith of the Church. For it leaves the Christian religion without authoritative content, and the Christian believer without an intelligent basis for his faith.

Several streams of philosophical and theological thought rising in the early nineteenth century, from Schleiermacher to Kierkegaard, have given thrust and direction to present-day opposition to the evangelical doctrine of inspiration. Hegel's divorce of faith from reason was further defined by Ritschl's divorce of religious from theoretic knowledge; and, grafted on to the extreme mysticism of Schleiermacher, this movement away from the Reformed tradition gathered momentum in Kierkegaard's teaching and in our day has reached full spate in the dialectical theology of Karl Barth.

The displacement of the authority of Scripture by that of human experience and enlightenment—a characteristic of this movement—has never been seriously challenged even by theologians who are ready to disown its most extreme conclusions. From this soil sprang classical liberalism, and in this soil all the branches of present-day liberalism have their roots. The underlying presuppositions of both neo-liberalism and neo-orthodoxy are derived from this source; however diversely they interpret the meaning and function of revelation, they unite in rejecting the identification of God's truth with any formulation given in the Scriptures. For that reason, we can group them together in opposition to the evangelical doctrine of inspiration. While in common with us they believe that God has intervened to save men in the Person of Jesus Christ, they do not believe that he has interpreted his redemptive action in a divinely mediated record bearing for us the authority of the Word of God.

I. THE MEANING OF INSPIRATION

The present anti-intellectual outlook in theology avoids a definition of inspiration. Much of the argument of opponents of the traditional doctrine of inspiration is based on a misunderstanding, and at times even on misrepresentation, of the position held by present-day evangelical theologians. Such terms as revelation, inspiration, and illumination, as widely used in Reformed circles, are then misapplied.

By revelation Protestant theology historically has understood the act of God by which he communicated to men a knowledge of himself and his will. By inspiration is meant that influence of the Holy Spirit on the minds of selected men which rendered them organs of God for the infallible communication of that revelation. By illumination is understood the divine quickening of the human mind in virtue of which it is able to understand the truth so revealed and communicated.

Modern theologians tend to confuse these terms and to use them interchangeably in a manner that does less than justice to any of them. Thus J. K. S. Reid speaks of "degrees of inspiration" when, we would think, a reference to degrees of revelation would be more accurate; inspiration as such does not admit of degrees, though obviously the light of revelation does. Inspiration keeps pace with the revelation and it is not its function to add to the light bestowed, nor to create the fact-materials that it handles. Dr. John Baillie similarly confuses inspiration with enlightenment. Of inspiration he says: "Its meaning and scope have often been misconceived through its being applied primarily to the prophetic and apostolic witness, and withal their written witness, to the revelation rather than to the illumination of the prophetic and apostolic mind which is an integral part of the revelation to which such witness is borne" (*The Idea of Revelation in Recent Thought,* p. 66). This enables Dr. Baillie to put revelation and inspiration on different levels, as when he says: "In what is given of God there can be no imperfection of any kind, but there is always imperfection in what we may be allowed to call the 'receiving apparatus'" (*ibid.,* p. 34). But the prophets never claimed that revelation came to them by way of personal illumination or in the form of a personal insight. Indeed, evidence occurs that their spiritual enlightenment enabled them only partly to understand what the revelation had conveyed to them and what inspiration enabled them perfectly to record (cf. I Peter 1:10 f.). Revelation has thus to do with the disclosure of truth; inspiration with its communication; and enlightenment with its understanding and interpretation.

By many contemporary writers "verbal inspiration" is frequently identified with dictation and mechanical writing. We presume this is because it is easier to challenge it in this form. Reformed opinion has never promulgated a doctrine of merely mechanical or automatic inspiration in which the Holy Spirit is the exclusive agent and the human writer a mere machine recording the communication. Peter asserted that "holy men of God spake as they were moved by the Holy Ghost." And the Church accepted the twofold truth that holy men of God spoke and that they spoke as they were borne along by the Holy Ghost. Both a divine and a human agency are recognized. While God is the moving Agent and responsible Author, the human writer is his free and conscious instrument, so that the words of Scripture are at one and the same time the consciously self-chosen words of the human writer and the divinely inspired words of the Spirit of God. Thus Scripture is all human and all divine, and this perfect harmony between the divine authorship and the human authorship is secured by inspiration.

The linking of inerrancy with "bare literalism" is another allegation that conservative theologians disown. Reverence for the text of Scripture as inspired does not mean that evangelicals are bound to a literal interpretation of it. The science of hermeneutics developed freely within the premises of verbal inspiration, and principles of interpretation whether literal, allegorical, or typological—were determined on grounds proper to the mode of revelation in each case. J. K. S. Reid's assertion that "the new doctrine of infallibility" is based on a literalism "allied to the expectation of finding in the Scriptures the same kind of thing that is so successfully applied by science" must be met by the retort that the doctrine actually makes imperative an acceptance of the teaching of the Bible as authoritative in whatever form it has pleased God to communicate it, and an application of those principles of interpretation that bring us closer to the mind of the Spirit in the Word. If literalism means that we insist, because of our belief in revelation and inspiration, on maintaining the literal sense of the great historical facts on which the Christian faith is founded, then we accept the imputation. It also means, moreover, that we repudiate inferences from the text of Scripture unsupported from the plain sense of Scripture but adduced to harmonize the Bible with twentieth century thought. If, with exegesis based on knowledge of both the principles of grammar and the facts of history, we interpret the text within the context of Scripture and the analogy of the faith, and not within the context of modern thought, we think we are dealing honestly with the Bible both as literature and revelation.

There is further misconception as to what conservative theologians understand by "verbal" inspiration. The term may be unfortunate inasmuch as it may appear to single out each separate word of the text as the proper subject of inspiration. No literature, however, can be subjected to such a process.

Words, in all literature, must be accepted as the vehicles of thought, and the arrangement of words that gives adequate expression to the thought is correct to the exclusion of any other arrangement that fails to do this. Only if the thought is verbally correct is the communication what it was intended to be. If the content of revelation is of God, its communication in writing obviously must ensure that it is given as God would have us receive it. In this case, writing communicates the content of revelation, and inspiration guarantees its veracity. But that does not mean that each word is inspired out of relation to all other words in the context. To deal with words in this arbitrary and abstract form is, of course, to destroy the organic unity of any book.

Forgetfulness of this fact permits J. K. S. Reid to assert that the evangelical doctrine of inspiration means that "God's word is petrified in a dead record" (*The Authority of Scripture*, p. 279). This is surely a misconception of the inspiration that is the living breath of the Spirit and that makes the Word of God "quick and powerful and sharper than any two-edged sword." The Spirit has an abiding relationship to the inspired word so that his vitalizing presence makes its words spirit and life. This living presence pervades the translated Word as truly as the original text. For this reason our Lord and his apostles did not scruple to quote, as possessing divine authority, what the Seventy of Alexandria had written in the Greek translation of the Hebrew Scriptures. This does not indicate that verbal inspiration petrifies or deadens the letter, though it does stabilize the content of revelation and give its communication permanent significance.

It is obvious, therefore, that inspiration must provide everything necessary for the communication of the truth. Since the Bible is a written revelation, it must be a revelation in words, and each word shares in the inspiration of the whole. Words are inspired in their proper relations to other words, not to ensure a "mechanical transmission" or to form a "petrified text," but to ensure that the revelation gains permanence in an authentic and authoritative record. Whether we use the word "verbal" or "plenary" matters little, for it is difficult at the end of the day to escape the conclusion of Bishop Westcott that "we come nearer to the meaning of Scripture by the closest attention to the subtleties and minute variations of words and order" (*The Epistles of John,* p. vi).

II. MODERN ANTITHESES

A study of modern theology suggests that its central ideas of inspiration are based on certain antitheses derived from the existential philosophy and dialectical theology basic to both neo-liberalism and neo-orthodoxy. These antitheses would not have arisen to create the tensions that disturb contemporary dogmatics if the Biblical account of the origin of Christianity and its exposition of redemptive revelation had been accepted in the obedience of faith.

The Scriptures and Divine Revelation

The first of these is the antithesis between the Scriptures as witness to the truth, and the divine revelation. For this antithesis the Biblical doctrine of inspiration provides not a synthesis but a solvent.

Neo-orthodoxy asserts that Scripture is not itself revelation, because by its very nature revelation, it is supposed, does not allow of inscripturation. That which is inscripturated, it is said, is put under the control of man, as if, to use Emil Brunner's words, the Spirit of God were "imprisoned within the covers of the written word." For that reason, whatever our doctrine of inspiration, we are told, there can be no "inspiredness" of the Biblical documents.

To understand the basis of this antithesis, we must recognize how modern theories of religious knowledge distinguish sharply between conceptual and existential knowledge. The claim that knowledge is always from subject to subject means that any objective knowledge of God is impossible. "All revelation," says John Baillie, "is from subject to subject, and the revelation with which we are concerned here is from the divine subject to the human." This means that "in the last resort it is not information about God that is revealed, but God Himself" (*op. cit.*, pp. 27 f.). Revelation must not, therefore, be equated with revealed doctrine, and there is no deposit of truth on which a system of theology can be built. Only existentially can we know God. All the events of revelation are thus placed outside the cognitive apprehension of man.

"The recovery of this fundamental insight," says Dr. Baillie, "is the first thing we notice as running broadly throughout all the recent discussions, marking them off from the formularies of an earlier period." He complains, indeed, that "from a very early time in the history of the Church the tendency has been manifested to equate divine revelation with a body of information which God had communicated to men" (*ibid.*, p. 29). Here neo-orthodoxy strikes a note neither new nor orthodox. Schleiermacher had already voiced this complaint and affirmed, moreover, that the "ideal dogmatic" would have nothing to say directly about either God or the world or anything outside us, but ought to confine its affirmations to what goes on in the Christian soul. And the position has been reasserted by liberal theologians often since his day. This theory completely destroys the intellectual aspect of evangelical faith as embracing a divine message containing information about God and man. It means that the Bible cannot be conceived as teaching any system of truth, and that no internal consistency can be looked for even in its testimony to Christ. This Emil Brunner makes very clear: "At some points," he says, "the variety of Apostolic doctrine, regarded purely from the theological and intellectual point of view, is an irreconcilable contradiction" (*Revelation and Reason*, p. 290). This in the last resort would seem to destroy all possibility of the knowledge of God by placing the events of revelation in the realm of the transcendental and outside our rational apprehension. It need scarcely be pointed out that this refusal to identify revelation with events that are accessible to the historian has very serious consequences for religion. It deprives that revelation of the capacity to teach anything about the world of everyday phenomena, to which man most immediately belongs. If he asks to be told authoritatively concerning his place in the divine scheme of things and the destination to which he and all history are moving, the Bible is disallowed to answer in terms of divine revelation. On these vital matters, though it may speak with authority, it is held to be fallible and erroneous in theology and ethics as well as in history and science. Most serious of all, God himself cannot then be objectively known. Propositions about him which the Bible presents must be discussed as non-divine and non-authoritative. God's self-disclosure is in no sense identical with the representation given in the record of Scripture.

This antithesis between special revelation and its Biblical witness the conservative theologian dismisses as false. The assumption that the revelation is divine and the witness to it merely human, or, put otherwise, that the revelation is infallible and its record fallible, raises the question whether the infallible revelation is of any consequence to man if it must be approached through a fallible record. Why God should "inspire" the revelation, and yet be unable or unwilling to inspire the witness sufficiently to make it a trustworthy bearer of revelation, does not admit of easy explanation. Dr. Baillie puts the case this way: "We cannot believe that God, having performed the mighty acts and having illumined the minds of prophets and apostles to understand their true import, left the prophetic and apostolic testimony to take care of itself. It were indeed," he impressively adds, "a strange conception of the divine providential activity which would deny that the Biblical writers were divinely assisted in the attempt to communicate to the world the illumination which, for the world's sake, they had themselves received." He concludes, therefore, that "the same Holy Spirit who had enlightened them unto their own salvation must also have aided their efforts whether written or spoken to convey the message of salvation to those whom their words would reach. That is what is meant by the inspiration of the Scriptures" (*op. cit.*, p. 34). We agree that it would be indeed strange if God had "inspired" the prophets and apostles to receive a revelation which was for all the ages and yet not inspired them to communicate that revelation to all for whom it was intended. But if inspiration, as here appears, is defined broadly as the "aid" which the Holy Spirit gave to those who received the revelation to enable them to communicate it, then the issue narrows to this: what manner of aid did the Holy Spirit give? We reply, as indeed we must, since we are dealing with God, that he gave all the aid necessary for correct transmission in a completely trustworthy record. To stop short of this is surely to limit the Holy Spirit and render such aid as he gave nugatory.

Even more serious is the charge that the believer in the infallibility of Scripture frustrates the function of faith. Heinrich Vogel of Berlin states the position thus: "The old Protestant doctrine of verbal inspiration transforms the living word of God into a sacred text, and its consequent denial of the human character of Scripture evades and fails to appreciate not only the possibility of offense, but at the same time the reality of faith" (*God in Christ,* p. 139). We do not trouble ourselves to reply to the erroneous contention that the Protestant doctrine of inspiration denies the "human character" of Scripture. But when the believer in the infallibility of Scripture is charged with "failing to appreciate the reality of faith," is this not tantamount to saying that faith cannot properly be exercised unless and until we recognize that there are fallible elements in the Scripture? If this defines the only condition in which faith can be exercised, then the Christian has seriously misread his New Testament. This tendency to put a premium upon credulity is all too common in modern thinking on religion. We find the late Dr. William Temple's mind working along the same lines when he wrote of Jesus Christ: "It is of supreme importance that He wrote no book. It is even of greater importance that there is no single deed or saying of His of which we can be perfectly sure that He said or did precisely this or that." Of the Bible as a whole he has this to say: "No single sentence can be quoted as having the authority of a distinct utterance of the All-Holy God" (*Nature, Man, and God,* p. 350). This indicates how far neo-liberalism has had to go in its attempt to divorce revelation from Scripture and to denigrate the Bible as the source of any adequate and reliable knowledge of God. Presumably, what makes it "of supreme importance" to Dr. Temple that we have no certainty regarding any "single deed or saying" of Christ is the allegation, just noted, that this gives greater scope for the exercise of faith. To us faith based on such uncertainties is mere presumption. Indeed, Dr. Temple's confidence that God is the "All-Holy" rests upon epistemological considerations that require the trustworthiness of the scriptural revelation.

That the truth cannot be communicated in propositional form is a reflection of the present-day anti-intellectual revolt against doctrinal theology. We may well ask: why should God not put propositions in our minds about himself if he is indeed the Truth and the goal of man's quest? Can man ever dispense with truth revealed in this form? The fact is that man falls back upon the propositional revelation of God in order to interpret the eventual or factual revelation.

The fallacy behind the modern theory of religious knowledge in its application to God is its failure to recognize the sovereignty of God in his self-disclosure. It too readily assumes that God and man are partners walking together on a plane of equality. Whatever validity the subject to subject theory may have in relations of subjects meeting on the same plane, it is not adequate in divine-human relations. Man is finite, fallen, and a sinner. To be a sinner means that his understanding is darkened, his heart is alienated, and his will impotent. His place is prostrate at the feet of his Lord, asking: "Lord, what wilt thou have me to do?" The only adequate response to God's self-disclosure is self-surrender as an act of man's *whole* being.

Revelation—Encounter or Communication?

The second antithesis created by the modern school of theology, both neo-liberal and neo-orthodox, is that between revelation as encounter and revelation as communication. This has led modern theologians to postulate a discontinuity between Scripture and authority which has driven neo-liberalism and neo-orthodoxy into sheer mysticism, if not indeed into religious agnosticism.

The evangelical position can recognize no such antithesis inasmuch as our encounter with God rests upon the mediation of his truth to chosen prophets and apostles. In virtue of divine inspiration that communication is for us completely trustworthy, introducing us to the living and true God.

Neo-liberalism, in its attempt to shift the basis of authority from what Scripture says from without to what experience says from within, avers that the doctrine of verbal inspiration is based on failure to recognize the operation of the Holy Spirit and his testimony within. We think Coleridge has put the position in classic form: "Whatever finds me bears witness for itself that it has proceeded from a Holy Spirit" (*Confessions of an Inquiring Spirit*, Letter I). Negatively, this would mean that what does not find me cannot be accepted as from a Holy Spirit. In either case, the norm of what is or is not of the Holy Spirit is within myself. It is thus the active response to the record of revelation that guarantees its validity, and so a man creates for himself, as H. Wheeler Robinson puts it, a Scripture within a Scripture. He substitutes an inspired experience for an inspired Scripture, and a truth is inspired only when it is inspiring. Not without point does Theodore Engelder twit the Barthians with "refusing to believe that God performed the miracle of giving us by inspiration an infallible Bible, but . . . ready to believe that God daily performs the greater miracle of enabling men to find and see in the fallible word of man the infallible Word of God" (*Scripture Cannot Be Broken*, p. 129).

This form of reasoning can be seen to lead, all too easily, to an irrationality that lands us in the quagmire of mysticism. When we are told that, in the giving of revelation, inspiration is "an effect of the operation of the Spirit of God through which a man learned to understand the nature of the facts given to him," we are asked also to believe that only to the extent that inspired knowledge can be gained from a fact or a word is that fact or word guaranteed for us as actual. Let us illustrate by applying this to the facts of the Gospel records. If, for example, the apostles through God's Spirit gained

inspired knowledge from the resurrection of Christ, then the actuality of the
resurrection is established for everyone who feels the witness of the Spirit in
the Scriptures. Or again, if the words of Christ and the oracles spoken through
the prophets have become the objects of inspired understanding, then for the
religious point of view their reality is proved. This, incidentally, is the argument, in practically identical terms, used by Reinhold Seeberg in a recent
volume (*Revelation and Inspiration*, p. 112). Kierkegaard has put it more
tersely in his maxim: "only the truth that edifies is truth for thee." But of
what use is it for us that "for the religious point of view" our experience of
religious effects arising from the apostles' narrative of the resurrection
guarantees for us the reality of the event, if critical disparagement of the
historical records should convince us that, in point of fact, Christ did not
rise from the dead from the scientific point of view? We cannot long continue to believe on the authority of our religious experience what we know to
be contrary to the finding of our scientific investigation (cf. Cornelius Van
Til on this point in his Introduction to B. B. Warfield's *The Inspiration and
Authority of the Bible*).

Similarly, Martin J. Heinecken, who, in a most superior tone, disparages
the "naive fundamentalist," dismisses the historical basis of the virgin birth
and resurrection of our Lord as of no interest to faith, for "just as with the
virgin birth, such an occurrence as the resurrection is highly improbable but
not impossible." Whether probable or possible is apparently an irrelevance
to faith inasmuch as "he who means to establish an objective certainty only
confuses the issue." The "fact to which faith witnesses is a final and complete
victory over death" (*The Moment Before God*, pp. 264 f.). Can naïveté, we
ask, go further? If Christ did not in fact rise from the dead, even if disciples
then and now credulously believe that he did, while in fact he is still in
Joseph's tomb, then his "resurrection" cannot be "a victory over death,"
complete or otherwise. This divorce of faith from factual reality lands us
only in the cloudland of make-believe, and the Christian faith is as un-
substantial as a daydream.

It can be seen that in reality this is an attempt to recover a basis of confidence in certain of the spiritual facts and ideas of the Bible without accepting its divine authority or even its historical trustworthiness. It implies that
Christian experience has a sufficient basis for confidence in the Christian
facts and events, while dispensing with the inherent authority of the Bible,
and confining its "authority" at best to its practical effectiveness as a means
of grace. J. K. S. Reid presses this point: "Its authoritative character . . .
lies not in itself . . . but finally and quite securely in the fact that it is the
means elected of God's free grace for the operation of God's free grace"
(*op. cit.*, p. 217). Thus when the Bible is not actively a means of grace it
has little or no authority for us as Christians, and none at all for the non-
Christian who approaches it.

All this does not explain how, if the Bible record is untrustworthy, we can accept the trustworthiness of a spiritual experience that is based on it. We are left in the impossible position of having to accept as true as a matter of religious experience what we must reject as false as a matter of objective reality. In no other department of human thought or research is truth based on subjective experience that lacks objective reality, yet this is what is offered us as the basis of religion.

Our only escape from this dilemma lies in the recognition that our experience is a testimony to the trustworthiness of the Biblical record only because our experience has roots in that inspired record. By the living encounter in the Word there comes the flash of identification between the written Word and Jesus Christ the Living Word. This is what Paul commends in his converts at Thessalonica to whom, as he tells us, he preached a very factual gospel: "For this cause we thank God without ceasing, because that when ye received the word of God which ye heard of us, ye received it not as the word of man but, as it is in truth, the word of God which effectually worketh also in you who believe" (1 Thess. 2:13). In this case, obviously, credence to the written or spoken word led to an experience of the Living Word, and this identification of the written Word with the voice of God is what we understand by "finding Christ" in the Scriptures. Thus a dual confirmation results: our experience confirming the authority of the Scriptures, and the Scriptures confirming the validity of our experience. But our experience would have nothing to confirm if we had not previously received and believed the facts contained in the Biblical record. In other words, the truth which becomes real to our subjective experience has its objective foundation in the written Word. We dare not reverse this order, because to see the facts first of all through the medium of our experience is not necessarily to see them aright. In many cases the facts are distorted as they pass through our own distorted personality, and without appeal to the Scripture norm we are left at the mercy of every hallucination that may possess us. The subjectivism that cannot be tested by the reality of Scripture truth thus opens the door to many spiritual perils, not least of all the possibility that the human personality may be invaded by influences within the spiritual world that are not of God. For that reason, were there none other, it would become necessary for us, as it was necessary for the first disciples of Christ, to refer back from the most exalted experiences to "the more sure word of prophecy" (2 Peter 1:17 f.). But this we cannot do if we lack a firm doctrine of inspiration. Invocation of the authority of the Spirit to contradict the authority of the Scriptures threatens, in fact, to become the particular blasphemy of the present age!

The Word of God and the Text of Scripture

The third antithesis postulated by modern theology is that between the Word of God and the text of Scripture.

Not only is a sharp distinction drawn between the Word of God and the text of Scripture, but they are conceived as discontinuous and placed in different categories. To think of Scripture as the Word of God is, Professor Reid remarks, an infringement of the sovereignty of God. While Barth draws a parallelism between God present in the Person of Christ and the Word present in the Scriptures, he claims that the analogy breaks down in that there is no corresponding unity between the Word of God and the Scripture witness. Man's "subordination" to Scripture is, therefore, strictly limited to its witness. The "absolute surrender," as in the seventeenth century, led to the setting up of a "paper Pope."

We are told that textual criticism has made infallibility untenable. To the evangelical scholar it is not a little perplexing to have the modern objection to inspiration thus placed in the realm of textual criticism. The text of Scripture he never regarded as sacrosanct: it derives its sacredness from the fact that it conveys the revelation of the true God to the souls of men. That is to say, the inspiration of the text is derivative and arises from the fact that the message it conveys is inspired. Since we are completely dependent upon the text, in the first instance, to understand the message, it follows that text and message stand or fall together. It is singular perverseness to put the Living Word and the written Word in sharp antithesis. The written Word bears testimony to the Living Word, Jesus Christ, in such an intimate way that to discredit the Scriptures is virtually to blot Jesus Christ out of the knowledge of men. Therefore, as Calvin puts it, "we owe to the Scriptures the same reverence which we owe to God, because it has proceeded from Him alone."

It is difficult, indeed, to understand why textual criticism should be supposed to make infallibility untenable. Brunner goes so far as to claim that the fundamentalists, confronted by the contradictions and inconsistencies unearthed by the critics, have had to resort to "an infallible original." This original he speaks of contemptuously as "an infallible Bible of which two things only are known; first, that it was the infallible Word of God, and, second, that although it was very different from the present one, it was still the same Bible." This he condemns as descending to "apologetic artifices." This is, of course, a gross misrepresentation. We are not appealing to a Bible of which we know little or nothing, or which "is very different from the present one." That original is all but identical with the text we possess, the margin of difference being so small that only one text in one thousand is open to uncertainty on textual grounds, while, moreover, no doctrine of the faith is thereby involved in uncertainty.

It is common knowledge that we do not possess the autographs of any of the books of the Bible. But even if the autographs were discovered that would not in the least affect the principle on which infallibility is claimed for the Scriptures. What we contend is that an infallible revelation has actually entered into history, and the existence of an infallible and perfect original text—even if not discoverable—is the grand presupposition of the science of textual criticism. We do not claim divine inspiration for the formation of the

Canon as we have it, nor for the preservation of the text, though we are ready to recognize a divine providence of a very impressive kind in both. The text of the Bible must, therefore, be subject to the same scientific analysis as that of any other literature, and the very highly developed state of this science is itself a tribute to the value placed upon the words of the original text as being the *ipsissima verba* of inspiration. The men who employ their skill in the tasks do so in the confident faith that they are on the road to discovering ultimate and final truth. In like manner, even Luther's somewhat reckless criticism of the Canon is a tribute, not to any laxity in his doctrine of inspiration, but rather to a high doctrine of inspiration to which, in his opinion, certain books in the Canon did not attain.

It is strange to hear believers in the infallibility of Holy Scripture described as "bibliolaters." Fundamentalism, we are told, deifies the Book and speaks of it as if "the Spirit of God were imprisoned within the covers of the written word." The fundamentalist, says Brunner, is "in bondage to the Biblical text," and this "makes the Bible an idol and me its slave." This is what is meant by calling the Bible the paper Pope of Protestantism. We can conceive of the applicability of this charge to the Pharisees as a class in our Lord's day. They searched the Scriptures, reverenced them as the final judge of all controversy, but they refused to bring their lives into conformity to their demands. We cannot conceive of the charge being applicable to evangelicals of the present day who are seeking to bring their lives to the light of the Word as to the judgment of God himself. But the sacredness of the Bible is to them, as we have already indicated, a derived quality and is not resident primarily in the pages of the Book. We recognize it as the words of men who were given a divine revelation and were inspired to communicate it to their fellows, and so, as Calvin puts it, "it is beyond all controversy that men ought to receive it with reverence." The Bible is for us the only sure and accessible repository of divine revelation and so of the knowledge of God that makes us wise unto salvation. Without it we would be in the position of the pagan world, left to grope after God if haply we might find him. We believe that if the living and true God revealed himself at all he revealed himself infallibly, and if he willed that the revelation should be in the possession of his Church for all time, we must believe that he had it in his power to give an infallible record of it. This he has done in the Hebrew-Christian Scriptures. And so we recognize and reverence the Bible as the Word of God written, and we bow before its authority as before the authority of its Lord. In so doing we think we are following the example of our Lord and Saviour who interpreted his mission, waged his conflicts, comforted his heart, and guided his steps, in dependence upon the written Word.

What we must reject, however, with the utmost emphasis, is the oft-repeated assertion that this doctrine of inerrancy is "a new doctrine." When A. G. Hebert says, in the strain of many modern writers, that "modern fundamentalism is asserting something that no previous age has under-

R. A. Finlayson: CONTEMPORARY IDEAS OF INSPIRATION   233

stood in anything like the modern sense" (*The Authority of the Old Testament*, p. 98), we point out that history is utterly against his contention.
The inspiration which we claim for the Scriptures is the inspiration which
the Scriptures claim for themselves, which the Apostolic Church claimed
for them, and what the Reformed Church understood by the Word of
God written.

It is a historical fact that not till the rise of the School of Saumur in the
mid-seventeenth century did any question arise within the Calvinistic or
Reformed Group as to the verbal inspiration of the Scriptures. And the
violence of the reaction to it is the measure of the shock it administered to
the Reformed tradition. Karl Barth began his meteoric career with the
slogan: Back to Calvin. The early Reformers, especially Luther, are frequently appealed to in order to give Reformed sanction to the modern
approach to the Scriptures by which revelation is emptied of its doctrinal
content.

But Luther's insistence on the inner witness of the Spirit as opposed to the
dead letter must be read in its historical setting as an insistence upon personal
faith in Christ as opposed to the mere intellectual homage to the letter of
Scripture deemed sufficient by the Roman Church. While it is true that the
Reformer saw no reason for elaborating a doctrine of inspiration, there is
nothing in his works that denies the verbal and plenary inspiration of the
canonical books of the Bible. On the contrary, we find in several places in
his writings that he equates the Scriptures with "the words of God," and it
was his custom to use the terms "Scripture says" and "God says" interchangeably. Nor is there any evidence that he recognizes degrees of inspiration.

As for Calvin, he makes this recognition of the divine authority of the
written Word the distinctive mark of true Christianity. "This is a principle,"
he says, "which distinguishes our religion from all others, that we know that
God has spoken to us and are fully convinced that the prophets did not speak
at their own suggestion; but that being organs of the Holy Spirit, they only
uttered what they have been commissioned from Heaven to declare. Whoever then wishes to prosper in the Scriptures let him first of all lay down this
as a settled point, that the Law and the Prophets are not a doctrine delivered
according to the will and pleasure of men, but dictated by the Holy Spirit"
(*Commentaries* on II Timothy 3:16).

The modern hostility to inspiration must be sought for in another direction
than that of Reformed tradition. And Martin J. Heinecken, writing of the
place of Kierkegaard as the forerunner of Barth, puts the case as succinctly,
perhaps, as any. "Without Kierkegaard," he writes, "there would have been
no Barth, no dialectical theology, no return to the Bible that would preserve
any kind of scientific respectability" (*The Moment Before God*, p. 19).
Without doubt "scientific respectability" is the *raison d'etre* of neo-orthodoxy. Has it attained it? Rather, its rearguard action involving retreat into

personal mysticism actually places it beyond the reach and interest of modern science. It has severed the Christian faith from its roots in history; bringing it down to the level of mystical experience, it has emptied Christian faith of its revealed doctrinal content and obliterated the distinction between truth and error, between orthodoxy and heresy, between faith based on knowledge and mere credulity. Most serious of all, it has impugned the trustworthiness of the historical Christ, and changed the heart-throbbing words of his message to the world into the mere echoes of other men's experience. Under its solvent the Person of Christ becomes elusive and illusionary, a mere intruder into history, as someone has put it, who has troubled men with his message but left no sure word for posterity. For it must be clearly understood that the battle being waged against the inspiration of the Bible is, in the last resort, an assault upon historic Christianity and its foundation, Jesus Christ. This is an impressive acknowledgment of the fact that Scripture is recognized to be the supreme bulwark of the historic Christian Faith.

THE PHENOMENA
OF SCRIPTURE

Everett F. Harrison

Everett F. Harrison is Professor of New Testament in Fuller Theological Seminary, California. He holds the A.D. degree from University of Washington, Th.B. from Princeton Theological Seminary, M.A. from Princeton University, Th.D. from Dallas Theological Seminary, and Ph.D. from University of Pennsylvania. He is author of The Son of God Among the Sons of Men. A Dictionary of Theology, *of which he is editor, is to be published in 1959.*

15. *Everett F. Harrison*

THE PHENOMENA
OF SCRIPTURE

D URING most of the centuries spanned by the history of the Christian Church it has been customary to speak of the Bible as the Word of God. Today many Protestants refuse to make this identification. One of the contributing factors in this change of attitude is the unwillingness to consider a record divine which is marred by inaccuracies. The Bible may contain the Word of God, or be the vehicle for the Word, it is said, but can no longer be equated with that Word itself.

It is maintained that the view of verbal inspiration could hold the field only so long as the divine factor in its composition was magnified to the neglect of the human. Obviously, if God be admitted as the Author of Scripture, error in the original text becomes unthinkable, lest the very character of God be impugned. The demand for more recognition of the human element in the Bible is sometimes fortified by an appeal to the theanthropic person of our Lord. In him the divine consented to be yoked to the human with all its limitations. So, it is contended, the divine factor in the making of Scripture was pleased to yoke itself to the human despite the frailties of the latter. The comparison is interesting, but if it is made from the standpoint of seeking to justify the ways of God in producing his Word through men who stained the record with errors, the comparison is quite inept, for it logically involves the imputation of shortcoming in one way or another to the person of Christ. It would be more appropriate to point to the phenomenon of the Christian worker, who may be labelled a man of God, despite his sinfulness, because of the operation of God upon him and through him, but in that case the analogy with a unique activity of divine inspiration breaks down.

The advocate of verbal inspiration quite naturally seeks on his own part to make use of the prestige of our Lord in order to buttress his position. This is done principally by appealing to Christ's blanket endorsement of the Old Testament as unbreakable Scripture, the very Word of God. Since many of the problems lie in the Old Testament field, this appeal takes on all the greater significance. The citing of Christ's attitude toward the Old Testament, however, involves a problem of its own. Criticism in the modern sense had not begun. We can hardly say that Jesus' pronouncements on the Old Testament were framed in anticipation of the attacks which would be made on it many hundreds of years later. Consequently, his affirmations on Scripture cannot be invoked with the same force as though the modern issues were in his mind. On the other hand, in view of the perfection of his humanity and the fullness of his wisdom, we rightfully expect that his comments on the Old Testament are fully reliable and like all his words shall never pass away and shall never be outmoded by advancing knowledge.

We turn from our Lord's own testimony to the modern debate over inspiration.

Most writers seem agreed that the modern formulation of the doctrine of verbal inspiration belongs not to the Reformers but to the dogmaticians who succeeded them. But certain statements in Luther are quite harmonious with the rigid position of his successors. More recent evangelicals have outlined the requirements of the doctrine of verbal inspiration in somewhat diverse ways. A. A. Hodge and B. B. Warfield, in a joint article, affirmed that, "A proved error in Scripture contradicts not only our doctrine, but the Scripture claims, and therefore its inspiration, in making those claims" (*Presbyterian Review*, Vol. II, p. 245). Francis L. Patton, on the other hand, declared, "It is a hazardous thing to say that being inspired the Bible must be free from error; for then the discovery of a single error would destroy its inspiration. Nor have we any right to substitute the word 'inerrancy' for 'inspiration' in our discussion of the Bible unless we are prepared to show from the teaching of the Bible that inspiration means inerrancy—and that, I think, would be a difficult thing to do" (*Fundamental Christianity*, pp. 163 f.). One must grant that the Bible itself, in advancing its own claim of inspiration, says nothing precise about its inerrancy. This remains a conclusion to which devout minds have come because of the divine character of Scripture. If a person has become convinced by the study of the Word that its majesty and perfection can only be accounted for on the basis that the text was free from error as originally given, such a person ought not to be charged with intellectual dishonesty if he refuses to let perplexing problems in the sacred record move him from this solid conviction. He may feel bound to seek explanation for the problems, and perhaps be dissatisfied with the explanations he receives, yet he continues to rest in his conviction, lest the abandonment of his position mean the forsaking of Scripture as the Word of God.

It is quite possible that one who stands firm in the belief that the Bible, being God's Word, must be free from error, may count it presumptuous to investigate the tension points very closely. He fears being drawn into the role of a critic of the Word of God instead of being submissive to its pronouncements. He does not deny the function of criticism in a theoretical sense, but practically he is hesitant to employ critical methods in the effort to determine whether or not mistakes do occur. One who follows Dr. Patton's lead is liable to admit the legitimacy of critical investigation but may not care to permit himself to go very far lest the vindication of his own principle of liberty of investigation should turn up difficulties which might embarrass him in continuing to hold a high view of Scripture. Consequently, it has been left largely to so-called liberals to expose and press the problems. It would seem that the only healthy attitude for conservatives is to welcome criticism and be willing to join in it. No view of Scripture can indefinitely be sustained if it runs counter to the facts. That the Bible claims inspiration is patent. The problem is to define the nature of that inspiration in the light of the phenomena contained therein.

Let no one imagine it is an easy task. Can we expect agreement, for example, on what constitutes error? The scientific age in which we live has put a premium upon precise accuracy. Must we impose our standard on an ancient Book? We think we know what truth is. The chances are we are thinking in Hellenistic terms, identifying truth with what corresponds to reality. But the writers of Scripture were not as greatly influenced by this conception of truth as by the Hebrew conception which identifies as truth what corresponds to the nature and purpose of God. Sin is truth if the one standard is applied, for sin is certainly real. But it cannot be truth in the higher sense of being in accord with the nature and purpose of God. The annalistic accounts of the kings of Judah found in the books of Kings take us into the realm of history as ordinarily understood. Here the customary standard of truth may fairly be applied. But in Chronicles the same period is presented from quite a different standpoint. The concept of God's covenant mercy mediated through David and his house dominates the treatment of the history. It is more internal than external. How can we say that one is more true than the other?

I. THE TEXT OF SCRIPTURE

Are we justified in appealing from our present text to supposedly infallible originals? Such a procedure is sometimes ridiculed on the ground that no one living has ever seen such infallible originals. True enough. But as Dr. Carl Henry once observed, no one has seen the fallible originals either. The one is as much a presupposition as the other.

But is inspiration not jeopardized by uncertainties about the proper reading to be followed in some passages? When it is alleged that there are thousands of variant readings, this situation can be made to sound well-nigh hopeless. Differences in the several English versions which have succeeded one another during the last 350 years reflect changes made in the Greek text by modern editors on the basis of manuscript discovery. But an elementary fact remains. There *is* a text of Scripture. The Bible is not an undefined literature which has attained its form by some hit-or-miss process, and which ought now to be completely remade by admitting a flood of variant readings. The vast bulk of the Word of God is not affected by variations of text at all. Many of the variants concern differences in spelling only. Others can be readily accounted for as scribal embellishment. It is true that as the wealth of materials increases, the task of certifying the proper reading in a given instance may be made more difficult. Yet, despite all this, comparatively little alteration in the text may be looked for in days to come.

The real problem for textual criticism lies in the difficulty of working back to the autographs. The pre-Massoretic period in the transmission of the text of the Old Testament and the first hundred years of the history of the New Testament text are the sore spots. The Dead Sea Scrolls of Old Testament books present examples of proto-Massoretic text, proto-Septuagint, and others which do not conform to either type. Perhaps still more ancient texts will some day come to light to aid the process of certifying the wording of Scripture. Meanwhile, we must rest in the fact that whereas copying has created some uncertainties, the great bulk of the Bible remains unchallenged and its spiritual message shines through to the reader undimmed.

II. CHRONOLOGY

Since the Biblical faith is rooted in the conviction of the activity of God in human history, events gain significance both in themselves and in relation to one another. Therefore the Bible is concerned with chronology. This is a difficult field, even for the specialist, so that agreement has not been attained on all points. But a good example of progress is the work of Edwin R. Thiele on the period of the divided kingdom (*The Mysterious Numbers of the Hebrew Kings*, 1951). He summarizes his findings as follows:

> When we once accept the premise of an original reckoning of reigns in Israel according to the nonaccession-year system with a later shift to the accession-year method; of the early use in Judah of accession-year reckoning, a shift to the nonaccession-year system, and then a return to the original accession-year method; when we begin the regnal year in Israel with Nisan and with Tishri in Judah; when we take into consideration the existence of a number of coregencies; and when we recognize that at some late date—long after the original records of the kings had been set in order and when the true arrangement of the reigns had been forgotten—certain synchronisms in II Kings 17 and 18 were introduced by some late hand strangely out of harmony with the original pattern of reigns—when all this is understood, we have shown that it becomes possible to set forth an arrangement of reigns for the Hebrew kings in which we

Everett F. Harrison: THE PHENOMENA OF SCRIPTURE   241

find both internal harmony and agreement with the facts of contemporary history (p. 268).

The findings of this scholar have been widely accepted, and should give encouragement for further progress in other areas of chronological difficulty.

III. NUMBERS

Are the figures given in the Biblical narrative trustworthy? To begin with, it should readily be granted that some numbers are not intended to be exact. For example, a clan in Israel was called a thousand. This is an arbitrary figure, and it is highly unlikely that it was anything more than an ideal figure—like a regiment which is often not up to full strength.

One of the complaints lodged against the Biblical narrative is that numbers are often exaggerated. For example, it is doubted that the children of Israel could have increased in Egypt to the point that they were a nation to be reckoned with, 600,000 men, besides women and children (Ex. 12:37). It is pointed out that the repressive measures of the Egyptians would have prevented any such increase. But the Scripture attests the futility of the effort to check the growth of the male population (Ex. 1:18) and expressly informs us that the more the children of Israel were oppressed the more they multiplied (Ex. 1:12). It was the enormous growth of the people which caused alarm among the Egyptians and led to harsh treatment (Ex. 1:7-11). If it be insisted that such a large number of people could not have survived the rigors of life in the wilderness, one can agree. The Bible does not assert that Israel maintained itself in the wilderness. Apart from God's supernatural care the sojourn there would have been impossible. If one cannot accept the miraculous he will naturally quibble at the numbers.

Another tension point is the population figures given for the towns captured by Israel at the conquest. The *tels* of these places, as they are examined today by archaeologists, are small and apparently quite incapable of containing such large numbers as the records assign to them. The problem is real. One factor in a possible solution is the fact that such population figures as 12,000 for Ai must surely have included the people who ordinarily dwelt outside the city and carried on agriculture in the surrounding country. They would rally to the city in time of siege.

More perplexing is the conflict in figures found in parallel passages of the same event. Professor H. P. Smith prepared a list of these (*Inspiration and Inerrancy,* pp. 250 f.). For example, it is stated in II Samuel 10:18 that David destroyed of the Syrians 700 chariots. In I Chronicles 19:18 the number is put at 7,000. Dr. Smith proposes that the Chronicler was desirous of enhancing the glory of Israel's golden age, which now lay in the past, and he did this by altering the figures. If so, it is strange that II Chronicles 9:25 should state that Solomon had 4,000 stalls for horses and chariots, whereas the earlier annalistic record of I Kings 4:26 states that he had 40,000 stalls.

242 REVELATION AND THE BIBLE

The pattern is not consistent. Some have thought that abbreviations were used for figures and that these were sometimes misconstrued by those who used the texts at a later time. No explanation that has been given is entirely satisfactory. Here one must simply confess to having insufficient data for a judgment. It is amusing to note that Dr. Smith's figures do not jibe with the text in the case of II Samuel 10:6, for he lists the men of Tob as 1,200, whereas the text has 12,000—an unwitting lesson to all of us about the difficulty of transcribing numbers precisely.

IV. THE GOSPELS

All will agree that the records of our Lord's life and ministry are central to the whole gamut of Scripture. But not all agree that they are trustworthy accounts, in which case they cannot have been inspired of God. One of the most devastating lines of criticism used to question the record is the contention that the tradition has been so thoroughly shaped by the viewpoint and needs of the early Church that we are practically without any reliable means for forming a truly historical picture of what transpired in the life and labors of Christ. This is one of the fruits of an extreme application of the form-criticism method. Granting that the interest of the Church may have been greater in some things that pertained to the tradition than others, because of the bearing on its own situation, this does not mean that the Church altered the tradition. Selection does not mean perversion. The tradition was grounded on the testimony of witnesses, men who had companied with Christ. It would be utterly inconsistent with such witness to alter the tradition, especially when many of these witnesses were still alive and active in the leadership of the Church. The tradition in written form, preserved in the Gospel records, cannot successfully be opposed to the oral tradition which preceded it, as though the tradition had lost its reliability by the time it was inscripturated. The only reason for putting the tradition into written form was to preserve that which had been the oral teaching of the Church from the time of its inception.

The first three Gospels possess certain marked similarities, having considerable material in common and looking at our Lord's ministry from essentially the same perspective. They are therefore called Synoptic Gospels. It is widely agreed today that these accounts make use of sources, whether written or oral or both. Mark is viewed as the basic account, for Matthew and Luke appear to have made liberal use of his narrative.[1] In addition, they utilized other sources. Attempts have been made to show that even Mark is composed from previously existing sources. All this sounds unbecoming to the notion of inspiration. What room is left for divine action? A moment's

---

[1]For the contrary view questioning the primacy of Mark and supporting the traditional priority of Matthew, see John H. Ludlum Jr.'s two articles on "New Light on the Synoptic Problem" in *Christianity Today,* Nov. 10 and No. 24, 1958.—ED.

reflection, however, will shed a different light on the situation. The Old Testament which was so heartily endorsed by Christ and so reverently held by the early Church to be the Word of God had already been constructed in part along similar lines, for the use of sources is often indicated throughout the historical books. We have no reason, therefore, to raise any a priori objection to this methodology in the composition of the Gospels.

If the Gospel writers imply their dependence upon one another's work by the similarity of the wording in many places, yes, even identity of wording, they also reveal something of their own reason for writing by the variations of their narrative when touching the same material. They have a special aspect of Christ which they wish to magnify. Or they have in mind a certain type of reader. So, for example, we may instance Luke's words in reporting the cries of the crowd at the triumphal entry of Christ—"Glory in the highest," instead of "Hosanna in the highest" as in the other Gospels. Luke knew that his Gentile readers would be unfamiliar with the word Hosanna, so he did his best to express its meaning in a way which would be intelligible.

Verbal alteration is not an isolated feature, for it occurs also in the parallel accounts of the Old Testament. It is present too in many of the quotations made by New Testament writers from the Old Testament. The more one emphasizes the alterations in the wording of the quotations, the more impossible it becomes to explain these deviations on the basis of carelessness or errancy. Schoolboys could do a better job of mere transcribing than the New Testament writers have sometimes done. It becomes necessary to suppose that a divine power was present in them, leading them in the interest of fulfillment and application to use language which differed at times from that of their Old Testament exemplars.

If the Gospel writers had been interested in presenting records which would meet the test of verbal agreement, they would certainly have labored to harmonize their accounts. There is nothing superficial or flippant about these accounts. Clearly they were written with all soberness and in the consciousness of handling truth. But that truth was capable of multiform expression which gained its unity from its great Subject and from its Author, the Spirit of Truth.

Verbal contradictions do occur in the Gospels. One of the most famous is the "staff" passage which recounts Jesus' directions to the disciples governing their preparation for the preaching tour they were about to undertake. According to Mark 6:8 a staff was permissible, whereas bread, pouch, and copper coins for the girdle were ruled out. The parallel passages in Matthew 10:9 and Luke 9:3 differ in that they include a prohibition of staff as well. Are we to take the common sense approach and say that staff and sandals (which the Markan account also allows) were necessary items, whereas bread and pouch and copper coin contained occasions of temptation to provide for oneself and even store up a supply in advance? If so, then the

244 REVELATION AND THE BIBLE

other accounts may represent what Swete calls "an early exaggeration of the sternness of the command." Or are we entitled to think that the more sweeping demands of Jesus in the Matthew and Luke accounts better suit the spirit of the narrative, with its note of urgency and complete dependence on God? It is odd that these two should agree together against Mark. Perhaps the text of Mark originally read as they do and it was altered at a very early date. Speculation cannot do much to resolve the riddle. Whatever be the explanation, this sort of thing is rare in the Gospels, for ordinarily they flow along together with only minor changes in terminology which do not materially affect the meaning.

Sometimes one Gospel appears to add to another something which alters the sense. In the report of the Sermon on the Mount, Luke has "Blessed are ye poor," whereas Matthew has "Blessed are the poor in spirit." We need not suppose that Matthew had Luke's text before him and consciously added to it. The saying, as it circulated in the tradition, probably had the form Luke gives it. Matthew's terminology is something of an interpretation which is also in the nature of a safeguard against a misunderstanding of the purport of Jesus' saying. Poverty is not in itself a blessing nor does it by itself convey a spiritual benefit. But redemption history reveals the truth that the poor are apt to be those who, though oppressed by their fellows, commit their case to the Lord and trust in him to vindicate them. They may even have become poor because their piety made them a target of ungodly and unscrupulous men who knew they would not use worldly methods to defend themselves. We should ask ourselves whether it would have been better for Matthew to leave the words of Jesus in the bald form found in the tradition, or whether the addition is not justified both in the mind of Christ and in the verdict of history. There does not appear to be any antecedent reason why interpretation, which is so prominent a part of the epistles of the New Testament where they touch the person and work of Christ, should not also find a place in the records of his life and work which the Gospels afford us. Particularly is this so when it is recalled that the epistles, in greater part at least, preceded the Gospels in order of composition. Their influence on the Gospels in this respect must not be ignored.

No further attention need be given to the factor of verbal differences in parallel accounts, since reason and experience teach us that the same thing can be stated in more than one way without loss of accuracy. Were the accounts slavishly similar, suspicion would be engendered that they had been made to agree out of an ulterior motive to furnish an appearance of harmony which the facts did not warrant.

A question may properly be raised about passages which stand in only one Gospel. This problem does not concern Mark, for practically all of his record reappears in some fashion in Matthew or Luke. But in the latter two Gospels we find not only individual sayings but whole blocks of material which are peculiar to the Gospel concerned. A very radical approach to the problem might conclude that because these items are not found in the basic Gospel of Mark, they are therefore to be suspected as alien to the original tradition. But on what basis can we judge that Mark is the sum total of legitimate early tradition? The words and deeds of Jesus were far bulkier than any of our Gospels or all of them put together. So, for example, the saying of Jesus in Matthew 16 about the Church has no counterpart in the other Gospels, but it can easily be defended as an authentic saying of Jesus rather than something read back into the tradition from a later time to justify the Church's existence and Peter's prominence in relation to it. As R. Newton Flew observes, "The Semitic colouring of these verses is unmistakable. The opening beatitude, the designation of Simon by his father's name, the Rabbinic expression of 'binding and loosing,' the eschatological struggle with the powers of the underworld—all these are indications of a primitive origin for the whole paragraph" (*Jesus and His Church,* p. 90).

In an inspired record we might expect to find events recounted in exactly the same order in parallel accounts. This is not the case, although the Synoptic Gospels do preserve a broad pattern of agreement in regard to the movements of Jesus as well as his utterances. But there are exceptions, such as the order of events in the Temptation and Jesus' rejection at Nazareth. This latter item is placed almost at the beginning of the Galilean ministry by Luke. Matthew and Mark have it much later. Generally speaking, there is no such thing as an inspired order of narration. As noted above, one may detect a broad chronological pattern unfolding in the Gospels, but it is obvious that within that framework the writers exercised considerable liberty in the placing of individual elements of the story. They can only be held blameworthy in so doing if they have committed themselves to a strict chronological sequence, and this they have not done.

Are the Gospel writers guilty of accretion? Have they added to the basic tradition imaginative or legendary elements, or have they been influenced to color their accounts by intruding material which derives from early Church usage but which is anachronistic for the period of the Gospels? This problem is another aspect of the comparative study of the Synoptics. To begin with we can rule out any suggestion that the tendency to accretion is such an organic thing that we can trace it through the various stages of the tradition. On the contrary, it is a well-known fact that in repeated instances the accounts which Matthew and Luke present are briefer than the account given in Mark, the basic Gospel. Examples are the story of the woman with an issue of blood, the Gerasene demoniac, John the Baptist's imprisonment, the cure of the epileptic boy. The Gospel writers were not afflicted with a mania to enlarge upon what was commonly received.

Matthew is the one chiefly accused of taking liberties with his material. In certain incidents he introduces two men where the parallel accounts have only one, as in the case of the Gerasene demoniac (Matt. 8:28) and the blind man at Jericho (Matt. 20:30). The animal used at the triumphal entry has a foal, which is not mentioned in the other accounts (Matt. 21: 2–7). But curiously enough, in the story of the resurrection, Matthew, like Mark, notes only one angel at the tomb, whereas Luke refers to two (the same is true in John's account). It would seem impossible, therefore, to find a pattern of accretion that is consistent. One could properly speak of error here if the texts which specify a single participant made it definite that there was one and only one. This is not the case. The possibility of a plurality can then be granted on principle.

An ecclesiastical interest has been detected by many writers in the case of Matthew's Gospel. It is said that the baptismal formula in connection with the Great Commission, to cite one example, is a reflection of the developed usage of the Church at a later time and cannot be attributed to Jesus himself. This sort of criticism is abritrary. What is the background for such a trinitarian statement as is contained in the apostolic benediction (II Cor. 13:14) unless it be the very utterance of Jesus referred to by Matthew?

Luke also is characterized by elements not found in the other Synoptic records. We are not thinking of blocks of material peculiar to his Gospel, but of additions where the narrative is held in common by the Synoptists. One example will suffice, the case of the two malefactors crucified with Jesus. Mark and Matthew are content to narrate the fact of the co-crucifixion. Luke alone tells of their conversation with Christ and with one another, climaxed in the repentance and faith of one of them. As a historian who made inquiry about the events of the life of Christ before setting his hand to writing, Luke must have learned of this development and so included it. We can hardly charge a man of his historical judgment with embroidering a story in order to give it greater human interest.

V. THE FOURTH GOSPEL AND THE SYNOPTICS

John's account of our Lord's ministry follows a path so completely different from the Synoptics that it overlaps in only about ten percent of the material. It makes the ministry longer than the express statements of the other Gospels require, and it locates the scene of Christ's labors preponderantly in Judea rather than in Galilee. Is this historically justified? Since the Gospel materials combined give us only about 30 days of activity, it is evident that the Synoptic tradition is by no means a complete account of our Lord's active ministry. An extensive Judaean ministry is not out of the question. In fact, it is demanded by the Synoptics themselves, for they present the visit to Jerusalem as involving a verdict of death for Jesus as a fact assured in advance. Only John's Gospel gives us the true explanation for this state of affairs, for it indicates that Jerusalem has had its opportunity to evaluate Jesus and that the decision has been negative. Incidentally, the Synoptics in their own way testify to the presence of Jesus in Judea before the final journey. The story of Martha and Mary is only one example of several which tend to establish his presence in the vicinity of Jerusalem on more than one occasion prior to the closing days.

A striking feature of John's Gospel is the discourse material. Here Jesus makes no use of the typical parabolic medium of the Synoptics. The addresses are mainly occupied with his own person and credentials. Sometimes they become dialogues between himself and his auditors. In many ways they reveal contrast to the discourses in the other Gospels. It is significant that Jewish scholars have experienced less difficulty in receiving these discourses as authentic than many critics of Christian persuasion, for they recognize how closely they parallel Rabbinic examples. Verbatim reporting was not expected on the part of a faithful disciple as he made available the sayings of his esteemed master. This freedom of expression did not necessarily involve unfaithfulness in the fulfillment of his task.

The basic question which keeps emerging even in the Synoptic report of Jesus' Galilean utterances is the person of Jesus in the sense that the very nature of the teaching involved an assumption of authority which was inseparable from the mystery of his being. In John's Gospel this question is more overtly discussed. The very openness of the discussion may be explained, at least in part, by the identity of those who heard our Lord. In the main, those who listened to the Johannine discourses were not the simple folk of Galilee but the custodians of Israel's traditions and hopes, the leaders of Jewry. Their position would require them to scrutinize his claims. This can be only a broad generalization, to be sure, for John 6 reports a discourse in which the common people were the auditors, and it is heavily Christocentric in its emphasis.

The cleansing of the temple is given an entirely different location in John than in the Synoptics. Instead of placing it at the close of the ministry, as they do, where it proves to be the event which crystallizes official Jewish opposition and triggers the developments which lead to Jesus' death, John puts it early. And since he has no cleansing of the temple at the close, he substitutes, as some think, the story of the resurrection of Lazarus as the occasion for the action of the Sanhedrin against Jesus. There is no necessity whatsoever for supposing that John invented the story of Lazarus' resurrection in order to provide a basis for official Jewish action against Jesus. The deepening opposition to him, attested both in John and the Synoptics, and the several attempts to capture him or put him to death during the course of his ministry, make it possible for events to have run their course even without a cleansing of the temple during the Passion week. But a proper understanding of the course of events is facilitated when we retain both cleansings. The former one helps to explain the exasperation of the Jewish hierarchy which is noted in connection with every subsequent visit to Jerusalem. It explains, too, why Jesus felt it expedient to leave Judea and pass through Samaria into Galilee, as stated in John 3 and 4. The second cleansing, on the other hand, comes in naturally as the sequel to the triumphal entry and the

prelude to the seizure and trial. Commercial traffic in the temple courts
could easily have been revived by the time our Lord came up to Jerusalem
for the final visit.

Into the much discussed question of the nature and the time of the Supper
mentioned in John 13 in relation to that mentioned in the Synoptics, we do
not propose to enter here, except to say that the key may still be missing for
the solution of the difficulty. John's references to the Feast as still future
from the standpoint of the meal eaten with his disciples (John 13:29;
18:28) may possibly be explained as pointing to the Feast of Unleavened
Bread, which was sometimes designated by the term Passover (Luke 22:1).
Some have conjectured that John was operating on a different calendar than
the Synoptists, perhaps reflecting the calendar dispute which the Qumran
community had with official Judaism. More light on this whole problem is
urgently needed.

It is our conviction that John wrote with full knowledge of the Synoptic
tradition, not to dispute it or displace it, but to build upon it and give it a
more definitely theological interpretation than his predecessors had supplied.

VI. THE ACTS AND THE EPISTLES

Opportunity for criticism in this area arises from the fact the same general
period is covered by the latter half of Acts and by the epistles of Paul. Acts
reports the movements of Paul and the founding of his churches. The
epistles reflect Paul's movements to some extent and reveal his principles
and methods. These writings are nearly all accepted as authentic in our time.
But a less favorable verdict has often been passed on the book of Acts. A
favorite testing point is the council of Jerusalem (Acts 15). Paul reports on
his contacts with the Jerusalem church in his epistle to the Galatians, and
includes an account of a visit to the holy city over the issue of circumcision
as it affected Gentile converts (Gal. 2:1-10). In many ways his account
differs from the report of Luke in Acts 15. Among other things, Luke makes
much of the decree which was sent to the Gentile churches as a result of the
conference. Paul is silent about this. Instead of jumping to radical conclusions about the unreliability of Luke, it is well to reflect how widely two
men may differ in their interest even when they are ideologically attuned.
Since Luke makes no mention of something very close to Paul's heart, the
fund raised by him in his churches for the poor saints at Jerusalem, though
he (Luke) gives a rather full report of the journey, including the listing of
Paul's traveling companions, and since he has nothing to say about Paul's
hope to visit Spain, though this was strongly in the apostle's mind and Luke
must have known of it because of his close association with the apostle, it is
then quite possible for him to emphasize a feature of the Jerusalem council,
namely the decree, which did not bulk nearly as large in the thinking of Paul
and therefore found no place in his letter to the Galatians.

VII. ERROR IN SOURCES?

We venture to embark on a delicate question which is involved in our general discussion. Does inspiration require that a Biblical writer should be preserved from error in the use of sources? Presumably when Stephen asserted that Abraham left Haran for Canaan after his father's death (Acts 7:4), he was following a type of Septuagintal text such as Philo used, for the latter has the same statement (*Migration of Abraham,* 177). The Hebrew text of Genesis will not permit this, since the figures given in Genesis 11:26, 32 and 12:4 demand that Terah continued to live for 60 years after Abraham left Haran. A similar approach may be made to the problem of Matthew's citation of Zechariah 11:12, 13 as though it were from Jeremiah (Matt. 27:9). No doubt other explanations are possible here, but we can understand that if this passage in Zechariah had already been associated with the name of Jeremiah in Jewish tradition, Matthew might readily fall into line with this practice. We are not affirming that this is a dogmatic requirement, but if the inductive study of the Bible reveals enough examples of this sort of thing to make the conclusion probable, then we shall have to hold the doctrine of inspiration in this light. We may have our own ideas as to how God should have inspired the Word, but it is more profitable to learn, if we can, how he has actually inspired it.

VIII. ETHICAL HARMONY?

To some minds the historical problems which tend to plague the defenders of inspiration are less important than the conflict in theological position which they find here and there in the Scriptures. A prime case is the contrary statement of II Samuel 24:1 and that of I Chronicles 21:1. The former passage states that the anger of the Lord was kindled against Israel and he incited David to number the people. This act brought divine retribution which the chapter describes. In Chronicles, on the other hand, it is stated that Satan rose up against Israel, inciting David to number Israel. Are we to think that the writer of Chronicles revolted against the idea that God would incite David to do something which would bring death to thousands of his subjects, so he changed his source to read Satan instead of God? This does not get us very far. Surely the Chronicler held a sufficiently high view of God that he would grant the divine awareness that Satan was inciting David. In that case, should not judgment have fallen on Satan rather than on the people? It seems clear that underlying both accounts is the recognition of the sinfulness of the nation. This is definitely implied in II Samuel 24:1. A nation that would repudiate its king for the usurper Absalom, to mention only one of its blemishes, was not pleasing to God. It is difficult to see any basis here for the thought that God is made to appear a capriciously angry deity, and that the Chronicler tries to get God off the hook by ascribing the trouble to Satan. God often used Satan and evil influences to bring judgment upon those who had disobeyed him or turned against him (see I Kings 22:19–23).

Another tension point is the divergent treatment of faith and works in Paul and James. Can these be harmonized? James 2:24 contains the crux of the discussion. It sounds anti-Pauline if it is allowed to stand in isolation. But the preceding verse demonstrates that for James, as for Paul, there is a justification based on faith alone (cf. Rom. 4:3–5). The point James is making is that true faith involves a manifestation in works. Only as these are present can faith be adjudged genuine. In this Paul concurs (Gal. 5:6). It is not at all clear that James is attacking teaching known to emanate from Paul. Certainly in the James passage there is no reference to works of the law such as Paul rules out in connection with justification. To teach that Paul and James are irreconcilable is not only to fail from the standpoint of penetrating exegesis but also to question the integrity of the honored expositors of the Word who have wrestled with this problem throughout the long history of interpretation and have concluded that the two representations are not fundamentally opposed.

Conclusion

Unquestionably the Bible teaches its own inspiration. It is the Book of God. It does not require us to hold inerrancy, though this is a natural corollary of full inspiration. The phenomena which present difficulties are not to be dismissed or underrated. They have driven many sincere believers in the trustworthiness of the Bible as a spiritual guide to hold a modified position on the non-revelation material. Every man must be persuaded in his own mind. James Orr once wrote, "It remains the fact that the Bible, impartially interpreted and judged, is free from demonstrable error in its statements, and harmonious in its teachings, to a degree that of itself creates an irresistible impression of a supernatural factor in its origin" (*Revelation and Inspiration*, p. 216). In this statement all believers should be able to concur. It is possible that if our knowledge were greater, all seeming difficulties could be swept away.

On an occasion when he was interrogated with respect to a theological problem, Jesus replied, "Ye do err, not knowing the Scriptures" (Matt. 22:29). How striking it is that the one allusion to error by our Lord in the days of his flesh was not to something in the Scriptures but to failure to know them and interpret them aright.

THE EVIDENCE OF
PROPHECY AND
MIRACLE

Bernard Ramm

Bernard Ramm is Professor of Religion and Director of Graduate Studies in Religion in Baylor University, Texas. He holds the B.D. and M.A. degrees from Eastern Baptist Seminary and the Ph.D. from University of Southern California. He has written Problems in Christian Apologetics, Protestant Biblical Interpretation, Protestant Christian Evidence, Types of Apologetic Systems, The Christian View of Science and Scripture, *and* The Pattern of Authority.

16. Bernard Ramm

THE EVIDENCE OF
PROPHECY AND
MIRACLE

AN UNBROKEN belief stretches from earliest Hebrew times to the present century that supernatural knowledge in the form of a fulfilled prophetic utterance, and supernatural power in the form of a miracle are *indicia* of a divinely given revelation. The Biblical appeal to this type of evidence is clear; the Church Fathers wrote extensively on the subject; and the witness of the fulfilled prophetic word and the accomplished miracle has been central in Christian apologetics in the subsequent Catholic and Protestant centuries. Few convictions in Christendom have such a sustained historical continuity.

However, the appeal to Christian evidences has been seriously questioned in modern times.[1] Philosophers have construed systems which have *ex hypothesi* excluded any supernatural events. Philosophers have also questioned the sufficiency of the grounds of Christian evidences, or the validity of the argument from evidences. Scientists are of the opinion that the supernaturalism of Christian evidences is incompatible with the naturalism of the scientific method. Religious liberals, having agreed with the scientists, added a religious objection: in that God assertedly *always* works from within nature, he *never* works on nature from the outside, i.e., supernaturally. Finally, theo-

---

[1] Christian evidences has a wider scope than fulfilled prophecy and miracles, but for the purposes of this essay we are restricting our discussion to these items. "Evidences" is not the best word; "indicia," or "witnesses," or "signs" is more Biblical, and apologetically, less ambiguous.

logians under the influence of Kierkegaard have urged that any obvious supernatural act of God would be destructive for faith, or inconsequential to it.

The result is that within and without the Church the traditional apology of the witness of prophecy and miracle receives scant attention. But if the *historical* revelation of God be accepted, how is the argument from prophecy and miracle to be assessed? Should this part of our apologetic be judged as outmoded? Or is the witness of the Christian centuries to the validity of this appeal to be maintained?

I. BIBLICAL MATERIALS

Whatever may be the doubts of modern theologians about Christian evidences, the Biblical witness is clear: *the fulfilled prophetic utterance and the accomplished miracle are the indicia of a supernatural revelation and redemption wrought by a Divine Person who is making himself known by these means.*

We are not speaking of a passage of one of the prophets which appears to have been fulfilled in some historical event. Much rather, we are appealing to the texts *which state the very structure of Christian evidences itself.* It is the Scripture itself which sets up the structure of Christian evidences, and not, to the contrary, the work of apologists who have imposed a structure upon Scripture. For example, in the discussion of the Great Prophet who shall come (Deut. 18) the difficulty created by the appearance of the false prophets is discussed. The Israelite must be able to distinguish the true prophet from the false. The text reads: "And if thou say in thine heart, How shall we know the word which the Lord hath not spoken? When a prophet speaketh in the name of the Lord, if the thing follow not, nor come to pass, that is the thing which the Lord hath not spoken, but the prophet hath spoken it presumptuously: thou shalt not be afraid of him." (vv. 21–22) The corollary *necessarily* follows: if the thing does come to pass, the prophet speaks from God. The fulfilled prophetic utterance points out the true prophet of God.

The subject matter of Isaiah 41 is God's contention with pagan gods. The Israelite not only had the problem of differentiating the true from the false prophet, but the true God from the gods of the surrounding nations. The word of Scripture again gives us the structure of the apologetic: If a god does not know the future, he is a dead god; if he knows the future, he is the living God. God through Isaiah thus taunts the idols: "Show the things that are to come hereafter, that we may *know* that ye are gods" (v. 23, italics supplied).[2]

---

[2] This structure is elaborated in Ezekiel. More than fifty times Ezekiel states that through some God-given *indicium*, Israel would know that her God is the living God.

The extent of the fulfilled prophetic word in Scripture is not within our province, but the materials are rather large. They stretch from Genesis 3:15 through the prophetic utterances of our Lord concerning the destruction of Jerusalem, and they proffer a rather indigestible surd to those theologians who have no place for the supernatural in their systems.

Not only is the *structure* of the appeal to the fulfilled prophetic word given within Scripture, but also the appeal to the manifestation of the divine power in miracles. For example, when Moses asks God how he (Moses) shall make it clear to the Israelites that he speaks from God and not from himself, he is assured of such miraculous signs as will remove doubt (Exod. 4:1 ff.). And what is true of Moses is true of many other prophets who were granted miraculous powers that it might be clear to Israel that they were God's spokesmen. Here again the *structure* of the apologetic is not foisted upon Scripture but found native to Scripture.

Our Lord himself claimed that his *works* witnessed to his divine origin and to the divinity of his teaching. His words in this connection are difficult to controvert. For example, he claimed that the power to heal implied the power to forgive sin, and the power to forgive sin implied the power to heal (Matt. 9:1–8). Cities in which he performed supernatural works were not complimented for failing to respond to a defective apologetic but were upbraided for rejecting the witness of the miracles (Matt. 11:20 ff.). When the disciples of John the Baptist came asking for clear evidence of his Messiahship, he satisfied them by pointing to his various miraculous acts (Lk. 7:19–23).

Our Lord, on one occasion, informed his listeners that if they could not accept his naked word, they should be properly impressed by his miracles, and so believe (John 10:38).

With regard to the miraculous signs given to the apostles, the witness of Hebrews 2:4 is unusually clear: "God also bearing them witness, both with signs and wonders, and with divers miracles, and gifts of the Holy Ghost, according to his own will" (The Greek text is especially emphatic: *sunepimartyrountos tou theou*—"God bearing a witness *along* with theirs and *in addition* to it"). And Paul affirms that the resurrection of Christ very strongly (*en dynamei*—"powerfully") marks (*horisthentos*) him out as the Son of God (Rom. 1:4).

The number of miracles recorded in Scripture is large, to be sure. But certain matters are apparent: (1) when the total time span of the Biblical record is considered, the number of miracles is few; (2) they tend to cluster around certain great events or persons; and (3) the maximum saturation is to be found in the life of Christ as we would expect it to be, for he supplies the climax of revelation and redemption.

If we are committed to a revelation of God *in history,* we are committed also to the mode in which God *professes to seal* his revelation. A theology which professes to accept this revelation, and yet rejects the structure of the

witness of the revelation itself to its divinity, comes short of complete loyalty
to the truth of God. For the structure of the apologetic from evidences is
contained within Scripture itself.

II. THE THEOLOGICAL PROBLEM

For a theologian committed to the Biblical revelation, the real problem is
not whether this apologetic structure exists, but rather, to determine its place
in a wider apologetic. While theologians have agreed that the Scriptures do
contain the fulfilled prophetic word and the accomplished divine miracle,
they disagree over the role such evidences are to play in a Christian apologetic.

The issue can be crystallized by presenting a painfully simple contrast of
the extremes in this matter: (1) Some theologians are convinced that Christian evidences must play a minor role in Christian apologetics. This has been
urged on two different grounds. One group argues that a man believes the
gospel simply because the Holy Spirit enables him to believe. Christian evidences can make no appeal *prior* to the Spirit's work, and the work of the
Spirit is so convincing that any appeal to evidences *after* the Spirit's work is
relatively unimportant. Another group of theologians thinks that the case for
Christianity is to be made by an adequate philosophical apologetic. Unless
a man accepts the total structure of Christian thought through philosophical
apologetics, he will not hear the witness of Christian evidences; but if he is
persuaded that Christianity is true on philosophical grounds then Christian
evidences will add little to his convictions.

However, (2) other theologians are convinced that Christian evidences
present an indubitable authentication of a divine revelation independent of
philosophical considerations. They are an appeal to the average man (not
the sophisticated man), and as such are conclusive. If the evidences are
rejected, the rejection is not due to any ambiguous element in the evidences,
nor to lack of cogency of the argument, but solely to the obstinancy of the
sinful mind.

We shall not attempt at this point a reconciliation of these two points of
view, each of which has a large and necessary fragment of the truth.

III. THE INNER AND OUTER WITNESS

The root of the issue in Christian evidences is the character of Christian
apologetics, and the doctrine of spiritual or religious certitude which must
accompany it. If the major outline of Christian apologetics can be traced,
then the narrower province of Christian evidences can be ascertained. For
a historical point of departure we turn to the thought of Augustine.

Augustine taught that truth of every kind is grounded in *The Truth*,
God himself. Any truth which man learns constitutes a species of revelation.

This revelation is two-pronged: there is the impartation of truth, and a capacity granted to receive it. Wherever men possess truth they possess it in virtue of the fact that God has supplied it and granted the illumination necessary for its apprehension.

This same pattern of revelation is true of the Christian faith but with necessary religious modification. God has imparted a revelation of himself to man, and this revelation is the truth. Man, blinded by sin, needs a special illumination in his heart enabling him to grasp the truth of God as truth. With every fruitful grasping of the truth of the gospel must be an inner illumination of the mind showing that the gospel is the truth. Thus the Christian's acquisition of truth, and his religious certitude about the truth *derive directly from God.*

While wrestling with the problem of religious authority John Calvin developed Augustine's insights Biblically rather than philosophically and produced for the Christian Church his great doctrine of *the inner witness of the Holy Spirit.* The sense of divine truth, and the religious certitude over divine truth which the Christian possesses, stem from the inner operation of the Holy Spirit upon the human heart (Gal. 4:6), or the human spirit (Rom. 8:16), or the human understanding (I John 5:19). Christian certitude is a creation of the Holy Spirit within the human heart by the instrument of the preached or read Word of God. This certitude is not man-made by human reason, nor created by the teaching of an infallible institution (the Roman Catholic Church), nor the product of a remarkable religious experience (as in religious fanaticism), but it is *God-made* through the Word and the Spirit.

If these premises are true, it means that there is no genuine religious life in the heart till the heart is stirred by the Holy Spirit. Neither the Church, nor human reason, nor religious experience can accomplish the work of the Spirit and the Word. Once the Spirit moves *in* the Word, there shine into the Christian heart *light, truth,* and *certitude.*

These conclusions may now be directly applied to our understanding of Christian evidences. Only the Spirit and the Word may break through the human shell of sin and unbelief.[3] Therefore the witness of miracle and prophecy apart from the Spirit's action falls upon deaf ears and dead hearts. In themselves alone evidences cannot move the heart to faith. It is improper to expect evidences to slay unbelief, to rout atheism, and to convert sinners. Saving faith is a gift of the Holy Spirit, and this is requisite for *all* acts of faith.

These theses are illustrated in the story told about Lazarus and Dives. Dives, in torment, asks that a messenger be sent by Abraham to his brothers

---

[3] Paul Feine has noted that this is the doctrine of the entire Scripture. Cf. *Theologie des Neuen Testaments* (achte Auflage; Berlin: Evangelische Verlaganstalt, 1949), p. 263. We have developed these theses at greater length in our own work, *The Pattern of Authority* (Grand Rapids: Eerdmans, 1957).

to warn them of the coming torment. Abraham replies that the brothers of
Dives possess the truth of God in the writings of Moses and the prophets.
But, Dives remonstrates, his brothers need something *extra* to rouse them out
of their sinful ways: *let one from the dead evangelize them!* Abraham
replies: "If they hear not Moses and the prophets, neither will they be
persuaded, though one rose from the dead" (Luke 16:31). The truth is
obvious: if these brothers would not hear the voice of the Spirit in the
Scriptures, they would not respond to a remarkable example of evidences.

It is the Spirit working in the Word which arouses man to spiritual life
and faith, and no appeal in isolation from the Spirit and the Word "gets
through," so to speak.

However, great care must be exercised at this point. It might be deduced
from what has been just said that Christian evidences are superfluous. It
could be said: they are ineffectual *before* faith, and inconsequential *after*
faith. The temptation—and it is a great one—is to rest the Christian apologetic completely upon the inner witness of the Spirit.

However, we do not believe that such a claim has fully pounded out the
issues. The Christian faith is the truth of God and it exists prior to any
man's experience of it, or personal certitude of it through the Holy Spirit.
The Spirit works in the Word, and the Word of revelation exists as a reality
separate from its realization in the hearts of men by the Holy Spirit. The
Holy Spirit does not create truth in his inner witness; he creates an *ability*
within the blind man to see the truth, and the *life* within a dead man to
apprehend it, and a *conviction* within a heretofore faithless mind that it is
the truth. This is an inner, spiritual religious certitude.

But another question must be asked: *what are the indicia of divinity in
the Christian religion itself?* What is the mark of divinity in the Truth to
which the Spirit bears a divine witness? The meaning of Christian evidences
is this: *there is a congruity between the divine witness in the heart and the
Christian religion.* Just as the Spirit puts a stamp of divinity in the believer's
consciousness, so God has put a stamp of divinity upon the Christian religion.
An apologetic which treats evidences lightly—a mere tipping of the hat in
passing—is therefore a curtailed apologetic.

It must be emphasized strongly that the prophetic word and the accomplished miracle are part of the Word of God in which the Spirit witnesses.
The Spirit of God may, therefore, witness to the gospel in those passages that
are prophetic or that contain an account of a miracle. The Spirit in using
these passages containing "evidences" is employing part of sacred Scripture.
On the other hand, when the Spirit bears his witness in other parts of Scripture, and the Christian perceives the divinity in those Scriptures, he is thus
prepared to perceive the divinity of Scripture in those Scriptures which deal
with "evidences." This is no luxury added to the witness of the Spirit but is
a necessity for the heart's *full* rest in the certainties of the Christian religion.
It is the nail at the *other end* of the board which certifies to the Christian

that he is neither the victim of some inward psychological phenomenon, nor of some outward socio-religious pressure. Therefore the inward witness of the Spirit and the divine indicia of the evidences must be properly related for a complete sense of Christian certitude.

This congruity is to be stressed in another direction. *The Christian has had a taste of the power indicated by the evidences.* The power which raised Christ from the dead is the same power quickening the believer from spiritual death to spiritual life (Eph. 2:1 ff.). The power that dispelled the gloom of cosmic darkness dispels the sinful darkness of the human heart (II Cor. 4:1 ff.). The power which took away the blindness of a Bartimaeus takes away the blindness of human sin in the believer's mind. The omniscience of God in prophecy is tasted by the Christian when he must confess that he did not know God, but God knew him. The Christian is partaker of the powers that have been—in the mighty acts of God in the past—and of the age that shall be.

The conclusions reached at this point of our discussion are: (1) the priority of the work of the Spirit excludes the adequacy of a purely "intellectual" faith stimulated by Christian evidences in isolation; and (2) that the reality of the fulfilled prophetic word and the accomplished miracle assures the Christian that the other end of the board, so to speak, is firmly nailed down.

A question left over is the query whether Christian evidences should be preached or not. To be sure, the gospel is the center of Christian preaching, but the minister is called to preach the total witness of God—the whole counsel of God. As stated previously, evidences are part of the Word of God. The Spirit may indeed use this aspect to bring illumination into the heart. The mistake of previous generations was not that it preached Christian evidences, but that it tacitly assumed that the evidences in and by themselves could do the work of the Holy Spirit. The point has been made that they cannot; but this does not mean that they have become useless. If evidences are preached as part of the Word of God with the full understanding of the priority of the witness of the Spirit, then evidences may be part of our preaching materials. That sinners have been saved by the preaching of evidences—and by the reading of works on evidences—is a matter of record.

IV. THE NATURE OF THE WITNESS

Having said this much it is now necessary to examine in greater detail the structure of the witness of Christian evidences. Prophecy and miracle take place in a world of *sinful* men, and in conjunction with a divine redemption and a divine revelation. It is in this context that the witness of the evidences occurs and if examined apart from this context the witness loses its meaning. According to Scripture, sin has effected a serious and wicked condition in the human heart. The possible manifestations of sin are countless, and each century has written its own record of its peculiar infamy. If God is the beatitude of man, then man's spiritual separation from God will inevitably result in man's self-corruption in sin. The most tragic manifestation of sin is the disappearance from the consciousness of man of *a knowledge of God;* and the most singular evidence of this tragic loss is the corrupt form of religious worship, or the very absence of worship.

Sinful man may turn art into smut, love into sensuality, and power into tyranny. He will use knowledge for his deviltry, and science for his cruelty. He is capable of corrupting to some degree every human faculty, every human institution, and every human relationship. Unless we take into assessment the complete dimensions of sin we cannot comprehend the Christian teaching of revelation, redemption, and Christian evidences. The divine remedy must be more than equal to the human perfidy, and wherever Christian evidences are underestimated or denied we must urge that in some manner or other the situation created by man's sinfulness has not been properly assessed. If the assessment is proper it will reveal how and why the prophetic word and the powerful miracle are a necessary and vital part of the *overcoming* of human sin.

For example, religious liberalism had little taste for Christian evidences, branding miracles not merely as impossibilities but as real hindrances to faith. But the religious liberal had so *redefined* sin that any sort of supernatural aid to sinful man appeared out of place. That religious liberalism had failed to plumb the radical depths of sin is acknowledged in much contemporary theological literature, and it is now judged that the older orthodoxy had a better estimate of human sin than religious liberalism did. But if man is *radically* sinful (in the original meaning of radical—pertaining to the roots) then the doctrine of redemption proposed by religious liberalism is too weak to cope with the sinful human predicament. On the other hand, if an orthodox theologian treats evidences cursorily it means that he has not realized *all* the measures the redeeming God must take to reach human consciousness.

Christian evidences—the supernatural word and the supernatural act—is part of the means whereby the loving and redeeming God reaches through to fallen and sinful consciousness with his saving truth. This *supernaturalism* is one piece with the supernaturalism of the creative word, and the powers of the age to come.

Commensurate with the doctrine of sin are the doctrines of revelation and redemption. The former concerns itself with the restoration to man of a true knowledge of God, and the latter with the restoration of man to a living fellowship with God. Each implicates the other. Thus the prophetic word and the miracle are *participants in revelation and redemption.* And it is not surprising that in the supreme Person of revelation, who is at the same time the climax of redemption—the Saviour—should be found the greatest concentration of supernatural phenomena in the entirety of sacred history.

Therefore these supernatural phenomena are not isolated events to be judged in themselves, but are parts of the whole fabric of divine revelation and divine salvation. A theologian is not true to the Biblical witness if he denies them, or ignores them, or neglects them.

One of the reasons why Christian evidences is the theological orphan of the twentieth century is that the nature of the various evidences as witnesses has not always been clearly stated. Let us now inspect the nature of this witness commencing with miracles. No matter where man has lived he has become directly acquainted with his own powers and those of his environment. He learns how much he can lift, how long he can work, and how far he can run. He has some sense of the strength of the wind, the bite of the frost, the heat of the sun's rays, the force of a flood, and the violence of a lightning bolt. His life is a constant pitting of his powers against those of his environment. The psychological intensity of this struggle is greatest at times of sickness and death. In his experiences with power—his own and that of nature—he develops an alphabet (or calculus) of power.

This alphabet is never the same with all peoples, and may change much within the historical existence of a particular people. But man is aware when something *transcends* his alphabet of power. Something which suddenly stands outside this alphabet speaks to him of a power greater than what he has heretofore experienced, and usually points man to an Omnipotent Spirit.

Christian evidences deals with the action of God in transcending the alphabets of power of the various cultures and periods into which his revelation came. When God so transcends an alphabet of power, he has prepared the situation. God has controlled the alphabet of power of the people to whom he shall speak; he has chosen, furthermore, to act supernaturally in connection with his plans of revelation and redemption. So the supernatural act is not to be compared to an airplane dropping down upon some primitive tribe and eliciting worship from the primitives. The opening of the Red Sea, for example, did not come from nowhere, so to speak. It was part of an entire nexus of redemption and revelation commencing remotely with the promises made to Abraham, and immediately with the ministry of Moses. The plans laid for the revelation to be given, and the salvation to be accomplished, included the supernatural means and the alphabet of power of the Egyptians and Israelites.

The same may be said for the life of Christ. The revelation in his life and word, the salvation wrought in his death and resurrection, and the *alphabet of power* of the people of that time are of one piece in the counsels of God.

By his display of power in transcending the alphabets of power at various times and places, God has put his stamp upon the revelation and redemption with which the display of power is intimately and necessarily associated. A miracle is a manifestation of the *omnipotence* of God. It *impresses* man because it transcends his alphabet of power. It is part of the divine program necessary for the reclamation of man. It is a powerful and dramatic means of bearing witness to a consciousness weakened and clouded by sin.

Man has similarly developed an alphabet of knowledge, and much of what we have said of the alphabet of power pertains to the alphabet of knowledge. Psychologically speaking, man feels his limitations of knowledge greatest when he faces decisions which seem to require detailed knowledge of the future. If an alphabet of power be transcended, it will be most singularly transcended in the area of future events *which do not exist as yet.* A transcending of an alphabet of knowledge points to an *Omniscient Spirit.* The fulfilled prophetic word is the witness of the action of the Living God.[4]

The Biblical notion is clear with reference to the fulfilled prophetic word: *The God of Israel is the Living God because he knows what shall be, and this omniscience differentiates the God of Israel from false gods, and the prophet of Israel from false prophets; and the religion of Israel from false religions.*

V. DOES IT MAKE ITS CASE?

Some generous soul might grant that the structure here presented is valid *as a structure,* but would doubt if there is a reality to which the structure conforms. Does Christian evidences make its case? Perhaps the exegesis behind the fulfilled prophetic word is wrong, or the document which contains the prophecy was written centuries after the events described. And might not the history of the documents which report miracles be suspect? And are there not several other possible explanations of miracles besides referring them to God?

Since we have elsewhere treated these problems extensively, in our work *Protestant Christian Evidences,* we shall not repeat the materials here. In the previous part of this essay we noted that we do not expect evidences to make their case apart from the Holy Spirit. But the authenticity of evidences as *witnesses* to revelation may be suggested by the following considerations:

(1) In its doctrine of God as Creator the Christian faith has the necessary prerequisite of the occurrence of supernatural events in this world. He who is Creator possesses the wisdom and the power to so act.

(2) The Christian faith also has the necessary justification for such supernatural acts in its doctrines of sin, revelation, and redemption. Human sin, divine redemption, and supernatural act are of one piece, and their impressiveness is seen in their interrelationship. The divine revelation and redemption illuminate the mind with reference to the *meaning* of the supernatural act. Biblical miracles are not historical oddities nor indigestible entities nor mythological tales; they are "lighted" from within by the meaning derived

---

[4] We are not in a position here to give a lengthy discussion of the entire character of the prophetic word. Our only purpose has been to present in simplest details the witness-bearing character of a fulfilled divine utterance. Nor do we have space to comment on the abuses of this witness in previous centuries.

from the doctrines of revelation and redemption. (Werner Elert has brilliantly pointed out that our entire notion of historical possibility or impossibility is profoundly associated with the character of our inner life. A Christian has no problem with the historical possibility of the resurrection of Christ because in the call of the gospel he has met the Risen Lord. A person who has not heard this gospel call does not have the inner possibility to judge the possibility or impossibility of this event. Cf. *Der Christliche Glaube,* pp. 159 ff.)

On the other hand, the supernatural act is an arrow, a witness, a signal which arrests our minds and stirs our hearts from their spiritual stupor. It is a necessary and dramatic means of calling attention to the redemptive drama, and without this dramatic witness we might let the redemptive drama go unnoticed. And while calling such dramatic attention to such an occurring redemption it also indicates its divine character.

(3) By careful exegesis of the Scripture text the divine fulfillment of the divine promise may be shown. Not even the radical redating of the Old Testament books destroys the force of the argument since numerous prophecies fall on the other side of these critical dates. By a study of the text and their contents the weight of evidence can be shown to lean towards the historicity of the miracles of Jesus Christ, and particularly to his resurrection. The life and writings of Paul are decisive at this point. Most critics accept the basic Pauline writings as authentic, and they give us an early and reliable witness to the resurrection.

The fulfilled promise of a prophetic word, the miraculous act of an apostle, are part of the divine *indicia* which inform the believing heart that the religion he holds within his heart by reason of the witness of the Spirit in the Word exists also in the world (prior to his personal experience) by the supernatural acts of the Living God.

THE HOLY SPIRIT
AND THE SCRIPTURES

J. Theodore Mueller

John Theodore Mueller holds the Th.D. degree from Xenia Theological Seminary, where he studied archaeology and apologetics under Melvin Grove Kyle. He taught theology at Luther College (New Orleans) and Wittenberg Academy. After seven years in pastoral ministry, he was called to Concordia Seminary, Missouri, as Professor of Systematic Theology and Exegesis, and still teaches on modified service. His three sons are Lutheran ministers.

17. J. Theodore Mueller

THE HOLY SPIRIT
AND THE SCRIPTURES

EVANGELICAL Christendom has always regarded the Holy Scriptures as the divinely inspired truth of salvation. While God has revealed himself to man universally by his law written in the human heart and his witness in nature and history, he can be known savingly only from the gospel set forth in the Holy Bible (John 5:39; II Tim. 3:15–17). The fundamental proclamation of Holy Scripture is summed up in John 3:16: "God so loved the world that he gave his only begotten Son, that whosoever believeth in him should not perish, but have everlasting life." The gospel thus centers in the incarnation of the Son of God and his vicarious atonement (John 1:29; II Cor. 5:18–21).

This saving gospel revelation the Scriptures ascribe, in particular, to the Holy Spirit as its mediator; for while the Father sent his Son to redeem fallen mankind (John 3:17) and the incarnate Son redeemed man from sin and its consequences by shedding his blood on the cross (I Cor. 6:20; II. Cor. 5:18–21), the Holy Spirit applies the free and full salvation procured through Christ's substitutionary atonement by implanting saving faith in the hearts of men through the gospel (Rom. 1:16). In agreement with this sanctifying work the Scriptures ascribe to the Holy Ghost also the giving of the divine Word by which alone perishing man can be saved.

I. THE SPIRIT THE MEDIATOR OF THE SCRIPTURES

The Bible is very emphatic in witnessing that the divine truth of salvation has been mediated to men by the Holy Spirit both orally and in the Scrip-

tures. He is the "Spirit of truth" (John 15:26). He moved the holy men of
God to speak (II Pet. 1:21). According to St. Peter, the Spirit of Christ testified beforehand the sufferings of Christ by the prophets just as he testified
them by his apostles (I Pet. 1:10–12). Of himself St. Paul declares: "Which
things [the gospel truths that were freely given to him by God, v. 12] also we
speak not in the words which man's wisdom teacheth, but which the Holy
Ghost teacheth" (I Cor. 2:13). The added participial clause translated in
the KJV, "comparing spiritual things with spiritual," can have but one
meaning: "Interpreting spiritual truths by means of Spirit-given words (cf.
the marginal note in the RSV: "Interpreting spiritual truths in spiritual
language"). The appended words evidently climax the Apostle's remarkable
statement that he was speaking the revealed gospel mysteries in words supplied to him by the Holy Spirit.

Because the Holy Spirit is the mediator of all divine truth, the Scriptures
are the "Word of God" or the "Word of the Lord," for he is true God with
the Father and the Son (Acts 5:3; Matt. 28:19). In this sense, the New
Testament, for example, quotes Ps. 95:7 ff., as spoken directly by the Holy
Spirit: "The Holy Ghost saith" (Heb. 3:7). In this sense St. Paul writes: "All
scripture is given by inspiration of God" (II Tim. 3:16); and again: "The
things that I write unto you are the commandments of the Lord" (I Cor.
14:37). In this sense the same apostle places the oral Word and the written
Word on the same level of divine inspiration when he writes: "Therefore,
brethren, stand fast, and hold the traditions which ye have been taught,
whether by word, or our epistle" (II Thess. 2:15). In this sense the Christian
Church has always accepted the canonical Scriptures of the Old and the
New Testament as the inspired Word of God; and in this sense conservative
theologians still "assert the verbal inspiration of the Bible, that is, its plenary
inspiration in the full sense of the word, absolute in phrasing and in particular words," declaring: "By virtue of its inspiration Scripture is the book of
God, wherein God infallibly and with divine authority tells us what to believe in matters of faith, what to do and what to forbear in matters of life
and practice [and] what to reject as error or falsehood" (*Concordia Cyclopedia*, 1927, p. 79).

II. THE SPIRIT THE INTERPRETER OF THE SCRIPTURES

As the Holy Spirit is the divine mediator of the Scriptures, so also he is
their divine interpreter. This truth is taught in those passages which affirm
that he, the Comforter, testifies of Christ (John 15:26), that he guides believers "into all truth" (John 16:13–14), that he teaches Christ's disciples
all things and brings to their remembrance whatever their Lord had taught
them (John 14:26), in short, that he illuminates the hearts of men and
moves them to believe the revealed truth of salvation. Christ states expressly
that the Holy Spirit "shall glorify me; for he shall receive of mine, and shall

show it unto you" (John 16:14 f.). This means that the Holy Spirit does not testify by the written Word anything against Christ, the incarnate Word. The two are never in opposition to each other, but always bear witness to each other. The written Word is the divinely inspired revelation concerning the incarnate Word, the Saviour of sinners, by which the Holy Spirit is operative toward their salvation.

On the basis of such passages as have just been quoted, Christian theologians have asserted the saving testimony of the Holy Spirit in the hearts of men by which he engenders and strengthens faith in them, glorifies Christ by them and sanctifies them in their daily life. This sanctifying witness of the Holy Spirit manifests itself in the believers by their sincere faith in Christ as their personal divine Saviour, their unshakable conviction of their sure salvation, their patient endurance in affliction, and their radiant hope of eternal life until by grace they finally obtain the crown of righteousness. In short, the testimony of the Holy Spirit makes men believers in Christ by an inward persuasion of the truth of the gospel and asserts itself in them to God's glory by their consecrated Christian life.

III. TWO AXIOMATIC TRUTHS

From the doctrine of Scripture, asserting the Spirit's sanctifying work in the hearts of believers, two very important axiomatic truths may be derived.

The first is that the illuminating witness of the Holy Spirit never takes place apart from God's Word as set forth in the Scriptures. Such as reject the Scriptures as the divine truth grieve the Holy Spirit and harden their hearts against his testimony of the divine truth (Acts 7:51). Our Lord recognizes but one way by which sinners are sanctified: "Sanctify them through thy truth: thy word is truth" (John 17:17). Of his own words—and these we now have in the Scriptures (II Thess. 2:15; I Pet. 1:10–12)—Christ says: "The words that I speak to you, they are spirit and they are life" (John 6:63). Those who reject the gospel of salvation, our Lord declares to be outside his kingdom of grace, as the "world" which "cannot receive the Spirit of truth, because it seeth him not, neither knoweth him" (John 14:17). The Holy Spirit therefore does not witness savingly in malicious unbelievers. Perverse rejecters of the divine Word may indeed voice fragmentary truths pertaining to the area of civil righteousness or social ethics, since the divine law is written also in their hearts to guide them in the affairs of this life; but to them the gospel is a stumbling block and foolishness (1 Cor. 1:23). At Corinth the Apostle brushed aside the "wisdom of this world," exalting itself over the divine wisdom of salvation as foolishness before God, exclaiming triumphantly: "Where is the wise? where is the scribe? where is the disputer of this world? hath not God made foolish the wisdom of this world? For after that in the wisdom of God the world by wisdom knew not God, it pleased God by the foolishness of preaching to save them

that believe" (I Cor. 1:20 f.). Thus the saving witness of the Holy Spirit
never occurs outside of or in opposition to the Scriptures. Whatever other
religious assurance or religious experience unbelievers may boast is at best
only self-deception. Luther's emphatic statement that whatever teaches anything apart from or against Scripture is the "perverse devil" (*der leidige
Teufel*) is in full agreement with God's Word which warns us against our
"adversary the devil," whom we are to "resist steadfast in the faith" (I
Pet. 5:8 f.).

The second axiomatic truth concerning the illuminating and sanctifying
witness of the Holy Spirit is that it does not take place in such as persistently
repudiate Christ's vicarious atonement. The gospel doctrine of Christ's aton-
ing death on the cross is the very core of the Scriptures. When our Lord
commanded his opponents to search the Scriptures because they testify of
him (John 5:39), he made himself known to them as the divine Saviour of
lost and perishing man. This same central gospel truth he impressed upon his
disciples especially before his last great suffering when he addressed them on
his saving mission as the world's divine Redeemer (John, chs. 13–17). In
this his final instruction he carefully explained to his followers also the witnessing function of the Holy Spirit, who was to bring to their remembrance
whatsoever he had said to them (John 14:26), testify of him (John 15:26),
guide them into all truth (John 16:13–15), and so strengthen their faith in
him as their divine Saviour. At the same time he added, by way of warning,
that the unbelieving world could not receive the Spirit of truth (John
14:17). The saving testimony of the Holy Spirit therefore does not take
place in those who obstinately reject Christ as their personal Saviour and his
vicarious atonement as their only hope of salvation.

IV. EFFECT OF THE SPIRIT'S WITNESS BY THE DIVINE WORD

Let those who reject the inspired Scriptures, either in whole or in part,
bear in mind that the Holy Spirit, witnessing by the divine Word, exercises
both an illuminating and a blinding, or hardening effect upon men.

Of the illuminating effect of the "statutes of the Lord" the inspired
Psalmist says that they "are right . . . enlightening the eyes" (Ps. 19:8).
Of the divinely inspired Word he writes: "Thy word is a lamp unto my feet,
and a light unto my path" (Ps. 119:105); and again: "The entrance of thy
words giveth light; it giveth understanding to the simple" (v. 130). The
"simple" are those who believingly and gratefully receive the divine Word,
hating "every false way" (v. 128).

But with the same clarity and emphasis the Scriptures tell us also of the
blinding, or hardening effect of the divine Word upon perverse unbelievers.
The Lord thus hardened Pharaoh's heart when obstinately he disobeyed his
Word and stubbornly refused to let the people go (Exod. 7:3, 14; 9:12). To
the Corinthians St. Paul writes: "For we are unto God a sweet savour of

Christ, in them that are saved, and in them that perish. To the one we are the savour of death unto death; and to the other the savour of life unto life" (II Cor. 2:15 f.). Here the line between the illuminated believing hearers of the Word and the blinded unbelieving hearers is sharply drawn. This blinding is directly attributed to God who judicially inflicts it upon them because of their unbelief. To this truth the Apostle clearly witnesses: "According as it is written, God hath given them the spirit of slumber, eyes that they should not see, and ears that they should not hear; unto this day" (Rom. 11:7). Unbelieving Israel is here pointed out as a warning to all who spurn the divine Word. The same truth is taught in the final chapter of Acts where St. Paul impressed upon his unbelieving Jewish hearers the warning of Isaiah: "Hearing ye shall hear, and not understand; and seeing ye shall see, and not perceive . . . lest they should see with their eyes, and hear with their ears, and understand with their heart, and should be converted, and I should heal them" (Acts 28:24–27). The same words of Isaiah our divine Lord proclaimed to the unbelieving Jews who refused to believe, even "though he had done so many miracles before them" (cf. John 12:37–41) The unbelieving Jews rejected the oral proclamation of the gospel, because they had first rejected the sacred Scriptures, which testify of the Redeemer and his gospel of salvation.

Both Luther and Calvin acknowledged this twofold effect of the divine Word upon men. Ronald S. Wallace in his recent book *Calvin's Doctrine of the Word and Sacrament* (Wm. B. Eerdmans Publishing Co., Grand Rapids, Mich., 1957) sums up Calvin's view on the twofold effect of the preached Word thus: "It can either soften or harden the heart. It can either save or condemn the hearer" (p. 93). He then quotes Calvin as saying: "The Gospel is never preached in vain, but has invariably an effect, either of life or death" (*Commentary* on II Cor. 2:15). Again: "As the Word is efficacious for the salvation of believers, so it is abundantly efficacious for the condemning of the wicked" (*Commentary* on Isa. 55:11). To these statements of the Genevan divine Mr. Wallace adds: "Calvin is, however, careful to add, when he speaks in this strain, that this negative effect 'does not belong to the nature of the Gospel, but is accidental.'" Its destroying effect comes "from the fault of mankind" (pp. 93 f. *Commentary* on II Cor. 10:8). That indeed is true, as St. Paul testifies when he writes to the Corinthians: "But if our gospel be hid, it is hid to them that are lost; to whom the god of this world hath blinded the minds of them which believe not, lest the light of the glorious gospel of Christ . . . should shine unto them" (II Cor. 4:3 f.). The expression "the god of this world" denotes Satan, under whose influence all unbelievers are. According to the context, St. Paul here argues: "The Holy Spirit desires to enlighten those who hear the glorious gospel of Christ, but if they persist in their unbelief he permits Satan to blind their minds so that they finally arrive at a stage where they are unable to perceive the divine truth." Whether the gospel truth is brought to men by Christ's mes-

sengers orally or whether it is presented to them in the Scriptures, is immaterial since it is always the same divine Word. For the Apostle his oral
Word and his written Word were equally inspired by the Holy Spirit (I Cor.
2:13; 14:37; II Thess. 2:15).

From the fact that the unbelieving Jews rejected Christ, just because they
rejected the Scriptures (John 12:37–41), it is obvious that what is true of
the perverse rejection of the incarnate Word is true also of the perverse rejection of the written Word. In both cases the blinding, or hardening effect
of the divine Word takes place. When Simeon blessed the Christ Child in
the temple, he said by divine inspiration: "Behold, this child is set for the
fall and rising again of many in Israel; and for a sign which shall be spoken
against" (Luke 2:34). The words "for the fall" evidently mean "for condemnation through the rejection of Christ," while the words "for the rising
again" means "for salvation by believing in Christ." The added explanation
"for a sign which shall be spoken against" signifies that Christ will always be
an object of peculiar derision to unbelievers who willfully deny him and his
divine truth. Thus Christ is a rock against which blind unbelief dashes itself
to pieces, and at the same time a rock upon which believers rise to glory.

Christ, however, is not a rock of rising or falling *per se,* but inasmuch as
he proclaims himself to be the appointed Messiah who came to seek and save
that which is lost (cf. John 6:60–66; 8:42–59). As such he is believed or
rejected both in his oral proclamation and his written proclamation in the
Scriptures. He thus could challenge his unbelieving opponents: "For had ye
believed Moses, ye would have believed me, for he wrote of me. But if ye
believe not his writings, how shall ye believe my words?" (John 5:46 f.). To
reject the Scriptures means therefore to reject Christ as the divine Redeemer.
Thus also the Scriptures become to unbelievers a rock against which they
dash themselves to pieces by their stubborn unbelief, while to all believers the
divine Word proves itself a rock of salvation by which, through faith in
Christ, they rise to everlasting life. St. Paul well describes the twofold effect
of the divine Word when he writes: "We preach Christ crucified, unto the
Jews a stumblingblock, and unto the Greeks foolishness; but unto them
which are called, both Jews and Greeks, Christ the power of God, and the
wisdom of God" (I Cor. 1:23 f.). So, then, as the Holy Spirit by an act of
divine grace enlightens the believers, by an act of divine judgment, he also
blinds or hardens those who maliciously refuse to believe the divine Word,
either in its oral proclamation or in the inspired Scriptures.

V. DENIAL OF PLENARY INSPIRATION IMPERILS THE
SPIRIT'S WITNESS

But we may say still more. All who deny the plenary inspiration of the
Scriptures and assume only a partial inspiration imperil the testimony of
the Holy Spirit. To his unbelieving hearers Christ proclaimed the im-

portant truth that they refused to accept him as their divine Lord just because they refused to believe the writings of Moses, i.e., the inspired prophecies of Moses concerning him as the promised Messiah (John 5:46 f.). Their perverse refusal to believe the Messianic prophecies in the writings of Moses made it impossible for them to regard Christ as their Saviour. Rejecting the Scriptures, they resisted the Spirit's testimony asserting itself also in the Lord's oral proclamation. Unbelieving readers of the Bible, who accept of the Scriptures only what pleases them and reject what is not in agreement with their critical minds, thereby exalt their perverted reason above the written divine Word and make it impossible for the Holy Spirit to guide them into all truth. And, as it happened in the case of the unbelieving Jews to whom the Saviour witnessed, the rejected divine Word may be the very fundamentals which they require for salvation.

God's Word declares emphatically: "All scripture is given by inspiration of God, and is profitable for doctrine, for reproof, for correction, for instruction in righteousness: That the man of God may be perfect, thoroughly furnished unto all good works" (II Tim. 3:16 f.). Whatever therefore is a part of Scripture is also divinely inspired and as such the divine Word by which the Holy Spirit witnesses to men the saving truth of Christ. Liberals may ridicule this conclusion, yet it is sound and unanswerable, resting upon the witness of the Scriptures no less than upon the infallible authority of the divine Christ, who acknowledged "all scripture" as God's Word and so as divinely authoritative, including such books, chapters and parts of the Old Testament long repudiated by destructive Bible critics as mythical (John 5:39). In Matthew 19:4–6 our Lord decisively refers to Genesis 1:27 and 2:24 to assert God's will and institution over against the Jewish unlawful divorce practice. To the omniscient Son of God, Adam and Eve were not mythical characters, but historical persons. Nor was the divine institution of holy wedlock, as reported in the first two chapters of Genesis, to him anything mythical, but something very factual and normative. Just so St. Paul in Romans 5:12–19 regards Adam as a historical person and the story of his fall as the divinely inspired truth standing in close relation to the gospel of salvation; for there he compares the first Adam, whose fall brought death into the world, with the second Adam, our blessed Redeemer, Jesus Christ, whose vicarious death brought life to lost mankind. So, then, our divine omniscient Lord and his inspired apostles recognized all the Scriptures of the Old Testament as the divinely inspired Word and as such the true source and rule of faith and life. Unless we are ready to disavow their authority we must regard all the canonical books of the Old Testament as the divinely inspired Word of God and the means of the Spirit's witness for the salvation of men.

If, in opposition to Christ and his inspired apostles, liberal theologians reject large parts of the Old and New Testaments as mythical, this unwarranted action is prompted by sheer unbelief and downright rebellion against God. Dr. F. Pieper in his *Christian Dogmatics* rightly calls this procedure an act of high treason by which the destructive critics challenge and violate the infallible judgment of the sovereign God and exalt their own fallible opinions over his inerrant divine truth. Where that is done willfully and persistently, there God in his righteous wrath and just judgment may ultimately withdraw his Holy Spirit so that the Spirit's saving witness is no longer perceived in their darkened hearts (Matt. 13:13–15; John 12:39–41). If by way of exception they still cling to Christ as their divine Saviour—as some profess to do—that is due solely to God's superabundant grace and undeserved longsuffering.

Christian believers do not tempt Christ by disobedience (I Cor. 10:9), but keep in mind his rule of true discipleship: "If ye continue in my word, then are ye my disciples indeed; and ye shall know the truth, and the truth shall make you free" (John 8:31–32). Genuine discipleship of Christ, created by the Holy Spirit's guidance into all truth (John 16:13), with the full understanding of the divine truth and the complete spiritual freedom of God's dear children, exists only in such as obediently continue in the divine Word, and for us today that is the divine Word of the Scriptures. This is the meaning of Christ's earnest words: "He that is of God heareth God's words; ye therefore hear them not, because ye are not of God" (John 8:44). This is the meaning also of our Lord's solemn threat: "Whoever shall break one of these least commandments, and shall teach men so, he shall be called the least in the kingdom of heaven" (Matt. 5:19). When God, after the departure of Moses, called Joshua to lead Israel, he commanded him: "Only be thou strong and very courageous, that thou mayest observe to do according to all the law, which Moses my servant commanded thee: turn not from it to the right hand or to the left, that thou mayest prosper whithersoever thou goest" (Josh. 1:7). This same divine command is found also in the last book of the Bible: "If any man shall add unto these things, God shall add unto him the plagues that are written in his book. And if any man shall take away from the words of the book of this prophecy, God shall take away his part out of the book of life . . . and from the things [promises] which are written in this book" (Rev. 22:15–19).

While St. John here speaks of "the prophecy of this book," he states a principle that applies to all the Scriptures as God's inspired Word. Men are not to add to God's sacred revelations, nor are they to take away from them, but they are to search the Scriptures believingly and faithfully, since they testify of Christ (John 5:39). The Scriptures are a gospel unit witnessing with one accord to our divine Redeemer so that they cannot be accepted in part and also be rejected in part. They must be received wholly as God's Word and not merely in part. Luther very strikingly compares the Scriptures with a golden ring which cannot be broken, for if it is broken in a single place the whole ring becomes unfit for use. In the same sense Luther also remarks that the Holy Spirit cannot be divided so as to speak the truth in one place and falsehood in another. Let all who condemn the Scriptures in part as untrue or mythical consider the great harm they do to Christendom as also the occasion of stumbling they give to the enemies of the cross of Christ who pride themselves on their atheism and rejection of the Scriptures. On Judgment Day we must give an account of our stewardship of the divine Word which God in his infinite mercy gave to perishing sinners for eternal salvation. "Be not deceived; God is not mocked; for whatsover a man soweth, that shall he also reap" (Gal. 6:7).

VI. DETACHMENT OF THE SPIRIT FROM THE SCRIPTURES

Church History has much to report on the many attempts made within Christendom to detach the Spirit's testimony from the divine Word as set forth in the Scriptures. We shall here refer only to a few manifestations of this trend.

It is not the least of Luther's achievements that he steered clear of the "enthusiasm" or "spiritualism" of his day, which asserted the Spirit's witness apart from or beyond the inspired divine word in the Scriptures. In his notable work *A History of Christian Thought* (Vol. I, p. 235), Dr. J. L. Neve presents Luther's doctrine on this point as follows: "The Spirit operates, and this is energetically emphasized (by Luther) against the spiritualistic tendencies, only *through* the Word and *in* the Word, as this Word awakens faith and at the same time becomes the bearer of the entire revelation for the awakened faith (cf. W. 18, 136, 9 ff.; 139, 18 ff.)." Dr. Neve adds by way of explanation: "By the term 'Word of God' Luther has reference primarily to the living Word as preached in the Church. . . . But the truth of this Word is conditioned by its dependence upon the written Word (*op. cit.,* p. 256)."

The fact that the truth of the oral Word is conditioned by its dependence upon the written Word of the Scriptures, Luther proved time and again by identifying the oral "Word of God" with the written "Word of God" set forth in the Scriptures. The preacher, Luther affirmed, must preach only the Word of Holy Scripture, for "the Bible is the very Scripture of the Spirit" (W. 7, 638; 46, 545; 47, 133). When in the Smalcald Articles Luther wrote: "The Word of God shall establish articles of faith, and no one else, not even an angel" (Part II, Art. II. 15), he had in mind, as the context shows, the sacred Scriptures. Just because the Scriptures are the Spirit's own divine word, they, according to Luther, approach man with his divine power for faith and salvation.

This almighty divine power, exerting itself by the Word, can, of course, be resisted, just as God's omnipotent power working by means can always be resisted. Thus a tree, which owes its origin and preservation to God's omnipotent power, may be hewn down by feeble man. So also the conception of human life may be prevented, though God is the omnipotent author of all life. Nevertheless, it is the Spirit's divine power, operative by the Word, which makes the gospel the power of God unto salvation to every one that believeth (Rom. 1:16; Eph. 1:19), just as it was the omnipotent power of God in his creative word: "Let there be light" which brought forth light at the creation of the world, or as it was the omnipotent power of God in the divine life-giving words addressed to dead Lazarus: "Lazarus, come forth," which caused him to come forth from the grave alive. Luther did not think of any "mechanical" power of the divine Word; he merely claimed for the divine Word the power for faith and salvation just because it is the Word of the omnipotent Lord.

Luther thus took very seriously such passages as teach that the gospel is the power of God unto salvation to every one that believeth (Rom. 1:16); that the Word of God works effectually in those that believe (I Thess. 2:13); that we are born again by the Word of God which liveth and abideth for ever (I Pet. 1:23); that the words of Christ are spirit and life (John 6:63) and others; for, as he said, they all declare that the Holy Spirit operates, converts, enlightens, justifies and sanctifies by the living divine Word. To Luther the written Word of the Scriptures is always indissolubly joined with the power of the Holy Spirit, who has made it for all times the means by which he operates on and in the hearts and minds of those who properly hear and read it. This truth he recognized in such passages as I Thessalonians 1:5; Psalm 19:8; II Timothy 3:16 f.; John 7:17 and others. Because Luther was in principle opposed to all forms of scholasticism, he never endeavored to present his doctrine of the efficacy of the divine Word in any Aristotelian category. He rather stated his teaching on the sanctifying operation of the Spirit in and by the divine Word in plain language, intelligible to the laymen of his day for whom he largely wrote, since he wished them to share in the blessing of the restored gospel.

To describe the relation of the omnipotent witness of the Spirit to the divine Word, Luther used the prepositions "by," "in," "with," and "under" to designate, first, that the Spirit and the Word are never identical, and second, that the Spirit and the Word are so intimately joined that in his witness the Spirit never goes beyond the written Word. In his great work *Die Lehre Luthers* (Vol. VII of his *Lehrbuch der Dogmengeschichte*) Reinhold Seeberg aptly describes Luther's thought on this point as follows: "The Spirit never enlarges the area of divine revelation; he merely conveys to the individual hearts what the words declare that proceed from Christ's mouth" (*op. cit.,* p. 383). While Luther thus adopted St. Augustine's distinction between the external Word and the internal Word, he at the same time clarified the relation and extent of the two (*op. cit.,* p. 383 f.).

Agreement of Luther and Calvin

It has been stressed time and again that there was a great difference between Luther and Calvin in their emphases on the Spirit's operation in and by the divine Word. This difference exists and must not be overlooked even though, as Dr. B. B. Warfield points out, Calvinism and Lutheranism "have infinitely more in common than in distinction" (*New Schaff-Herzog Encyclopedia of Religious Knowledge,* II, p. 160). The difference manifests itself especially in Calvin's theological view of the sacraments, though on this point the Genevan was far removed from Zwingli's more extreme position.

In *Calvin's Doctrine of the Word and Sacrament,* Ronald S. Wallace quotes Calvin at great length to clarify his view on the relation of the Spirit to the divine Word. He writes: "Calvin seldom refers to the preaching of the Gospel without speaking of it in such exalted language and without exhorting the readers to prize beyond all other gifts of God to the Church this incomparable treasure set in our midst by the grace of God, for it is the Word which is able to save the human soul" (p. 89). He then quotes Calvin's words: "It is a high eulogy on heavenly truth that we obtain through it is a sure salvation; and this is added, that we may learn to seek and love and magnify the Word as a treasure that is incomparable" (*Commentary* on Jas. 1:21). Again: "The Gospel is not preached that it may only be heard by us, but that it may, as a seed of immortal life, altogether reform our hearts" (*Commentary* on I Pet. 1:23). Despite such expressions, Calvin, however, held that the Spirit works when and where he wills, though not apart from the divine Word. He thus writes: "The work of the Spirit, then, is joined to the Word of God. But a distinction is made, that we may know that the external Word is of no avail by itself, unless animated by the power of the Spirit. All power of action, then, resides in the Spirit Himself . . . and thus all power ought to be entirely referred to God alone" (*Commentary* on Ezek. 2:2; *op. cit.,* p. 89 f.). The reader easily detects in these statements that Calvin was eager to deprecate any "mechanical power" of the Word and ascribe all glory for the believer's conversion to God. He writes, for example: "Saving is not ascribed to the Word, as if salvation is conveyed by the external sound of the voice, or as if the office of saving is taken away from God and transferred elsewhere" (*Commentary* on Jas. 1:21). Again: "God sometimes connects Himself with His servants and sometimes separates Himself from them. . . . He never resigns to them His own office" (*Commentary* on Mal. 4:6). Whereas Luther might be accused of "mechanizing" the Word, Calvin might be charged with separating the Spirit from the Word. Against such misinterpretation of their doctrines both, however, protested.

Despite their differences, both Calvin and Luther firmly held to the canonical Scriptures as God's inspired Word to which everyone desiring to be saved must submit in willing and consecrated obedience. As a matter of fact, on account of the special situation which Calvin faced in Switzerland, he and his followers developed the doctrine of verbal and plenary inspiration of the Scriptures much more systematically than did Luther, who in this matter regarded himself as in no special opposition to Romanism, against which he primarily directed himself, except, of course, that he rejected the

Apocryphal writings as non-canonical and maintained the distinction of the ancient Christian Church between *homologoumena* and *antilegomena*.

Luther therefore agreed with Calvin in rejecting "heavenly prophets" and other "swarmers" (as Luther called them) who boasted special revelations from God outside and apart from the Scriptures. The reason why Luther spoke of the "spiritualists" as swarmers (*Schwaermer*) was because they, like bees, were swarming in the air without any certain place upon which to rest. The swarmers, he said, were aimlessly flying around in the cloudland of their own dreams and refused to base their faith on the Bible. Luther, just as Calvin, wanted the teachings of the Church to rest upon clear passages of the Scriptures, or lucid and unmistakable divine words which could not be shaken. Thus the Protestant leaders of Wittenberg and Geneva, whatever their other differences, were in full agreement in teaching that the divinely inspired Scriptures are the only source and norm of the Christian faith and so the divine means by which the Holy Spirit leads men into all truth. Both opposed the detachment of the Spirit from the Scriptures.

Modern Forms of Detachment

In the revolutionary spiritualism of his day, Luther encountered the detachment of the Spirit from the divine Word in various forms. One of the earliest spiritualists was Andreas Karlstadt, his colleague at Wittenberg, who had supported his challenging theses against Rome and had attended his decisive disputation with Dr. Eck at Leipzig as his trusted friend. Soon, however, Karlstadt became a religious evolutionist, encouraging incendiary methods of reformation. He almost succeeded in destroying Luther's work at Wittenberg by his extreme seditionary procedure, for which he cited the Spirit's promptings. Fortunately the great Reformer, who meanwhile had been busy at the Wartburg translating the New Testament into the language of the people, was informed of Karlstadt's erratic behavior and, boldly returning to Wittenberg, soon restored peace and order by means of a few timely sermons. Luther's sane and sober guidance of the disturbed people was based upon clear Scriptures passages, whereas Karlstadt boasted of being led by the Spirit's inward prompting in his social and spiritual agitations. His example shows that the pretended guidance of the Spirit without the inspired Scriptures may lead to unspeakable confusion.

More calamitous was the appeal to the Spirit, apart from the Scriptures, in the case of Thomas Muenzer, whose personality and talents so favorably impressed Luther that the Reformer recommended him to his friend John Silvanus for promotion at Zwickau, Saxony, where in 1520 he was appointed a pastor. But before long Muenzer began to raise objections to Luther's spiritual Reformation of the Church. He pretended to be moved by the Spirit to surpass Luther as a reformer. To this end he depreciated the Bible, which Luther esteemed as "the treasure of all treasures." Following his "inner light," he set out to destroy the godless in the world and establish a kingdom of peace ruled by Christ. His fanaticism fanned into burning flames the prevailing unrest among the peasants, caused by many social and economic evils, and finally led to the Peasant's War. In a short time the disorganized peasants were defeated and their "prophet," as Muenzer was known among them, was executed. Karlstadt and Muenzer, no doubt, were extreme enthusiasts in their appeal to the "inner guidance of the Spirit" apart from the written divine Word. While the invocation of the Spirit has not always proved itself so utterly disastrous, the two cases show the dangers inherent in this trend. Wherever the Scriptures are set aside and man's faith is based upon some alleged "inner prompting of the Spirit," there commonly the gospel truths of the Christian faith are set aside and social pursuits are put in the place of the spiritual teachings of Christ's saving gospel.

The dangerous tendency of detaching the Spirit from the Scriptures may be illustrated also by the failure of neo-orthodoxy to restore to the Christian Church the gospel of Christ in the sense of Biblical theology.[1] Without doubt Christendom owes a debt of gratitude to Karl Barth. In the arid desolation of bankrupt humanism he called thinking religious leaders to a new appreciation of theology as also to a new appraisal of basic Christian values. His slogan, "Back to Luther and Calvin!" challenged the theologians of his day to go beyond Schleiermacher and the crass rationalists, and once more to review the theology of the Reformation as a new starting point. But Barth went back neither to Luther nor to Calvin. His doctrine of the Scriptures is

[1] As P. T. Forsyth recognized, the danger of "spiritual vagrancy" coheres in emphasis on the "Spirit of Christ" rather than on the letter of Scripture (*Faith, Freedom and the Future,* pp. vi-ix). While Forsyth, despite his departure, stayed rather near the "letter," others did not. Daniel Jenkins professes that the Spirit gives insight for "discriminating between what is true and false" in the traditions of the past (*Tradition, Freedom and the Spirit,* pp. 65, 70). Contemporary illumination of believers is thus exalted above apostolic inspiration. H. H. Farmer affirms that the Bible is an indispensable record which confronts us reliably with the concrete individuality of the historic Christ ("The Bible: Its Significance and Authority," in *The Interpreter's Bible,* Vol. I, p. 156), yet he disparages its infallibility and appeals to the Spirit as compensation for its fallibility: the Holy Spirit takes the things of Christ and shows them to scholars (*ibid.,* p. 17). But does not genuine Christian faith first take its rise from the conviction that Jesus of Nazareth is the Christ, and not from the Spirit apart from the Gospel history? If trustworthy knowledge of Biblical events is dependent upon modern scholars specially illumined by the Spirit, the Bible itself becomes unprofitable for the ordinary reader and the ordinary believer. The fact is, however, that the transition from an inerrant Bible to a Bible trustworthy in its main outlines cannot really be made by a decisive appeal to the Spirit, for in dealing with special historical revelation our concern is not with an immediate divine activity but, rather, with something historically determinable. Neo-orthodox theologians who make the Spirit rather than Scripture the locus of revelation (even if they locate that revelation on the "rim" of Scripture) exaggerate the fact that the Spirit conveys personal conviction and certainty into the notion that the Spirit is the immediate source of revealed truth. While they insist that the Spirit is not to be sundered from Scripture, they mean little more than that the Bible serves as the frame within which the Spirit existentially encounters man; surely they do not affirm the revelation-status of Scripture itself.—ED.

very definitely at variance with that of the Wittenberg and Genevan divines
who, for example, did not regard large portions of the Scriptures as mythical
and unhistorical, as does Barth. They accepted the canonical Scriptures as
the divinely inspired Word of God which is both infallible and inerrant.
Barth regards only that as the Word of God which the Spirit impresses upon
the individual human mind as such, or, we may say, the Bible is God's Word
only so far as God speaks through it. If God does not speak through the Scriptures they are not God's Word, but merely man's word (cf. *The Doctrine of
the Word of God,* p. 123). Thus neo-orthodoxy denies the objectivity of theological truth and so has no "sure word of prophecy." To Barth divine truth
is all the more subjective, since the Bible, according to his view, was written
by erring men and so is itself errant. He writes: "The prophets and apostles
even as such . . . in their spoken and written word [were] capable of error
and actually erring men like us all" (*Kirchliche Dogmatik,* Vol. I, Part II,
pp. 563 ff.). But Luther and Calvin esteemed the Scriptures as God's infallible Word because they were given by divine inspiration. The Spirit never
errs and therefore the Scriptures are God's inerrant Word even if men refuse
to believe them. But according to Barth "the inspiration does not lie before
us as the Bible lies before us. The Bible is God's Word [only] so far as God
lets it be His Word" (*ibid.*).

To what deplorable aberrations from conservative Biblical theology the
neo-orthodox "doctrine of the Word" will lead is shown by Barthianism in its
more liberal manifestations. Emil Brunner, for example, oriented Barthian
theology to what has been called "Anglo-Saxon liberalism." He writes: "I
myself am an adherent of a rather radical school of Biblical criticism which,
for example, does not accept the gospel of John as a historical source and
which finds legends in many parts of the synoptical gospels" (*The Theology
of Crisis,* p. 41). Or: "Whosoever asserts that the New Testament gives us a
definite consistent account of the Resurrection is either ignorant or un-
conscientious" (*The Mediator,* p. 577). Brunner rejects the Christian doctrines of the inspired, inerrant Scriptures and of Christ's virgin birth and
propitiatory atonement. In its more liberal aspects neo-orthodoxy conforms
to modernism, which denies the gospel truths held by the Christian Church.
For this sort of theologizing neo-orthodoxy certainly cannot claim the Spirit's
guidance into all truth; it is a movement away from the Scriptures, and no
appeal to the guidance of the Holy Spirit will avail in its behalf.

VII. THE ABIDING SPIRIT IN THE ABIDING WORD

When Christ promised his disciples the Holy Spirit to guide them into all
truth, he addressed them as sincere believers. The Comforter was to be theirs
as the Spirit of truth which the world cannot receive because it seeth him not,
neither knoweth him. But the believing disciples knew him, for he dwelled
with them and in them and was to abide with them forever (cf. John 14:16

f.). Here, then, we have two basic truths concerning the Holy Spirit: first, the Spirit forever abides with all true believers in Christ; and second, the world cannot receive him, because it refuses to accept him. But believers in Christ also *keep his words* (John 14:23), as these are now set forth to us in the Scriptures. It is the peculiar nature of Christian believers that they are built "upon the foundation of the apostles and prophets, Jesus Christ himself being the chief corner-stone" (Eph. 2:20).

This divine foundation of the apostles and prophets, the sacred Scriptures, will endure till the end of time, and through the divine Word the Holy Spirit will gather into Christ's kingdom of grace and glory God's elect whom no man shall pluck out of his hand (John 10:20). Human speculations and heresies are doomed to pass away. But the promise of our divine Lord stands forever: "My words shall not pass away" (Matt. 24:35). Resting upon that sure promise of the living triumphant Christ, the communion of Christian believers will always hold fast to the inspired divine Scriptures and the gospel message of Christ's perfect vicarious atonement. Led by the Holy Spirit, Christ's followers will be more than conquerors in their battle for the divine truth. In his immortal Reformation hymn Luther penned defiant words: "We tremble not, we fear no ill, they shall not overpower us." God's communion of believers cannot fail, because the triumphant Christ and his Holy Spirit, working with the divine omnipotent Word, cannot fail. "And I will pray the Father, and he shall give you another Comforter, that he may abide with you forever; even the Spirit of truth: whom the world cannot receive, because it seeth him not, neither knoweth him" (John 14:16 f.). By this unfailing divine promise the Church of Christ will be triumphant till the end of time.

THE PRINCIPLES
OF INTERPRETATION

Ernest F. Kevan

Ernest F. Kevan is Principal of London Bible College in England. He holds the B.D. and M.Th. degrees from University of London, and is an accredited minister of the Baptist Union of Great Britain and Ireland His writings include The Saving Work of the Holy Spirit, The Law of God in Christian Experience, The Evangelical Doctrine of Law, *and* The Puritan Doctrine of Conversion. *He served as joint editor of* The New Bible Commentary.

18. *Ernest F. Kevan*

THE PRINCIPLES
OF INTERPRETATION

AFTER it has been established that the Bible is the Word of God, there can be no more important subject for consideration in Biblical studies than the inquiry into the principles, laws and methods of its interpretation. To be without an understanding of these principles is to be, as it were, before an ancient chest containing treasures of rare value, but without a key with which to open it.

The surest way to an understanding of the true principles of interpretation is to give first attention to what the Scripture itself reveals.

I. DATA SUPPLIED BY THE NEW TESTAMENT

It seems possible to classify the New Testament use of the Old in a four-fold way: the historical, the propositional, the homological, and the illustrational.

Historical Use

By this is meant the New Testament habit of referring to persons and events of the Old Testament in a way that takes their historicity for granted. It has been computed that the New Testament alludes to over 100 Old Testament events; among these are the creation of Adam and Eve, the murder of Abel, the Flood, the call of Abram, the destruction of Sodom and Gomorrah, the birth of Isaac, the choice of Jacob, the selling of Joseph into Egypt, Pharaoh's oppression, the leadership of Moses, the Exodus, the passage through the Red Sea, the 40 years in the wilderness, the giving of the

Law, the capture of Jericho, the career of David, the building of Solomon's temple, Elijah's ministry, the experience of Jonah, and the steadfastness of Daniel.

This body of evidence bears witness to a factual and objective understanding of the Old Testament as a literally true and reliable history. The New Testament regards the Biblical events as having occurred and as having occurred in the manner described.

Propositional Use

That familiar phenomenon of the Gospels associated with recurring phrases as "that it might be fulfilled which was spoken" and "then was fulfilled that which was spoken" may be placed under this heading. Instances of these prophetical propositions are noted, for example, in connection with Bethlehem as the place of Christ's birth, Galilee as the area of his ministry, and his being numbered with the transgressors.

The propositional use of the Old Testament by the New goes much farther than this, however. Unequivocal statements of the Old Testament are employed in the New either for the support of doctrine or as the basis of behavior. The Lord appeals to the primeval marriage state of Genesis 2 in his reply to a question about divorce; the Ten Commandments are accepted as the unchallengeable foundation of man's duty to God and his neighbor; the doctrine of the resurrection is supported by appeal to the divine statement, "I am the God of Abraham, the God of Isaac and the God of Jacob"; the unity of the Godhead is substantiated from the teaching of Deuteronomy; the atonement is expounded in terms of the "Suffering Servant"; the universality of sin is proved by passages from the Psalms and the Prophets; justification by faith finds its evidence in Genesis; and the demand for sanctification is based on Leviticus. Statements made in the Old Testament are thus regarded as authoritative for the proof of doctrine, and this establishes a pattern for the construction of principles of Biblical interpretation.

It would be negligent to ignore what Dr. A. G. Hebert calls

a certain antinomy running through the Christian acceptance of the Old Testament. St. Paul, writing to the Galatians, solemnly warns them that they must on no account undergo the circumcision which the Law commands; to the Romans he says that no peace with God is to be attained by the observance of the Law; in Ephesians, that the exclusion of the Gentiles from the privileges of Israel, symbolized by the Wall of Partition in the Temple, has been broken down. The readers of Hebrews are told that the day of the Temple sacrifices is over. St. John makes it clear that the Jews who reject Jesus are no true sons of Abraham. Behind all this lie the actions attributed to Jesus himself in the synoptic Gospels: He had broken the rules of Sabbath observance; he had called the Pharisees hypocrites; he had declared the laws of ritual uncleanness to be no longer binding, annulled the Mosaic permission for divorce, and had performed, as the last act of his ministry, a rite, independent of the Levitical sacri-

fices, in which he had declared the New Covenant to be inaugurated
through his blood (A. G. Hebert, *The Authority of the Old Testament,* p. 200).

This amounts to saying that in their propositional use of the Old Testament
the Biblical writers are cognizant of transition from the dispensation of the
Old Covenant to that of the New.

Homological Use

The novelty of the notion of homology in the context of Biblical interpretation may perhaps justify an explanation. The concept of homology belongs
strictly to the realms of mathematics and science and stands for "the state or
quality of identity of nature, make-up, or relation." Homology differs from
analogy; in analogy there is resemblance without identity of nature, but in
homology the resemblance is based on identity. This concept has recently
been lifted out of its normal context and used by Dr. Phythian-Adams in the
service of Biblical interpretation. Expositors have customarily spoken of
"analogy" and "metaphor" when confronted in the New Testament with
certain expressions belonging to the Old. Phythian-Adams writes:

> But surely, the truth is that St. Paul did not go to the Old
> Testament for appropriate figures of speech: he went to it—or
> rather he lived in it—because he read there a story of Redemption which was *repeating itself* in the events of the New Age of
> Christ. It was for him no mere *analogy* that there was a new
> Israel, a new deliverance from bondage, a new Covenant, a new
> Inheritance: and what is true of St. Paul is equally true of the other
> writers of the New Testament. . . . How shall we describe this
> interpretation of the Old Testament? At the risk of seeming
> pedantic I would urge that we need a special term. To speak of
> "analogy" and "metaphor" in this connection is not merely inadequate, it misses the mark at which the writers were aiming. The
> relation which they perceived between the old and the new Dispensation was, in fact, wholly unique and cannot be indicated in
> quite ordinary language. But there is another term, less common yet
> not entirely unfamiliar, which may help us, namely, "homology." By
> "homology" we mean that there is between two things not a mere
> resemblance but a real and vital—in this case, an "economic"—
> correspondence: and this seems to be precisely what the writers of
> the New Testament expound (W. J. Phythian-Adams, *The Way of
> At-one-ment,* pp. 10 f.).

Phythian-Adams is not strictly the pioneer in the use of this term, for Dr. F.
W. Farrar employed it earlier in his account of Theodore, who "believed that
the relation of the Old to the New Testament lay mainly in the homology of
facts due to a sort of pre-established harmony" (F. W. Farrar, *The History
of Interpretation,* p. 218).

Phythian-Adams recognizes that the time-honored expression for this
fundamental unity between the Old Testament and the New is, of course,

the word "type" or "typical," but the ambiguity attaching to this term, and the abuse of the idea in illegitimate directions make it desirable to find another. For this reason Phythian-Adams "baptizes" homology, employing it to express the identity and correspondence which exist between things under the Old Covenant and things under the New. The beginnings of homology can be seen in Jeremiah's prophecies of a second "exodus" and a "new covenant," but, says Hebert, "it is only in the New Testament that 'homology' comes fully into its own, and the thought is clearly worked out that the pattern of God's working, under two dispensations, is one and the same" (*op. cit.*, p. 219).

Representative homologies include such features as the following: "the last Adam," "Abraham's seed," the "Israel of God," the "great high priest," "Christ our Passover," "sacrifice," "my blood of the new covenant," "redemption," and "Mount Zion . . . the heavenly Jerusalem." The entire range of material relating to the Messianic hope is also of this same homological kind, as also the imagery of the Apocalypse.

Illustrational Use

Indisputably the New Testament employs historical material for illustrating truth and for enforcing moral lessons. Examples are found in the reference to David's eating of the shewbread, Jonah and the great fish, the Flood, Elijah sent to Zarephath, the serpent of brass, the patience of Job, and Elijah's prayer for rain.

Illustrational use of the Old Testament is not confined to persons or events but is found in the quotation of sayings. For example, when the Apostle in I Corinthians 9:9 cites the Old Testament injunction, "Thou shalt not muzzle the mouth of the ox that treadeth out the corn," in connection with his demand for the adequate support of the ministry, he must not be understood as implying that the passage from Deuteronomy was written to *teach* that the ministry must be adequately remunerated, but only that the humanitarian treatment of animals provides an excellent illustration of the greater importance of caring for the servants of God. It is in keeping with the "much more" argument of Christ in Matthew 6:30.

The border line between the typical and the illustrational is difficult to draw. It is possible that some Old Testament persons and events have been wrongly interpreted as types when they were intended to be understood as no more than illustrations. In the foregoing paragraph, for example, the allusion to Jonah has been classified as an illustration, though some expositors speak of Jonah's entombment in the fish as a "type" of Christ's three days within the grave. The distinguishing characteristics of types, and the question whether they merge into homologies on the one side or illustrations on the other, require an examination of each separate instance, but the presence of types in the Scripture is undeniable.

Another form of the New Testament's illustrative use of the Old is allegory, found in such places as Galatians 4:22–31 and Hebrews 7:1–3. In Galatians 4:24 Paul says he is speaking "with another meaning" (Greek) and uses a historical event of the Old Testament as an analogy of things in the New. The literal sense is not denied or destroyed but itself forms the basis of the spiritual realities which Paul seeks to illustrate. Again, the reference to Melchizedek being "without father, without mother, without descent, having neither beginning of days, nor end of life" is an allusion, not to a physical fact about Melchizedek, but to the way he appears on the page of Scripture. This designed absence of reference to parentage and birth—a matter of such importance in the line of the Aaronic priesthood—is taken as illustrative of the eternity of the person of Christ.

II. SURVEY OF INADEQUATE METHODS

During the long years of Biblical study many methods of exposition of Scripture have been evolved. No one of them seems adequate, however, to the demands of Scripture itself. Farrar finds a testimony to the grandeur of Scripture in that it remains undiscredited by the dangerous uses to which it has been perverted (*op. cit.,* p. ix). These inadequate methods may be surveyed as follows.

Superstitious

This is perhaps a question-begging title for this group of methods, but few scholars today would challenge the correctness of the description. Its beginnings are found in the interpretative principles of Palestinian Jews who sought for "all possible hidden meanings" (Oesterley and Box), and which allowed oral tradition so to dominate the written word that arbitrary interpretations were forced upon Scripture. The Cabbalists of the twelfth century went to the length of assuming that the Massoretic text with its verse enumeration, its vowel-points and its accents was divinely given to Moses, and that the "numbers of the letters, every single letter, the transposition, the substitution, had a special, even a supernatural power" (Louis Berkhof, *Principles of Biblical Interpretation,* p. 17). Jewish exegetical methods degenerated into "a mere art of leading astray" (Farrar, *op. cit.,* p. 105). Certain modern methods approximate to this superstitious approach, such as those of Ivan Panin and the Concordant Version.

Criticism need go no farther than to point out, first, that this type of interpretation proceeds on false views of inspiration and, indeed, of revelation; and second, that it has no support in Scripture itself.

Allegorical

This exceedingly old device still maintains an amazing hold upon certain minds in the present day. From the philosophical treatment of the Greek myths it passed into Biblical interpretation through Philo. Clement of

Alexandria propounded the theory of a threefold sense of Scripture—mystic, moral, prophetic (or fourfold, by adding the literal sense). His successor Origen projected an analogy from the alleged tripartite nature of man and spoke of the bodily sense (grammatical), the psychic sense (moral) and the spiritual sense (mystical). All passages, he held, carry a mystical sense, but not all bear a literal sense; in many instances, therefore, the apparently literal had to be spiritualized. Origen appealed to New Testament precedent for the allegorical method, particularly to Galatians 4:21–31, I Corinthians 10:1–4 and Hebrews 7:1–3. In point of fact, none of these passages is strictly allegorical in method even though, as Paul suggests in Galatians, they are allegorical in appearance; as already observed, they are purely illustrational. Further, in none of these examples is allegory employed in proof of doctrine, nor does the Apostle assert that the relevant Old Testament passage teaches the truth he is expounding. The "allegorical" use, then, is either an argument *ad hominem,* as Hebert suggests (*op. cit.,* p. 209) or it is purely illustrational. No warrant exists, therefore, for the claim that the allegorical method finds support in Scripture (cf. J. B. Lightfoot, *Commentary on Galatians,* pp. 199 f.).

A closer definition of allegory, and its comparison with "homology" or "type," is now appropriate. The Greek verb employed by Paul in Galatians 4:24 is *allēgoreō* and means "to speak so as to imply other than what is said." *Allēgorein,* then, merely implies that in addition to the plain grammatical meaning of the words, something more is to be perceived. The term is capable of covering all forms of metaphor, parable or illustration and supremely, so far as Scripture is concerned, homology or type. The presence of the word *allēgoroumena* in Paul's writings does not of itself determine the nature of the *allēgoria* used; the form could possibly be any one of the above (cf. J. B. Lightfoot, *ibid.,* p. 180). In its stricter use, however, an allegory is a story *composed for the purpose* of instruction and is thus clearly to be distinguished from the illustrational use of an event of history. *The Pilgrim's Progress* is an undisguised example of allegory in this strict sense: it is a story composed for the sake of its moral and one in which the descriptions and incidents are but accessories.

Clement and Origen and their long line of imitators employed the allegorical principle in its stricter sense and not after the Pauline manner. They were ready to throw away the literal sense of a passage if they thought it unacceptable. To the charge that they were throwing away the Word of God, their reply doubtless would have been that they were doing nothing of the kind; professedly they were rejecting only the outer shell which surrounded the truth. They insisted that there are many meanings to a passage, and that the literal meaning is the least valuable, and possibly not a meaning at all. Indeed, Origen held that the difficulties in the literal sense were interposed specially by God as a kind of wire across the interpreter's path, causing him to stumble and to look for some secret meaning (*De princ.* IV, ii. 7–9).

Sheer allegorism of the Alexandrian kind introduces nothing but chaos into speech and destroys all objectivity of truth: it is "fantasy unlimited." Historically it led to the wildest forms of interpretation and became an arbitrary instrument for making the Old Testament say whatever the expositor wished; it brought serious study to a standstill and awarded the prizes to the most ingenious. It is small wonder, therefore, that this arbitrary handling of Scripture provoked a reaction. Alexandria was confronted by Antioch, the center from which healthier methods of exegesis began to emerge under the guidance of men like Theodore and John Chrysostom. Theodore studied passages as a whole and not as "an isolated congeries of separate texts": his procedure was first to consider the sequence of the thought, and then to examine the phraseology and the separate clauses. The impulses given at Antioch were a long while gaining ascendancy; indeed, it would be true to say that even yet they have not fully won the day. The delightful art of allegorization dies hard, and many allegedly evangelical expositors in the present day prefer glamourously to display their inventive powers rather than patiently to plod the unspectacular paths of conscientious work on the Biblical text.

Dogmatic

Those who immediately followed the Reformation retained the sound principle of the interpretation of Scripture by Scripture. While they refused, however, to submit exegesis to the domination of ecclesiastical tradition as formulated by councils and popes, they nonetheless *"were in danger of leading it into bondage to the confessional standards* of the Church. . . . Exegesis became the hand-maid of dogmatics, and degenerated into a mere search for proof-texts" (Berkhof, *op. cit.,* pp. 28 f.). The domination of interpretation by dogmatics is sometimes called the interpretation of Scripture according to "the analogy of faith." This term is quite incorrectly lifted from Romans 12:6 where, of course, the reference is to the subjective aspect of faith. The phrase came to be employed, however, for the necessity of conforming Scripture to the dogmatic formulations of the Church. It is certainly wise on the part of the inexperienced expositor to check his findings by reference to the common Christian faith, and he may rectify many idiosyncrasies of his interpretations in this manner. But this is something quite other than forcing all passages of Scripture to echo the same dogmatic truth.

Rationalistic

The rationalistic method of interpretation persists whenever the authority of human reason is exaggerated. Its normal procedure is to deny what cannot be speculatively understood nor proved and to reject the supernatural and miraculous as legendary accretion. All endeavors to produce a non-supernatural Gospel have failed, however; the liberal or rationalistic method stands condemned by its own impotence to account for the Scriptures. The main rationalistic argument is that its human historical origin requires also that the Bible be historically conditioned. From this, much of the content of the Bible is inferred to be ephemeral in value and mixed with error. The Bible is assigned the inspiration of religious genius, representing man's highest thoughts about God; it is nevertheless regarded as a human production to be explained and interpreted by naturalistic principles. Dr. John Lowe remarks, "The humanistic and rationalistic tendencies of many of the critics became a fixed bias which distorted interpretation. What should have been a provisional working hypothesis, a legitimate reluctance to admit the supernatural so long as a natural explanation was possible, became an unquestioned axiom" (*The Interpretation of the Bible*, edited by C. W. Dugmore, Chapter VI, "The Recovery of the Theological Interpretation of the Bible," p. 113). This is undoubtedly the indictment that must be brought against such prejudiced criticism.

Mythological

The allegorical method has reappeared in recent days in the guise of Dr. Rudolf Bultmann's plea for the "demythologization" of Scripture. Bultmann argues that the New Testament is written in "myths," that is to say, in existential allegories of the thought and experience of those whose lives had been touched by the vitalizing and redeeming power of Jesus, but whose mental images were restricted to the New Testament world. This, says Bultmann, accounts not only for the unscientific language offensive to the modern man, but for the theological concepts which trouble modern readers of the New Testament. "The thesis of Bultmann is that something has to be done with what he calls the mythology of the New Testament. As long as this is taken at its face value as literally true, Christianity remains meaningless to modern man. It is useless to summon him to decide for or against Christ because an undemythologised Christianity is simply not a live option for him" (Ian Henderson, *Myth in the New Testament*, p. 9).

Bultmann seeks to differentiate his position from the rationalistic criticism of the Bible prevalent at the end of the nineteenth century. Whereas liberalism eliminated the "mythological" (the supernatural) and ignored the fact of Christianity as an event, he reasserts both myth and event, simultaneously interpreting them in his special way. He contends rightly, of course, that what Christ has done is more than something historical (*historisch*) : it is of experiential and religious significance (*eschatologisch* or *geschichtlich*). That this is so can be clearly seen from the fact that Christians refer to the death of Christ not only as an event which occurred under Pontius Pilate but also as the sacrifice of "the Lamb of God which taketh away the sin of the world." To affirm the latter, moreover, contends Bultmann, is to speak mythologically: it is a theological allegory to convey the idea of what Christ's saving power means to the Christian. It becomes the task of the interpreter, on this approach, to strip the gospel of this mythological form of speech and to translate it into the forms of experience of Christ which are familiar to a man of the present day.

This demythologization of the Scripture seems little different from the "de-allegorization" of earlier generations and it must be rejected for the same reasons. What Bultmann is pleased to call "myth" is in many instances more appropriately understood in terms of homology, but it is in any case the historical and human medium through which God has chosen to speak to man. What lies behind the forms of Christian theology is not existential thinking, but divine action in historical events bearing an eschatological significance.

III. FOUNDATIONAL PRINCIPLES

Dr. Farrar does not weary of reminding his readers of his opinion that the interpreter's view of the nature of the Bible and its inspiration largely determined the methods of interpretation. This opinion is on the whole true, but it is not to be applied in the one and only direction that Farrar delights to apply it in his antagonism to the doctrine of verbal inspiration. The Cabbalists and other similar Jewish interpreters produced their systems as a result of their superstitious view of the nature of Scripture. The Alexandrians and their successors interpreted Scripture in accordance with their view that Scripture cannot be held to contain anything inharmonious with their view of God and of spiritual reality. The Dogmatists and the Rationalists likewise came to Scripture with their own presuppositions. It is not, therefore, a peculiarity of conservative evangelical theologians that they also are guided in their view of the Bible by what they think of it. Presuppositions there must be, but the difference between the presuppositions of conservative theology and the presuppositions of the other groups is that those of the former are provided by the Scripture itself whereas those of the other groups are not.

The presupposition of conservative theology is that the Bible demands an approach in reverence and faith. It claims to be the Word of God and must be examined and interpreted in that light. This does not carry with it any preconceived notions of what it ought to contain, but merely anticipates that the book will be studied for what it has to say. This respectful attitude will therefore not require a resort to allegory to remove the "inharmonious" or to invent the fanciful in an eisegetical manner; nor will it require that the supernatural be eliminated, as attempted by rationalism, nor the objective factor destroyed, as by neo-orthodoxy.

The basic principle of Biblical interpretation which emerges from this point of view is that the sense of Scripture is to be found in the grammatical meaning of the words. To respect the grammatical sense is the fundamental rule in the study of all books, and the Bible, though rightly revered as "the Book of books," is nevertheless still a book. It is no magical object left mysteriously lying in man's path and requiring occult methods for extorting its powers. Every word is therefore to be accepted in its normal meaning and in the context of the style of writing in which it appears. Law, history, poetry and prophecy, each has its own literary style, and the interpreter will not be unmindful of these characteristics when endeavoring to reach an understanding of any given passage.

Legal and documentary material is necessarily found in the form of plain prose, but common speech is enlivened by metaphor, simile and parable to a degree far greater than is generally realized. The prophetic writings of the Bible are full of such figures of speech; so also are its poetical and apocalyptic portions. The presence of metaphor and symbol must be recognized, but this does not require the abandonment of the principle of obedience to grammatical sense. The words must still be taken in their grammatical sense, though that sense will vary as the style of the writing departs from prose and conforms to one or other of the modes of figurative speech. This recognition of metaphorical style is not to be thought of as a return to allegorization, nor is it a "spiritualizing" of the passage. When a writer employs metaphor he is to be understood metaphorically and his metaphorical meaning is his literal meaning: that is to say, it is the truth he wishes to convey. The term "literal" stands strictly as the opposite of "figurative," but in modern speech it often means "real," and it is used in this way by those who want to be sure that they know what the writer really and originally meant. In this sense a metaphorical saying is "literally" true. To avoid the ambiguity in this word "literal" and at the same time to find an expression to denote an idea which is nonmetaphorical, it might be useful to return the word to what might conceivably have been its first shape and spell it "letteral" or "letteralistic." Hebert has recourse to the word "literalistic" (*op. cit.*, p. 271) in the endeavor to remove the ambiguity. Thus a metaphorical statement is "literally" true but cannot be "literalistically" true. The "literal" meaning, then, is what the particular writer intended, and although he used metaphor, no one familiar with the language in which he expressed himself could reasonably misunderstand him.

The bearing of all this on Biblical interpretation must now be clear. When it is affirmed that the Bible is literally true, it is not implied that it contains no metaphorical elements, but merely that what was said metaphorically must be understood to be its real meaning. The question is occasionally asked whether it is right to believe in the literal fulfillment of prophecy. The answer, of course, is affirmative, but that affirmative answer does not require that the fulfillment shall be "letteralistic."

To have discovered the grammatical sense of a passage is by no means to have exhausted it, for the grammatically understood sentence must be interpreted theologically. In seeking the theological sense of a passage, it is important to recognize the historical principle in revelation. Earlier methods of exegetical study seem occasionally to have neglected this feature of historical development, and to have been held down by a static conception. But the Bible cannot be treated as a mere "word-book," "as a compendium of homogeneous doctrines, as 'an even plane of proof texts without proportion, or emphasis, or light, or shade'" (Farrar, *op. cit.,* p. x). The most elementary application of the historical principle requires the interpreter to transpose himself to the time and place of the author, and this can be achieved only by historical study. This history, however, is no mere ordinary history. Rather, it is sacred history, made by the movements of the self-revealing God, known in earlier times through the laws and institutions of worship he gave to the chosen nation of Israel and subsequently manifested in the person and work of the Lord Jesus Christ. The former is sometimes called the Old Dispensation and the latter is called the New Dispensation.

The word "dispensation" raises in the minds of some readers the disputations associated with the "dispensationalist" viewpoint so-called. But "dispensationalists" have no monopoly of the term and it has a connotation of its own independent of any particular school of thought. Strictly taken, of course, the word does not refer to a period of time, but rather to a manner of working; it points to the sovereign way in which God has been pleased to "dispense" his grace to his people. *A passage of Scripture has theological meaning according to its dispensational place;* that is to say, its true significance as part of the revelation of God is to be discovered by paying heed to its position in the unfolding of God's progressive self-revelation.

There is deep harmony and unity between the Old and the New Testaments; though written in different tongues they speak a common theological language. They speak the same truths, but what was in outline in the one is fully-painted in the other; what was shadow in the former is substance in the latter; what was typified in the Old is realized in the New. The unifying principle of interpretation is the homological; that is to say, the clearly discernible prearrangement of things in the one dispensation "corresponds" to things in the other. It is on the principle of homology that the entire Bible may be said to be a Christian book.

The homological principle which binds the meaning of the two dispensations points the way to the theological significance which lies within. This theological significance is sometimes called the "mystical" sense, but it is not for one moment to be thought of as a "second" sense not based on the literal meaning of the words. Where a mystical sense is found, writes Berkhof, it "does not constitute a second, but the *real sense* of the Word of God" (*op. cit.,* p. 140).

The crux of the problem raised by the allegorical method is whether secret and independent senses of Scripture exist, as it were, in their own right—or whether there is but one sense only, from which derivative senses may be inferred. Only the second of these alternatives can meet the demands of the facts. Scripture is not *multiplex,* but *simplex;* and this unity of meaning resides in the grammatical sense. This grammatical or literal meaning forms the basis of derivative meanings, and in relation to these subsequent interpretations the grammatical and literal must be regarded as primary while the others are secondary. The School of Antioch, and such teachers as Augustine, Luther and Calvin have always insisted that the theological sense is found only *in* the literal.

That Scripture contains inner and deeper meanings must not be denied; for the Bible is no ordinary book and has the profundities of the mind of God in it. While, therefore, allegorization in the strict sense must be repudiated, the search for an inner significance of a homological or typical kind must be held to be part of the legitimate study of the Bible.

On the importance of the principle of mystical interpretation Dr. Darwell Stone writes, "This interpretation is closely bound up with the permanent value of the Old Testament. If the Old Testament is to fulfill its purpose as 'written for our admonition' (I Cor. 10. 11), something much more than its merely literal and historical meaning is needed" (*A New Commentary on Holy Scripture,* article on "The Mystical Interpretation of the Old Testament," p. 695). "Christ in all the Scriptures" may perhaps be a slogan which some expositors have abused, but its essential truth is verified in the words of Christ (John 5:46). The devout and spiritually-minded reader of the Bible will find more in it than the bare literal sense: he will discern the deeper truth of timeless applicability which lies within the meaning originally intended by the author as he addressed his contemporaries. The reverent reader will not ignore or discredit the literal and historical meaning, but neither will he fail to search for the eternal truth that it enshrines.

A Practical Rule for Interpretation of Prophecy

Prophecy had to be spoken within the framework of the present and the past; that is to say, in the terms of the old dispensation. This determines its outward material forms. In all their statements about the kingdom of God, even when uttering the most spiritual and glorious truths regarding it, the vocabulary which the prophets employ is always that of the kingdom of God in the forms in which they knew it in their own day. Interpretation must first discover these "dispensational forms," namely, the historical and circumstantial factors of the prophecy, and then, and only then, can it make the necessary inferences. Putting this succinctly, the rule is that a passage must be examined for its dispensational place.

The prophetic pronouncements against Assyria are a good illustration of this principle. Says Dr. Davidson:

> Certainly the prophet, so far as his own mind was concerned, did not use the term "Assyrian" merely as a symbolical name for the foe of the Church. He meant the Assyrian—who, no doubt, was the foe of the Church. . . . It is safer to say, not that Assyria is a symbol or type of all enemies of God's kingdom, but that the truth expressed by the prophet in regard to Assyria is, of course, not limited to

Assyria, but may be applied to all foes of the people of God. It is a truth which may be generalized. . . . This way of stating the case conserves the literal sense of the prophet's words, and allows us to perceive how he thought and spoke, as one would naturally do in the circumstances in which he was placed (A. B. Davidson, *Old Testament Prophecy,* pp. 187 f.).

With regard to a prophecy uttered with reference to Old Testament conditions and peoples, but as yet unfulfilled, Davidson wisely says: "The true way to regard prophecy is to accept it literally as the meaning of the prophet —the only meaning which in his time he could have—but to say, as to fulfillment, that the form of the kingdom of God is now altered, and altered finally, never to return to its old form; and so fulfillment will not take place in the form of the prediction, but in an altered form; but still the truth of the prophecy will, no doubt, be realized" (*ibid.,* p. 169). In this way the fulfillment of what the prophet spoke may greatly transcend what he knew.

The valuable and important principle to be learned from this is that a prophecy undergoes transmutation when it passes from one dispensation to another. The understanding of this "transmutation" must be guided by New Testament principles. The light of later and clear revelation is to be brought to bear on the earlier or the more obscure, and Old Testament descriptions of the Day of the Lord and its issues are subject to modification by fuller revelations given to subsequent generations. "Such modifications," says Dr. Beasley-Murray, "are not cancellations of the prophetic word but amplifications, glimpses of broader streams of grace than the narrower rivulets of former days" (G. R. Beasley-Murray, *The Evangelical Quarterly,* July 1948).

Obedience to this rule will yield the following working method.

(1) If the prophet's words apply only to the Old Testament dispensation, and are to be fulfilled in it, they will, no doubt, be fulfilled literally in terms of the Old Testament dispensation.

(2) If the prophecies refer to things to be realized only in the New Testament dispensation, then it will be the interpreter's duty to strip from them the Old Testament form, which arose from the dispensation and time when the prophet lived, and look for their fulfillment in a way corresponding to the spirit of the New Testament dispensation and the altered conditions of the world.

(3) If a great general principle be expressed, capable of several fulfillments, that fulfillment which took place in Old Testament times will be sought in terms of Old Testament economy, and that which either has taken place or will take place in New Testament times will be understood in accordance with the spirit and principles of Christianity (cf. Davidson, *op. cit.,* p. 192).

All this means that it is the interpreter's task to distinguish between what is of permanent validity and what belongs to a stipulated period. "It is fatal," says J. Stafford Wright, "to assume that every Scripture is of permanent

validity irrespective of the circumstances in which it was given." The Levitical prescriptions are an example of this.

Prophecy is governed by the law of organic fulfillment. Fulfillment is real:
that is to say, what the prophets forecast will come to pass. There is a
genuine correspondence between prophecy and the fulfillment, though it will
not necessarily be "literalistic" in the sense of a letter-by-letter mechanical
correspondence of form in both prediction and fulfillment. The fulfillment of
the acorn is the oak, and the fulfillment of the apple blossom is the apple.
Thus, so long as the *reality* of the fulfillment is not abandoned, it might be
safe to affirm that the best word for the true interpretative rule is "ideal-
istic"; that is to say, it is the embodied "idea" which lives on in the fulfillment, after the "form" has been shed like a husk. The "idea" is latent in the
"form," and it is the "idea" which is imperishable. The formula yielded by
these considerations can be stated thus: when an Old Testament prophecy
passes into the New Testament its *form* is transcended, and its *substance* is
transmuted.

The Bible is the world's greatest book. It expresses the thoughts and
purposes of God as he has chosen to reveal them stage by stage to the believing man. The interpreter's prayer must ever be for a mental capacity big
enough to span the whole, lest he fail to see the wood for the trees. He needs
a mind alert to the modes of divine expression and a heart open to the
spiritual purposes which God has disclosed.

ARCHAEOLOGICAL
CONFIRMATION OF
THE OLD TESTAMENT

Donald J. Wiseman

Donald J. Wiseman has served since 1948 as Assistant Keeper of the Department of Egyptian and Assyrian (now Western Asiatic) Antiquities of The British Museum. Educated at King's College, London, and Wadham College, Oxford, he has excavated at Nimrud, Iraq, and Harran, South Turkey, and has served on archaeology survey teams in other Near Eastern countries. He edits the journal Iraq, *and is author of* The Alalakh Tablets *(1953),* Chronicles of Chaldaean Kings (626–557 B.C.) in the British Museum *(1956),* Cappadocian Tablets in the British Museum V *(1957),* The Vassal-treaties of Esarhaddon *(1958) and many articles in Assyriological, archaeological and Old Testament studies.*

19. Donald J. Wiseman

ARCHAEOLOGICAL
CONFIRMATION OF
THE OLD TESTAMENT

Biblical archaeology is a specialized branch within the developing science of archaeology which has itself been described as an "expanding universe." It includes the study of the material remains of antiquity of Palestine and of those countries which from the earliest time to the first century of the Christian era were brought into relation with it. These comprise the remains of buildings, art, inscriptions and every artefact which leads to an understanding of the history and life not merely of the Hebrews or of Palestine but of those countries, especially Egypt, Syria, Jordan, Asia Minor, "Mesopotamia" (Sumer, Babylonia and Assyria) and Persia (Iran), which bear more or less closely on the Biblical record.

I. THE NATURE OF OLD TESTAMENT ARCHAEOLOGY

It is little more than a century since organized surface exploration in these countries began. At first these were mainly directed to the identification of sites well-known from the Bible itself. Manners and customs, languages and traditions, were noted before they were lost under advancing Western influences. The geography of Bible lands and visible remains of antiquity were gradually recorded until today more than 25,000 sites within this region and dating to Old Testament times, in their broadest sense, have been located. Several hundreds of these long-buried ruins have been sounded, but less than a hundred have been thoroughly explored, none exhaustively.

Among the finds are about half a million clay documents in the cuneiform script, dating from about 3,300 B.C. to 50 A.D., widely used throughout the area. In addition there are numerous papyri and inscriptions on stone potsherd and other substances. Types of settlement examined range from the earliest camp and cave sites to villages and royal cities. This unprecedented abundance of material should not, however, divert attention from certain limitations which accompany the progress of archaeology as a science. The knowledge of some periods and places is still very defective, a reminder of the unreliability of any hypothesis or argument from silence. Unlike the steady increase in our knowledge from the written documents, the methods of excavation have only recently been developed to the point where stratigraphy, the succession of levels of occupation, and typology, the study of groups of related objects, can be considered reliable. Thus many earlier reports of discovery need revaluation. In this way the fallen walls of Jericho, often quoted both as an outstanding evidence of the truth of a Biblical historical fact and as evidence for dating the entry of the Israelites into Canaan, have recently been by more modern methods as confidently dated to about the time of Abraham. Nevertheless, much of the advance in our understanding of the Old Testament, its language and history, its places and peoples, can be attributed to archaeological discovery.

II. INSCRIPTIONS

By far the largest mass of evidence for comparison with the Scriptures is to be found in the Ancient Near Eastern inscriptions. Few contemporary documents of Old Testament times have been found so far in Palestine itself, so that illustrations must be drawn from the writings of neighboring countries.

The Early Narratives of Genesis

These have long been compared with Sumerian and Akkadian (Babylonian and Assyrian) epics. Their story of creation (*enuma eliš*) survives in several versions (from the twentieth century B.C. and later) which are themselves probably copies of earlier Sumerian originals of which fragmentary clay tablets survive. In these their view of the origin of the universe and of man is stated. The whole creation was for them a divine act *e nihilo*. At first the earth was covered with a watery chaos; light is mentioned before the existence of luminaries; heaven and earth are distinct divisions of the firmament and the luminaries precede the creation of plant and animal life. Finally comes the special and deliberate creation, made from the earth's clay and blood, which was called Man, whose primary duty is the service of the gods. These similarities with the Genesis accounts, however, have to be rescued from a host of extraneous matter which fill the ancient poem. The differences between it and the Biblical record are too numerous for the latter to have evolved from the Mesopotamian epics and the similarities might well be explained by both versions going back to the common element of a primary historical fact.

As with the creation epics, the Babylonians wrote of a great Flood. This was included, as the eleventh tablet, in a series now called the Epic of Gilgamesh which sets out an individual's search for eternal life. As the story unfolds it is impossible not to be struck by the resemblances with Genesis 6–9, even though the majority of the text is far different. Details are given of the construction of the ark to accommodate both men and beasts; the flood waters come from above and below, birds are released to test how far the waters have receded before the ark finally lands "upon one of the mountains of Urartu" (so Gen. 8:4). As with the creation story, it may also be argued that this "myth" also reflects an historic fact. The flood is mentioned and marked in a number of these early documents as cutting right across the early history of mankind. Archaeological evidence of flood-deposits at Ur and Kish, though interpreted by their discoverers to be the flood of this Sumerian legend which they equate with the Flood of Genesis (C. L. Woolley, *Ur Excavations,* IV, 1956, pp. 15–19) is much questioned and thought by other scholars to represent some unusual local inundation. A. Heidel concludes in his study of the Gilgamesh epic that,

> as in the creation epic we still do not know how the Biblical and Babylonian narratives of the deluge are related historically. The available evidence proves nothing beyond that there is a genetic relationship between the Genesis and Babylonian versions. The skeleton is the same in both cases, but the flesh and blood and, above all, the animating spirit are different. It is here that we reach the most far reaching divergencies between the Hebrew and Mesopotamian stories (*The Gilgamesh Epic and Old Testament Parallels,* 1945, p. 268; see also his *The Babylonian Genesis,* pp. 139 f.).

The stories of creation and the flood have no close parallels in Egyptian literature, so most scholars have assumed that Israel borrowed these traditions from the East during the period of the greatest Assyrian influence (ninth to seventh centuries B.C.) or even in the later Jewish exile in Babylonia. However, a fragment of the Gilgamesh Epic dated to the second millennium B.C. has recently been found at Megiddo, and this, combined with such traditions as that of the Tower of Babel which may well refer to the ziggurat of Babylon at some time when that city flourished between the third millennium and its destruction about 1600 B.C., has led to a renewed appraisal. It is now confidently stated that these narratives, whether imported and adapted by, or indigenous to, the Hebrews, could be dated in the second millennium. The same is said of the substance of the Table of Nations in Genesis 10, which represents the state of knowledge towards the end of that millennium, if not earlier. A further factor which has induced this change has been the recent publication of Sumerian texts which, in a number of instances, provide earlier parallels with the Hebrew stories than was hitherto possible. Among these is an epic which possibly describes the state of life in "paradise" which was naturally irrigated (Gen. 2:6). Birth was without pain or travail and a curse followed the eating of a plant. Perhaps more striking, as also more certain as a reading, is the description of the specially created woman named Nin-ti, a Sumerian word which can be equally translated "the lady of the rib" and "the lady who makes alive," reminding the reader of Eve, "the mother of all living," fashioned from the rib of Adam (S. N. Kramer, *From the Tablets of Sumer*, pp. 169–175). Another text describes the time when all men spoke in one language and unitedly served the gods.

The Patriarchal Period

A revolution of thought about the historicity of the patriarchal period is now being brought about following the discovery of more than 70,000 inscribed clay tablets from ancient Alalakh and Mari in Syrian (eighteenth to seventeenth centuries B.C.) and Nuzi in C. Iraq (fifteenth century B.C.). These now provide a detailed view of the historical, social, legal and economic background of these times. Opinions as to the placing of the patriarchs within the first half of the second millennium vary, Albright and De Vaux placing Abraham between 1900–1700 B.C.; Rowley in the eighteenth to seventeenth centuries and Cyrus Gordon as late as the Amarna age (fourteenth century). Part of the uncertainty is due to the current controversy over the exact date of Hammurabi of Babylon (Albright, 1728–1686, Sidney Smith 1792–1750 B.C.). The tablets reflect the composite population of the Upper Euphrates (northwestern Mesopotamia), an area in which Genesis 11:10 ff. locates Abram's ancestors. Harran flourishes at this time and the Mari texts link Turakhi (Terah), Sarugi (Serug) and Nahur (Nahor) as names of districts perhaps derived from the families or tribes who once inhabited them. It has already been shown that some scholars consider the early chapters of Genesis as showing a formative influence from this same area (W. F. Albright, *Recent Discoveries in Bible Lands*, p. 73).

Many parallels between the predominantly Hurrian (Horite) tablets of Nuzi have been described by Gordon and Speiser. Thus the relation of Eliezer and Abraham, as adoptee to a childless couple who yields his right to the real heir, is now explained (Gen. 15:2–4), as is the action of Sarah in providing Hagar for her husband. Moreover, Abraham may have felt able to break with contemporary custom in driving Hagar away only when given a special assurance by God to do so (Gen. 21:12). The possession of *teraphim* (household gods) constituted the right to the chief inheritance and honor in the family (Gen. 31:19, 30–35). It was common practice for a man to work for his bride, as did Jacob among the Aramaean tribe of Laban. Oral blessing having legal force, and levirate marriage, the right of a daughter to inherit property, and a form of sale-adoption (cf. Exod. 21:7–11) are other customs found at this time. The force of these parallels is all the stronger since the Alalakh texts show that throughout the Upper Euphrates region in the early second millennium there was an essentially homogeneous culture with a Sumerian basis but a mixed Amorite-Hurrian development. The Nuzi texts reflect a later stage in this culture. It must be continually remembered that the Old Testament implies, as do these documents, a mixed population in Palestine including Hittites whose early infiltration there is now shown by the Alalakh texts. M. R. Lehmann has shown how applicable the Hittite laws are to the negotiations by Abraham for the cave of Machpelah (Gen. 23). The distinctive features of legal contracts (*nathan* with the meaning "to sell"); the patriarch's concern over obtaining a title to the land free from feudal obligations; the designation of details including the trees, are all characteristic of these Hittite business documents. As Dr. Lehmann has rightly emphasized,

> We have thus found that Genesis 23 is permeated with the knowledge of intricate subtleties of Hittite laws and customs correctly corresponding to the time of Abraham and fitting in with the Hittite features of the Biblical account. With the final destruction of Hattusas about 1200 B.C. these laws must have fallen into oblivion. This is another instance in which a late dating must be firmly rejected. Our study again confirms the authenticity of the "background material" of the Old Testament, which makes it such an invaluable source for the study of all the social, economic and legal aspects of the period of history it depicts (*Bulletin of the American Schools of Oriental Research*, Feb. 1953, pp. 15 ff.)

This increase in the knowledge of the patriarchal age from the texts, combined with the archaeological evidence, has led scholars of many shades of religious opinion to affirm the "historical" nature of the patriarchal narratives. There is, however, a wide divergence in their definition of "history" (Albright, *op. cit.*, p. 72). Professor H. H. Rowley claims that "it is not because scholars of today begin with more conservative presuppositions than their predecessors that they have a much greater respect for the Patriarchal stories than was formerly common, but because the evidence warrants it."

Egypt and the Exodus

Daily life in ancient Egypt is abundantly illustrated in many tomb paintings, papyri and objects. For some periods, however, there are few historical texts and one of these is that part of the Second Intermediate Age (about 1786–1550 B.C.) in which Joseph himself is probably to be placed (Dynasties 15–16, about 1700 B.C.). There can be no doubt, however, that some of the customs recounted in Genesis 34 to 50 are characteristic of this period. Similarly, there is increasing evidence for situating many names, terms and episodes in these narratives at this time also, though much further study is required (K. Kitchen, *The Joseph Narratives,* Tyndale Old Testament Lecture, 1957). One papyrus of a century before Joseph (as dated here) describes the prison system of the period and, on the verso dated only about

40 years before Joseph was sold into Egypt, lists 79 servants in an Egyptian household of whom 45 were Asiatics bearing distinctive west-Semitic names (e.g., Shiprah, Menaham), probably sold into slavery as was Joseph himself. This list adds the Egyptian names given to the slaves in addition to notes about their office (e.g., "chief over the house," "house-servant") and their sex (W. C. Hayes, *A Late Middle Kingdom Papyrus in the Brooklyn Museum,* 1955). It is also to be noted that at this period a number of descriptive stories are found both in the papyri (Senuhe) and in the Babylonian tablets (Idrimi).

Evidence for the entry of Israel into Palestine is mainly archaeological (see p. 17). The "Hebrews" might well be among the semi-nomadic bands of *habiru,* who infiltrated into the open lands between the city-states at this as at earlier times. The earliest mention of Israel in contemporary documents is a reference in the stele of the Egyptian king Merneptah (1222 B.C.) which shows that the Israelites, though poor, were already in the land. The manners and life of the Canaanites and other groups already in the land are now known from the tablets of Ras Shamra (Ugarit), the most prosperous Canaanite seaport of the fourteenth century, and from documents found at Alalakh (level IV) and Amarna (Egypt). The Ras Shamra texts include many in a unique alphabetic script and a language closely related to the Hebrew of this period. Myths, historical and business documents reveal the religion and ritual of the northern Canaanites with its emphasis on fertility and sex (J. Gray, *The Legacy of Canaan, The Ras Shamra Texts and their Relevance to the Old Testament,* 1957).

The Monarchy

It is, however, only when the Israelites are in contact with the Assyrians and Babylonians that, so far, direct allusions are made to Biblical persons and historical events. Shalmaneser III, king of Assyria (859–824 B.C.) lists the "200 chariots and 10,000 men of Ahab, the Israelite" who supported Irhurleni of Hamath at the Battle of Qarqar in 853 B.C. He also describes his defeat of Hazael of Damascus near Mt. Senir (Hermon, the Shenir of Deut. 3:9). In 841 B.C. he received the submission of Jehu, king of Samaria (called Beth-Omri in these Assyrian texts as Damascus is sometimes designated Beth-Hazael). Jehu may have been trying unsuccessfully to seek Assyrian support against Hazael (II Kings 10:31 f.; 21:3, 22 f.). His submission is not directly referred to in the Hebrew records; the illustration of it on the Black Obelisk in the British Museum does, however, provide the only extant contemporary portrayal of a person mentioned in the Old Testament. Tiglath-pileser III (745–727 B.C.), called by his native name Pul(u) in both Babylonian texts and II Kings 15:19, met opposition from "Azariah of Judah" and received tribute from Menahem of Samaria in 739 B.C. The amount of 50 shekels paid by each of the Israelite leaders is the current price of a slave, here paid to avoid deportation (II Kings 15:20). A few years later Tiglath-pileser claims to have marched through "the borders of Israel" against Phoenician and Philistinian towns. These operations seem to have been carried out in answer to an appeal for help from the pro-Assyrian Ahaz (whom he calls by his full name Jehoahaz) who paid tribute in 734 B.C. The Assyrian annals tell how Pekah was replaced by Hoshea; while an inscribed sherd, found in the ruins of Hazor (destroyed by the Assyrians in 732 B.C. when they overran Galilee) bears his name (Pqh). When it is realized that the historical documents which survive from the reign of Tiglath-pileser III are incomplete, the extent of these parallels in agreement with the Hebrew history is most instructive.

The resistance of Israel to Assyria soon brought Shalmaneser V to besiege Samaria in 724 B.C. but he died before the city fell and his successor, Sargon II, claims the final capture in his first year (722/1 B.C.; so [unnamed] II Kings 17:6). Amongst the booty he claimed the capture of "the gods in whom they trusted," an interesting and corroborative allusion at this time to the polytheism of Israel and Samaria which was continually criticized by contemporary Hebrew prophets (D. J. Wiseman, *Journal of the Victoria Institute,* 1955, pp. 28 f.). This same text of Sargon bears an account of the desolation of Babylon strongly reminiscent of the language of Isaiah 13. Sargon records the resettlement of Samaria with persons brought from other parts of his empire (cf. II Kings 17:24) and tablets from Guzana (Gozan, Tell Halaf) show that Jewish exiles were later living there. Israel was now broken and absorbed into the Assyrian provincial system so that Judah faced Assyria alone. Sennacherib, son of Sargon, attacked Judah in 701 B.C., and records his capture of Lachish and the surrounding villages both in his annals and on his palace-reliefs (so II Kings 18:13 f.). His inscriptions agree with the Biblical record also in stating that Hezekiah initially paid him tribute, the variations in the weight of tribute being perhaps due to the different system of measurement then prevailing. Both accounts agree that Jerusalem was besieged at this time, Sennacherib claiming that he "shut up Hezekiah, the Jew, in his royal city like a bird in a cage." The absence of any statement in the Assyrian history relating the fall of the city could be taken as acquiescence in the Judaean claim to victory. There are, however, some difficulties in aligning the Assyrian and Hebrew accounts chronologically. Albright considers that the Hebrews conflated the accounts of two invasions and that the siege of Jerusalem came nearer the end of Sennacherib's reign in 681 B.C.; the writer has elsewhere tried to show the inadequacy of this view (in *Documents from Old Testament Times,* D. Winton Thomas, ed., 1958, where he discusses the relation between Assyrian and Babylonian historical records and the Old Testament). Sennacherib's assassination (II Kings 19:37) is the subject of both Assyrian and Babylonian texts. Sennacherib, according to his personal letters, directed much of his effort against the Chaldaean rebel Marduk-apla-iddin II (Merodach-Baladan), who, when temporarily reigning in Babylon in 703/2 B.C., sought Hezekiah

as an ally when it appeared that further war with Assyria would end successfully (Isa. 39:1 ff.). Esarhaddon of Assyria (681–669 B.C.) included among
his tributaries "Menasseh, king of Judah." According to the terms of treaties
to which such vassals subscribed, they had to accept the god of Assyria as
their god and bind their followers "for ever" to allegiance to Assyria. Assyrian
letters tell how "the inhabitants of Judah sent 10 manas of silver" as part of
their annual dues. The study of these treaties does much to show the background of thought in the Biblical period. Like the Biblical "covenants" they
are arranged in direct speech with a historical prologue, divine witnesses
followed by stipulations and end with curses and blessings. This form goes
back to the second millennium B.C. The distinctive aspect of the Old Testament covenants at all periods is, of course, that they are made and witnessed
by the one God directly with his people and the purpose is spiritual (G. E.
Mendenhall, *Law and Covenant in Israel and the Ancient Near East,* 1955;
D. J. Wiseman, *The Vassal-Treaties of Esarhaddon,* 1958).

Babylonian tablets also help to elucidate the history of Judah before the
Exile. The Babylonian Chronicle, a unique, reliable and contemporary
historical source, recounts the movement of Egyptian troops to support the
Assyrian rearguard action at Harran after the fall of Nineveh in 612 B.C.,
graphically described as in Nahum. It will be observed that, as often, the
non-Hebrew texts and the historical interpretation of Scripture (II Kings
23:29 as an instance of *'al* with the force of *'el* "against") are explained now
by details given of the Battle of Carchemish in 605 B.C. The same chronicle
records the attacks on the Arab tribes of Qedar and Hazor prophesied by
Jeremiah (Jer. 49:28 ff.). These oracles were formerly said to be a late
reflection of attacks made on these tribes in 648 B.C. or a confusion with
Nebuchadrezzar's raids there in 681 B.C. "On the second day of the month
of Adar he (Nebuchadrezzar) captured the city and arrested the king. He
appointed a king of his own choice, received heavy tribute and sent them
(the booty and prisoners) off to Babylon" (Babylonian Chronicle). This is a
direct reference to a crucial point of Biblical history, the divine punishment
on the broken covenant foretold by Isaiah and Jeremiah and marked by the
Jewish exile which now begins. The captured king was Jehoiachin, whose
presence as an exile in Babylon is also attested by a number of ration-tablets
found there. The Babylonian nominee was Mattaniah-Zedeqiah. The date
(16th March 597), now precisely known for the first time, is in accord with
the Biblical notes (II Chron. 36:10; II Kings 24:12), which place the event
in the spring, at the change over from reckoning Nebuchadrezzar's seventh
to eighth regnal year. These same texts had mentioned the fall of Ashkelon
in 604 B.C., an event which must have added weight to the prophecies of
Jeremiah to the approaching disaster, for in the same month a solemn fast
was proclaimed in Jerusalem (Jer. 36:9). A great battle in 601 B.C., in
which Egypt defeated the Babylonians, is also recorded. This event, which
was unsuspected from either Biblical or non-Biblical sources, explains why

Jehoiakim, against the advice of Jeremiah, now put his trust in Egypt and broke with Assyria. The scantiness of extra-Biblical sources for an understanding of this period or of the times of the Exile preclude undue weight being placed on the numerous hypotheses which abound. In 587, after a long siege, reflected in the Lachish letters, Jerusalem was destroyed. Apart from the few references to Jehoiachim and Judaeans among the exiles in Babylonia, there is no reference to this event in contemporary documents. This is not surprising, for many similar exiles brought from many different countries to Babylonia as a result of Nebuchadrezzar's extensive campaigns are listed in the same texts. Moreover, from this time onwards the Babylonians were increasingly using more perishable writing materials inscribed in Aramaic which have not survived. Cyrus has left details of his policy of religious toleration which encouraged the restoration of holy places formerly destroyed or neglected by the Babylonians. A glimpse of Jewish life and customs abroad in the time of Ezra or Nehemiah is afforded by the Elephantine papyri from Egypt.

One of the major historical problems of the book of Daniel has been the reference to "Darius the Mede." Persian and Babylonian records make no reference to any intervening ruler of royal status but clearly state that Cyrus himself took over the Neo-Babylonian Empire from Nabonidus after 15 days in which the city was under a military governor Gubaru (Gobryas). As a result there is a general agreement among scholars that "he [Darius the Mede] has no place in history, and that he is a fictitious creation out of confused traditions" (H. H. Rowley, *Darius the Mede*, p. 5). The recent discovery of a stele inscription from Harran naming a "king of the Medes" as late as 540 B.C. reopens the whole question. One suggestion put forward is that Cyrus had a separate throne-name (Darius) as conqueror and king of the Medes.

III. EXCAVATIONS

The evidence of the archaeological excavations and researches at Biblical sites provides no less valuable, even if often more general, evidence for comparison with the statements of the Old Testament. As a result of developing techniques, sites are now located, identified and explored, their successive periods of occupation traced and dated by characteristic types of objects (e.g., pottery, implements, seals, architectural and art styles) with greater precision than formerly. Thus the first entry of the semi-nomadic Hebrews under Abraham into the hill-country of south Palestine seems to have taken place early in the second millennium B.C. when such towns as Bethel, Shechem and Dothan, associated with the early patriarchs, are seen to have been in existence. Hebron was not yet occupied (so Gen. 23:2; 35:27). From the material remains it would seem that about 2000 B.C. there were few towns but that in the following century a new era (M. Bronze II) began and sites like Jericho were reoccupied. Gezar, Megiddo and Hazor were already flourishing Canaanite cities with high places and altars. Kyle and Albright have shown that Sodom, Gomorrah and Zoar in all probability now lie beneath the southern waters of the Dead Sea and they, as Glueck later, found adjacent sites in this once densely populated area abandoned about this same time. It appears that the population hurriedly left older settlements and returned to semi-nomadic life. Genesis 14 is now considered "historical," since the route taken by the coalition of kings followed the existing "Kings Highway" (east of Jordan, Num. 20:17) marked by a line of fortresses of which the remains can be dated to this time. Although the kings themselves cannot be certainly identified, the personal names (e.g., Tudhalia, Ariuku— the identity of Amraphel with Ammurapi is unlikely) and the place-names fit well with the contemporary onomastica. Albright considers that this chapter cannot be dated later than the sixteenth century and states:

> It is very striking to note that none of the important religious centers of Israel in the time of the monarchy whose remains do not show any occupation at so early a date, appears in connection with the narrative of the Patriarchs. If the Patriarchal stories grew up round cult-centers, we should expect to find the Patriarchs playing a bigger role in them" (*op. cit.,* p. 75).

The Exodus and Conquest

Archaeological evidence for the period of the Israelite sojourn in Egypt is only of a general illustrative nature; that is, many of the customs and details mentioned in the Joseph narratives can be compared with tomb paintings or objects from earlier or later periods. Excavations do show, however, the major building activity of Dynasty 19 in the Delta area where Rameses II set up his capital about 1290 with the aim of controlling his Asiatic Empire.

The store-city of Raamses (Exod. 1:11), built by Israelite labor-gangs, is the "House of Raamses" in the splendid city-ruins identified by the majority with Tanis, later Zoan (by others with the nearby ruins of Qantir). Pitham is Tell Retabeh and the "Reed Sea," crossed by the Israelites in the first stage of their exodus, the area of papyrus marshes east of Tanis and Succoth (excavated by Naville at Tell el-Maskentah). Their route to the Sinai range of mountains is today marked by Merkah and Serabit-el-khadim with its turquoise mines in which proto-sinaitic (early alphabetic) inscriptions have been found. Both were occupied during this century. The survey of (Trans)- jordan by Glueck and Lankester-Harding shows that before the thirteenth century Edom and Moab were sparsely populated by groups of semi-nomads who then settled down in fortified villages and were able to prevent the direct transit of the Israelites. South Canaan is found to be a land of city-states (principally Jerusalem, Lachish, Hebron, Gezer) between which the semi-nomadic peoples infiltrated as is shown also by the constant reference in the Amarna, Alalakh and Ras Shamra tablets to the Habiru. The Israelites, perhaps a group of the "Habiru," were armed only with light weapons, and having no siege equipment avoided the heavier fortified localities. Excavations at Jericho (Tell es-Sultan) since 1952 show that the ruins of the late bronze age city (after 1500 B.C.) suffered considerable denudation and very little remains. An Iron-Age foundation has survived only because it was dug deep into earlier levels. The evidence allows the presumption that Jericho, too, fell in the Late Bronze Age at the same time as other southern cities. The fallen walls, once confidently ascribed by Garstang to Joshua's day, are now known to be 300 years earlier in date. Another city, the destruction of which Joshua claimed, presents difficulties in relation to the Biblical evidence. Ai ("the ruins," if the same as Et-Tel) has been found to have lain unoccupied after 2400 B.C. except for a temporary settlement of Israelites there about 1000 B.C. A number of theories are put forward to explain this; that the later Israelites explain the "ruins" by attributing them to Joshua; that the neighboring Bethelites used it as an outpost in their defense against the invaders (but there would hardly then have been a "king of Ai" as in Josh. 8), or even that the story of the conquest of Bethel was later attributed to "Ai." The difficulty remains, but further evidence may provide some more adequate explanation. Bethel (only indirectly mentioned in the conquest narrative) was excavated in 1934 and found to have been violently destroyed by fire in the late thirteenth century, a date for the conquest of the land to which much evidence again points. The finely built Canaanite houses were succeeded by Israelite buildings and occupation of a poorer quality. The same situation has been found at Lachish (Tell ed-Duweir) where the destruction is further marked by an inscribed and dated sherd (1220 B.C.). Debir (Tell Beit Mirsim) was razed to its foundations by invaders between about 1250 and 1200 B.C. Y. Yadin, at present clearing the vast ruins of Hazor in Galilee, has uncovered a large Canaanite settlement and shrines of this same period, the destruction of which he attributes to Joshua. All this points to a planned campaign as outlined in Joshua 10. Unbroken occupation of the Egyptian-dominated strongholds of Taanach and Beth-shan confirm that the Israelites with their tribal organization avoided these large fortresses which guarded the Esdraelon plain.

The Monarchy

Before the entry of the Israelites, the Philistines, a branch of the "Sea Peoples" entering the eastern Mediterranean at this time, had established themselves in East Cyprus (Sinda) and on the Palestinian coast. Their presence is marked by pottery bearing characteristic patterns, found at Gezer, Beth-Shemesh, Tell Qasilah and other sites, but their origin is still obscure. By 1050 B.C. traces of the destruction caused by these same peoples are found at Shiloh and distant Beth-Shan. Discoveries at Bethel and Tell Beit-Mirsion in Palestine and Ras Shamra in Syria show the wealthy local Canaanite culture based on an extensive trade and Egyptian influence. In contrast, the poorer Israelites who succeeded them have left a cruder art, poorer pottery and more vulnerable town walls. Their daily life is by now well-known from the excavations at Ai, Mizpah (if identical with Tell-en-Nasbeh), Beth-Shemesh and Beth-zur. The Philistines seem to have introduced the technique of iron-working into Palestine and thus to have had an economic hold over Israel (I Sam. 13:19–22) until their defeat by Saul and David. Saul's fortified palace at Gibeah yielded the first iron implement yet discovered in the hill country. Life in Gibeah was simpler in the days before it too fell to the Philistines. With the turn of the tide of military power an industrial revolution took place in David's day (the beginning of the Iron Age I period). Iron replaced flints in sickles and weapons, and iron nails enabled improved building techniques to be used (I Chron. 22:3). The excavations show a steadily increasing standard of living even for the country folk under David (about 1000 to 961 B.C.); otherwise archaeology reveals nothing of the king's work unless some of the fortifications of Jerusalem (Ophel) can be attributed to him.

Solomon built extensively and to do this used his power as a merchant-prince controlling the trade routes from Arabia to Syria and the East. At Ezion-geber (Gulf of Aqabah) he developed large copper and iron smelting plants and a harbor. This trade is marked by a sherd found at Tell Qasileh marked "from Ophir," and chariots traded from Egypt and breeding-horses from Cilicia (so I Kings 10:28 f.) increased the nation's wealth. Heavy taxes led to a reorganization of the administrative districts where the governors had dwellings, as found at Beth-Shemesh and Lachish, where taxes could also be stored. More than 500 horses could have been stabled at Megiddo where accommodation was provided for them and for the provincial administrators. The taxes and forced labor gangs were employed on the reconstruction of Hazor, Megiddo and Gezer (I Kings 9:15) and at each of these places identical gateways of the Solomonic period have been recovered.

The Temple, being built under the direction of foreign (Phoenician) craftsmen, followed the current trend and was divided into an outer court, from which a single door between two pillars led directly into a large holy place or room (*hekal*) and in turn into a small inner sanctuary or "holy of holies" (*debir*). This plan is clearly traced in the temple found at Hazor in 1957 and in a smaller temple at Tell Tainat in Syria. The decorations of *cherubim,* palm trees and open work can be seen in contemporary ivory working and the temple furniture (lavers, censers, fleshhooks) seen in the objects found at a number of Palestinian and Syrian sites.

The period of the divided monarchy to which there are references in the secular inscriptions is becoming better known from actual excavations. The work of De Vaux at Tell el Far'ah (Tirzah) confirms that the site was no longer in active use after Samaria had become the northern capital. The Harvard expedition to Samaria uncovered six successive Israelite levels of occupation; the original foundation and building (I) of fine workmanship by Omri-Ahab with ivories used in decorating and furnishing the royal palace (I Kings 22:39; Amos 6:14); and the pool where Ahab's chariot was probably washed down (I Kings 22:38). The citadel of Jehu with its strong walls (II) was destined to survive until replaced by a Hellenistic construction about 150 B.C. Here were found 63 inscribed ostraca or accounts of exports and imports of wine and oil showing that Samaria was still an active trading and administrative center. The occupation of Jeroboam II (about 786–746 B.C.) and his Israelite successors can be traced in levels IV–VI. Destruction levels in various cities can be attributed to the invasions of Tiglath-pileser III in 734–732, the ruin at Hazor (level V) and Megiddo (level III) being particularly heavy. The change of regime at Samaria when it fell to Assyria in 722 is described, in archaeological terms, by a poorer and partial reoccupation shown by pottery types imported by the new settlers brought in from the East (II Kings 17:24). As Israel was henceforth incorporated in the Assyrian provincial system, such traces as have been found show an increasing external influence.

In Judah, excavations at Lachish (1932–1938) have revealed the very city walls, gateway, ramp and weapons depicted on the reliefs of Sennacherib at Nineveh which parade his siege of that city in 701 B.C. A vast communal burial pit may mark the resting place of many of the defenders. Hezekiah's ability to withstand successfully the Assyrian siege of Jerusalem may well be due to the precaution taken to ensure the water supply through the 1700 foot "Siloam tunnel" discovered in 1880. It bore a Hebrew inscription describing this remarkable engineering feat, but the work was probably eased by the use of earlier Canaanite tunnels similar to those found at other sites. The lintel of a large tomb cut out of the rock at Jerusalem for "Shebna, who is over the house," much criticized by Isaiah (22:15), is now in the British Museum, if the interpretation of the inscription made by Avigad is accepted.

The Egyptian resistance to the increasing Babylonian power is shown by the destruction of Megiddo (level II) by Necho II of Egypt. It was here that Josiah was slain while vainly trying to maintain his independence. The fall of Carchemish to Nebuchadrezzar is shown by the excavation there conducted by Sir C. L. Woolley in 1931–32. In 598 the Babylonians advanced for the final siege of Jerusalem, destroying Lachish and many other towns, most of which were never reoccupied, or only sparsely so, after the return from exile. During the Exile, stamped sealings marked "Eliakim, steward of Yaukin (Jehoiachin)" show how the royal estates were managed while the Judean king was held hostage in Babylon. The seals of Jaazaniah (Jer. 11:8) and Gedaliah, governor of Judah after Jerusalem fell in 587 B.C., have been found at Tell-en-Nasbeh and Lachish respectively. The period of the Exile itself both in Palestine and Babylonia is obscure. In the latter it was a time of gradual decline both economically and culturally, and the texts show that it was a period without literary distinction or innovation. For this reason the commonly accepted view that the Exile was a period of great influence on the Jews themselves must remain a theory. The state of the

Jews and their religion is only known, from extra-Biblical evidence, in the
excavations and texts of distant Elephantine (Egypt). The archives of the
fifth century from Nippur prove little beyond the fact that a handful of Jews
remained there when many of their brethren had returned to Judah. Archaeological discoveries show that the reoccupation of Judah was slow and
that though Gezer, Lachish, Gibeah, Bethel, Beth-zur and Hazor show traces
of settlement in the Persian period the land did not flourish until the Greek
period. Under Persian influence coins (marked *Yhd*—"Judah") first appear.
By contrast with the scriptural account of these same periods, this survey
shows how little, and often general, is the evidence afforded by archaeology
as distinct from the inscriptions.

IV. THE TEXT OF THE OLD TESTAMENT

One result of the inscriptional and archaeological discoveries briefly summarized above has been the gradual reappraisal of the literature of the Old
Testament and a fresh attempt to place it in its contemporary setting. This
is still a very difficult task by reason of the virtual absence of writings surviv-
ing from Palestine itself and of the necessarily subjective nature of this form
of literary criticism. Thus, for example, Albright, in the light of the poetic
forms of the Ugaritic texts, now dates such Hebrew poems as the song of
Deborah (Judg. 5) and the song of Miriam (Exod. 15) to the time of Moses,
the oracles of Balaam (Num. 22-24) to the thirteenth century and the
blessings of Jacob (Gen. 49) and the blessings of Moses (Deut. 33) as not
later than the eleventh century. Similarly, in opposition to the widely accepted results of literary criticism, he would assign many psalms, including
Psalm 68, to this early date. "This Psalm," he writes, "has often been attributed to the Maccabean period (second century B.C.) in spite of the fact
that Jewish scholars who translated it into Greek in the same century did
not understand it any better than did the Massoretes a thousand years later.
This is typical of much so-called 'critical' work in the biblical field" (in
Religion in Life, 21, 1952, pp. 543 f.). It has already been shown that other
narratives (e.g., Genesis 10, 23, Isa. 13) bear the marks of earlier composition than has been hitherto generally allowed. It is to be expected that, as the
understanding of the languages, vocabulary, literary forms and methods
increases as a result of the great body of written material available from both
Egypt and "Mesopotamia," further studies of this kind will be made (e.g.,
D. J. Wiseman, *New Discoveries in Babylonia about Genesis*, 1956). The
important part played by scribes in the Ancient Near East and the methods
and materials they employed should continue to act as a check on the more
extravagant theories of the compilation of ancient texts (G. R. Driver,
Semitic Writing, 1948). Thus, students of Akkadian literature find it difficult
to endorse the place given to oral tradition by many Old Testament scholars
today, for in the second millennium oral tradition supplements and does not

exclude or supersede the written word (e.g., J. Laesse, *Oral Tradition in Mesopotamia,* 1954).

The discoveries first made in 1947 of manuscripts of the Old Testament at Qumran and neighboring sites are now well-known. These include the first copies of the Hebrew text dating from the pre-Christian era (except for fragments like the Nash papyrus of about 100 B.C.) and now represent more than 100 individual Biblical scrolls. Every book of the Old Testament, except Esther, is found either complete (like the famous "Dead Sea Scroll" of Isaiah) or represented by fragments. It is clear that the most copied books were Deuteronomy, Isaiah and the Psalms, the books of the Law, Prophets and Writings used for popular instruction and thus the most commonly quoted by Jesus Christ in his ministry. The texts date from between about 200 B.C. to 68 A.D. (about 128 A.D. at Murabba'at)—a date corroborated by archaeological evidence—when they were stored away for safety in time of war. These discoveries are of great importance for the study of the Biblical text and, unlike the sectarian documents found with them which are currently the subject of much controversy, their value and testimony are apparent. Textual variants exist as in all groups of manuscripts from the Ancient Near East and show that more than one textual tradition is in question at this time before the establishment of the authoritative Hebrew text in the late first century or early second century A.D. Some show a close affinity to the Massoretic text, some to the long neglected old Samaritan recension and others to the Alexandrian Septuagint, the historical worth of which is now established (F. M. Cross, *Bulletin of the American Schools of Oriental Research,* No. 141, pp. 9–13). The texts bear little on the dating of Biblical books except that some of the latest datings (e.g., Ecclesiastes at 200 B.C.) are excluded (G. Wright, *Biblical Archaeology,* pp. 212–217). It is already clear that the Qumran scrolls have inaugurated a new and welcome period of Old Testament textual studies and give promise of further such discoveries at any time.

V. THE NATURE OF ARCHAEOLOGICAL CONFIRMATION

From the preceding summary it is hoped that it will be obvious that archaeological researches have done much to illustrate the Biblical record, its life and times, its places, peoples, customs, literature and even words. This is the very purpose of such research and its expected result. Regrettably, Biblical archaeology is treated by many as an uncoordinated body of knowledge summoned as an ally to defend or confirm the Scriptures as they understand them, and a vague idea thus abounds in some quarters that the Bible is confirmed, or proved increasingly, with each discovery. There is rightly a general agreement that an increased understanding of Bible history has come principally from the field of archaeology and that this has tended to bring a return to a more conservative attitude in some questions, notably the histori-

cal creditability of the patriarchal age and a disposition to credit more
Biblical narratives, now comparable with early narratives from the Ancient
Near East, than formerly (H. H. Rowley, *The Old Testament and Modern
Study*, 1951, pp. xx–xxi). It has also led to a general appreciation of the
greater reliability of the Massoretic Hebrew text than was allowed earlier in
this century. On the other hand, by the very nature and limitations of archaeology as a science, many problems are also raised in the interpretation of
the evidence produced, and these are not denied even if not stressed here.
Similarly, difficulties may arise from a misunderstanding or misinterpretation
of the Bible itself and it is only when the facts, not the theories, found by
extra-Biblical research are related to the facts of the Bible, itself rightly
understood, that a valid comparison may be made and agreement expected.
Those who stress that the value of the Old Testament lies not in its historical
or literary but in its religious teaching would here contend that the great
spiritual themes lie outside the scope of archaeological research. In part this
is true.

They would argue that religious truth is one thing and historical fact
another, that neither necessarily presupposes or accompanies the other
(Millar Burrows, *What Mean These Stones?*, pp. 2–4). It would not seem
right to belittle any evidence which directly corroborates the historicity and
accuracy of the Bible at any point any more than it would be right, as sometimes happens, to interpret the evidence either of archaeology or of the Bible
itself out of context in order to find proofs of Biblical accuracy. The evangelicals, believing that the Lord God has revealed himself in history and supremely in Jesus Christ, have always supported those who investigate those
times and places in which the revelation was made. They encourage research
both into the Bible itself and into archaeology as a branch of science. They
should not be content with a mere suspension of judgment in the face of
difficulties and apparent discrepancies, though this may often be necessary,
but should be in the forefront of any work which seeks to reach the truth.
For them the truth is supremely the revelation of God in Jesus Christ and
therefore their attitude to the Old Testament is dominated by him as he
interprets and fulfills it in the New. Ultimately the truth or "confirmation"
of the Old Testament rests in God and does not depend on the human
science of archaeology, valuable though it is.

ARCHAEOLOGICAL
CONFIRMATION OF
THE NEW TESTAMENT

F. F. Bruce

F. F. Bruce is Professor of Biblical History and Literature in Sheffield University, England. He holds the B.A. from Cambridge University, M.A. and D.D. from Aberdeen University. His published works include The Acts of the Apostles, The Spreading Flame, Are the New Testament Documents Reliable? Second Thoughts on the Dead Sea Scrolls, *and* The Books and the Parchments. *He has been editor of* The Evangelical Quarterly *since 1950 and of the* Palestine Exploration Quarterly *since 1957.*

20. *F. F. Bruce*

ARCHAEOLOGICAL
CONFIRMATION OF
THE NEW TESTAMENT

BIBLICAL archaeology, for most people to whom the expression means anything, is almost exclusively associated with the Old Testament. There are several reasons for this. One is that the historical setting of the New Testament—the Graeco-Roman world of the first century A.D.—was well-known from the writings of classical authors of the period, and there was no need for archaeological research to recover the record of vanished civilizations such as form the historical setting of the greater part of the Old Testament narrative. Another reason is that many archaeological discoveries relating to the Old Testament have impressed the public imagination to a degree unparalleled in the New Testament field. For a hundred people who have some idea of the flood-line at Ur or the excavations at Jericho, there is barely one who knows anything about the Oxyrhynchus papyri or the warning inscription from the temple at Jerusalem. There is a picturesqueness about the cuneiform tablets which is not shared by the rough notes on Egyptian ostraca of a later date. The reported discovery of the tomb of St. Peter has excited more stir than most finds from the early Christian period, but this may be due as much to its supposed bearing on ecclesiastical controversy as to its purely historical interest. The Dead Sea Scrolls have received much more public attention than is usually given to written documents from the Near East of Graeco-Roman days, but interest in them has been stimulated by the widely publicized suggestion that their evidence in some way or other has weakened the authority of Christianity.

I. THE NATURE OF NEW TESTAMENT ARCHAEOLOGY

New Testament archaeology is for the most part a matter of written documents. These may be public or private inscriptions on stone or some equally durable material; they may be papyri recovered from the sand of Egypt recording literary texts or housewives' shopping lists; they may be private notes scratched on fragments of unglazed pottery; they may be legends on coins preserving information about some otherwise forgotten ruler or getting some point of official propaganda across to the people who used them. They may represent a Christian church's collection of sacred Scriptures, like the Chester Beatty Biblical Papyri; they may be all that is left of the library of an ancient religious community, like the scrolls from Qumran or the Gnostic texts from Nag Hammadi. But whatever their character, they can be at least as important and relevant for the study of the New Testament as any cuneiform tablets are for the study of the Old.

Again, if New Testament archaeology cannot boast of the excavation of long-buried cities, it has enabled us, by less spectacular but not less convincing means, to identify a large number of sites mentioned by the apostles and evangelists. At times it has succeeded in pinpointing the location of an ancient city whose name and whereabouts had long since disappeared from popular memory. At other times a tomb, a monument, or the foundations of a building have come to light and helped us to understand better some New Testament incident associated with the place in question.

II. PAPYRUS DISCOVERIES

Papyrus documents have been discovered from all ages of ancient Egyptian history, but we are concerned here with those which belong to the later centuries B.C. and the earlier centuries A.D., when there was a large Greek-speaking population in Alexandria and other parts of Egypt. This Greek-speaking population was literate in all its strata. The common people wrote letters and kept the ordinary commercial accounts of daily life on pieces of papyrus; for odd jottings some of them found an even cheaper writing-material in broken pieces of pottery, or ostraca, as they are commonly called.

These scraps of papyrus and pieces of pottery soon found their way to the local rubbish heaps, where they lay undisturbed for centuries. It was towards the end of last century that scholars began to take an interest in them. Unlike the papyri containing literary texts, of which many have been found, the papyri which have thrown most light on the New Testament are those which contain the writing of ordinary people in their everyday vernacular. For this everyday vernacular presents remarkable similarities to the Greek in which a good part of the New Testament is written. Scholars had for long recognized the differences between New Testament Greek and the Greek of classical literature, but they were not sure how to account for them. Richard Rothe in 1863 could refer to New Testament Greek as "a language of the Holy Ghost," from which it might be inferred that it was a form of Greek divinely produced for the purpose of recording the Christian revelation. But in that same year Joseph Barber Lightfoot, lecturing in Cambridge, declared his belief "that if we could only recover letters that ordinary people wrote to each other, without any thought of being literary, we should have the greatest possible help for the understanding of the New Testament." His words were prophetic. For when the attention of scholars was turned a few years later to the vernacular papyri, they discovered that the "language of the Holy Ghost" was not very different from the language of the common people.

The pioneer in comparing the language of the New Testament with that of the papyri was the German scholar Adolf Deissmann. The study was taken up by others, among whom special mention should be made of two British scholars, James Hope Moulton and George Milligan, who between them produced a monumental work, *The Vocabulary of the New Testament illustrated from the Papyri and other Non-literary Sources* (Edinburgh, 1914–30), in which the results of this comparative study were made accessible to the student.

There was at first a natural tendency to go too far in assuming that the language of the New Testament could be entirely explained in terms of the new discoveries. The New Testament idiom is indeed vernacular when it deals with everyday affairs, although much of it (as we might expect) has a Semitic flavor not found in the Egyptian papyri. But there is also a large literary element in the New Testament for which we must seek parallels in the later Greek authors; while in order to understand what we may call the theological vocabulary of the New Testament, we must pay special attention to the Septuagint, the Greek version of the Old Testament which was made in Alexandria in the closing centuries before Christ.

Great excitement was aroused towards the end of last century by the discovery of two papyrus fragments at Oxyrhynchus in Egypt, containing a number of isolated sayings of Jesus, each introduced by the words, "Jesus said." Some of these were similar to sayings of Jesus preserved in our Gospels; others had no known parallels. One of the most striking was the frequently quoted one: "Jesus said: Wherever there are two, they are not without God, and wherever there is one alone, I say, I am with him. Raise the stone, and there thou shalt find me; cleave the wood, and there am I." The fragments belong to about A.D. 140.

The substance, though not the diction, of these sayings has affinities with the teaching of Jesus in St. John's Gospel. One of the Oxyrhynchus sayings was previously known from a reference by Clement of Alexandria (c. A.D. 180), who quotes it as coming from *The Gospel according to the Hebrews,* a

322 REVELATION AND THE BIBLE

work which was current in Egypt in the early Christian centuries. This saying has now been identified afresh in the recently discovered Coptic version of the *Gospel of Thomas*. This work (which is quite different from the apocryphal *Gospel of Thomas* hitherto known) is a comprehensive collection of sayings of Jesus of the same character as those found on the Oxyrhynchus papyri, and the first saying in the collection is the one quoted by Clement: "Whosoever listens to these words shall never taste death. Let not him who seeks cease until he finds, and when he finds he shall be astonished; astonished he shall attain the kingdom and when he attains it he shall rest. . . ."

The authenticity of these uncanonical sayings attributed to Jesus must, of course, be carefully assessed. Several of them are clearly the product of Gnostic reconstruction of the original Christian message; others are the fruitage of pious but undisciplined imagination. In *Unknown Sayings of Jesus* (London, 1957), Joachim Jeremias isolates 21 sayings unrecorded in the Gospels which in his judgment have a specially high claim to authenticity, and considers their significance in detail. Such a study does not indeed confirm the New Testament record, but plainly any sayings which may reasonably be traced back to Jesus deserve to be considered by every Christian with great interest and attention.

Along with the *Gospel of Thomas* just mentioned there was found about 1945 a whole library of Gnostic literature—at Nag Hammadi on the west bank of the Nile (the ancient Chenoboskion). This library consists of 13 papyrus codices, comprising 48 Gnostic treatises, mostly translated from Greek into Coptic. While the codices themselves belong to the third and fourth centuries A.D., the Greek originals were composed a century or two earlier. One of these treatises, and that a most important one, has been published thus far—the Valentinian *Gospel of Truth,* which was composed about the middle of the second century and is mentioned by Irenaeus a few decades later (*Against Heresies* iii.11.9). Such works do not help us to understand the New Testament better, but they do indicate how the New Testament was understood in some very significant and influential circles in the early days of Christianity.

What was believed to be a previously unknown Gospel was discovered among Egyptian papyri purchased from a dealer in 1934 and promptly published in *Fragments of an Unknown Gospel and other Early Christian Papyri,* by H. I. Bell and T. C. Skeat (London, 1935). The fragments of the "unknown Gospel" (Egerton Papyrus 2), dated on palaeographical grounds around A.D. 150, appear actually to have belonged to a manual designed to teach people the Gospel stories. This manual drew upon all four of our canonical Gospels, and thus makes its contribution to the evidence that the fourfold Gospel was generally accepted in the Church at the middle of the second century.

In 1931 news was published of the discovery of a collection of papyrus texts of the Greek Scriptures which have come to be known as the "Chester

Beatty Biblical Papyri." This collection evidently formed the Bible of some outlying church in Egypt; it comprises eleven fragmentary codices, three of which in their complete state contained most of the New Testament. One contained the Gospels and Acts, another Paul's nine letters to churches and the Epistle to the Hebrews, and a third the Revelation. All three were written in the third century; the Pauline codex, the oldest of the three, was written at the beginning of that century. Even in their present mutilated state, these papyri bear most important testimony to the early textual history of the New Testament; they have provided most valuable evidence for the identification of the "Caesarean" text-type.

The oldest known fragment of any part of the New Testament is a scrap from a codex of St. John's Gospel, to be dated in the first half of the second century, and therefore probably less than fifty years later than the actual composition of that Gospel. One side exhibits John 18:31–33, the other side verses 37 and 38 of the same chapter. It was included in a miscellaneous lot of Egyptian papyri bought for the John Rylands Library in Manchester in 1920, and was published in *An Unpublished Fragment of the Fourth Gospel in the John Rylands Library,* edited by C. H. Roberts (Manchester, 1935).

More recently another papyrus text of St. John's Gospel has been discovered and published, later in date than the Rylands fragment (for it belongs to the end of the second century) but much more comprehensive (for it preserves most of John 1–14, while fragments of the following chapters have also been identified). This text has been published by V. Martin in *Papyrus Bodmer II: Évangile de Jean,* Chap. 1–14 (Bibliotheca Bodmeriana, 1956), Chap. 15–21 (1958). For two-thirds of this Gospel it adds to our knowledge of the text current in Egypt a century and a half before the date of the great vellum uncials, Vaticanus and Sinaiticus.

When archaeology provides us with the material for tracing the text of the New Testament farther back and establishing it on a firmer basis, it renders an inestimable service to Biblical studies.

But it happens from time to time that papyrus texts which have no direct relation to the New Testament help nonetheless in its interpretation. Thus, the statement in Luke 2:3, that in pursuance of the imperial census-decree which preceded our Lord's birth, "all went to be enrolled, each to his own city," is illustrated by a papyrus in the British Museum, recording an edict of A.D. 104 in which the Roman prefect of Egypt gives notice: "The enrollment by household being at hand, it is necessary to notify all who for any cause whatsoever are outside their own administrative districts that they must return to their own homes, in order both to carry out the customary procedure of enrollment and to continue steadfastly in the agriculture which belongs to them."

One final and problematical papyrus document must be mentioned: a letter written by the Emperor Claudius in A.D. 41 to the people of Alexandria in Egypt, and now preserved in the British Museum. There had been serious outbursts of violence between the Greek and Jewish communities in Alexandria; Claudius bids them keep the peace and exercise mutual tolerance. Then, addressing himself to the Jewish community, he goes on: "Do not introduce or invite Jews who sail down to Alexandria from Syria or Egypt, thus compelling me to conceive the greater suspicion, or else I will certainly take vengeance on them as fomenting a general plague for the whole world." The language used here reminds us of similar language provoked in official quarters by the spread of the Christian movement, and it may be that the introduction of Christianity into the Jewish community of Alexandria was leading to riots of the same kind as broke out in Rome some years later—"at the instigation of Chrestus," says Suetonius—when "Claudius commanded all the Jews to leave Rome" (Acts 18:2). Was Apollos forced to leave Alexandria for much the same reason as forced his friends Priscilla and Aquila to leave Rome? It may be so; we wish the evidence were more explicit.

III. INSCRIPTIONS

Another enigmatic decree of Claudius has been preserved, not on papyrus but on stone. A slab of white marble in the Louvre, coming originally from Nazareth (so far as can be ascertained), records an edict of a Roman emperor ordaining, on pain of death, "that graves and tombs remain undisturbed in perpetuity for those who have made them for the cult of their ancestors or children or members of their family." The character of the Greek script and a consideration of historical circumstances point to Claudius as the emperor in question. It is suggested by some scholars that, concerned about the "general plague" which was infecting Alexandria and Rome, and indeed the whole world, Claudius (who was in any case a man of antiquarian interests) investigated the history of the trouble and found that it went back to one Jesus of Nazareth who was crucified, and whose body was shortly afterwards found to be missing from the tomb in which it had been laid. Again, we must suspend final judgment until more evidence comes to light.

There is no such enigma about another edict of Claudius, inscribed on limestone at Delphi in Central Greece. This edict is to be dated during the first seven months of A.D. 52, and mentions Gallio as being proconsul of Achaia. We know from other sources that Gallio's proconsulship lasted only for a year, and since proconsuls entered on their term of office on July 1, the inference is that Gallio entered on his proconsulship on that date in A.D. 51. But Gallio's proconsulship of Achaia overlapped Paul's year and a half of ministry in Corinth (Acts 18:11 ff.), so that Claudius's inscription provides us with a fixed point for reconstructing the chronology of Paul's career.

A fragmentary door-inscription in Greek from Corinth, belonging to this general period, appears to have read when complete "Synagogue of the

Hebrews"; conceivably it belonged to the synagogue in which Paul "reasoned every sabbath" (Acts 18:4) after his arrival in that city, until his presence was no longer tolerated there and he moved to the house of Justus next door. In the course of excavations in Corinth in 1929, a pavement was uncovered which bore the inscription in Latin: "Erastus, procurator for public buildings, laid this pavement at his own expense." The pavement evidently existed in the first century A.D., and we wonder if it was laid by Paul's friend Erastus, city treasurer of Corinth, whom he mentions in Romans 16:23. Yet another Corinthian inscription refers to the "meat market" (Gk. *makellon*), mentioned by Paul in I Corinthians 10:25.

Our reference to Gallio reminds us how frequently Luke, in his Gospel and Acts, has occasion to mention men who occupied official positions in various parts of the Roman Empire. The student of Roman history is aware of the bewildering variety in the titles held by these men, and he cannot fail to be struck by the confident accuracy with which Luke uses them. He tells us, for example, that Paul's opponents in Thessalonica laid information against him and his friends before the *politarchs,* for thus he denotes the civic authorities (Acts 17:6). This term *politarchs* is not found in any classical author, but it is found in some nineteen inscriptions, ranging from the second century B.C. to the third century A.D., as a title of magistrates in Macedonian cities. In five of these inscriptions Thessalonica is the Macedonian city in question; it had five *politarchs* at the beginning of the first century A.D., and six in the middle of the following century.

Another example is the designation which Luke gives to Publius, the chief man in Malta. He calls him literally "the first man of the island" (Acts 28:7), and inscriptions have been found in both Greek and Latin which show that "first man" (Gk. *prōtos,* Lat. *primus*) was indeed his proper title.

Luke's narrative of the riot in Ephesus (Acts 19:23 ff.) represents the *ecclesia* or civic assembly of that place as meeting in the theatre. That it did in fact meet there is shown by an inscription in Greek and Latin, found in the Ephesian theatre, which records that a Roman official, Vibius Salutaris, presented a silver image of Artemis ("Diana" of KJV and ASV) and other statues "to be set up in the theatre during a full session of the *ecclesia.*" The mention of the silver image of Artemis reminds us of the leading part played in the riot by Demetrius, president of the guild of silversmiths, which boasted Artemis as its patron goddess. The great open-air theatre of Ephesus, when excavated, proved to have room for about 25,000 people.

In Acts 14:11 we are told that, when Paul and Barnabas visited Lystra in Asia Minor during their first missionary journey, and healed a lame man, the local inhabitants shouted in their Lycaonian vernacular: "The gods have come down to us in the likeness of men!" They identified the apostles with two deities, calling Barnabas Zeus (KJV and ASV "Jupiter") and Paul Hermes (KJV and ASV "Mercurius" or "Mercury"), "because he was the chief speaker." These two gods had a traditional association with that part

326   REVELATION AND THE BIBLE

of Asia Minor. The Roman poet Ovid, for example, relates how they once came to that district incognito, and found no hospitality except in the hut of an aged and impoverished couple, Philemon and Baucis. More precise evidence came to light in 1910, however, when W. M. Calder found near Lystra an inscription recording the dedication to Zeus of a statue of Hermes, along with a sundial, by men with Lycaonian names. Sixteen years later Calder and W. H. Buckler found in the same vicinity a stone altar dedicated to the "Hearer of Prayer" (presumably Zeus) and Hermes.

The city of Derbe is closely associated with Lystra in the narrative of Acts, but its site was unknown until 1956. In that year Michael Ballance discovered a dedicatory inscription set up by the council and people of Derbe in A.D. 157. The inscription was found at the mound of Kerti Hüyük (some thirteen miles N.N.E. of Laranda) in circumstances which make it practically certain that Kerti Hüyük is the ancient Derbe. Previous tentative identifications had been made several miles to the west of that, on the supposition that Acts 14:20 implies that Paul reached Derbe from Lystra in one day. It is now clear that the end of this verse should be translated: "on the next day he set out with Barnabas for Derbe." Mr. Ballance gives an account of his discovery in *Anatolian Studies* 7 (1957, pp. 147 ff.).

On Paul's last visit to Jerusalem, a riot broke out because it was rumored that he had taken a Gentile into the temple with him (Acts 21:28). Gentiles were forbidden on pain of death to penetrate beyond the outer court of the Jerusalem temple; notices in Greek and Latin were posted at intervals on the barrier surrounding the inner courts which warned Gentiles of the penalty for such sacrilegious trespass. Two of these inscriptions have been found, both in Greek—one in 1871 by Charles Clermont-Ganneau, and another one, in a more fragmentary condition, in 1935. The inscriptions read: "No foreigner may enter within the barrier which surrounds the temple and enclosure. Anyone who is caught doing so will be personally responsible for his ensuing death."

The writings of Luke lend themselves to this sort of illustration more than other parts of the New Testament because Luke, more than any other New Testament writer, relates his narrative to the context of contemporary events. It is unnecessary to remind readers at this time of day how thoroughly Luke's accuracy in detail has been vindicated when tested by evidence of this kind. The early researches of the late Sir William Ramsay made valuable pioneer contributions to the establishment of Luke's credit as a serious historian, although in his later writings there was an unfortunate tendency for the popular apologist to swamp the scientific archaeologist. Much useful information is presented by Henry J. Cadbury in *The Book of Acts in History* (New York, 1955), a volume whose worth is all the greater because Dr. Cadbury disclaims any apologetic motive.

Even where Luke has been suspected of nodding, he has a habit of being vindicated in due course by some new item of evidence. For example, his reference in Luke 3:1 to "Lysanias the tetrarch of Abilene" at the time when John the Baptist began his ministry (A.D. 27) has been regarded as a mistake because the only ruler of that name in those parts known from ancient historians was King Lysanias whom Antony executed at Cleopatra's instigation in 36 B.C. But a Greek inscription from Abila (18 miles W.N.W. of Damascus), from which the territory of Abilene is named, records a dedication by one Nymphaeus, "freedman of Lysanias the tetrarch," between A.D. 14 and 29, around the very time indicated by Luke.

Much study has been devoted to the statement in Luke 2:2 about the imperial census which was first held "when Quirinius was governor of Syria." We know that Quirinius was governor of Syria from A.D. 6 onwards, but the census referred to in Luke 2:1 ff. must have been held before the death of Herod the Great in 4 B.C. It is widely admitted that such a census may have taken place in Herod's reign, may have formed part of an empire-wide enrollment, and may have involved registration at one's original home (cf. the papyrus mentioned on p. 323). It has been argued also that Quirinius was governor of Syria for the second time in A.D. 6, and that the census of Luke 2:1 ff. took place during an earlier governorship of his. It is, however, very difficult to fit such an earlier governorship into what we know of the history of the province of Syria in the last decade B.C., and the Latin inscription (on the *Lapis Tiburtinus*) which has usually been invoked as evidence that Quirinius was governor of Syria twice proves only that he twice governed a province as imperial legate; it does not prove that his earlier governorship was exercised in Syria, as his later governorship certainly was. It is more generally accepted nowadays that his earlier governorship was exercised in Galatia. In that case it may be best to follow those commentators who, following a hint in Tertullian, read "Saturninus" instead of "Quirinius" in Luke 2:2. Sentius Saturninus was governor of Syria in 8–6 B.C.

While inscriptional evidence illustrates the accuracy of Luke in details, more impressive—and in fact more important—is the sure confidence with which he can convey the right atmosphere and local color of one place after another with a minimum of descriptive words. Here is an author who can see the places and events which he portrays, and can enable his readers to see them too.

IV. OSSUARIES

In 1945 the late Eleazar L. Sukenik discovered two ossuaries—receptacles for bones in the vicinity of the Jerusalem suburb of Talpioth exhibiting graffiti which he claimed to be "the earliest records of Christianity." The burial chamber in which the ossuaries were found was in use during the years preceding A.D. 50. The two graffiti, scratched in charcoal in Greek letters, read *Iesous iou* and *Iesous aloth*. Sukenik suggested, with a considerable measure of plausibility, that both inscriptions referred to Jesus; he supported this argument by the presence of four crosses on the second ossuary, but their significance is much more problematical. But while Sukenik supposed that the inscriptions expressed a lament over the crucifixion of Jesus, it is more probable that the first is a prayer to Jesus for help, and the second a prayer to Jesus that the person whose bones are contained within may rise from the dead. (Sukenik was caused considerable embarrassment at times by those who misunderstood him to mean that he had found Jesus' own ossuary —which, of course, he never suggested.) It is possible, then, that here we have relics from the Christian community in Jerusalem during the first twenty years of its existence. (See B. Gustafsson, "The Oldest Graffiti in the History of the Church," *New Testament Studies* 3, 1956–7, pp. 65 ff.)

In 1923 an ossuary of the same period was found in the Yemenite quarter near Bezalel in Jerusalem, bearing the name Sapphira in Hebrew and Greek letters. Joseph Klausner proposes to identify this Sapphira with the wife of Ananias in Acts 5:1 (*From Jesus to Paul*, London, 1944, pp. 289 f.), but we cannot be sure of the identification.

V. COINS

The coin record of New Testament times is a fascinating study, not only for general illustrative interest, but also because Roman coinage supplies an outline of the successive phases of imperial policy towards the Jews for the two centuries between 63 B.C. and A.D. 135, while the legends on the coins struck by the emperors to mark special occasions express those hopes of abiding peace which the emperors might promise but which Christians found to be realized in Christ (cf. Ethelbert Stauffer, *Christ and the Caesars*, London, 1955, *passim*).

Occasionally the coin record, or its absence, throws light on a point of New Testament history. For example, the reference in II Corinthians 11:32 to the ethnarch of King Aretas who guarded the gate of Damascus to seize Paul has been correlated with the fact that, while coins of Damascus have been found with the insignia of the Emperors Tiberius and Nero, none have been found thus far with the insignia of Gaius and Claudius, who between them ruled from A.D. 37 to 54. Should we infer from this that during Paul's residence at Damascus that city was not within the imperial frontier but directly governed by the Nabataean king? We cannot be certain; the argument from silence is always liable to be reversed.

Again, a crucial question in the chronology of Paul's career is the date of Felix's replacement by Festus as procurator of Judaea (Acts 24:27). The fact that a new Judaean coinage begins in Nero's fifth year, before October of the year 59, may point to the beginning of the new procuratorship; A.D. 59 is a date probable on other grounds for the arrival of Festus.

VI. THE QUMRAN TEXTS AND THE NEW TESTAMENT

The "Dead Sea Scrolls" found at Qumran have introduced us to the literature of a Jewish community which flourished between 100 B.C. and A.D. 68 and resembled the primitive Church in these respects: it regarded itself as the true remnant of Israel, supported this claim by a distinctive exegesis of the Old Testament writings, and interpreted its divine vocation in strongly eschatological terms. A comparative study of two contemporary movements of this character is bound to throw fresh light on both, quite apart from the possibility of establishing direct contact between them. Thus far the most promising attempts to establish direct contact have centered around the person and ministry of John the Baptist, although nothing in the way of real proof has yet been forthcoming. Alongside the resemblances, we must take account of the differences between the two communities, the chief of these being that, whereas the Qumran sect expected the Messiah (or Messiahs) to come, the primitive Church maintained that he had come—in the person of Jesus of Nazareth.

These documents have at least provided us with a new background for New Testament study, and certain phases of New Testament study have already taken on a new appearance against this background. The Johannine literature and the Epistle to the Hebrews in particular may be illuminated in important respects by this discovery. It is impossible to enter into details within the scope of this chapter, but reference may be made to the symposium *The Scrolls and the New Testament,* edited by Krister Stendahl (New York, 1957), although at this stage it can be looked upon as no more than an interim report.

VII. SACRED SITES

The identification of "sacred sites" is an important and fascinating branch of New Testament archaeology. But, while we can usually be sure of the general location of the places where Christ and the apostles lived and worked, it is rarely possible to fix the scenes of some of the great New Testament events within a matter of square yards. Tradition goes quite far back, but seldom far enough. The destruction of Jerusalem in A.D. 70, and the foundation of a new pagan city on the site in A.D. 135, make it particularly difficult to identify the places in Jerusalem mentioned in the Gospels and Acts. The temple area, of course, is certain. The place called Gabbatha, the Pavement (Greek *lithostrōton*), in John 19:13 has been identified with the court of the fortress of Antonia, a Roman pavement of nearly 3,000 square yards. The pool of Bethesda (John 5:2) can be identified with a fair measure of certainty in the northeast quarter of the old city (the area called Bezetha, or "New Town," in the first century A.D.), where traces of it were discovered in the course of excavations near the Church of St. Anne in 1888.

The fourth Evangelist knew Jerusalem as it stood before A.D. 70. The pool of Siloam (John 9:11) still stands south of the temple area as it did when Jesus sent the blind man to wash there.

The most important of Jerusalem's sacred sites, the place where Christ was crucified and buried (John 19:41), cannot be located with absolute certainty. The traditional site, covered by the Church of the Holy Sepulchre, was pointed out to Constantine in 327; but there is some doubt whether it actually lay outside the "second wall" of Jerusalem, as Golgotha must have done. A good popular examination of the problem is provided by André Parrot in *Golgotha and the Church of the Holy Sepulchre* (London, 1957). But, interesting as the problem must be to every Christian, it is not of the first importance; wherever our Lord's sepulchre is to be located, "he is not here, for he has risen."

Among other Palestinian sites mentioned in the Gospel record none is more certain than Jacob's well, near Balatah (the ancient Shechem). The third-century synagogue at Capernaum is visible; it was possibly built on the same site as the synagogue where Jesus did the mighty works recorded in Mark 1:21 ff.

Rome, unlike Jerusalem, has preserved its Christian tradition unbroken from the first century. Its early Christian cemeteries, however, belong to a later period than the New Testament narrative. Towards the end of the second century the presbyter Gaius claimed that he could point out at Rome the "trophies" (i.e. burial-places) of the apostles Peter and Paul on the Vatican hill and the Ostian road respectively. Within recent years the monument which he described as the "trophy" of Peter has almost certainly been found in the course of excavations beneath St. Peter's; it appears to go back to the time of Marcus Aurelius (161–180). A full account is given by Jocelyn Toynbee and J. Ward Perkins in *The Shrine of St. Peter and the Vatican Excavations* (London, 1956). It is only to be expected that the places where the apostles were executed and buried should be remembered by the Roman Christians a century later.

Another early visitor to Rome was Simon Magus (cf. Acts 8:9 ff.) ; he is said to have founded a heretical sect there and opposed the apostles. Justin Martyr, who lived in Rome in the middle of the second century, tells us that this sect, the Simonians, paid divine honors to Simon and had erected a statue to his memory with the inscription *Simoni deo sancto* ("To Simon the holy god"). Possibly Simon did receive divine honors, but the story of the inscription is evidently a mistake, based on a misreading of an old Roman dedication *Semoni Sanco deo fidio* ("To Semo Sancus the god of oaths"). The Simonians may have regarded this inscription as providentially applicable to Simon, and used it in their worship.

VIII. THE NATURE OF ARCHAEOLOGICAL CONFIRMATION

Generally speaking, "confirmation" is not the best word to use of the bearing of archaeology on the New Testament. In fact, in both Testaments it is better to regard archaeology as illustrative than as confirmatory. In places (say) where Luke has been suspected of inaccuracy, and his accuracy has been vindicated by some inscriptional evidence, it may be legitimate to say that archaeology has confirmed the New Testament record. But for the most part the service which archaeology has rendered to New Testament studies is the filling in of the contemporary background, against which we can read the record with enhanced comprehension and appreciation. And this background is a first-century background. The New Testament narrative just will not fit into a second century background.

But when we talk of background, or even when we think of the exact confirmation of historical details, we have not touched the heart of the New Testament message. To the New Testament writers, as to Christians of today, the heart of the message is the Son of God, incarnate in the Man Christ Jesus, the Saviour of the world. Archaeology may illuminate the historical context in which he was manifested in flesh, but how could it confirm the claim that life and salvation are available as God's free gift to those who believe in him? It may throw greater light than we possess thus far on the place where he was crucified and buried; it can add to our knowledge of the significance which his death and burial, together with his resurrection, had for his followers in the early Christian centuries; but how can it confirm the validity of that significance? In our gratitude for the aid which archaeology affords to Biblical studies, let us bear in mind its limitations, and not try to make it prove more than it can. Christianity is a historical revelation; archaeology can illuminate the history, but it is not by means of archaeology that the revelation itself is apprehended as truth.

REVERSALS OF
OLD TESTAMENT
CRITICISM

Nic. H. Ridderbos

Nicholas H. Ridderbos is Professor of Old Testament in the Free University of Amsterdam, The Netherlands, where he once pursued theological studies and received the D.D. degree in 1939. He was appointed to the chair of Old Testament in 1950. He is author of several books, including De 'werker der ongerechtigheid' in de individuele Psalmen *(The 'worker of unrighteousness' in the personal Psalms),* Israels profetie en 'profetie' buiten Israel *(Prophecy in Israel and 'prophecy' outside Israel),* and Is there a Conflict Between Genesis I and Natural Science?

21. *Nic. H. Ridderbos*

REVERSALS OF
OLD TESTAMENT
CRITICISM

FOR MANY centuries Bible criticism played no important role, at least not among those who wished to be known as Christians. But gradually this situation began to change. In the course of the nineteenth century, Bible criticism came to exert more and more influence. About the turn of the century, we might say, criticism of the Old Testament reached a high point.

I. CRITICISM AT THE TURN OF THE CENTURY

About that time the Wellhausian school had attained great influence. It is true, of course, that orthodox scholars opposed the conclusions of that school on fundamental grounds, and even among those who accepted Bible criticism in principle some scholars held themselves more or less aloof from Wellhausen's theories. But a conspicuously large measure of agreement prevailed nonetheless among influential Old Testament scholars of that period.

According to Wellhausianism, Israel's worship of God, like that of every other religion, had a very primitive beginning. Israel's ancestors were fetish worshippers and polydemonistic. Under Moses' leadership the tribes were united into one people accepting Yahweh (Jehovah) as their common God. Scholars differed over whether this Mosaic religion required the exclusive worship of Yahweh, and whether its moral character was higher than that of the religions of surrounding peoples, but general agreement prevailed that the religion that emerged in Mosaic times was not really monotheistic.

After Israel's entrance into Canaan the worship of Yahweh was influenced measurably by the prevailing Baal worship of the country. Assertedly, this had not only disadvantages, but many advantages as well. "The Yahweh of the nomads was a power hostile toward culture, a god of thunder, of war, of the holy ban, in the first place a destroyer and, for the rest, a god of the monotonous, empty steppes. Such a religion could never have become that of a cultured people, let alone of all mankind. Baal worship brought this religion what it lacked; now for the first time Yahweh attained to the beneficent Godhead who, in Hosea's words, also supplies corn, oil and wine (Hosea 2:8). So it has also been a providential circumstance that Israel first for a long time had to worship the Baals" (cf. J. Ridderbos, *Israel en de Baäls; afval of ontwikkeling*, second ed., 1928, pp. 10 ff.).

A later phase in Israel's religion is assertedly reached in the appearance of the great prophets. With increasing clarity they preached the doctrines of ethical monotheism. As follows from what has been said, that was "something new"; hence there is more reason to designate them as revolutionaries than as reformers.

Slowly thereafter the Law acquired greater significance until, after the Exile, the Law completely ruled the religious life of the Jews. Their worship (cultus) was regulated in detail. Strong emphasis was laid on the necessity of observing the Law's dictates even to the smallest minutiae.

This representation of the evolution of Israel's religion, it is apparent, went hand in hand with a particular view of the writings of the Old Testament.

The Pentateuch had long been regarded as a unity, and, for the most part, was ascribed to Moses. But after the middle of the eighteenth century, scholars in increasing measure began to dispute this view. As the result of the work of the Graf-Kuenen-Wellhausen school an entirely different conception came to great influence.

The Pentateuch was now regarded as assembled from four different documents. The earliest was the Yahwistic document (J), characterized by its use of the name Yahweh for God; this document was regarded as dating back to the early monarchical period, about the middle of the ninth century B.C. The second document was the Elohistic document (E), characteristic of which were the references to God as Elohim; the date of this document was placed at about the middle of the eighth century B.C. Deuteronomy (D) was the book of the law, assertedly discovered during the time of King Josiah, 622 B.C. (cf. II Kings 22:8). The last document was the Priestly code (P), dating to the period of the Exile and directly afterward.

Of central significance was the determination of the date of D (Deuteronomy). What was new in this theory was not the identification of the book of the law of Josiah with Deuteronomy, but the assertion that D had *originated* in Josiah's time. The reasoning was as follows: D calls for the centralization of worship (cultus) in one place; but the older books of the Old Testament, the legal portions as well as the historical portions, imply that before Josiah's time the multiplicity of holy places was legitimate; therefore D must have originated at the time of Josiah.

P (the Priestly code) is repeatedly identified with the book of the law that Ezra had with him when he came from Babylon to Canaan about the middle of the fifth century B.C. (cf. Ezra 7:14). During the Exile the priests had no occasion to exercise the worship rites and therefore applied themselves to theory. The largest part of P is to be found in the second portion of Exodus (the description of the tabernacle), in Leviticus and in Numbers.

Not only the Pentateuch but also the other books of the Old Testament were now dated according to a new pattern. Roughly stated, the traditional sequence was: Law (the five books of Moses, the Pentateuch)—the Psalms—the Prophets. In place of this, the following chronological order was substituted: Prophets—Law—the Psalms.

As is apparent from what has been said, this school had an evolutionistic view of the development of Israel's religion. There is again and again a development from the lower to the higher, from the simple to the complex. Wellhausen was under the influence of Hegel via Vatke. It is worth noting that the well-known conception of Hegel—thesis-antithesis-synthesis—also appears repeatedly in Wellhausen's system. In this manner he speaks of the successive development of nomad religion, rural religion, and prophetic religion. And of conclusive significance for his system is the sequence of nature religion, prophetic religion, and priestly religion. There is a time wherein a plurality of altars is legitimate; a time in which an attempt is made to attain to the unity of sanctuary; and a time in which the unity of sanctuary is an accomplished fact; and so on.

II. METHOD OF APPROACH

In the above we have attempted to give some impressions of the pattern of views that prevailed about the turn of the century (1900 A.D.). Since that time there have been important changes in Old Testament scholarship. If we wish to delineate these reversals, we shall encounter no small difficulties. Our picture of Old Testament criticism as it obtained about 1900 is not entirely adequate, since certain severe simplifications have had to be employed. But it is even more difficult to give a picture of the present status of Old Testament criticism. To depict the status of knowledge or scholarship in any field a half century in the past is generally easier than to portray the contemporary scene, for we find ourselves in the middle of the prevailing currents. Only time will show which currents are deep and lasting and which are temporary. And an additional observation must be made. At the turn of the century much more unanimity of opinion prevailed among Old Testament scholars than is to be observed today. This very phenomenon is, in fact, one of the typical changes that have come about in Old Testament scholarship.

Therefore, we shall not directly pose the question: what is the current status of Old Testament criticism? But we shall consider two other questions, namely, what are the causes, and what is the significance, of the changes of view? In answering these we hope also to shed some light on the current position of Old Testament criticism.

III. CAUSES OF REVERSALS IN OLD TESTAMENT CRITICISM

How are the important reversals in Old Testament scholarship to be explained? There are many reasons. But two complexes of causes are of special importance.

The Changes in Spiritual Climate

In the first place, it must be pointed out that the dominant spiritual currents in our times are totally different than at the beginning of this century. Belief in direct-line evolution today grips people's minds less than it did 50 years ago. At the start of the century many persons could still make a plea for the pursuit of objective scholarship; at the present time a consciousness has impressed itself that objective scholarship is an illusion, a contradiction in terms. Nowadays many are convinced also that simply to analyze the Old Testament and to trace the development of Israel's religion is insufficient, and that the most important question is: What is the *message* of the Old Testament? This is likely connected with the fact that the realization of the need to get at this Biblical message is stronger with our generation than with a generation that still expected so much from human knowledge and human ability.

We need not speak further here about these changes in spiritual currents, since their consideration falls more appropriately into other chapters of this volume. But it goes almost without saying that these changes have influenced Old Testament scholarship. One conspicuous instance of this is the remarkable fact that the evolutionistic interpretation of the history of Israel's religion, as expressed by Wellhausen, has now to a large extent been abandoned.

At this point two restrictive remarks are in order: First, no one likely would wish to deny that Wellhausen erected his conception constructively, that he stood under the influence of Hegel, that he held evolutionistic views. Nevertheless, these lines do not depict Wellhausen in totality; with good reason a reminder has appeared recently not to underestimate the influence of Herder upon Wellhausen (cf. H. J. Kraus, *Geschichte der historisch-kritischen Erforschung des Alten Testaments,* 1956, p. 248). Wellhausen draws this line: natural religion—prophetic religion—priestly religion. He conceives this as a development in which the spirit more and more releases itself from nature. Notwithstanding, Wellhausen regards the third phase as a phase of rigidity, and he writes about natural religion with obvious sympathy.

Second, we must note that students of the Old Testament today continue to see apparent lines of development in the Old Testament. It is difficult to deny that, in a certain sense, we can and must speak of development in the Old Testament. From of old, orthodoxy has spoken of the history of revelation, of God revealing himself with increasing clearness.

New Data and New Methods

As a second set of causes of reversals in Old Testament positions, we must mention the uncovering of new data and the projection of new methods. The discovery of new data we owe to the excavations of the archaeologists. We shall not treat this aspect in detail because it is handled in other parts of this book. The result of these excavations will find occasion for passing mention, however, at several relevant points later in this chapter. There is no occasion to deal here with textual criticism, so I do not treat the scrolls found at Chirbet Qumran.

Something must be said in detail, however, about the new methods that have been brought into use. In his instructive book, *The Old Testament in Modern Research* (1956), Herbert F. Hahn deals with such themes as "The anthropological approach to the Old Testament," "The sociological approach to the Old Testament," and so forth. Here we shall consider especially the new methods for Old Testament study that can be grouped together under the term "form-criticism."

One of the fathers of form-criticism was Hermann Gunkel. This scholar accepted the source-analysis advanced by Wellhausianism, but attempted to penetrate to what lay behind the documents J, E, D, and P. He asked that special attention be given to the smaller units. By examining the form in which the transmitted material has come down to us, he attempted to establish the various types and genres of tradition. He asserted that each type and genre was closely associated with a specific situation in the life of the people.

Form-criticism found many followers. Today it still exercises a strong influence. As has been said, form-criticism can be combined with the analysis of documents advanced by the Wellhausian school. But with this the followers of form-criticism attach great importance to oral transmission. Through constant repetition the oral traditions had already acquired a certain form. From this the conclusion was drawn that although the definitive version of a document may have come late in history, the document might nonetheless contain very ancient material.

Many authors are of the opinion that for a great deal of the orally transmitted materials the cult was the primary situation in life. Originally the Psalms were sung as part of the rituals performed at the shrines. But this was not all. At the shrines priests recounted the sacred stories; according to some scholars, portions of the transmitted materials were presented in the form of a cultic drama. On the occasion of cultic ceremonies the priests presented the laws to the people; these laws grew in the course of the centuries and were again and again adapted to the modified circumstances. There is a school of thought also which regards some of the prophets as members of the cult personnel; their prophecies were assertedly preserved through associations of cult prophets, to which they had belonged; these associations transmitted the prophecies to the people, adapting them to the altered circumstances.

A specially strong emphasis on oral transmission exists in various Scandinavian scholars, among them I. Engnell. Despite strong criticism of the Wellhausian school, Engnell in large measure accepts that school's analysis of the Pentateuch. In a certain sense he speaks also of J, E, D, and P, but when he refers to these he means something different than Wellhausen. For Engnell, J, E, D, and P stand for circles of traditionists, by which the principal materials were transmitted orally. In Engnell's judgment, all the sources of the Pentateuch are old as well as recent, recent in the sense that they obtained their literary fixity, anyhow their definitive literary fixity, only after the Exile; old, in the sense that all the sources contain ancient material. According to Engnell, such a phenomenon as the centralization of worship (cultus) may not be used for dating the sources. Rather, we must assume that various circles of traditionists existed side by side, each circle with different spheres of interest. In the one circle, interest might exist in the centralization of the cultus, but not in others. Deuteronomy speaks of this centralization, while J and E do not; yet this does not necessarily indicate that J and E are more ancient than D.

IV. SIGNIFICANCE OF THESE REVERSALS

In this section we shall attempt especially to answer the question: Have orthodox scholars reason to rejoice over the recent reversals in Old Testament criticism? Here I make the statement that in my view it is not possible to answer this question with a simple yes or no. In considering this question I will discuss subjects of various natures. With all this we shall need to go into further detail regarding the question, how far are we entitled to speak of reversals in Old Testament criticism?

Investigation of the Psalms

We may begin with a few remarks concerning a more limited aspect of our subject, namely, the study of the Psalms, for in this manner we can more easily arrive at a proper impression of the changes in Old Testament scholarship.

Bernh. Duhm regarded it as likely that Psalm 137 is the *oldest* poem in the Psalter (*Die Psalmen,* second ed., 1922 [first edition, 1899!], pp. XX, 454); but according to Engnell, it is the *most recent* of the Psalms (*Studies in Divine Kingship in the Ancient Near East,* 1943, pp. 175 f.). One who reads this might infer that a large change assuredly has taken place in Old Testament criticism, and that orthodoxy has indeed ground to rejoice over this altered situation. For the orthodox scholar finds himself again and again in opposition to the late dating of a large portion of the Old Testament, because it conflicts with some aspect of the Old Testament account, in this instance with the Old Testament record that David is author of many of the Psalms, and also because the late dating of historical sections, as a rule, is combined with doubt regarding their historical trustworthiness.

To mention only the views of Duhm and Engnell, however, would give a very one-sided impression. There was never such a time when Duhm's conceptions were universally accepted. And there is missing even more of a general acceptance in our time of Engnell's views. A new plea is even made in our day for the post-exilic origin of many of the Psalms. This attempt comes not from the side of extremely critical scholars, but from some Roman Catholic authors such as A. Robert and A. Deissler ("The Anthological School").

Are we not justified then in speaking of reversals in the study of the Psalms? Indeed, we must certainly take account of reversals, provided we keep in view the complexity of the contemporary situation. About the turn of the century (1900) a strong movement called for the recent dating of the Psalms; many of the Psalms were dated in the Maccabean period. This was not only a question of dating, but influenced the very conception of the Psalms as well; and it went hand in hand with viewpoints held by scholars concerning the evolution of the religion of Israel. Since that time, new factors already mentioned have become operative, especially new data and methods. It has been discovered that the people surrounding Israel—Babel, Egypt, Ugarit—had a very old poetic literature that in greater or lesser measure displayed relationship with the Old Testament Psalms. Under the influence of the discoveries of recent excavations, and of other factors, the Psalms, too, have been placed in close connection with religious worship (cultus). In many of the Psalms several authors now see religious formulas which were used in Temple worship in Jerusalem before the time of the Exile. So now some critics are ready to accept the fact of Davidic and even of pre-Davidic Psalms in our Psalter (cf. J. J. Stamm, *Ein Vierteljahrhundert Psalmenforschung, Theologische Rundschau,* XXIII, 1955, pp. 1–68).

Speaking generally, therefore, one is justified in noting a current tendency to acknowledge for the Psalms a date earlier than scholars were inclined to concede at the beginning of this century. However, this more ancient dating in many instances is correlated with an exegesis that gives reasons for many serious objections. G. Widengren, who belongs with Engnell to the leaders of the Uppsala school, contends that several of the Psalms originally were part of a cultic drama, in which the king played the role of a dying and resurrecting Godhead!

In the present-day investigation of the Psalms, diverse tendencies are therefore to be noted. Among these tendencies, some can certainly bring us to better understanding of the Psalms. Especially will it be fruitful, in the writer's personal opinion, to lay emphasis upon the connection between the Psalms and the cultus, and also on the connection between the Psalms and the king.

Continuity and Reversals

1. After these remarks on a rather limited aspect of our subject, it is proper now to turn to more general observations. First, we would call attention to the fact that, despite the aforementioned reversals, certain viewpoints are still regarded by most Old Testament scholars as lasting results of the critical investigation of the nineteenth century. For instance: that Isaiah, chapters 40 and following, is not attributable to the prophet of that name who lived about 700 B.C.; that the prophecies of Daniel, at least in part, came out of the Maccabean period; that the story of the book of Jonah is not history, but a parable or allegory—these conclusions seem to be accepted by virtually every critical scholar. This is not to say that investigation of the above-named books has stood still since 1900, nor that universal agreement has now been reached on these subjects. Radically differing viewpoints are still adduced concerning these books. And sometimes these viewpoints contain gratifying elements. So a greater realization has arisen that, despite all the differences, important points of similarity exist between Isaiah 1–39 and 40–66; this is then explained by the theory that chapters 40 to 66 arose in prophetic circles that considered themselves in a peculiar pupil-relationship to Isaiah. (Cf. O. Eissfeldt, *Einleitung in das Alte Testament,* second ed., 1956, p. 419. For further literature on Isaiah, cf. E. J. Young, *Studies in Isaiah,* 1955, pp. 9–101.) But this does not alter the fact that critical scholars have cast aside the traditional viewpoints concerning these books.

Amidst all the reversals an undeniable continuity—and sometimes a remarkably far-reaching continuity—persists in critical scholarship. No one opposed Wellhausen more vehemently than did Engnell—A. Bentzen, when in a discussion with Engnell he quoted Wellhausen, wrote a mocking "Forgive me, that I quote this old condemned dragon" (*Messias, Moses redivivus, Menschensohn,* 1948, p. 24)—but nonetheless when it comes to the source-splitting of the Pentateuch that became fashionable during the nineteenth century and was carried through to certain set conclusions by Wellhausen, even Engnell goes along in considerable measure. We have already pointed out, however, that Engnell regards J, E, D, and P in a rather different way than did Wellhausen and his followers. But the majority of the present-day critical investigators stand closer to Wellhausen than to Engnell. As we saw above, Engnell insists that we cannot invoke the centralization of the cultus for dating the sources, but a great many contemporary authors do that nevertheless. That is not to say that in this respect nothing is altered. Around the turn of the century it was commonly said that the discovery of the book of the law under Josiah was "a pious fraud"; the book of the law had allegedly been prepared just for this occasion; the "discovery" of the law-book was thus merely a fiction. Today the critics no longer speak so easily about a "pious fraud"; it is now deemed more likely that the book of the law was written earlier, e.g., under Manasseh, and that it contained much of still older material (cf. H. H. Rowley, *The Growth of the Old Testament,* 1953, pp. 29 ff.). But the notion is still widely held that the laws of Deuteronomy were *proclaimed* for the first time under the reign of Josiah and that they acquired their authority at that time.

Perhaps it is useful to note in this connection that a certain measure of fluctuation is evident in the representation given of J, E, D, and P. The older Wellhausians regarded them largely as authors who wrote with a definite purpose in mind. Under the influence of form-criticism, the emphasis arose that the documents transmit older materials; hence J and E came to be viewed as the work of mere compilers who had gathered and arranged the multifarious legacy of oral tradition essentially in the form in which they found it. Today, certainly, emphasis falls upon the more ancient material that these supposedly later documents contain, but it is noteworthy that they are now regarded once more as authors, or groups of authors, whose works evidence a purposeful character. H. F. Hahn has written: "This recognition of the unifying religious motivation of Hebrew historiography was the most important development in Old Testament criticism of the last two decades" (*op. cit.,* p. 266).

2. There is occasion, therefore, to speak of continuity as well as reversals in Old Testament criticism. We may note this more fully in respect to the Priestly document (P). As we have seen, this document was viewed at the beginning of this century either as exilic or post-exilic; it was thus the most recent of the sources in the Pentateuch. But recent archaeological excavations have brought to light the remarkable similarity of the terminology of this document with that of the worship sacrifice that prevailed in Ugarit about 1400 B.C. From the side of the critics this is now admitted, although differences of feeling occur as to how far this similarity extends.

We must caution the reader again, however, not to overvalue the significance of the reversals in Old Testament criticism in the last half century. First of all, it is noteworthy that a large area of critical agreement still exists on the question of which segments should be ascribed to P. And likewise, if acknowledging that P contains ancient material, even very ancient material, the majority of critical scholars still accept a post-exilic date for the definitive literary fixity of P, and still contend that P is the youngest of the sources. It must be added that Kuenen and Wellhausen themselves held that P contained some older material.

Nonetheless a reversal of considerable significance has eventuated in this area. G. von Rad contends that critical investigation has now established the position that P in its present form is not to be understood historically with-

344   REVELATION AND THE BIBLE

out the preceding pre-exilic history of the cultus (G. von Rad, *Theologie des Alten Testaments*, I, 1957, p. 248). And Hahn writes: "Wellhausen had maintained that the priestly spirit of minute regulation that animated the system was an entirely post-exilic phenomenon without any roots in the Hebrew past. Now it appeared that this very spirit had been a dominant force throughout the evolution of the system" (*op. cit.*, p. 112).

Here again it should be emphasized that this shift does not bear simply on the question of dating. The change involves these results also, that scholars now do more justice to the value of the so-called "P-portions"; that they see more clearly the large place of the cultus in the entire period of Israel's history; that they have a larger regard for the unity of the Old Testament. We shall return later to the significance of this latter development.

Historical Trustworthiness of the Old Testament

The following question is next in order: Has the historical trustworthiness of the Old Testament, or more sharply formulated, has the historical exactness of the Old Testament through these reversals in contemporary criticism been vindicated? While this question is handled more comprehensively in another chapter, we cannot forego discussion of it at this juncture.

Here again discussion will profit from an example. Wellhausen expressed the well-known viewpoint: The accounts of the patriarchs are historically of importance to us only in so far as they reveal to us the times in which they were written. Nowadays, however, to find anyone who would take responsibility for such an expression would be difficult. Through the excavations at Mari, Nuzu, Ugarit, and elsewhere, it has become clear, for instance, that the social-economic circumstances that are described in the stories of the patriarchs are very old (we employ this general term because many difficulties still cling to chronology) ; and still other considerations could be mentioned in this connection. But this does not mean that the majority of present-day critics think the stories of the patriarchs therefore are in all respects historically trustworthy. Many critics still share the opinion that the patriarchs were not historical persons, but only personifications of tribes. And although Abraham, Isaac, Jacob and Joseph, for example, be accepted by some critical scholars as actual historical persons, these scholars are mostly of the opinion that, viewed historically, we can make only some general statements about them. The genealogical connection which these four patriarchs have toward one another, according to the Old Testament, is presumed to be unreal, because the tradition regarding this genealogical connection is seen as a result of the collection of originally independent folk tales. Many Old Testament stories regarding the patriarchs are viewed as legends which originally belonged to the Canaanite places of worship and only later were connected with the figures of the patriarchs (cf. M. Noth, *Geschichte Israels*, 1950, pp. 105 ff.).

An observation of more general import will not be amiss at this point.

Through excavations we now possess rather conclusive evidence that the ancestors of the Israelites emigrated to Canaan out of northwest Mesopotamia. But that this occurred on orders from God, and with a world-embracing promise from God, naturally disregards all historical arguments and all historical dispute. Nonetheless it is exactly this fact of divine direction that finally gives value to these narratives.

Let us put what we have said in a somewhat wider perspective, referring once again to form-criticism. G. von Rad says: "The path from the presentations of the source documents to the historical events has for us become longer, because the simple picture of the source documents, which for the originators of the literary division of the sources was the starting-point for their investigations, must now be viewed as the end-station in which a long history of the interpretation of Israel's early history has finally come to rest" (*op. cit.*, p. 14). Naturally, this position has its consequences. The Wellhausian school held fast in the main to the historical sequence of the events recounted in the Old Testament: the period of slavery in Egypt, Sinai, the journey through the wilderness, entrance into Canaan, and so on. But scholars like Noth, von Rad, and others, regard this as unjustified. As they see it, various masses of tradition became connected with one another only in a secondary stage. The traditions regarding the events at Sinai, for instance, are regarded as having originally no connection with the traditions regarding the exodus from Egypt and the entrance to Canaan. What happened at Sinai—there can certainly be little told about what happened there—was not experienced by the tribes that came out of Egypt. And it follows that for the scholars named above, the figure of Moses is much more nebulous, much less historically real, than he was for the old Wellhausians.

Writers like Noth and von Rad are not extreme critics whose views we can ignore; they are well qualified Old Testament scholars wielding great influence especially in Germany but also outside. On the other hand, their views do not reign unchallenged. When one reads the writings, for example, of W. F. Albright, an entirely different impression is gained concerning these matters. With what we may perhaps call "a winning American optimism," Albright proclaims insistently that the latest discoveries strikingly confirm the Israelite traditions. He certainly ascribes much more to the trustworthiness of the Old Testament materials than do Noth and von Rad. But this does not mean that Albright warns simply against the dangers of hypercriticism; he warns also against an over-reliance on tradition (cf. W. F. Albright, *From the Stone Age to Christianity*, second ed., 1946/48, p. 193). Albright himself describes his point of view as "rational conservatism" (*Recent Discoveries in Bible Lands*, 1955, p. 133). As a matter of fact, Albright accepts fundamentally the methods of Alt and his followers (writers such as Noth and von Rad), but he means only to say that they go much too far (cf. *From the Stone Age to Christianity*, p. 210). For the relationship of the views of Albright and Noth see Albright's review of Noth's *Geschichte Israels* in

Erasmus, IV, 1951, pp. 490–493. Albright writes there: "Though we are often very uncertain as to exactly how things happened, we may rest assured that the historical facts were generally closer to the Israelite tradition than our modern reconstructions" (p. 492). Nevertheless, the instances in which, according to Albright, the Old Testament is historically untrustworthy are not few.

The complicated questions that are posed for us by Israel's exodus from Egypt and entrance into Canaan are dealt with, for example, in the book *From Joseph to Joshua,* by H. H. Rowley, which appeared in 1950. This volume demonstrates that even a moderate critic such as Rowley regards considerable Old Testament data as untrustworthy. Reading this book will also confirm the impression of the difficulty of harmonizing all the data of the Old Testament and the results of recent excavations.

The Religio-Historical Approach

Archaeological findings have exercised influence on Old Testament scholarship and not in the last place in this way, that they have brought to light again the religions of ancient peoples who lived round about Israel. We must delve into this more closely.

1. When the religions of the surrounding peoples were once more brought to light, scholars were at first struck by remarkable similarities between these religions and that of Israel. For a time, therefore, the tendency prevailed to view everything of value in the Old Testament as having been borrowed from other peoples; in this connection the first thought was of Babel (cf. the "Panbabylonism" of such writers as Hugo Winckler, Friedrich Delitzsch, and others). These extreme viewpoints did not hold favor very long. But the danger of too much emphasis on Israel's dependence upon its neighbors in religious matters is certainly not obviated once and for all. One need only mention the "myth and ritual school" (S. H. Hooke, I. Engnell) which advances the view that a certain pattern of myths and rituals was widespread in all of the ancient Near East, and that this pattern was also to be seen in Israel. Proceeding from this line of thought, this school advanced to the reconstruction of all sorts of myths and rituals that are supposed to have been common in the life of Israel.

Many scholars, however, entertain sounder ideas. They emphasize that to obtain a good picture of the religion of Israel it is more important to observe in what respects this religion *differed* from other religions, than to be preoccupied with the *similarities* between the religion of Israel and other religions. Also it must be noted that whenever Israel borrowed a notion or a practice from other peoples it acquired a different content than it had originally, because it now functioned in an entirely different totality.

Precisely through the rediscovery of the neighboring religions it has now become more possible to focus attention upon what was *unique* in Israel's religion. This must be regarded as a distinct gain. Perhaps the warning here is not presumptuous, however, that evangelical scholarship should not make too much of an apologetic use of this possibility; that we should not try to prove that the Old Testament brings us the special revelation of the only true God by pointing out the differences between the religion of Israel and the religions of the neighboring nations. That the Old Testament brings us the special revelation of the only true God is something that lies in an entirely different area; it is not something to be proved but can only be seen with the eye of faith. We need mention only this: uniqueness is not alone applicable to the religion of Israel; the religion of Babel, of Egypt, in fact, the religion of every people, is in some respects also unique (cf. on this point my *Israels profetie en "profetie" buiten Israel,* 1955, p. 45 ff.).

2. Archaeological discoveries have prompted many scholars to reject the evolutionistic viewpoints that Wellhausianism had advanced regarding the origin and development of Israel's religion. Even before Israel was established as a nation, it now appears, the surrounding nations had forms of religion which can be characterized as highly developed. Naturally, however, this does not in itself prove that the ancestors of Israel already had a highly developed worship of God. But, to put it mildly, there is certainly no warrant here for the representation that the forerunners of Israel were polydemonistic, fetish worshippers, and so forth.

In these matters also we must be careful not to overestimate the significance of the reversals since the turn of the century. We must not lose sight of the fact that Wellhausian literary analysis of the sources and their dating still carries a great influence. Still widely accepted is the view that the Canaanization of the belief in Yahweh was a necessary stage that indicated a step forward. Many today remain of the opinion that the demand for the centralization of worship (cultus) received its authority at the time of Josiah. The most important turnabout in this respect probably lies in this, that the greater attention is now focused on the fact that the essential character of the belief in Yahweh remained the same throughout the centuries. Various authors have thus accepted the idea that the germs of "ethical monotheism" already were present in the Mosaic religion (cf. H. H. Rowley, *Mose und der Monotheismus, Zeitschrift für Alttestamentliche Wissenschaft,* L I X, 1957, pp. 1–21). Albright has gone the farthest in this direction, in that he is willing to designate Moses as a monotheist (*op. cit.,* pp. 196–207). For the rest, the presentation of Albright also has its drawback. Referring to Albright's expression, "The period between 1350 and 1250 B.C. was ideally suited to give birth to monotheism," H. H. Rowley remarks, rightly, "This is to present biblical monotheism not as something attained by divine revelation to Moses and his successors, but as something that belonged to the *Zeitgeist* of the age of Moses" (*Journal of Semitic Studies,* II, 1957, p. 428; in a review of W. F. Albright, *From the Stone Age to Christianity: Monotheism and the Historical Process,* second ed., with a new Introduction, 1957).

The "Theological" Approach to the Old Testament

Of the various changes or reversals in Old Testament scholarship, the most important of all is perhaps this, that at the present time much more attention is again being paid to what is generally designated as "the theology of the Old Testament." A half century ago many scholars regarded the study of the Old Testament as only a narrower department of the more general study of the religions; the purpose was to uncover the development of Israel's religion. Today many see that alongside this or in its place—and this is a very important difference!—the purpose of such study is to answer these questions: What is the message of the Old Testament? How are we to understand the relationship between the Old and New Testaments? What is the meaning of the Old Testament for modern man?

Earlier we intimated, as a possible cause of these changes in viewpoint, the strengthening of the consciousness that man has need of a message from God. One factor that has brought about these changes is certainly this, that the exposition of a "theology of the Old Testament" is now regarded as a more fruitful prospect because a greater fundamental unity has been discovered in the Old Testament. In other words, a greater realization now obtains that the distinguishing characteristics of Israel's religion have remained the same throughout the centuries. This is not the place to treat this increased attention to the "theological" approach to the Old Testament more fully, since we are here concerned, not with changes in Old Testament scholarship in general, but with the reversals in Old Testament criticism. But it is important to take cognizance of this new approach, with its growing awareness that, while Old Testament criticism has a definite value, it cannot, however, be allowed the last word in Old Testament study.

One thing is regrettable in this respect. Many quarters are inquiring into the message of the Old Testament. The answer to this question, admittedly, cannot be given by way of an "objective unprejudiced science." But when literary or historical questions are involved, scholars seem to think they can go to work with an objective, scientific method; in other words, in these respects it seems that the Old Testament must be handled as any other book. It is difficult to deny that here there lies an inconsistency. C. A. Keller recently has posed the demand that in order to come to a proper historical understanding of the events of Moses' time, we must take reckoning of the personal intervention of Yahweh, of which the sources bear witness, and that we must work out a scholarly historical method that takes account of this intervention (cf. C. A. Keller, "Von Stand und Aufgabe der Moseforschung," *Theologische Zeitschrift,* XIII, 1957, pp. 430–441; esp. 438–441). It is sincerely to be hoped that such a challenge will be accepted.

In this connection a reference in greater detail to the previously mentioned work of G. von Rad (*Theologie des Alten Testaments,* Vol. I) is relevant. Von Rad writes as follows: "The object with which theology occupies itself is not the spiritual-religious world of Israel and its psychological situation, also not its realm of faith . . . but only that what Israel itself directly has professed concerning Yahweh" (pp. 111 ff.). And he follows with the statement that the witnesses of the Old Testament "limit themselves to presenting the relationship of Yahweh to Israel and to the world really only in one way, namely, as a *continued divine working in history* (italics mine).

From this approach von Rad writes a "Theology of the Old Testament" that differs fundamentally from what usually appears under this title. This is a very significant attempt which we cannot now discuss further. But through this viewpoint von Rad necessarily directly confronts the question of the historicity of the Old Testament narratives. He speaks of this repeatedly (cf. pp. 116 f., 300 ff., 329 f.). The clearest answer he gives to this question is in his commentary on Genesis (*Das erste Buch Mose,* I, third ed. [A T D], 1953, pp. 22 ff.). There he denies that the narratives of Genesis are no more than wordings of religious truths of universal significance, that the representation of the godliness of the patriarchs constitutes their main purpose, and he argues that these narratives have the character of what happened only once-for-all in the history of salvation. But they are not historical in the strict sense; the experiences of the community in the course of centuries are condensed or synthesized in these narratives. The final conclusion that von Rad gives to the question is unsatisfactory, but that the question of historicity is raised anew can perhaps be taken as an encouraging sign.

V. CURRENT POSITION OF ORTHODOX SCHOLARSHIP

What, in view of all these reversals in Old Testament criticism, is the contemporary position of orthodox Old Testament scholarship? By "orthodox Christians" I mean in this connection those who desire to bow before the divine authority of the Bible and who realize that their views with regard to questions of literary-historical criticism must be dominated and characterized by their acceptance of the divine authority of the Bible. Is the position of orthodox Old Testament scholarship easier than it was a half century ago? This question cannot be met by a direct answer. In some respects its position has become more encouraging. The tone of the critical scholars is repeatedly less self-assured than it was at the turn of the century. Orthodox scholars too will again and again be able to gain an advantage from new data and new methods. Interchange is certainly possible, especially in the realm of Old Testament theology. An orthodox Christian can often learn a great deal from and through the books of critical scholars in the field of Old Testament theology, even though he cannot agree with the literary-historical criticism that underlies such books, and although this is often strongly felt.

Yet the orthodox Old Testament scholar still finds himself in as much of an isolated position as at the end of the nineteenth century. In all likelihood we must say that he finds himself more isolated than ever before. One thinks here about the position of the Roman Catholics; at the beginning of the century the critics were being officially opposed, but today many Roman Catholic authors are indulging in Biblical criticism and this meets with more or less official approval. (While it is impossible to give further details here regarding the position of the Roman Catholics, the reader is referred to an informative work, *Introduction à la Bible*, I, edited by A. Robert and A. Feuillet, 1957. So also we shall not survey the newly unfolding Jewish Old Testament scholarship. Orthodox Christian Old Testament students will do well to follow attentively the development of Jewish Old Testament studies; often the Jewish scholars surpass critical Christian scholars in their regard for the traditions contained in the Old Testament.)

Perhaps the situation can be stated in this manner: At the beginning of this century it was clearer than now that criticism of the Old Testament contained a danger for the faith of the Church of all ages, especially because of the critics' evolutionary starting-point. Due to the strong constructionist character that the critical position then carried, it was also easier—at least so it appears to us now!—to oppose it; today the methods of the critics are much more refined and they work with a far greater amount of factual material.

At any rate, orthodox Old Testament scholarship, as in the past, will have to go forward along its own path, without allowing its way to be prescribed by Old Testament criticism, neither by the recent reversals in this field. That many difficult questions face it need not be concealed. Two dangers especially are present. The first is that it may fall short in its regard for the authority of God's Word. But another danger is that orthodox Old Testament scholarship exists in too great a degree on the reaction against Old Testament criticism. Even though the critic often presents analysis of the books of the Bible in an unacceptable manner, this does not necessarily mean that every analysis thereof must be rejected. There is also the possibility that one is too hesitant in acknowledging the parallelisms that exist between the Old Testament and the religions of the peoples that surrounded Israel.

We may ask whether the new data and the new methods already discovered, and those still to come, will affect critical Old Testament scholarship in such a way as to carry it still farther from the critical positions of 1900. This possibility exists, but no one can predict whether this will make the position of the orthodox Old Testament student easier.

May God give us, in the present and in the days to come, men who will take up the study of the Old Testament both in believing subjection to God's Word and in keeping with the new challenges which each changing period of history imposes on this enterprise of scholarship.

REVERSALS OF
NEW TESTAMENT
CRITICISM

Merrill C. Tenney

Merrill C. Tenney is Professor of New Testament and Dean of the Graduate School in Wheaton College, Illinois. He holds the Th.D. degree from Gordon College, A.M. from Boston University and Ph.D. from Harvard. His published writings include Resurrection Realities, John: the Gospel of Belief, Galatians: the Charter of Christian Liberty, The Genius of the Gospels, The New Testament: History and Archaeology, Philippians: the Gospel at Work, *and* Interpreting Revelation.

22. *Merrill C. Tenney*

REVERSALS OF
NEW TESTAMENT
CRITICISM

For NEARLY two centuries the science of Biblical criticism has played an increasingly important part in the thinking of Protestant Christianity. Influenced by the uninhibited attacks of the Encyclopedists of the French Revolution and by the rationalists of the "Enlightenment," the scholars of the Church felt compelled to study the Scriptures more carefully in order to answer the questions that had been raised concerning their truthfulness and authenticity. The resulting examination of the written text evoked numerous theories, widely promulgated and vigorously argued, concerning its authorship, composition, and reliability. Tradition was thrown to the winds as legendary and consequently unreliable; the deductions of critical study were regarded as "assured results." Some of these results have proved to be of permanent value; others have been long since discarded in favor of other theories. Many scholars who digressed from traditional belief honestly admitted that their theories were only provisional, and that new evidence would doubtless bring new conclusions. Others changed their minds when the evidence confronting them did not support their conjectures. Some, however, have clung to a negative criticism as tenaciously as their forbears did to inherited tradition.

As a matter of fact, Biblical criticism is a paradox. If all of the books of the Bible contained a categorical statement like the title-page of a book, giving the name of the author, his connection with Christianity, the date at which he wrote, the place where he lived, and the circumstances under which his book was composed, historical criticism would be unnecessary. It is the absence of the full historical data that compels the scholar to search out all the minute points that bear on the case, and to formulate from them some coherent conclusion about the document that he is studying. His task is legitimate, and is forced on him by the paucity of the evidence.

Ironically enough, it is this selfsame paucity that makes his conclusions uncertain, and that has brought the science of Biblical criticism into disrepute. A shaky case in court can be defended more adequately by competent witnesses than by astute lawyers, although both may be necessary. Similarly, the scarcity of data concerning the authorship of a book like Hebrews may lead to a dozen different learned suppositions or arguments about it; but the real settlement of these arguments will never be reached until positive information is available.

Unfortunately, such decisive evidence on the details of historical introduction is not always easy to obtain. The writers of the Bible were much more concerned with making history than they were with writing history. Even when they did offer some information about themselves and their works, they assumed that their readers knew who they were and what their circumstances were, and so they omitted many details that seem necessary to the modern scholar.

Of course, one should remember that Scripture was not given by God to entertain scholars but to convey a message. Nor was the scholarly approach wholly lacking; for Luke, in his well-known preface in Luke 1:1–4, stated plainly both the process and the intent of his work. Paul states in several passages (Gal. 1:11–12, I Cor. 15:1–11, I Thess. 2:13) that his writings were not simply his own opinions, but that they were to be received as the Word of God. There is no dearth of evidence that the writers of the New Testament looked upon their own works as authoritative, but often the precise details of origin are missing. Consequently, in order to reconstruct the framework of these writings many theories have been proposed. The evaluation of some of these proposals in the field of New Testament research will be the main burden of this chapter.

I. THE SYNOPTIC PROBLEM

The place of honor in the long history of New Testament criticism should be assigned to the Synoptic Problem. How can the Gospels of Matthew, Mark, and Luke resemble each other so closely if they are totally independent of each other, and how can they be so distinctive if they are simply copies of each other, or of some common source? The literary phenomena of the Gospels have been minutely studied for a century and a half, and in that time certain conclusions have been reached which have been almost universally adopted.

Modern Synoptic criticism began with Lessing (1729–1781), a German philosopher and essayist, who held that there was an original Aramaic Gospel which Matthew condensed and which Mark and Luke enlarged. Herder (1744–1803), a pupil of Kant, suggested that Mark was the first of the trio, and that later on an Aramaic Gospel was written which appeared in Matthew and which was used by Luke. The theory of an oral tradition as the basis for the Synoptics was proposed by Gieseler (1792–1854), and in substance it was carried on in the nineteenth century by Westcott (1825–1901). Numerous other solutions have been proposed, but the one most universally held today is that Luke and Matthew derived their content largely from Mark, which they contain almost in its entirety, and from a collection of the sayings or teachings of Jesus which for want of a better name is called "Q," from the German *Quelle,* meaning "source."

So firmly entrenched has this latter theory become that Sanday, as long ago as 1911, began an essay on "The Conditions under Which the Gospels Were Written" by saying:

> We assume that the marked resemblances between the first three Gospels are due to the use of common documents, and that the fundamental documents are two in number: (1) a complete Gospel practically identical with our St. Mark, which was used by the evangelists whom we know as St. Matthew and St. Luke; and (2) a collection consisting mainly but not entirely of discourses, which may perhaps have been known to, but was probably not systematically used by St. Mark, but which supplied the groundwork of certain common matter in St. Matthew and St. Luke (*Studies in the Synoptic Problem,* p. 4).

Sanday's statement of the case represents quite fairly the chief assumption of the majority of critical scholars for the last 50 years. Even such conservative writers as A. T. Robertson in America and W. Graham Scroggie in Britain have espoused the Two-Document theory in one aspect or another. In recent times, however, some new developments of thought have shaken confidence in it considerably.

For one thing, the rise of the Formgeschichte school has brought back the old concept of oral tradition into the forum of discussion. In an attempt to get behind the two documents of the current hypothesis, the analysts of the text began to consider the units that composed it. These units consisted of sayings or stories or blocks of teaching that could have been circulated individually and later collected into the "sources" or documents mentioned above. A little reflection, however, brought further questions. Who would have circulated these stories? How would they have been used? For what purpose would they have been employed? If they were really widely current among Christian believers, and were used as illustrations or texts for Christian preaching, why was it necessary to predicate that the persons who collected and assembled them were other than the traditional Gospel writers? Undoubtedly there are scholars who hold to the Formgeschichte theory as concomitant with the Two-Document theory, but there is a perceptible trend away from it back to some form of the theory of oral tradition.

Not only does the Formgeschichte theory offer a positive alternative to a documentary theory, but there is also a trend toward the abandonment of the hypothetical Q. Its existence has always been shadowy. Although the verbal similarities existing between sections of Matthew and of Luke have been interpreted as reflections of a non-Marcan original which both Evangelists used, such a document has never been found. Of course, a very early collection of the sayings of Jesus and of some stories concerning him remains possible. One such fragment appeared among the papyri of Egypt, and has already been published by Grenfell and Hunt (1897) under the title, "The Logia of Jesus." Another, "A Fragment of an Unknown Gospel," was edited by Bell and Skeat (1935). Neither Q nor any approximation of it has yet been discovered, however, nor is there any record of such a source in patristic literature.

While it is true that the foregoing reasoning may have the disadvantage of being based on an argument from silence, it is also true on the positive side that some modern scholars are challenging the existence of Q. A. M. Farrer, in an essay entitled "On Dispensing with Q," published in 1955 (*Studies in the Gospels,* D. E. Nineham, Ed.), has propounded that the critical study of the Synoptic Gospels can simplify its process by dispensing with Q. It is, he avers, quite unnecessary to hypothecate it unless we assume that St. Luke never read St. Matthew. Both of these Gospels, he says, were composed in the same literary region and about the same time, between A.D. 75 and A.D. 90. Mark's Gospel was extant and known in the same place and at the same time. It would be quite possible for the Evangelists to have known each other directly, and to have interchanged information or manuscripts, had they chosen to do so.

Not only is Q non-existent as a separate document, but no attempt to recover it from the Gospels has been successful. No two reconstructions are alike. There is no unanimity among those who propose the theory as to what the contents of the original document might be, except that it consisted chiefly of discourses and teachings. Furthermore, if Q had been written containing only a collection of Jesus' sayings and a few scattered narratives, it would not have reflected at all the general trend in gospel teaching characteristic of its age. Farrer observes that when Luke referred to his sources of information he spoke of Gospels; and Q was not a Gospel.

In another work published in 1957, a posthumous volume by Wilfred C. Knox on *The Sources of the Synoptic Gospels: Matthew and Luke,* the author suggests that the material may not have come from a single source, but that there may have been a number of short tracts used for teaching which the writers of these Gospels combined in their works. Without making any commitment on the validity of Knox' theory, one may say that he has at least presented a plausible alternative to the Two-Document theory that supplants the hypothetical Q.

II. THE DATE OF ACTS

A second important subject of historical criticism has been the book of Acts. Its historicity was assailed by F. C. Baur of Tübingen, who, under the influence of Hegel and Schleiermacher, became a thorough-going rationalist. He contended that Acts was produced about the middle of the second century for the express purpose of glossing over a long standing dispute between the Pauline or universalizing party in the Church, which advocated Gentile liberty, and the Petrine or Judaizing party, which held to a strict observance of the Law. The book of Acts was thus not an actual history of what had taken place in the first century, but was historical romance written for propaganda purposes. Baur remarked that "[its] statements . . . can only be looked upon as an intentional deviation from historical truth in the interest of the special tendency which they possess."

The same general opinion was reiterated by Weiszäcker in 1902 in his *Apostolic Age,* and in more recent years has been held by Kirsopp Lake and John Knox, although neither of these men would necessarily follow the Tübingen school in all details. They agree, however, on the historical unreliability of Acts, and to a date of writing that places it somewhere between A.D. 90 and 150.

Counter to this dismissal of Acts and its writer as unreliable is the teaching of Sir William Ramsay (1851–1939). Trained in the German historical school of the mid-nineteenth century which followed the Tübingen theory, he entered upon his career as a classical scholar and archaeologist. He became interested in the antiquities of Asia Minor, and spent a number of years in traveling through the country, studying its people, its terrain, and the remains of classical civilization. To his surprise he discovered that the most valuable guide to Asia Minor of the first century was the book of Acts. After examining carefully the actual territory over which Paul and the writer of Acts presumably traveled, and after comparing the book with the results of his historical and geographical investigations, Ramsay said:

> The boundaries of the districts mentioned in Acts . . . are true to the period in which the action lies . . . they are based on information given by an eye-witness, a person who had been engaged in the action described. . . . The present writer takes the view that Luke's history is unsurpassed in respect of its trustworthiness (*The Bearing of Recent Discovery on the Trustworthiness of the New Testament,* pp. 79 f.).

An even more astounding reversal of opinion was that of Adolf Harnack (*Luke, the Physician,* 1907), who could not by any stretch of the imagination be described as a conservative in Biblical criticism. Writing in 1907, Harnack said:

> Ten years ago, in the preface to the first volume of the second part of my "History of Christian Literature" I stated that the criticism of the sources of primitive Christianity was gradually returning to the traditional standpoints. My friends [of the rationalistic school] have taken offence at this statement of mine, although I had in part established its truth. . . . Let me, therefore, now express my absolute conviction that many traditional positions are untenable and must give place to new and startling discoveries. . . . We can now assert that *during the years 30–70 A.D.*, and *on the soil of Palestine*—more particularly in *Jerusalem—this tradition as a whole took the essential form* which it presents in its later development. . . . This result of research is becoming clearer day by day, and is steadily replacing the earlier "critical" hypothesis [the Tübingen theory] which assumes that the fundamental development of Christian tradition extended over a period of some one hundred years, and that in its formation the whole Diaspora played a part as important as that of the Holy Land and its primitive churches (*Luke, the Physician,* 1907, pp. vi, vii).

After an intensive and highly detailed study of the Greek text of Luke and Acts he came to the conclusion that both were written by the same author; that the author was a companion of Paul; and that he must have been Luke the physician, whom Paul mentions in his epistles. He affirmed that Acts was written in A.D. 62 or earlier, and that it is an accurate historical statement of the events which it describes.

Recent archaeological and historical discoveries have tended to confirm these judgments. At no point has archaeological evidence contradicted Luke, though not all of his statements have yet been corroborated. His use of the proper titles for contemporary officials, his accuracy in describing cities, and in locating provincial boundaries which changed frequently during the first century, and his vivid description of ancient navigation in Acts 27 bespeak an essential historical truthfulness that is quite the opposite of the careless partisan writing of which he had been accused.

III. THE FOURTH GOSPEL

A similar change has begun to take place in the critical attitude toward the Fourth Gospel. The traditional view, founded largely on the testimony of the Fathers of the second century, Justin Martyr, Tatian, and Irenaeus, assumed that the Gospel was the product of John the son of Zebedee, who wrote it in his extreme old age at Ephesus. This view was generally held by the church with very few exceptions down to the last of the eighteenth century, when it was first challenged by Evanson, a clergyman of the Church of England, who questioned both the authorship and validity of the Gospel. In 1826 Bretschneider, a German writer, published the first systematic criticism of the book. He reached the conclusion that it was written by an unknown Greek using the name of John, who lived in Egypt in the middle of the second century, and that the Gospel was first introduced to Rome and to the world by Gnostics. Baur, of Tübingen fame, followed much the same method of approach and came to the same conclusion that the Gospel was a document belonging to the second century.

Along with the acceptance of a late date there followed inevitably the corollary that the Fourth Gospel was not of apostolic authorship and that it was not historical in content. It came to be regarded as a theological interpretation of the life of Jesus written from a mystical or philosophical standpoint, representing the effect upon Christianity of a fusion of Greek philosophical speculations and of Jewish Messianism. The problem of its relation to the Synoptic Gospels was particularly acute. Many of the differences in statement and in attitude seemed irreconcilable. F. C. Burkitt (*The Gospel History and Its Transmission,* 1906, p. 225), after a survey of the divergence between the accounts of the life of Jesus given by Mark and that given by John, said:

> This is something more than mere historical inaccuracy. It is a deliberate sacrifice of historical truth; and, as the Evangelist is a serious person in deadly earnest, we must conclude that he cared less for historical truth than for something else. To render justice to his work we must do more than demonstrate his untrustworthiness as a chronicler.

Burkitt adds also:

> It is quite inconceivable that the historical Jesus could have argued and quibbled with opponents, as He is represented to have done in the Fourth Gospel. The only possible explanation is that the work is not history, but something else cast in historical form (*ibid.,* p. 228).

Burkitt's position was supported in this country by Benjamin W. Bacon and others of his school. He said in *The Fourth Gospel in Research and Debate* (1910), "On this question we are driven unavoidably to the alternative: Either Synoptics or John" (p. 3). This verdict epitomizes the critical thinking on the Fourth Gospel for most of the first half of the current century.

Both the critical views of the late date and of the unhistorical content have been modified considerably in recent years. The most vigorous rebuttal of the second century date was provided by J. B. Lightfoot in his *Biblical Essays.* He gave a convincing demonstration that the extant external evidence made a late date impossible, and made the following prediction: "We may look forward to the time when it will be held discreditable to the reputation of any critic for sobriety and judgment to assign to this Gospel any later date than the end of the first or the beginning of the second century" (p. 11).

Lightfoot's prediction has been amply justified by more recent developments in discovery and criticism. In 1935 a small fragment of a papyrus codex of the Fourth Gospel, containing John 18:31–33, 37, 38, was published by the John Rylands Library. It had come into their possession with a mass of other papyri from Professor B. P. Grenfell in 1920, and was identified in the process of cataloguing. This tiny fragment, about 2½ by 3½ inches in size, was unquestionably a genuine part of a very early copy of the Gospel written in codex form. Obviously it was intended to be read frequently, rather than to repose in the orderly oblivion of some library. When examined by palaeographers for the style and age of its handwriting, it was found to have close affinity with documents of the second century. Its editor says:

> On the whole we may accept with some confidence the first half of the second century, A.D. 100–150, as the period in which P. Ryl. Gk. 457 was most probably written—a judgment which I should be much more loath to pronounce were it not supported by Sir Frederic Kenyon, Dr. W. Schubart, and Dr. H. I. Bell who have seen photographs of the text and whose experience and authority in these matters are unrivalled.

This fragment proves that the Fourth Gospel circulated in Egypt by the first half of the second century. To be circulated at this time it must have been composed previously, and must have been known in the Church for at least a few years. The date of the writing of the Gospel must therefore have been in the last decade of the first century—quite certainly not later than the time of Trajan.

Even apart from such objective evidence as the Rylands Fragment recent critical theories have been changing. A. T. Olmstead, late professor of Oriental History in the University of Chicago, asserted in his work on *Jesus in the Light of History* (1942) that the narratives of John were written in Aramaic before A.D. 40, and were the oldest and most authentic accounts of Jesus' life. He did not submit extensive proofs for his view, but at least he allowed that an early date was possible. Erwin R. Goodenough, in an article on "John, A Primitive Gospel" (*Journal of Biblical Literature*, LXIV [1945] II, 145–182), concluded that there is no reason why the Fourth Gospel could not have been composed as early as A.D. 40. He discarded an evolutionary view of Christianity as "a hypothetical creation," pointing out that if Paul's Christology can be assigned to the sixth decade of the Christian era, there is no inherent reason why John's should be later. As positive arguments for such an early date, he presented (1) the author's apparent ignorance of the Synoptic tradition, (2) the absence of reference to the Virgin Birth, (3) and unfamiliarity with the Eucharist as taught by the Synoptics.

William F. Albright has taken much the same viewpoint in his published works. In *The Archaeology of Palestine* (p. 141) he shows that the court where Jesus appeared before Pilate, called Gabbatha or the Pavement (John 19:13) was the court of the Tower of Antonia, the Roman military headquarters in Jerusalem. It was destroyed in the siege of A.D. 66–70, and the rebuilding of the city in the time of Hadrian left it buried under the rubble of the ruins. The clear allusion of that Gospel to this place means that the writer knew the condition of the city before A.D. 70, and that he was probably writing from first-hand experience.

Again, in an essay on "Discoveries in Palestine and the Gospel of John," published in *The Background of the New Testament and Its Eschatology* as recently as 1956, Albright contends that there was a complete decline of Aramaic literature in Palestine under the Seleucids. The Jewish civilization of Palestine was wiped out in the First Revolt. He says:

> . . . if there are correct data in the Gospels or Acts of the Apostles which can be validated archaeologically or typographically, they must have been carried from Palestine in oral form by Christians who left that land before or during the First Jewish Revolt (p. 156).

Albright's observation suggests two conclusions: first, that the Gospel of John was written by a person who lived in Palestine before A.D. 70 and who was acquainted with the data about Jesus as they were circulated in Aramaic; and second, that it was originally written in Greek for a constituency that existed during his later lifetime. It must, therefore, have been written not later than the beginning of the second century, and more probably in the first century.

The Dead Sea Scrolls have cast some light on the Johannine problem. They have shown that Aramaic manuscripts existed in the time of Christ, but if the proportion of Aramaic literature to Hebrew were the same outside of the Qumran community as within it, it must have been sparse. There are relatively few Aramaic writings that appear among the Scrolls. The actual publication of an Aramaic John is not impossible, but is rather improbable. On the other hand, the Scrolls have shown that the vocabulary of John is not alien to the thinking of the earliest Christian community of Palestine. F. F. Bruce has brought out the fact that such expressions as "sons of light," "the light of life," "walking in darkness," "doing the truth," "the works of God" appear in the literature of the Qumran settlement (*Second Thoughts on the Dead Sea Scrolls,* 1956). These phrases show that the Gospel may reflect the pietistic religious terminology of first century Palestine which was used in the Qumran settlement, rather than the mystical language of the Greek world of Alexandria or Ephesus. If so, another objection to the early date of John has been dissolved.

The trend of Johannine criticism today is toward an earlier dating and a Palestinian provenance. The authorship is still debated warmly, for first century dating does not necessitate that John the son of Zebedee wrote the Gospel. There is, however, less objection to ascribing the Fourth Gospel to the disciple of Jesus who leaned on his breast at the last supper than to the "great unknown" hypothecated by Biblical criticism a century ago.

IV. THE CRITICISM OF THE PASTORAL EPISTLES

The Pastoral Epistles of Paul form a united group which possess marked characteristics of their own. Their content bespeaks a settled Church, rapidly becoming institutionalized, with recognized leaders and with increasing internal problems, both ethical and doctrinal. They differ considerably in content from the Travel Epistles, which reflect small groups of Christians who had not yet adjusted to the life of the world around them, and are trying to gain their balance in a novel and confusing situation.

Historical criticism has not been slow to seize upon these differences and to challenge the Pauline authorship. Marcion, in the second century, rejected them from his canon, and did not list them with the epistles of Paul which he accepted as authoritative. His judgment was doubtless prompted more by feeling than by an historical reason, since the teaching of the Pastorals against asceticism would have run counter to the Gnostic philosophy which he held.

In 1807 Friedrich Schleiermacher rejected the Pauline authorship of I Timothy. F. C. Baur in his work on the Pastorals in 1835 contended that it was inconsistent to reject I Timothy and to accept the Pauline authorship of II Timothy and Titus. He excluded all three from the Pauline Canon. The general verdict of New Testament scholars, with a few exceptions, has been the same down to the present day, and in many works on introduction the non-Pauline character of these books is taken for granted.

The arguments for this position are fivefold. First, the Pastorals differ in language and style more radically from the books of the acknowledged Pauline Canon than any one of the latter does from the rest. P. N. Harrison (*The Problem of the Pastoral Epistles*, 1921) argues at length from an exhaustive study of the vocabulary of the Pastorals that it bears a much stronger resemblance to the literature of the second century than it does to the Pauline writings. Of the 848 words used in them which are not proper names, 306 are not found in any of the ten Pauline epistles. Harrison concedes that some passages in the Pastorals are strongly Pauline, and that they probably represent genuine brief notes included in the larger works assertedly written by a later author.

The second objection to the Pauline authorship is that the church polity of the Pastorals is more advanced than that of the pioneer conditions in which Paul labored. The Pauline Church was in its infancy; the Church of the Pastorals is reaching adulthood. Church government had acquired a fixed form, and the officers had well-defined functions rather than being simply itinerant preachers.

Again, the errors combated by these epistles seem to have been more closely related to the heresies of the second century than to those which Paul discussed in his earlier epistles. These doctrinal digressions were the result of a reaction against an accepted standard rather than individual misapprehensions of the initial preaching of the gospel.

In conjunction with the foregoing argument is the corollary that the doctrinal content of the Pastorals reflects a body of truth which has become codified in a creed. The atmosphere does not reflect the creative formation of a new theology in Christ, as does Galatians, but rather the repetition of what has become settled belief.

Finally, the argument has been advanced that the Pastorals cannot be fitted into any known pattern of Paul's life. Their geographical and personal references do not accord with itineraries and contacts mentioned in Acts, and cannot, therefore, belong legitimately to his biography.

On the basis of the preceding arguments general critical opinion has rejected the genuineness of the Pastorals. There have been some notable exceptions, however. Theodor Zahn (*Introduction to the New Testament*) pointed out that the personal references to Paul's companions could hardly be free creations, especially since some of the allusions are uncomplimentary. Legend almost invariably lauds its subjects, and seeks to make them appear saintly. Zahn also questioned why the Pastorals, if they were written in the second quarter of the second century, did not reflect the autocratic rule of the bishops as Ignatius describes it. He asserts that there is no trace of such an attitude in these epistles.

From the historical standpoint Sir William Ramsay remarked:

> Incidentally we may here note that the tone of the Pastoral Epistles in this respect is consistent only with an early date. It is difficult for the historian of the Empire to admit that they were composed after that development of the Imperial policy towards the Christians which occurred . . . under the Flavian Emperors (*The Church in the Roman Empire,* 1903, p. 248).

While it is true that the Pastorals describe an ecclesiastical organization different from that of Thessalonians, it is by no means impossible that the change could have taken place within the span of fifteen years, which would be half a generation of growth. The offices mentioned were not to be understood wholly by modern definition. A "bishop" was merely an overseer; not the church official that he is now. Sometimes there was more than one bishop in a given church.

Pherigo, in an article published in 1951, "Paul's Life after the Close of Acts," in the *Journal of Biblical Literature,* argued that Paul must have been released after the two-year imprisonment chronicled in Acts, and that he died later in Rome under Nero, as tradition states. He avers that a forger would not have assumed release and imprisonment had there not been good reason for believing in them. Genuine or spurious, the Pastorals thus speak of a chapter in Paul's life that the New Testament does not record elsewhere. There is, therefore, room for the writing of the Pastorals by Paul between A.D. 62 and 65 in the general pattern of his career.

F. J. Badcock in *The Pauline Epistles* (1937) attacked the problem of the vocabulary which had been posed by P. N. Harrison. "I shall try to prove," he said, "(1) that there are no words employed which might not well have been in use in St. Paul's time . . .; and (2) more generally, that Dr. Harrison has set himself an impossible task" (pp. 115 ff.).

Accepting the list of words and phrases given in the appendix to Thayer's *Greek-English Lexicon of the New Testament* as peculiar to the Pastoral Epistles, he started with a count of 197. From these he deducted ten that were alternate or erroneous readings in the text, or as occurring elsewhere in the New Testament. The words used in common with the Septuagint, which would be available to any Christian writer in the apostolic period, may also be subtracted, amounting to 73. Thirty more are used in the classical authors; Aristotle and Strabo supply nine more; and ten are used by non-Christian authors contemporary with the apostolic age. Of the remaining vocabulary, a large part can be accounted for on the basis of analogy with known terms or by formulation from the needs of church life. He comes to the conclusion that there are no terms in the Pastorals that are demonstrably later than the first century. Harrison's thesis that the Pastorals must be late because of their language is not supported by the facts. Badcock concludes that the Pastorals "belong to the time anterior to the First Epistle of Clement, and are at least substantially Pauline."

Although Badcock takes the view that "The hand is the hand of an editor or redactor, but the voice is the voice of Paul, and no other" (p. 129), it is obvious that he has been compelled by the force of the content of the epistles to concede that they are essentially Pauline. He suggests that they are notes left by Paul which one of his assistants put into epistolary form after his death in Rome.

While Badcock does not completely reverse the critical position on the Pastorals, the concession that he makes shows that he is not fully convinced of its truth. A more positive attitude is assumed by E. K. Simpson in his commentary on *The Pastoral Epistles* (1954). He shows that many words and features appear that are distinctly Pauline, and that the dissimilarities between these documents and the uncontested Pauline writings are really no greater than the disparities between Tennyson's *In Memoriam* and his *Northern Farmer*. Simpson champions boldly the Pauline authorship.

Even more recently William Hendriksen in his *New Testament Commentary: The Pastoral Epistles* contends that in this controversy the burden of proof is wholly on the negative side. His discussion is extensive, and he holds that many phenomena which have been interpreted as fatal to the Pauline origin of the Pastorals may really be in its favor.

For instance, he points out that out of the 306 new words found in the Pastorals that do not occur in the ten undisputed epistles of Paul, only nine are found in *all* three letters. "If dissimilarity in new vocabulary proves different authorship, something can be said for the proposition that a different author would have to be posited for each of the Pastorals" (p. 8).

Thus the argument that a large proportion of new words must necessarily call for a different author proves too much, for the Pastorals are generally acknowledged to have been written by the same man.

Hendriksen notes that the Pastorals have many positive Pauline features. The author's attitude of concern for his addressees is Pauline. His use of figures of speech, of lists of virtues or vices, his occasional play upon words, his employment of long compounds, and the frequent allusion to individuals by name are all Pauline characteristics (pp. 13–17).

While he concedes that the Pastorals differ in many ways from the other Pauline epistles, he shows that there are no insuperable objections to the Pauline authorship, and he makes a good case for their acceptance in the Pauline Canon.

V. THE NEW TREND IN TEXTUAL CRITICISM

Ever since the printing of Erasmus' Greek Testament in the beginnings of the Reformation there has been a steady attempt to improve and to clarify the text of the New Testament. From the *Textus Receptus* of Stephanus, hastily patched together from the first convenient manuscripts that scholars could find to provide a basic text, to the carefully formulated text of Westcott and Hort, there has grown a Greek Testament which presumably is a close approximation of the original. Westcott and Hort edited the manuscript evidence by a set of principles which gave an objective basis for choice of variant readings, and which sifted them as accurately for error as any procedure could.

Through their genealogical method which classified the texts of the manuscripts, versions, and fathers into groups which could be evaluated as units, Westcott and Hort succeeded in eliminating some of the grosser mistakes and in making a closer approach to the original. They demonstrated that the bulk of the manuscripts followed the "Syrian" text of the fourth century, a revision made in Antioch which was antedated by the "Western," "Neutral," and "Alexandrian" families of text. Since the "Alexandrian" consisted chiefly of numerous small refinements of the "Neutral," it could not be given much separate weight. Consequently, the choice lay between the "Western" text, a somewhat cruder but more detailed text existing chiefly in the Old Latin, Old Syriac, and in the Latin fathers. The "Neutral" text was supposed to have been the oldest and purest of all. The editors so named it because they thought it to be free of perversions and corruptions. They based it chiefly on Codices Sinaiticus and Vaticanus, which were at that time the oldest complete vellum manuscripts known.

The text which they produced is still probably the best critical text available, but it cannot be considered as a final criterion of what the original manuscripts were. In the first place, the whole genealogical method has been called in question. One might almost as well attempt to reconstruct the features of his great-grandfather by adding together the features of his descendants as to reproduce exactly the original text from the faulty copies which have descended from it. It is true that when a series of manuscripts are copied from one original their united worth is no more than that of the archetype from which they were drawn. The subjective factors of judgment are still great, however; and the possibility of individual variants apart from family relations is so great that Ernest C. Colwell has argued for individual critical judgment upon each variant rather than judging by use of the family to which the variant belongs ("Biblical Criticism: Lower and Higher" in *Journal of Biblical Literature,* LXVII, 1948, pp. 1–5).

A second problem was posed by the discovery of the "Caesarean" family. The term is probably a misnomer, for the examples of this type of text have been found in Egypt as well as in Caesarea. It is supposed to have been the text used in Caesarea by Origen, perhaps according with the type of Testament that he found there. It has been reconstituted for a part of Mark by Lake and Blake, and on the Westcott and Hort theory makes a new family in the manuscript tradition. Its variants show that there was another class of text available in the third century which had not previously been taken into consideration when the supremacy of the "Neutral" text was accepted.

The discovery of the Chester Beatty papyri (p 45, 46, 47) of the Gospels, Acts, and Revelation, and of the Bodmer papyrus of John (p 66) has raised new questions about the finality of the Westcott and Hort text. Since the manuscripts of the "Neutral" text belong to the fourth century at the earliest, the newly discovered papyri, which belong to the third century, antedate it by a hundred years. It is possible that where the WH text differs from the papyri, it might be wrong. The papyri do not accord exactly with any of the "families," and since they are older, they may approximate more nearly the originals than Westcott and Hort.

A third factor in revising the standing of the WH text is the new estimate of the "Western" readings. Westcott and Hort admitted that this text was equally as ancient as the "Neutral," but thought it to be more loosely copied, and hence more corrupt. As a matter of fact, it was used more widely than the "Neutral," and despite its oddities, in some passages was conceded even by Westcott and Hort to be more trustworthy. The most recent venture in the field of textual criticism, the creation of a larger critical text of the New Testament based on the *Textus Receptus* and including collations of all the major manuscripts, will doubtless show that the WH text was not infallible, although it was undeniably the best up to its time.

The foregoing changes in the conclusions of New Testament criticism are sufficient to show that while much has been learned from the application of its principles, it is still in a fluid state. As new facts become available, the "assured results" of yesterday must often be altered or abandoned. In the attempt to fill the gaps of knowledge by hypotheses some errors are inevitable, and there is little room for insisting dogmatically that the theories are correct when their foundations are so often unsure.

To assert with finality that Q existed in a certain form, or that Acts is unhistorical, or that John is a product of the late second century simply because the conclusion logically follows from a theory is unsafe indeed. It is just as naive to accept the latest theory because it is new as to cling to tradition because it is old. Insufficient information may make the premises of the theory faulty, and consequently unreliable.

From the earliest period of the Church's history the Scriptures have been exposed to critical scrutiny. Their friends have sought to protect them from attack, and their enemies have sought to discredit them by the use of the same tool. Biblical criticism has stimulated a fuller investigation of the background of the Scriptures, and to an evangelical thinker it provides a powerful tool for apologetic preaching. The instrument is a useful servant, but it may become a bad master; for the "critical mind" may become so critical that it loses the truth it is trying to illumine.

Two things become increasingly apparent as the critical process of developing hypotheses and the consequent verification or contradiction of them continues: speculative theories and attacks upon the veracity and authenticity of the Scriptures tend to lose their support as the field of knowledge broadens, and fuller research increases the tenability of a conservative attitude in Biblical studies. Time is on the side of the believer who has confidence in the eternal truth of God revealed in the Scriptures.

AUTHORITY AND
THE BIBLE

J. Norval Geldenhuys

J. Norval Geldenhuys is Secretary of Publications of the Dutch Reformed Church of South Africa. He holds the B.A. and B.D. degrees from Pretoria University (South Africa) and the Th.M. from Princeton Theological Seminary. He is author of Supreme Authority *and* Commentary on the Gospel of St. Luke. *Also among his published works are two volumes in Dutch,* Onwrikbaar Seker, *a work on the divine origin and authority of Scripture, and* Die Bybel en Opgrawings, *a work on Biblical archaeology.*

23. J. Norval Geldenhuys

AUTHORITY AND
THE BIBLE

ALL ULTIMATE authority rests in God. As Creator and Sustainer of the universe he has the absolute right over all created beings and an all-embracing authority in heaven as on earth. This final and supreme authority gives him the unlimited prerogative to command and enforce obedience, to unconditionally possess and absolutely govern all things at all times in all places of the universe.

Modern science has made possible a deeper insight into God's unfathomable greatness, power and wisdom. Astronomy reveals astounding facts about the vast numbers not only of stars but of galaxies of stars. Scientific discoveries about the amazing structure of the atom compel us to stand in awe before the incomprehensible might and wisdom of God. Viewed in the greatness of God's creation our world is only an insignificant speck and all human beings, considered corporately or individually, are as particles of dust before the Almighty. It is actually undeniably true— man is in himself a being of little significance in this great universe of God. Therefore, the authority of the almighty Creator over us is absolute and final. Aware of our own nothingness we bow in awe and reverence before him, the King of kings and the Lord of lords.

As Christians we believe that this almighty God has spoken to us in and through Jesus Christ, his eternal Son. God's authority thus confronts us in and through him who, with the Father and the Holy Ghost, reigns over all things from eternity to eternity.

From the very beginning the unreserved acceptance of the supreme authority of Jesus Christ as Lord and Saviour undergirded the Christian

Church. Judas rejected his authority and died a shameful death. When the Jewish nation as a nation refused to acknowledge the authority of the Lord even after his resurrection, after the outpouring of his Spirit at Pentecost and after the missionary activity of his apostles, Jerusalem and the Jewish state were finally destroyed in 70 A.D. To this day the people who rejected the authority of their true Messiah have never again possessed the old Jerusalem.

The Roman Empire of the first three centuries A.D. chose to worship deified emperors and repeatedly tried to eradicate all loyalty to Jesus Christ. Soon the great worldly Empire was relegated to the past. It remained for Constantine, one of the greatest Roman emperors, to finally acknowledge and proclaim the supreme authority of the Lord.

The Roman Catholic Church elevated (if not in theory then in practice) tradition, the Church, the clergy and the Pope to the place of authority which belongs rightfully only to the Lord of all authority. The result was corruption and bondage. When other things, such as the error of the authority of tradition, the Church or the clergy, overshadowed acceptance of the authority of the living Lord, spiritual darkness ensued. And when, after the Reformation, some branches of the Church fell into mere bibliolatry, numerous sects and factions arose, with a resultant chaos of cults.

Refusing to bow before the supreme authority of the Lord and his Word, so-called nineteenth and twentieth century liberalism ended in spiritual bankruptcy and utter confusion.

Thus it helped to usher in such pagan philosophies as Communism, Nazism, Fascism and Nihilism. The arrogant rejection of Jesus' authority by atheistic Communism has inevitably forced and is continuing to force millions of people to become slaves of monstrous tyrants. Imperious Nazi and Fascist leaders, whose end was one of pathetic misery and total ruin, temporarily proclaimed themselves as national saviors, clothed with absolute authority.

The life of churches, of nations, of civilization itself, and of every individual human being, revolves about the inescapable challenge of the supreme authority of Jesus Christ. Where his authority is rejected, chaos and destruction inevitably follow.

In contrast to the seemingly mighty ones who rejected our Lord, a few simple fishermen and peasants of Palestine who accepted his authority after the first Pentecost went forth to establish the indestructible Church of Jesus Christ. Yielding completely to his authority, no earthly power, no scourge of persecution, could quench their enthusiasm, destroy their faith or stay them from establishing the Church in many lands until indeed it became a worldwide fellowship. Throughout the past nineteen centuries and today as well, millions have accepted the divine authority of him who died on the cross, was raised from the dead, and with the Father and the Holy Ghost reigns over all in heaven and on earth. Whenever and wherever the supreme authority of Jesus Christ is acknowledged as the ruling force in the life of the churches, there follow true revival of evangelical life, a greater unity among Christians, and extension of the frontiers of the Christian Church through new victories for the Lord of glory.

The acceptance or rejection of the unique, divine authority of our Lord and of his Word is thus of the utmost importance not only for those who are still outside the Church but also for the foundation and life of the Church as a whole in all ages and for every individual Christian. One of my life's most fascinating experiences has been to study the New Testament and Christian writings of the first three centuries A.D. to ascertain to what extent the authority of Jesus Christ was accepted by individual Christians, and by the corporate Church during those earliest days of our Christian era. Especially can we discern what a determining influence unconditional acceptance of Christ's authority as Lord and Saviour had upon the Church's acknowledgment of the Old and the New Testament Canon as the authoritative Word of God.

But before we inquire to what extent our Lord's authority was acknowledged and proclaimed during his earthly ministry and in the first centuries of our era, let us first see how Jesus Christ himself claimed and manifested supreme authority.

I. THE LORD UNEQUIVOCALLY CLAIMED UNIQUE AUTHORITY

The Old Testament prophets asserted only a delegated, secondary authority and introduced their messages with such phrases as, "Thus saith the Lord" or "The word of the Lord came to me saying. . ." Quite in contrast, and in a manner unlike that of anyone before or after him, Jesus spoke with a direct, unmistakably divine authority. "Verily, verily, I say unto you" were typical words from his lips. Never did he say "Thus saith the Lord" or "The message of God came to me." His manner of speaking leaves no doubt that he claimed to be one with God. He differentiated himself completely from all others as belonging not to their number but only to God, his Father. In speaking for himself, he never spoke of God as our Father but consistently spoke of "my Father" and of "your Father," making a clear distinction between his natural and eternal Sonship and the derived sonship of the disciples (cf. Mark 12:1–12, John 20:17). His claim that his unique Sonship entitles him to the throne of God, to absolute divine authority, is revealed by declarations such as "All things have been delivered unto me by my Father" (Matt. 11:27), and especially by the majestic words in Matthew 28:18: "All authority hath been given unto me in heaven and on earth." Thus we see that in many of his utterances our Lord claimed an absolutely comprehensive authority that gave him the divine right, the freedom and the power to demand and enforce obedience, to exercise unreserved possession, rule and dominion over everything in heaven and on earth. He placed himself in the very center of all things as the One possessing supreme authority even over the eternal destinies of men (cf. Matt. 25:31–46).

Only because he is the Son of God, one with the Father and with the Holy Ghost, could Christ claim in such a natural but uncompromising way what the Gospels record, namely, his supreme, divine authority.

II. THE LORD REVEALED HIS AUTHORITY IN PRACTICE

In complete harmony with his unique claims to divine authority, our Lord unmistakably and positively demonstrated this authority.

He did so in his merciful deeds of healing the sick, restoring sight to the blind, and saving many others from suffering. To the woman bound by infirmity for 18 years he said, "Woman, thou art loosed from thine infirmity. And he laid his hands upon her: and immediately she was made straight and glorified God." He raised even the dead. He took Jairus' daughter, who was already dead, by the hand and called, saying, "Child, arise." And her spirit returned, and she arose at once (Luke 8:55).

He revealed his authority also over nature, e.g., in changing water into wine, walking on the water, stilling the storms. Even when dying on the cross, in the darkness that covered the land, the earthquake that split the earth, and in the rending of the temple curtain, his authority over nature was revealed.

Jesus revealed his power also over men. When in the Nazareth synagogue he declared himself the fulfiller of Scripture, the Jews became enraged and determined to kill him. They "rose up, and cast him forth out of the city, and led him unto the brow of the hill whereon their city was built, that they might throw him down headlong." Humanly speaking, there was no possibility of escape. But Jesus, "passing through the midst of them went his way" (Luke 4:30), thereby revealing his authority over men.

Other incidents similarly revealed Jesus' authority over men. Even before his death and resurrection he exercised the divine prerogative to forgive men and women their sins. He did this so entirely in his own name that he did not even mention the name of God. He thus claimed to be one with the Father and demonstrated rights which belong only to God and which, according to the Old Testament, would remain God's prerogative even in the Messianic age (Isa. 43:25; Jer. 31:34; Ezek. 36:25). When the Pharisees charged him with blasphemy for acting as if he were God, and asked: "Who can forgive sins but God alone?," our Lord, by forthwith healing the palsied man, provided the unequivocal proof that he indeed has the right and the power to accomplish that which God alone can do (Matt. 9:3, Mark 2:10).

When on the cross he revealed his divine authority by forgiving the repentant thief, he once again exercised the exclusive prerogative of God

Almighty. "What things soever the Father doeth, these also doeth the Son likewise" (John 5:19).

Our Lord revealed his supreme authority also over the world of spirits. He overcame demonic hosts, the powers of Satan who tried to destroy the Saviour's work and hurled all their strength against him while he lived and suffered as man among men (see the writer's detailed discussion of the problem of demoniac spirits in *Commentary of the Gospel of St. Luke,* 1951). We mention one example: "And in the synagogue there was a man, which had a spirit of an unclean demon; and he cried out with a loud voice, Ah! what have we to do with thee, thou Jesus of Nazareth? art thou come to destroy us? I know thee who thou art, the Holy One of God. And Jesus rebuked him, saying, Hold thy peace, and come out of him. And when the devil had thrown him [the man] down in the midst, he came out of him, having done him no hurt. And amazement came upon all, and they spoke together, one with another, saying, What is this word that with authority and power he commandeth the unclean spirits, and they come out?" (Luke 4:33–36).

But our Lord revealed his divine power and might supremely by rising from the dead, appearing to his disciples as their risen Saviour, ascending into heaven and fulfilling his promise of the Holy Ghost. And by changing the small group of helpless disciples at Pentecost into men and women aflame with a living faith in a triumphant Saviour, and into world-conquerors in the best and highest sense of the word, he manifestly proved the validity of all his claims to be one with the Father and the Holy Ghost.

Before his ascension into heaven he declared: "All authority in heaven and on earth has been given to me. Go therefore and make disciples of all nations, baptizing them in the name of the Father and of the Son and of the Holy Spirit, teaching them to observe all that I have commanded you." Then he ended these words by making the explicit promise: "Lo, I am with you always, to the close of the age" (Matt. 28:18–20). He has fulfilled this promise through more than nineteen centuries, thus undeniably revealing his heavenly power and authority. In all these years men and women of all races and of all ages and conditions have experienced, and still continue to experience, that Jesus Christ is indeed the living Saviour and the Lord of lords who is ever with us to guide and help in all the vicissitudes of life.

In the book of the Acts we observe how the Lord as the Head not only founded the Church as a living organization but through his Spirit enabled the apostles and other followers to overcome even in the most trying circumstances. The dramatic conversion of arch-persecutor Saul of Tarsus is illuminating proof that the risen Christ continued to act with authority in guarding the welfare of his Church. Through the ages to our own time he has continually revealed his divine might and power by upholding believers individually and his Church generally; even the most terrible persecutions, trials, and dangers have not been able, and are not now able, to destroy the

Christian Church. Thus he fulfills his promise that, built on the rock of faith in him as Lord and Saviour, his Church shall not be overthrown, not even by the worst powers of darkness.

In another very positive and undeniable way our Lord revealed his authority, namely, by fulfilling the explicit prophecies he made during his earthly ministry. Luke 21:20–24 illustrates this point. Jesus clearly foretold Israel's suffering as a result of continued rejection of him as the true Messiah of God. He not only warned of Jerusalem's destruction and of the inhabitants' death or dispersion among all nations, but in verse 24 also clearly prophesies that Jerusalem would be so utterly lost to the Jews that the "holy" city would "be trodden down by the Gentiles, until the times of the Gentiles are fulfilled." The first part of our Lord's prophecy was fulfilled when the Romans destroyed Jerusalem in 70 A.D., killed possibly as many as one million Jews in and around the city, and took many thousands as captives to Rome and elsewhere. But history also proves that this Messiah-rejecting nation has never possessed the old Jerusalem. Although possessing a large section of Palestine and even a part of the modern Jerusalem, modern Israel today is still trying in vain to rule the old, actual city of Jerusalem. The Moslem temple on the site of the old temple of Solomon is evidence that Jerusalem is literally still being "trodden down by the Gentiles" and proves the divine authority of him who was rejected by Israel, but who is the Only-begotten of the Father and the King of kings.

Another explicit and tremendously important prophecy of our Lord is that in Matthew 24:12: "And this gospel of the kingdom will be preached throughout the whole world, as a testimony to all nations; and then the end will come." While the fulfillment of the first·half of this prophecy once seemed quite impossible, our lifetime has witnessed how the Lord of all creation has so guided the history of nations and the skills of men that it is possible for the Church in our time to complete the task of preaching the gospel throughout the whole world.

Many recent developments and signs of the times in general reveal Jesus Christ the Lord of history preparing all things for the great consummation of the ages, his return in glory. Then his authority will be revealed fully and majestically, and every knee shall bow before him as the One to whom the Father has given all authority in heaven and on earth.

III. DIVINE AUTHORITY ACKNOWLEDGED AND PROCLAIMED

We have seen how Jesus claimed and revealed divine authority. The question now arises, to what extent did his contemporaries and men through the ages perceive and acknowledge his authority? Already from the very beginning of his public ministry people were "astonished at his teaching; for he taught them as having authority" (Mark 1:22; cf. Matt. 7:28 f., John 7:6). He acted with such evidence of divine authority in healing the sick and in saving people from the power of Satan that both individuals and multitudes were amazed. In Luke 9:43, for instance, we read that after our Lord's healing the boy with the unclean spirit, the people "were all astonished at the majesty of God." And after he had raised the widow's dead son, "fear took hold on all: and they glorified God saying, A great prophet is risen among us: and God hath visited his people" (Luke 7:16).

The fact that even the demons and demon-possessed acknowledged his authority is vividly pictured in Mark 5:6–8: "And when he [the demoniac] saw Jesus from afar, he ran and worshipped him, and crying out with a loud voice, he saith, What have I to do with thee, Jesus, thou Son of the Most High God?"

However much they hated him, even his enemies had to acknowledge that he acted with authority. When Jesus, filled with holy wrath against the awful abuse and desecration of the temple, cleansed it by force and thus exercised yet another prerogative which the Old Testament ascribes only to God himself, his enraged enemies, not daring to capture him, nevertheless asked: "By what authority doest thou these things? or who gave thee this authority to do these things?" When finally Judas directed the emissaries of Jesus' enemies to capture him, we read: "When he said to them, I am he, they drew back and fell to the ground" (John 18:6). Instinctively even these rough men realized that he was clothed with unique authority.

It was above all, however, his true followers and those whom he saved from spiritual or physical distress who unreservedly acknowledged his supreme authority. We need only mention the tribute that followed Jesus' power over nature revealed by his walking upon the water and stilling the storm: "They that were in the boat worshipped him, saying, Of a truth thou art the Son of God" (Matt. 14:33).

The acknowledgment of Jesus' divine authority by his disciples reached a climax when, in speaking for them all, Peter, in response to the Lord's question "Whom say ye that I am?", said: "Thou art the Christ, the Son of the living God" (Matt. 16:16).

It was only after the resurrection and the ascension, however, that the apostles clearly recognized the supreme authority of Jesus. When they saw the risen Lord, they worshipped him (Matt. 28:17). Even doubting Thomas, when confronted by the living Saviour, in absolute surrender cried: "My Lord and my God" (John 20:28). After his ascension the disciples worshipped him and waited in utter obedience for the gift of the Holy Spirit. From the day of Pentecost on, the divine authority of Jesus Christ became for them a living and abiding reality. Thenceforth, clothed with his Spirit, they fearlessly proclaimed the supreme authority of their Saviour as the Lord of lords. Even to this day the central feature of the faith of Christians around the world has been Peter's proclamation on that first Christian Pentecost: "Let all . . . know assuredly, that God hath made him both Lord and Christ, this Jesus whom ye crucified" (Acts 2:36).

Before citing additional evidences to show that from the earliest beginnings of the Christian Church all true believers acknowledged and announced Jesus' supreme divine authority, we first wish to note this significant fact: God, the Father, unequivocally proclaimed that he himself had given all authority to Jesus, and that Jesus' claim to supreme authority is thus a genuine claim. The Father had already done this at the baptism of Jesus by saying: "Thou art my beloved Son; with thee I am well pleased" (Luke 3:22). Furthermore, he gave the Son power over sickness, death, the forces of nature and the life of men. And after the Transfiguration, God explicitly declared from heaven: "This is my Son, my Beloved; listen to him!" But, above all, it was by raising Jesus and exalting him to the place of honor at his right hand that God proclaimed to all the world that Jesus Christ his Son has supreme authority.

Turning again to early Church history we find that belief in the absolute divine authority of our Lord was the very cornerstone and foundation of the life of the Church and of every individual believer's faith. The apostles and other early Christians went forth not only proclaiming the teachings of Jesus, but preaching that the living Christ, their Sovereign Lord, was with them always, directing their lives and ruling over his Church.

While being stoned to death, Stephen, the first of many Christian martyrs, said: "Behold, I see the heavens opened, and the Son of man standing on the right hand of God" (Acts 7:56). From under the hail of stones he called with his last breath: "Lord Jesus, receive my spirit."

Peter's words in Acts 10:36, "Jesus Christ is Lord of all," give typical expression to the place of absolute authority given to our Lord in the early Church. The New Testament epistles and the book of the Revelation as well proclaim the same sovereign Lord as the Acts of the Apostles.

By calling him "the Lord" and even "God" and by applying to him Old Testament texts which in their original context pertain to God, the New Testament books clearly declare Jesus' divine authority.

Paul, who after the Saviour's appearance to him so dramatically changed from a persecutor of the Church into a devoted believer in Christ, calls himself "the slave of Jesus Christ" (Gal. 1:1; Rom. 1:1). He thereby expresses the complete character of his surrender to the authority of our Lord. And no wonder, for in Colossians 2:9 f., he declares that in Christ "dwelleth all the fulness of the Godhead bodily . . . [he] who is the head of all principality and power." In Ephesians 1:20 and following, Paul writes that God has made Jesus "to sit at his right hand in heavenly places, far above all rule, and authority and power, and dominion, and every name that is named, not only in this world, but also in that which is to come; and he put all things in subjection under his feet, and gave him to be head over all things to the Church." This impassioned description by Paul of the absolute and all-comprehensive authority of Jesus portrays the very foundation of Christianity, the living faith of the first Church. The apostle reiterates the same facts in Philippians 2:9-11: "God highly exalted him, and gave him a name which is above every name: that in the name of Jesus every knee should bow, of things in heaven and things on earth and things under the earth, and that every tongue should confess that Jesus Christ is Lord to the glory of God the Father."

In James 2:1 Jesus is called the "Lord of glory"; in Jude 4 "our only Master and Lord." In I Peter 3:22 we read: "Jesus Christ who is at the right hand of God, having gone into heaven; angels and authorities and powers being made subject unto him." The entire book of the Revelation mightily proclaims the supreme divine authority of Jesus Christ, who as "the King of kings and the Lord of lords" (19:16) is one with the Father and the Holy Spirit, and reigns over all. At the appointed time he will reveal his absolute authority in a final and decisive way.

That our Lord possesses ultimate authority in all his sayings, works and being is further clearly taught by the opening words of the letter to the Hebrews: "God, having of old time spoken unto the fathers in the prophets by divers portions and in divers manners, hath at the end of these days spoken unto us in the Son, whom he appointed heir of all things, through whom also he made the ages, who being the effulgence of his glory, and the impress of his substance, and upholding all things by the word of his power, when he had made purification of sins, sat down on the right hand of the Majesty on high."

The consistent and unequivocal presentation in every New Testament writing of Jesus as the triumphant, living Lord of all power and authority binds all the books into a remarkable unified whole.

In the writings of the Apostolic Fathers and in those of other early Church authors, the same unconditional acknowledgment of the authority of the Lord and of his Word prevails. In these writings Jesus is most often designated by the same name as God ("the Lord"). Clement of Rome (A.D. 96) calls Jesus "Our Lord, to whom be glory for ever and ever." Ignatius (A.D. 110) speaks of "Jesus Christ our God," and Polycarp wrote to the Church at Philippi (around A.D. 110): "Ye believed in him that raised our Lord Jesus Christ from the dead and gave unto him glory and a throne on his right hand; unto whom all things were made subject that are in heaven and that are on earth; to whom every creature that hath breath doeth service; who cometh as judge of quick and dead; whose blood God will require of them that are disobedient unto him."

Because the early Christians worshipped Jesus as God, one with the Father and the Holy Spirit, it followed quite naturally that they unreservedly believed and accepted his authority as final. To them he represented ultimate authority in all that he said, did and was.

So far, on the one hand, we have indicated that Jesus Christ claimed and positively revealed supreme divine authority and, on the other, that from earliest times believers and the Church acknowledged and proclaimed his authority. Together with all true believers of more than 1900 years, we

Christians today also unconditionally accept as our God the Lord who is one with the Father and the Holy Spirit. We unreservedly bow before his authority.

IV. THE LORD'S AUTHORITATIVE TEACHING

But now the question arises: Where can we find a reliable and authoritative account of God's self-revelation in and through Jesus Christ, his Son, and of the Lord's teachings, work and person?

Because Jesus as the Son of God possessed and eternally possesses supreme authority, we are already assured that an adequate, completely reliable account of his revelation and an authentic proclamation of the purpose of his life, death, resurrection and ascension would be preserved for all time.

That the Lord who has been given all authority in heaven and on earth so regulated the history and life of the early Church that a genuine all-sufficient and authoritative New Testament Canon was formed, corresponds to the fact that God's self-revelation in Christ was final and "once for all."

When we turn to the New Testament and other early Christian documents, we find that our Lord did, in fact, very carefully take all the necessary steps during his ministry on earth and the first years after his resurrection to ensure the New Testament's formulation, its acknowledgment and reverence by the Church. This he did by first calling disciples, and after a time by choosing and appointing apostles. The whole record of his dealings with the twelve conclusively shows they were not appointed to be merely his "messengers" or "heralds," but rather, his fully authorized representatives. The apostles were to be delegates whom he would send into the world with the commission to proclaim the gospel, to teach and to act in his name with authority.

In all four Gospels we see that comparatively early in his public ministry Christ began to teach his apostles that the time would soon come when he no longer would be in their midst (as man among men); they must needs go into the world as his witnesses and representatives. Therefore, he first made them his special, intimate disciples, in order to teach them intensively, to lead them to a full knowledge of himself as their Lord and Saviour, so that at the right moment they could act as his *apostles*.

On a few occasions even before his death he gave the apostles opportunity to act as his authorized representatives. We read in Luke 9:1–10: "And he called the twelve together, and gave them power and authority over all demons, and to cure diseases. And he sent them forth to preach the kingdom of God and to heal the sick. . . . And [said Jesus to them] as many as receive you not, when ye depart from that city, shake off the dust from your feet for a testimony against them." Here we see that the Lord gave the apostles power and authority not merely to teach and preach, but also to act as his delegates and in his stead. This fact is clearly emphasized by his words to the apostles in Matthew 10:4: "He that receiveth you receiveth me."

As the end of his earthly ministry drew ever nearer, the Lord taught his disciples more and more explicitly that they whom he had already appointed as apostles would need also to act as his authoritative representatives. Could he have expressed the fact of their coming unique responsibility any more clearly than, for example, in Matthew 18:18: "Verily I say unto you, what things soever ye shall bind on earth shall be bound in heaven: and what things soever ye shall loose on earth shall be loosed in heaven"?

This and much else in the Gospels conclusively prove that our Lord appointed the apostles not merely to be his missionaries, but also to lay the foundation of his Church with authority. As his work of redemption could not be repeated but had a "once for all" character, so also the apostles were given unique power and authority to lay the foundation of the Church in a conclusive way.

That the apostles in themselves were completely unable and unworthy to fulfill such a tremendous task goes without saying. Therefore, the Lord not only called and appointed the twelve to be his apostles but promised that the Holy Spirit would so teach and equip them that he could use them to establish, guide and build his Church on a secure foundation. In John 14:25 f., he said: "These things have I spoken unto you, while yet abiding with you. But the Paraclete, the Holy Spirit, whom the Father will send in my name, he shall teach you all things, and bring to your remembrance all that I said unto you." These words clearly teach our Lord's promise of the enlightening work of the Holy Spirit by whom the apostles would be able to remember Christ's teachings, and understand the significance of what he said and did. Therefore, they would be able to teach others all truth pertaining to him. This is stressed in John 16:12–14: "I have yet many things to say unto you, but ye cannot bear them now. Howbeit when he, the Spirit of truth, is come, he shall guide you into all truth: for he shall not speak from himself: but what things soever he shall hear, these shall he speak: and he shall declare unto you the things that are to come. He shall glorify me: for he shall take of mine, and shall declare it unto you." The apostles were promised enablement to understand the whole truth concerning the Lord, that they would be given the necessary prophetic insight, and would be adequately equipped in every way to teach and to act as his delegates.

After his resurrection, our Lord even more explicitly commissioned the apostles to be his uniquely authoritative representatives, as we read in John 20:21 f.: "Jesus therefore said to them again, Peace be unto you: as the Father hath sent me, even so send I you. And when he had said this, he breathed on them and said unto them, receive ye the Holy Ghost: whose soever sins ye forgive, they are forgiven unto them, whose soever sins ye retain, they are retained."

To enable them to lay the foundation of his Church in such a unique and "once for all" way he "opened their minds that they might understand the scriptures" (Luke 24:45). To accomplish their task it was essential that

382 REVELATION AND THE BIBLE

the apostles have the correct understanding of the Old Testament as the authoritative Word of God which Christ came to fulfill.

At Pentecost our Lord's promise to send the Holy Spirit to give necessary power, insight and wisdom to teach and act as his apostles was mightily and dramatically realized. From that very moment the apostles were new men; clothed with extraordinary power and authority, they began laying the foundations of the Christian Church for all the ages. They preached, taught and worked like men confident of being called, equipped and divinely commissioned as authoritative representatives of their living and triumphant Lord and Redeemer.

Under the Holy Spirit's guidance, Matthias was chosen to replace Judas. Thereafter no one was ever appointed to take the place of any of the original twelve apostles, with the possible exception of James, the brother of Jesus, who later took up the work of the martyred James, the son of Zebedee.

After the remarkable revelation of the Lord's power at Pentecost, the Church spread rapidly throughout the Jewish world under the leadership of these twelve apostles, and even beyond the boundaries of Palestine (Acts 8). The Lord founded it, however, to become his world-wide church. With this in view the living Saviour called, equipped and sent forth to be his special apostle to the Gentiles, Paul of Tarsus, clothed with his authority to teach and act as his delegate and representative (Acts 26:16 f.). As with the twelve, Paul was called and appointed to apostleship directly by the Lord himself and filled with the Holy Spirit (Acts 9:17-20). And through the mighty working of his Spirit, the exalted Lord enabled Paul to teach and act as his apostle in the highest sense of the word. In his divine name, on the Lord's authority and through his power, Paul founded Christian congregations in many parts of the world, and together with the other apostles and closely associated Christian leaders such as James, the brother of Jesus, he too was used by the Lord to lay the foundation of the Christian Church for all times.

V. APOSTOLIC AUTHORITY CLAIMED AND VINDICATED

That the apostles were keenly aware of their being called and commissioned as authoritative representatives of the Lord is abundantly clear. They consistently claimed to have and concretely exercised that unique authority which characterized only the true apostles of the Lord of all authority.

On that first Pentecost the apostles preached Christ with power, thousands of people came to believe in Jesus, received forgiveness of sins and eternal salvation (Acts 2:37-47; 4:33). Thus began the fulfillment of our Lord's promise to the apostles that through them he would found and build his Church.

He vindicated their apostleship also by enabling them to perform the same kind of miracles he had accomplished. "In the name of Jesus Christ of Nazareth, walk," said Peter to the lame man at the temple. "And he took him by the right hand, and raised him up. . . . And all the people saw him walking and praising God . . . and they were filled with wonder and amazement at what had happened to him" (Acts 3:6–10). That this and the healing of Aeneas (9:34), the raising of the dead Tabitha to life (9:40), and similar miracles, were not merely a few isolated cases is proved by the words: "By the hands of the apostles were many signs and wonders wrought among the people" (9:12). These miracles and the spiritual power evident in the apostles' lives and words showed they were indeed the deputies and unique representatives of the Lord. They so definitely claimed to be and so manifestly acted as the authoritative delegates of the ascended Lord that, whereas in the Gospels they are usually called disciples and only under special circumstances apostles, in the book of Acts they are consistently called apostles.

In his epistles, Paul also consistently declares himself an apostle of Jesus Christ (cf. Rom. 1:1: "Paul, a bond servant of Jesus Christ, called to be an apostle"; I Cor. 1:1: "Paul, an apostle not from men, neither through men, but through Jesus Christ"). When Paul mentions another person or persons as joint-author at the beginning of a letter, he explicitly calls himself an apostle but the others merely believers. Thus Colossians 1:1 reads: "Paul, an apostle of Christ Jesus . . . and Timothy, the brother" (cf. also 2 Cor. 1:1 and Gal. 1:1). Nevertheless, he unequivocally acknowledged the apostleship of the twelve. In Galatians 2:8 Paul says: "He that wrought for Peter unto the apostleship of the circumcision wrought for me also unto the Gentiles" (cf. also I Cor. 15:1–16).

In a few isolated cases in the New Testament persons other than the twelve and Paul are called apostles, but then only in the sense of persons sent to be the authoritative representatives of a church or of believers (cf. II Cor. 8:23; Phil. 2:25).[1]

All available evidence points overwhelmingly to the fact that in the highest sense of the word, only the twelve and Paul were called and appointed to be the original and unique foundation-laying apostles of Jesus Christ.

That the twelve were uniquely equipped to lay the foundation of the Church in an authoritative and "once for all" manner follows from the facts already mentioned: They had personally been with Jesus throughout his public ministry; after his resurrection he had appeared to them repeatedly;

---

[1] The only possible exception, as already noted, is Galatians 1:19 where, according to some, James, the brother of Jesus, is called an apostle. The fact that after his resurrection our Lord appeared in a special way to James, I Corinthians 15:7, and that later (after the martyrdom of James the son of Zebedee) this James the brother of Jesus played a leading role in the early Church, may have led to regarding him as a special apostle of the Lord.

at Pentecost he had filled them with the Holy Spirit in a unique way and, from that moment, wrought mighty works through them. While Paul was not one of the original disciples of Jesus, this fact was set aside by the extraordinary way in which the living Christ appeared to him, and by the Lord's endowing him with exceptional grace and power to fufill his apostleship (cf. I Cor. 15:10). Paul was able to say of his own work: "Truly the signs of an apostle were wrought among you in all patience, by signs and wonders and mighty powers" (II Cor. 12:12).

Many considerations indicate that this was a unique group of men and that never again could there be any so well qualified to act as the plenipotentiary apostles of Jesus Christ. The New Testament and the history of the early Church consistently teach that, just as the revelation of God in Christ is "once for all," so the risen Lord in a "once for all" manner laid the foundation of his Church through his chosen apostles.

Paul and the other apostles were supremely conscious of being called to fulfill this tremendously responsible task. In Ephesians 2:20 Paul speaks of the Church as "being built upon the foundation of the apostles and prophets, Christ Jesus himself being the chief corner stone" (cf. also I John 1:1-5, I Cor. 12:28, Rev. 21:14).

Nothing in Scripture suggests that these apostles ever wavered regarding Christ and his gospel. They all proclaimed the same Jesus Christ, the Son of God. In smaller practical details, such as the terms on which the Gentiles should be admitted to the Church, some of the apostles needed enlightenment from those to whom the ministry to the Gentiles had been specifically entrusted. They all spoke the gospel with power and authority, being taught and guided by the Holy Spirit. For this reason, the Apostle John could write: "If any one cometh unto you, and bringeth not this teaching, receive him not in your house, and give him no greeting" (II John 10).

VI. AUTHORITY CLAIMED FOR APOSTOLIC WRITINGS

Seeing that the Lord appointed the apostles to act as well as to teach as his authoritative representatives, it naturally follows that not only their spoken words but also their writings in their apostolic office were clothed with authority. The Apostle Paul leaves no doubt about this. Even by the way he begins his letters Paul clearly reminds his readers that he writes as the specially called apostle of Jesus Christ and therefore demands obedience. He consistently claims to write in the name and on the authority of the Lord. In I Corinthians 14:37 he writes: "If any man thinketh himself to be a prophet, or spiritual, let him take knowledge of the things which I write unto you, that they are the commandment of the Lord." So also in II Corinthians 10:11: "What we are by letters when we are absent, such we are also in deed when we are present." His letters are to substitute for his own presence as an authoritative apostle of the Lord. This he emphasizes in the words: "So then, brethren, stand fast and hold the traditions which ye were taught, whether by word, or by epistle of ours" (II Thess. 2:15). And in II Thessalonians 3:14 he even writes: "And if any man obeyeth not our word by this epistle, note that man, that ye have no company with him, to the end that he may be ashamed." He could demand such obedience only because it was true of him as a specially appointed apostle of the Lord, as of the apostles, that as stated in II Corinthians 12:19, "in the sight of God speak we in Christ" (cf. also I Pet. 1:1; II Pet. 1:1; I John 1:1–5; Rev. 1:11, 19, 2:14, 14:13, 19:9, 21:5, 22:18–19).

Because the apostolic writings were clothed with divine authority, it naturally follows that Paul would write words like those in I Thessalonians 5:27: "I adjure you by the Lord that this epistle be read to all the brethren." All available evidence shows that the early Church not only acknowledged wholeheartedly the unique authority of the writings but also treasured these documents written by apostles or by their most intimate and faithful followers. As Paul wrote in I Thessalonians 2:13: "For this cause we also thank God without ceasing, that, when ye received from us the word of the message, even the word of God, ye accepted it not as the words of men, but as it is in truth, the word of God."

Since the history of the New Testament Canon is treated elsewhere in this book, we need not describe its formation here. Our discussion has sufficiently indicated that Jesus Christ as the Lord of all authority and as the living Head of his Church used his apostles to lay the foundation of his Church for all time. He did this not only by enabling them to win converts and to form and organize churches in many parts of the world, but also through the Holy Spirit guiding and inspiring them, and a number of their closest followers, to write the books which comprise our New Testament. Thus the New Testament is clothed with his supreme authority and commands our unconditional obedience. The Lord himself saw to it that the authoritative preaching and teaching of his apostles be crystallized in written form, and that his Church recognize, acknowledge and preserve these writings for all time. It was accordingly not the Church that made the New Testament books authoritative. On the contrary, the Church humbly confessed these books to be clothed with the authority of the Lord, and therefore they require the unconditional obedience of all believers. It was not the Church that clothed the New Testament with authority but it is the Word of God, first proclaimed directly by the authoritative delegates of the Lord and subsequently in written form, that established and built the Church. The living Lord, who through his Spirit enabled the apostles to proclaim the gospel in unadulterated form, also illumined his Church through the Holy Spirit that she should recognize the New Testament books as authoritative.

VII. THE AUTHORITY OF THE OLD TESTAMENT

The New Testament writings teach that the Lord himself and his apostles emphatically proclaimed the divine authority of the Old Testament. For Jesus Christ the Old Testament was the word of God which "could not be broken" and "had to be fulfilled." He used Old Testament Scriptures to repel the onslaughts of Satan and to disarm his enemies among the Pharisees and Sadducees. He explicitly taught that he did not come to destroy the Law and the Prophets but to fulfill them. His whole life was steeped in the writings of the Old Testament, and even in the hours of death, words from the Old Testament were in his heart and on his lips. He continually taught that the Old Testament witnesses to him and that all the Old Testament prophecies concerning him would be fulfilled. During the 40 days before his ascension, he especially helped his disciples to understand the Old Testament and explicitly taught that all these Scriptures pointed to him.

Our Lord not only taught that the Old Testament is the authoritative Word of God, but by his life, death, resurrection, ascension and continued presence with and in his Church, demonstrated and proved that it is indeed the Word of the living God. All the Old Testament prophecies regarding his first coming (as Saviour and Lord) have been fulfilled in and through Jesus in such a manifest way that the divine authority of the Old Testament is unequivocally confirmed. Claims of the Old Testament writers of being commissioned to proclaim the words of God have not only been fully acknowledged as valid by the Lord, but have been fully vindicated by the certain manner in which our Lord has fulfilled the message and prophecies of the Old Testament.

The apostles and the early Church comprehended this clearly and therefore never wavered in acknowledging the authority of the Old Testament as the Word of God. Only heretics like Marcion ventured to reject the Old Testament.

VIII. OLD AND NEW BOUND IN UNBROKEN AUTHORITY

Because both the Old and the New Testaments proclaim Jesus Christ as Lord and Saviour and are clothed by the living Lord with his authority, we have a Bible of unbroken unity in the highest sense.

The mighty works of God in Christ form the center of the whole Bible. Through this divine Word, the Holy Spirit witnesses to Christ as the One who was to come, who has come, who is continually coming. At the consummation of all things he will finally come to be revealed as the Lord of lords to whom all authority in heaven and on earth has indeed been given. Thus the Bible comes to us with supreme authority as the Word of the triune God to whom be the glory and the power for ever and ever.

THE UNITY OF
THE BIBLE

Frank E. Gaebelein

Frank E. Gaebelein is Headmaster of the Stony Brook School, Long Island, New York. A Phi Beta Kappa graduate of New York University with an A.M. from Harvard, he holds honorary degrees from Wheaton College and Reformed Episcopal Theological Seminary. His many published works include Christian Education in a Democracy, The Pattern of God's Truth *and* Problems of Integration in Christian Education.

24. Frank E. Gaebelein

THE UNITY OF
THE BIBLE

THE PERENNIAL debate about the inspiration and authority of the Bible is a strong, though indirect, evidence of the uniqueness of the book. Other writings have been studied with the most minute care witness, for example, the Variorum Editions of Shakespeare, although even such close study of the greatest of English authors can hardly compare with the microscopic scrutiny to which Scripture has been subjected by scholars of all shades of theological conviction. As Karl Barth has said of his own work, when it comes to the writing of his commentaries, such as the *Römerbrief,* he has to take every word of the Bible seriously. And so also all responsible scholars, whether liberal or orthodox, must take every word seriously if they are to deal fairly with Scripture.

Not only has the Bible been more closely studied than any other book; it has also been the subject of a kind of inquiry quite different from that directed toward other works of literature. It is important to establish the most reliable text of the classics like Plato and Aristotle. But no one asks about Plato or Aristotle, Dante, Shakespeare, Goethe, or any other great writer the questions that are persistently asked about the origin and authority of the Bible. The plain truth is that the Bible is studied in a way and for a purpose that puts it in a class by itself.

The reason for this is clear. Whatever else may be said of it, we must admit that the Bible makes certain self-claims. Over and over it represents itself as being the Word of God. (For a marshalling of the Biblical evidence see the article, "Inspiration," by B. B. Warfield in *The International Standard Bible Encyclopedia,* Vol. 3, pp. 1473–83.) Within its pages Christ and the apostles declare it to be of divine authority. And it is beyond dispute that throughout its long history the Christian Church has accepted these claims as true, and that Israel also accepted the Old Testament as the very Word of God. Until the rise of the higher criticism in the eighteenth century, there was such widespread agreement regarding the divine origin and ver- acity of Scripture that what has become an arena of controversy was almost everywhere taken for granted. Moreover it is significant that even now, at a time when all kinds of Biblical criticism flourish, the great questions about where the Bible came from, what it really is, and what relationship it sus- tains to the living God will not down. They are still being raised in books and articles; they are still being discussed in classrooms all over the world.

I. THE BIBLE'S OWN CLUE TO ITS UNITY

Now in all this discussion one of the crucial issues is that of the unity of the Bible. In the case of Scripture, unity and authority are closely linked, just as unity and inspiration are near relations (cf. J. K. S. Reid, *The Authority of Scripture,* New York, Harper & Bros., 1957, pp. 18 f.). In a special sense, therefore, an understanding of the nature of the Biblical unity provides a clue to what the book really is.

How, then, do we go about investigating the unity of a literary work, whether Scripture or any other book? To this question there is an obvious answer. We investigate the unity of a work of literature by looking inside the work. In other words, we seek the integrating factor within the book itself. There is no other valid way to find the unifying principle of the Bible or of any other book. And if the charge is levelled that to do this is to reason in a circle, the answer is that internal evidence is always the essential subject matter of criticism. No one would accuse *The New York Times* book- reviewers of circular reasoning because they judge books on the basis of their contents. Nor would anyone question the right of a music critic to derive his evaluation of a new symphony from hearing the work, or the right of an art critic to look long and hard at a painting before writing about it.

But books are different from symphonies and paintings in that their authors may state within their pages what they intend to accomplish. Con- sider, for instance, such a work as Sir Winston Churchill's *History of the English-Speaking Peoples* with its preface making plain what Churchill is setting out to do. The responsible critic will take careful notice of the author's intention and will then decide whether it has been adequately ful- filled.

The same principle applies to the Bible, as Warfield pointed out (*The Inspiration and Authority of the Bible,* pp. 204 ff.). For Scripture contains its own doctrine about its nature and purpose—not, to be sure, in the form of a preface, yet in clear and definite terms. There is nothing ambiguous in the teaching of the Bible about itself. It is plainly stated within its pages that Scripture is the Word of God and that through it God speaks to men. Moreover, the great, central subject of the Bible is clearly set forth throughout the book. Thus it is our responsibility to examine in the light of Scripture's self-claims the phenomena of Scripture, such as the manifold facets of its historical, philological, and stylistic characteristics; and then, on the basis of this examination, to study the relation of these phenomena to the self-claim. But always the self-claim has prior consideration.

II. THE NATURE OF BIBLICAL UNITY

So with the all-important matter of the unity of the Bible. When it comes to the identification of the integrating factor of the book, we must go to Scripture itself. As Pascal said in the *Pensées,* "He who will give the meaning of Scripture and does not take it from Scripture, is the enemy of Scripture" (*Pensées* [899], translated by W. F. Trotter, New York, E. P. Dutton & Co., 1931, p. 266). But in doing this, we face several questions. What kind of unity is it that we are looking for in the Bible? Is it a unity of separate parts whereby the parts, as they are identified and classified, are recognized as fitting into the whole? Or is it a unity growing out of a single integrating principle that lies at the heart and center of the book?

Now there are those (e.g., Floyd E. Hamilton, *The Basis of Christian Faith,* Chapter IX; Arthur T. Pierson, *The Bible and Spiritual Criticism,* Chapters IV, VIII, IX), who have sought to formulate the unity of Scripture from an examination of such things as the consistency of its literary emphases, the congruity of its typology, and the harmony of its symbolism. On such grounds they have shown that the Bible exhibits a measure of unity far beyond what might be expected of a collection of the writings of men separated from one another by many years.

Such an approach is akin to the argument from design which sees behind the order and purpose of the natural world the mind that planned it all. Thus it moves from the literary phenomena of the book to the divine Author behind it. But useful though this approach is in its place, that place is not the first place. For to attempt to ascertain the central unity of the Bible in this way is like trying to discover the basic structure of a cathedral from the ornamentation of its exterior. Not that the two—basic structure and ornamentation—are wholly unrelated, but simply that there is a better clue than this.

Therefore, we go on to ask what other approaches to the unity of Scripture are possible. Now there are several answers to the question. There is the approach by way of doctrine, the approach through what is sometimes called "the drama of redemption," and the approach through a central person. Let us look at these with a view to identifying the one that is most in accord with Scripture.

First, then, the approach by way of doctrine. The Bible is the primary source-book of Christian doctrine. The great theologians, as distinguished from the religious philosophers, have all based their systems upon Scripture. But by the same token the Bible does not fully systematize its own doctrine. It presents the material out of which theologies are constructed. Not that doctrine as found in the Bible is haphazard; the New Testament epistles, especially the major Pauline letters, show the error of such a misconception. On the other hand, the doctrinal element in Scripture is not presented under a systematic theological unity. Actually the Bible is much too living a book for its unity to be centered in doctrinal formulation, however vital and dynamic the doctrines are. To say this does not imply that doctrine and theology are unessential; nor does it suggest that the Bible is not implicitly doctrinal and theological. It simply means that doctrine by itself is not the integrating factor within the Bible.

This being the case, we look next at "the drama of redemption," by which is meant the saving activity of God revealed in the Bible. To refer to this record of the redemptive history as "drama" does not necessarily mean that it is mythical or fictitious; rather is it a vivid term for the divine acts leading up to and culminating in all that God did for man through the crucifixion and resurrection of His Son, our Lord Jesus Christ. While to speak of these mighty works as "the drama of redemption" may seem to avoid certain contemporary prejudices against authoritative doctrinal and theological formulation, behind the phrase there still remain the essential historical facts upon which Christian doctrine rests. This approach does indeed bring us to the threshold of the unifying factor we are seeking, but it is not in itself that factor. Because it deals so directly with living persons, in contrast with the intellectual formulation of Biblical truth, it points us in terms of personality to the object of our search.

III. THE INTEGRATING PRINCIPLE CHRISTOLOGICAL

We turn, therefore, to the third approach to the unity of the Bible—that by way of the central person. And when we ask who that person is, we are confronted with what the apostle calls "the mystery of our religion" (I Tim. 3:16, RSV), using the word "mystery" in the special New Testament sense of something hitherto concealed but now revealed—i.e., "an open secret." What is this "open secret"? It is Jesus Christ himself, who, as Paul goes on to say, "was manifested in the flesh, vindicated in the Spirit, preached among the nations, believed on in the world, taken up in glory."

The Bible is par excellence the book of human nature. No other work tells us so much about man as it does. Here is humanity uniquely portrayed with a realism that penetrates beneath what men seem to be to what they are. But although the Bible is unique in that it reveals human nature in the unclouded mirror of truth itself, it is first and foremost the book of the divine Nature. Therefore, its unifying principle is nothing less than the Person of our Lord Jesus Christ, the incarnate Son of God and the Saviour of the world of men whose lost condition in trespasses and sins is so faithfully disclosed within its pages. It was Luther who, in commenting on the words of the 40th Psalm—"In the volume of the book it is written of me"—asked "What Book and what Person?" and replied by saying, "Scripture; and only one Person, Jesus Christ" (quoted by Adolph Saphir, *Christ and the Scriptures,* p. 7). So all the Bible, both Old Testament and New, is integrated in Christ.

To this fact the strongest witness is our Lord himself. Engaged in controversy with the Jews, he said to them, "Search the scriptures: for in them ye think ye have eternal life: and they are they which testify of me" (John 5:39). And in the same context he went on to say, "Had ye believed in Moses, ye would have believed me: for he wrote of me" (John 5:46). Not only so, but he constantly referred to the Scriptures as pointing to himself. For example, in Matthew 21:42–46, he climaxed the parable of the householder, with its indictment of Israel for rejecting their Messiah, by applying to himself Psalm 118:22, 23, "Did ye never read in the scriptures, The stone which the builders rejected, the same is become the head of the corner: this is the Lord's doing and it is marvelous in our eyes?" Likewise after the Last Supper he said to the disciples, "All ye shall be offended because of me this night: for it is written, I will smite the shepherd, and the sheep shall be scattered" (Mark 14:27), thereby showing himself to be the subject of Zechariah 13:7.

These are only a few of numerous incidents in which Christ made clear the fact that Scripture finds its unity in his Person. For it is beyond dispute that he knew that the Old Testament Scriptures were centered in him. To the two disciples whom he met on the Emmaus road the first Easter afternoon, he said: "O fools, and slow of heart to believe all that the prophets have spoken: Ought not Christ to have suffered these things, and to enter into his glory?" (Luke 24:25 f.). Whereupon, Luke tells us, "Beginning at Moses and all the prophets he expounded unto them in all the scriptures the things concerning himself" (vs. 27). In the appearance that night to the ten in Jerusalem he made the definitive statement regarding his centrality in the Old Testament: "These are the words which I spake unto you, while I was yet with you, that all things must be fulfilled, which were written in the law of Moses and in the prophets, and in the psalms concerning me" (Luke 24:44). To which the evangelist adds the significant statement, "Then opened he their understanding that they might understand the scriptures," indicating that apart from Christ there is no real comprehension of the Old Testament.

That the apostles follow our Lord in seeing him as the center of the Scriptures is evident from the sermons recorded in Acts. At Pentecost Peter used Psalm 16:8–11 and Psalm 110:1 as the basis of his proclamation of the risen Christ (Acts 2:25–36); and in his second sermon he identified him with the prophet of whom Moses wrote in Deuteronomy 18:15, 18, 19 (Acts 3:20–22). When the Ethiopian eunuch asked Philip the Evangelist the meaning of Isaiah 53, Philip "began at the same scripture and preached unto him Jesus" (Acts 8:30–35). At Antioch in Pisidia Paul preached Christ (Acts 13:32–37) from Psalm 2, Isaiah 55 and Psalm 16. And that his preaching was based upon the centrality of Christ throughout Scripture is plain from the description of his method in Acts 17:2, 3, which reports that "Paul, as his manner was, went in unto them, and three sabbath days reasoned with them out of the scriptures, opening and alleging, that Christ must needs have suffered, and risen again from the dead; and this same Jesus, whom I preach unto you, is Christ." As for his wider ministry to the churches with their preponderance of Gentile members, the same appeal to Christ in the Old Testament is part of the very warp and woof of the Pauline epistles.

What was true of Paul was true of others also. So we read that when the Alexandrian Jew, Apollos, had been instructed by Paul's pupils, Aquila and Priscilla, he "mightily convinced the Jews, and that publicly, showing by the scriptures that Jesus was the Christ" (Acts 18:24–28). Peter in his epistles, John in his epistles, the writer of Hebrews; James and Jude and the Revelation—all have this Christocentric orientation. Indeed, the statement in Revelation 19:10, "The testimony of Jesus is the spirit of prophecy," relates not just to the prophetic books but to the Bible as a whole.

It is significant also that this principle of Christ as the unifying center of the Bible was at the heart of the Reformation with its dynamic recovery of the Word of God. Said Luther: "All Scripture teaches nothing but the cross." And Calvin's undeviating conviction was that "Christ cannot be properly known in any other way than from the Scriptures" (quoted in *Calvin's Doctrine of the Word and Sacrament*, Ronald S. Wallace, Grand Rapids, Wm. B. Eerdmans Publishing Co., 1957, p. 98). As a recent writer concludes, Calvin "makes Christ central in the whole of Scripture in a way that is scarcely possible to a modern thinker [a revealing admission]. This made it appear as a unity incapable of contradicting itself. . . ." (A. Dakin, *Calvinism*, Philadelphia, Westminster Press, 1946, pp. 193 f. Quoted by J. K. S. Reid, *The Authority of Scripture*, p. 52).

But enough has been said to demonstrate that the integrating principle of the Bible is unquestionably Christological. The key to Biblical unity is not its consistency of literary phenomena, not its doctrine and theology, not its redemptive history. It is nothing less and none other than a Person, the living Lord, who only among the world's religious leaders dared say: "I am the way, the truth, and the life: no man cometh unto the Father but by me" (John 14:6). The integrating factor of the Bible is, in the words of Pascal, "Jesus Christ, whom the two Testaments regard, the Old as its hope, the New as its model, and both as their center" (*Pensées* [739], p. 223). Or, to paraphrase a greater thinker than Pascal, "There is neither Old Testament nor New, prophetic writings nor apostles, but they are all one in Christ Jesus."

The moment we see this, we pass from a theoretical unity to an organic unity. For integration in a person means integration in life. And when that Person is Jesus Christ, the unity, quite in keeping with the eternal horizons of the Bible, takes on infinite dimensions. Consequently, we see that Scripture, in the light of its Christological unity, is more than a combination of 66 sacred books, closely knit in theme and structure. As Francis L. Patton said, it is "an organism and not a miscellaneous collection of writings" (*Fundamental Christianity,* p. 169).

IV. IMPLICATIONS OF THE BIBLE'S UNITY

And now, having identified the unity of the Bible as being in the Person of Jesus Christ, we are ready to examine the implications of this unity. For implications there are, and they touch every aspect of the Bible and illuminate the deep questions regarding what kind of book it really is.

These implications involve first of all the crucial issue of the veracity of the Bible. Contemporary thinking about the Bible is haunted by the spectre of inerrancy. The orthodox view of Scripture held by the Church down through the ages has become the heterodoxy of the present; in most theological circles today, if there is one thing to be avoided like the plague it is the classical doctrine of verbal inspiration. Under the impact of world tragedy the modern theological mind has turned back, in part at least, to the great Biblical insights of the Reformation. But so scandalous has verbal inspiration become that some scholars feel obligated at all costs to remove the skeleton of inerrancy from the Reformers' closet, even though to do so requires prodigies of special pleading. Repelled by a certain kind of fundamentalism that has made for the Bible exorbitant claims, the contemporary theological mind persists in equating the view of the Bible held by scholarly conservatives today with the crudest forms of mechanical dictation. When it comes to those who are committed to the doctrine of Scripture believed by Christ and the apostles, taught by the Reformers, and expounded in a former generation by meticulous scholars like B. B. Warfield and J. Gresham Machen, both neo-orthodoxy and liberalism represent conservative belief by a strawman. Not only so, but the strawman is of such frightful, obscurantist mien as to scare even his makers!

The situation would be amusing were it not so serious. Here, for example, is Dean Bernhard W. Anderson of Drew Theological Seminary, writing a book on *Rediscovering the Bible.* In it he refers to the Inter-Varsity Christian Fellowship as bringing "crusading fundamentalism" to the college campus. "The key 'fundamental' of the faith, according to this group, is," he says, "the inerrancy of Scripture. In the words of a representative statement, it is 'an essential doctrine of the Word of God and our standards that the Holy Spirit did so inspire, guide, and move the writers of the Holy Scripture as to keep them from error'" (Bernhard W. Anderson, *Rediscovering the Bible,* New York, Association Press, 1951, p. 15).

So far Dean Anderson's statement is fairly objective. Now observe the strawman he immediately sets up: "This means," he continues, referring to the definition of inerrancy he has quoted, "that the words of the Bible are the very words of God himself. The writers of the Bible were mere passive secretaries who mechanically transcribed the divine words. . . . Because God is literally the author of Holy Scripture, the whole Bible 'from cover to cover' is held to be absolutely infallible. In popular practice fundamentalists have claimed infallibility for a particular version of the Bible: the King James Version of 1611!" (p. 15).

But the Inter-Varsity view of the Bible does not mean mechanical dictation. Nor is it justly mentioned in the same breath with the obscurantism that attributes inerrancy to the King James Version. It would not be difficult for a writer like Dean Anderson to consult such a work as *The New Bible Commentary*, recently published by Inter-Varsity, a cooperative endeavor of some of the best conservative scholarship in Europe and America (London, 1953; Grand Rapids, 1953). Plain intellectual honesty demands admission of the fact that it is quite as possible for responsible scholars today to stand for the inerrancy of Scripture and at the same time recognize that it was not written by "passive secretaries who mechanically transcribed the words," as it was for Calvin constantly to affirm the verbal infallibility of Scripture and at the same time recognize its human element.

Surely the time has come for those who hold the modern view of the Bible to lay aside the ghost of mechanical dictation in respect to conservative scholarship and to make a serious effort to learn what those who are committed to plenary inspiration really believe about the Bible. In short, what is needed is for scholars of differing points of view to take the trouble really to understand what the other side thinks.

The foregoing discussion of the current confusion regarding inerrancy provides a background for dealing with the relation between the veracity of Scripture and its Christological unity. The fact of this unity is not, of course, the exclusive discovery of those who view the Bible from the traditional conservative position. On the contrary, it is common ground with others who, although differing about the nature and extent of inspiration, recognize the Bible as being in some special sense the Word of God. A case in point is J. K. S. Reid's recent volume, entitled *The Authority of Scripture*. This is a valuable study of the Reformed view of the Bible, in which the author clearly sees Christ to be the center of the book (p. 236 ff.). But the significant thing is that in his thinking he combines this strong insistence upon the centrality of Christ in the Scriptures with a repudiation of the inerrancy of the written Word.

Nevertheless, the fact remains that our Lord placed complete reliance upon the full veracity of the Word. For it is simply not possible to read back into Christ's handling of Scripture anything less than his full recognition of its supreme trustworthiness, as Warfield has shown by examination of all the passages in which Christ uses the Old Testament (*op. cit.,* pp. 138 ff.). This being the case, the only way in which Christ's authority can be reconciled with a fallible Old Testament is through resorting to a strongly kenotic view of his Person, whereby he is seen as a child of his age, sharing the mistakes and superstitions of his people. But this accords ill with the crucial issues our Lord made to hang upon the very words of Scripture, and it certainly is inconsistent with a high view of his Person.

On the other hand, the difficulties attendant upon an acceptance of our Lord's estimate of Scripture as the unbreakable Word of God (John 10:35) must be faced. There are discrepancies; there are historical problems and ethical and spiritual questions that stubbornly resist the most thorough-going efforts to reconcile and solve them. What, then, of the veracity of Scripture? Is its inerrancy to be scrapped?

The answer is twofold. In the first place, there is the attitude of suspended judgment toward Bible difficulties. Such an attitude is constantly being vindicated, as archaeology has solved one Biblical problem after another, and as painstaking re-examination of discrepancies has finally led to answers. Illustrations of the former are too numerous to specify, but these words of Dr. Nelson Glueck will show the trend of archaeology: "The reviewer has spent many years in biblical archaeology, and, in company with his colleagues, has made discoveries confirming in outline or in detail historical statements in the Bible. He is prepared to go farther and say that no archaeological discovery has ever been made that contradicts or controverts historical statements in Scripture" (*The New York Times* "Book Review," Oct. 28, 1956. Dr. Glueck, a distinguished Jewish archaeologist, points out in his review of Keller's *The Bible As History* that the Bible, being essentially a theological document, does not, accurate though it is historically, depend on external proof). For the latter, recent research affords a striking illustration in the solution by Dr. Edwin R. Thiele of one of the thorniest problems in Old Testament chronology—that of discrepancies in the parallel accounts of the reigns of the kings of Israel and Judah (*The Mysterious Numbers of the Hebrew Kings,* Chicago, University of Chicago Press, 1951).

In the next place, there is another way of dealing with Biblical veracity as it is involved with the Christological integration of Scripture. And that is nothing less than a rethinking of the whole concept of inerrancy and verbal inspiration. Truth is truth, absolute and unchangeable. Yet truth is bigger than our knowledge of it, which should never be static but always growing. Our Lord, who claimed to be the truth, is far greater than our understanding of who he is. Just as the final formulation of the mystery of his Person, based upon the inspired data of Scripture, has not yet been made, so the perfect solution of the tension between Christ's own view of the Bible and the difficulties inherent in certain portions of the written Word is still beyond our grasp. This is not to say, however, that progress toward solution cannot be made. Instead, one of the great needs of the day is for scholars to re-examine in the light of all the data the concept of inerrancy as applied to Scripture. Moreover, such re-examination cannot be done hastily. If there is valid ground for criticism of the prevalent attitude of much contemporary theology toward a high view of inspiration, it is that the question has been disposed of prematurely. But the same criticism must be made of conservative theology when it insists upon what may be a rigid formulation of a position that, though accepted on faith, yet needs clarification and redefinition.

Furthermore, the Christological unity of the Bible requires the believer to take his stand with his Lord when it comes to the full reliability of the Word. Truth, although it has innumerable facets, belongs to God. And because Christ is one with God, he who said, "I am the truth," is the Lord of truth. And because Scripture finds its unity in him and is inspired by the Spirit whom he called "the Spirit of truth," it is the Word of truth. Therefore, the Christological integration of the Bible guarantees its veracity.

Bishop H. C. G. Moule, who was both a distinguished exegete and a humble saint, put in noble words the ground for our reliance upon the utter truthfulness of Scripture when he said: "He [i.e., Christ] absolutely trusted the Bible, and, though there are in it things inexplicable and intricate that have puzzled me so much, I am going, not in a blind sense, but reverently to trust the Book because of *Him*" (John Battersby Harford and Frederick Charles MacDonald, *The Life of Bishop Moule,* London, Hodder & Stoughton, Ltd., 1922, p. 138). To which should be added that the Christian who in his view of the Bible stands on any lower ground than that on which his Lord stood does so at his spiritual peril.

V. THE SPIRIT'S WITNESS IN SCRIPTURE

Once the master-principle of the Christological unity of the Bible is grasped, all Scripture may be seen in the perspective of the central Person. And it is here that the Holy Spirit plays an indispensable part. According to our Lord's own declaration in the *locus classicus* of John 16:13–15, the function of "the Spirit of truth" is to "guide you into all truth: for he shall not speak of himself; but whatsoever he shall hear, that shall he speak: and he will show you things to come. He shall glorify me: for he shall receive of mine, and shall show it unto you."

The discernment, therefore, of the far-reaching application of the unity of the Bible in Christ is more than an intellectual discipline; it is a spiritual adventure. This is not to say that it is irrational, but simply to point out that, along with the use of the mind in understanding the Word, there is available for the believer the guidance of the Spirit who inspired it. The Reformers recognized the inner witness of the Spirit (*Testimonium Spiritus Sancti internum*) to the truth of Scripture, a principle that fundamentalism in its preoccupation with defending the formal inerrancy of the Bible has too largely overlooked. Yet the reality of this witness of the Spirit urgently needs recovery today.

When we come to particular applications of the integration of the Bible in Christ, limitations of space permit only brief mention of certain significant areas. There is, for one thing, the panorama of Biblical history. Here Christ is the master-key, because in one way or another he is the focus of God's dealings with men through the ages. From the dawn of history in Eden, where the Redeemer is promised in the protevangel (Gen. 3:15), down through the arrival of Paul in Rome (Acts 28) to the picture of the early Church derived from the later epistles, Christ is central. Israel is important not just for Israel's sake, but for the sake of the Messiah who is to come from within her and of whose truth she is to be the vehicle. The nations surrounding Israel are important because of their relation to the chosen people from whom Christ was to come. The Roman Empire is important because it was the locale of the incarnation and the beginnings of the Church. The whole world is important because it is the field in which the gospel must be preached. Always the essential frame of reference is Christ.

Or consider the great doctrines of the Bible, having to do with such subjects as man, sin, sacrifice, redemption, love, judgment, heaven, hell. Just to think of them in relation to Christ immediately brings to mind the fact that they too have their focus in him. Without doubt the doctrines of Scripture, even though not, as we have already seen, systematically organized within Scripture itself, find in Christ their orientation. Even more, it is true in doctrine as in everything else, that "by him all things hold together" (Col. 1:17).

So also with prophecy and eschatology. Again the focus is Christ. What has been called "the harmony of the prophetic word" is nothing less than a harmony in and through Jesus Christ (cf. *The Harmony of the Prophetic Word* by A. C. Gaebelein). The scope of prophecy is vast; not only Judah and Israel, but also Egypt, Assyria, Babylonia, Ethiopia, Persia, Greece, and Rome, to say nothing of the lesser nations, have their place in the prophetic Scriptures. Yet towering over the kings and empires of the Bible is the King of kings and Lord of lords, in whose pierced hands is the ultimate destiny of all men and of all nations. In him prophecy is centered; in him it has been and will yet be fulfilled in the consummation of all things when he comes again.

Likewise with the literary phenomena of the Bible. To take a particular instance, typology has its Christological orientation, either directly or indirectly. Abel's "better sacrifice" points to the "full, perfect, and sufficient sacrifice, oblation, and satisfaction for the sins of the whole world" (*The Book of Common Prayer,* Service of Holy Communion) made by Christ. The ark, bearing Noah and his family through the flood, portrays safety in

Christ from judgment. Abraham, the founder of the nation of whom Christ came, prefigures the atonement in the story of his willingness to offer Isaac on Mount Moriah. So with incident after incident in the lives of the other patriarchs and in the great succession of Old Testament heroes. To mention only two, there is no more perfect individual type of Christ than Joseph, while Jonah, with his unique experience, is on the authority of Jesus himself the great Old Testament type of his death and resurrection (Matt. 12:38–42). The elaborate system of sacrifices and offerings set forth in the Pentateuch typifies Christ in various aspects of his redeeming work; yet leprosy, which is the type of sin, speaks, through the eloquence of need, of the One who only can cleanse the sinner from his spiritual malady. The wilderness experiences of Israel contain definite Messianic types—"They did all drink the same spiritual drink; for they drank of the spiritual Rock that followed them: and that Rock was Christ" (II Cor. 10:4). Even the furniture of the tabernacle has its Messianic reference (Heb. 9:1–10).

But, as every Bible student knows, these are only a few instances of the way in which Scripture is unified in Christ. To see him in all parts of the Word, from Genesis to Revelation, requires no labored exegesis. It asks only the willingness, through careful study and the leading of the Spirit, to recognize him who is already there.

VI. THE LIVING UNITY OF THE GREAT BOOK

The time has come, however, to step aside from a close examination of our subject and to look at it in the large. And there is probably no better way to do this than to conclude our discussion of the unity of the Bible by facing the accusation of bibliolatry that is so often made against those who hold to the complete reliability of Scripture. Such biblicism and literalism are, we are told, nothing short of turning the Scriptures into a "paper pope."

Putting aside such things as the assumption, which we have already considered, that all views of inerrancy necessitate mechanical dictation, let us ask ourselves whether there ever has been or is now on the part of those committed to a highly conservative view of Scripture any tendency whatever toward bibliolatry. And if we admit, as in common honesty we must, that there are those who have with the best of motives sometimes veered in this direction, let us also ask what can be done to correct the recurrence of such a tendency.

In a book (*Christ and the Scriptures*) published over half a century ago, Adolph Saphir, the distinguished Presbyterian Hebrew-Christian who had a notable ministry in England, saw this tendency with prophetic insight. He wrote:

> The charge of Bibliolatry (worship of the Bible) has been of late frequently preferred against those who maintain the supremacy of Scripture. As far as this objection is urged by those who do not

fully and clearly acknowledge the divine authority and inspiration of Scripture, it is easily refuted. But . . . we may do well to consider whether our opponents are not giving utterance to a truth which they themselves do not fully see, and [which] warns us against a danger the existence of which we are apt to overlook. In other words, never mind whence and for what purpose the charge of Bibliolatry is made,—consider the thing itself; is there such a tendency, such an evil, such a danger? I know that many Christians will reply at once, "We cannot value, and reverence, and cherish the Bible sufficiently." And this is quite true. The danger is not of a reverence too deep, but of a reverence untrue and unreal (pp. 115 f.).

These are discerning words. And Dr. Saphir goes on with the same clearness of sight to say, "By Bibliolatry I understand the tendency of separating, in the first place, the Book from the Person of Jesus Christ, and in the second, from the Holy Spirit, and of thus substituting the Book for Him who alone is the light and guide of the Church" (pp. 116 f.).

The quotation has been given at length because it comes from a man who held with passionate conviction to the utter reliability of the Bible, and because it points not only to the problem but also to the solution. The solution is, plainly enough, the principle of the unity of the Bible in Christ. If the Bible finds its true and vital integration only in the Person of our Lord Jesus Christ, then there can be no bibliolatry in any form, shape or manner on the part of any of us, no matter how stoutly we adhere to the inerrancy of Scripture. For Scripture, great as it is, is never to be equated with Deity. In all its perfection and truth, it is still a creature, albeit unique among books. According to its own self-witness, it is an instrument of the living God—the sword of the Spirit, the seed incorruptible whereby we are born again, the law of the Lord that converts the soul, the mirror in which we see ourselves in the blazing light of God's truth, the hammer that crushes our hardness of heart. But, great as it is, it is an instrument, an inspired and unique means to an end, not an end in itself. As such it can never in and of itself be the object of worship any more than God's other great book, the Book of Nature, can ever be the object of worship.

The center of the Bible is the living Christ. Throughout its pages God the Holy Spirit who inspired it bears witness to the Person who unites all the manifold strands of history, prophecy, poetry, symbolism, and doctrine to bear witness to him and his saving work. Let us, therefore, rejoice that Christ is the center of the Bible, that in him alone it finds its living unity. Let us reverence the Bible as the only written revelation of God, the only completely truthful book, realizing that we reverence it most fully and honor it most highly when we see within its pages the Lord Jesus Christ and when we make him in whom its unity is centered the center of our own life and service.

A SELECTIVE
BIBLIOGRAPHY

1. GENERAL AND SPECIAL DIVINE REVELATION

J. H. Bavinck, *Religieus besef en Christelijk geloof* (Religious Consciousness and Christian Faith). 1949.

G. C. Berkouwer, *General Revelation*. Grand Rapids: Wm. B. Eerdmans Publishing Co., 1955.

————, *De mens het beeld Gods* (Man the Image of God). (To be published in translation by Wm. B. Eerdmans Publishing Co.) 1957.

H. Kraemer, *Religion and the Christian Faith*. Philadelphia: Westminster Press, 1956.

William Masselink, *General Revelation and Common Grace*. Grand Rapids: Wm. B. Eerdmans Publishing Co., 1953.

2. SPECIAL DIVINE REVELATION AS RATIONAL

Loraine Boettner, *The Inspiration of the Scriptures*. Grand Rapids: Wm. B. Eerdmans Publishing Co., 1937.

John Calvin, *The Institutes of the Christian Religion.*

Gordon H. Clark, *A Christian View of Men and Things*. Grand Rapids: Wm. B. Eerdmans Publishing Co., 1952.

————, *Thales to Dewey*. New York: Houghton, Mifflin Co., 1957.

Paul K. Jewett, *Emil Brunner's Concept of Revelation*. London: James Clarke & Company, 1954.

3. SPECIAL REVELATION AS HISTORICAL AND PERSONAL

Paul K. Jewett, "Ebnerian Personalism and Its Influence upon Brunner's Theology," in *The Westminster Theological Journal*, May 1952, pp. 113–147.

————, *Emil Brunner's Concept of Revelation.*

Martin Kahler, *Der sogenante historische Jesus und der geschichtliche biblische Christus*. Leipzig, 1896.

James Orr, *The Problem of the Old Testament*. New York: Charles Scribner's Sons, 1921.

4. SPECIAL REVELATION AS OBJECTIVE

Gordon H. Clark, "Logic and Language," in *The Gordon Review*, February, 1956, pp. 3–9, and December, 1957, pp. 141–150.

Robert E. Longacre, "Linguistics and Inspiration," in *Bible Presbyterian Reporter*, March, 1958, pp. 10–12.

Eugene A. Nida, "Language, Culture, and Theology," in *The Gordon Review*, December, 1957, pp. 151–167.

5. SPECIAL REVELATION AS SCRIPTURAL

Oscar Cullmann, "The Tradition," in *The Early Church*. Philadelphia: The Westminster Press, 1956.

Abraham Kuyper, *Principles of Sacred Theology*. Grand Rapids: Wm. B. Eerdmans Publishing Co., 1954.

John Murray, "The Attestation of Scripture," in *The Infallible Word*. A symposium by members of the faculty of Westminster Theological Seminary (Philadelphia, 1946; Grand Rapids, 1953).

Herman Ridderbos, *Heilsgeschiedenis en Heiligie Schrift van het Nieuwe Testament*. Kampen: Kok, 1955.

Ned B. Stonehouse, "The Authority of the New Testament," in *The Infallible Word*.

Geerhardus Vos, *Biblical Theology, Old and New Testaments*. Grand Rapids: Wm. B. Eerdmans Publishing Co., 1948.

6. CONTEMPORARY VIEWS OF REVELATION

Louis Berkhof, *Reformed Dogmatics: Introductory Volume*. Grand Rapids: Wm. B. Eerdmans Publishing Co., 1932.

Paul K. Jewett, *Emil Brunner's Concept of Revelation*.

Paul G. Schrotenboer, *A New Apologetics: An Analysis and Appraisal of the Eristic Theology of Emil Brunner*. Kampen: Kok, 1955.

Cornelius Van Til, *The New Modernism*. Philadelphia: The Presbyterian & Reformed Publishing Co., 1947.

————, "Introduction" to B. B. Warfield, *The Inspiration and Authority of the Bible*. Philadelphia: The Presbyterian and Reformed Publishing Company, 1948; London: Marshall, Morgan & Scott, 1951.

John W. Walvoord (ed.), *Inspiration and Interpretation*. Grand Rapids: Wm. B. Eerdmans Publishing Co., 1957.

7. THE WITNESS OF SCRIPTURE TO ITS INSPIRATION

G. B. Bentley, *The Resurrection of the Bible*. London: Dacre Press, 1940.

L. Gaussen, *Theopneustia: The Plenary Inspiration of the Holy Scriptures* (David Scott's translation, revised by B. W. Carr, with a preface by C. H. Spurgeon). London, 1888.

B. B. Warfield, *The Inspiration and Authority of the Bible* (earlier edition, *Revelation and Inspiration*. New York: Oxford University Press, 1927; London: Marshall, Morgan & Scott).

————, "Revelation," "Inspiration," in *The International Standard Bible Encyclopedia*. Chicago: Howard Severance Company, 1915.

8. OUR LORD'S USE OF SCRIPTURE

R. C. H. Lenski, *The Interpretation of the New Testament*. Columbus, Ohio: The Wartburg Press, 1943.

L. M. Sweet, "Quotations, New Testament," in *The International Standard Bible Encyclopedia*. 1949.

R. V. G. Tasker, *Our Lord's Use of the Old Testament*. London: Westminster Chapel, 1953.

J. W. Wenham, *Our Lord's View of the Old Testament*. London: Tyndale Press, 1955.

9. NEW TESTAMENT USE OF THE OLD TESTAMENT

Wilhelm Dittmar, *Vetus Testamentum in Novo*. Goettingen: Vandenhoeck & Ruprecht, 1903.

E. Earle Ellis, *Paul's Use of the Old Testament*. Grand Rapids: Wm. B. Eerdmans Publishing Co., 1957.

Patrick Fairbairn, *Hermeneutical Manual*. Edinburgh: T. & T. Clark, 1858. (See especially pp. 354–460.)

R. V. G. Tasker, *The Old Testament in the New Testament*. London: Student Christian Movement, 1954. Second edition revised.

C. H. Toy, *Quotations in the New Testament*. New York: Scribner, 1884.

B. B. Warfield, *The Inspiration and Authority of the Bible*.

10. THE CANON OF THE OLD TESTAMENT

William Henry Green, *General Introduction to the Old Testament, The Canon*. New York: Scribner's, 1898.

R. Laird Harris, *The Inspiration and Canonicity of the Bible*. Grand Rapids: Zondervan Publishing House, 1957.

Edward J. Young, "The Authority of the Old Testament" in *The Infallible Word*, pp. 54 ff.

11. THE APOCRYPHA

Bruce M. Metzger, *An Introduction to the Apocrypha*. New York: Oxford University Press, 1957.

W. O. E. Oesterley, *An Introduction to the Books of the Apocrypha*. New York: Macmillan Company, 1935.

Merrill F. Unger, *Introductory Guide to the Old Testament*. Grand Rapids: Zondervan Publishing House, 1951.

12. THE CANON OF THE NEW TESTAMENT

Oscar Cullmann, "Scripture and Tradition," in *Scottish Journal of Theology*, June 1953.

Hermann Diem, *Das Problem des Schriftkanons*. Zollikon, Zurich, 1952.

F. W. Grosheide, *Algemene Canoniek van het Nieuwe Testament*. Kampen: Kok, 1925.

W. G. Kümmel, "Notwendigkeit und Grenze des neutestamentlichen Kanons," in *Zeitschrift für Theologie und Kirche*, 1950.

Herman Ridderbos, *Heilsgeschiedenis en Heilige Schrift*.

Symposium, *De Apostolische Kerk*, pp. 39–97. Kampen: Kok, 1954.

H. Strathmann, "Die Krise des Kanons der Kirche," in *Theologische Blätter*.

E. Flessemann-van Leer, *Tradition and Scripture in the Early Church*. The Netherlands: V. Gorkum Assen, 1953.

B. B. Warfield, "The Formation of the Canon of the New Testament," in *The Inspiration and Authority of the Bible*, pp. 411–416.

13. THE CHURCH DOCTRINE OF INSPIRATION

Kenneth S. Kantzer, "The Knowledge of God and the Word of God in John Calvin" (unpublished Ph.D. dissertation, Harvard University, 1950).

M. Reu, *Luther and the Scriptures*. Columbus, Ohio: The Wartburg Press, 1944.

John F. Walvoord (ed.), *Inspiration and Interpretation*.

B. B. Warfield, "The Church Doctrine of Inspiration," in *The Inspiration and Authority of the Bible*, pp. 105–128.

14. CONTEMPORARY IDEAS OF INSPIRATION

G. W. Bromiley, "Barth's Doctrine of the Bible," in *Christianity Today*, Dec. 24, 1956, pp. 14–16.

James Orr, *Revelation and Inspiration*. London: Hodder & Stoughton, 1910.

James I. Packer, *Fundamentalism and the Word of God*. London: Inter-Varsity Fellowship, 1958.

Robert Preus, *The Inspiration of Scripture*. Edinburgh: Oliver & Boyd, 1955.

Cornelius Van Til, *The New Modernism*.

B. B. Warfield, *Revelation and Inspiration*.

15. THE PHENOMENA OF SCRIPTURE

A. B. Bruce, C. A. Briggs, L. J. Evans and H. P. Smith, *Inspiration and Inerrancy*. London: James Clarke, 1891.

R. Laird Harris, *The Inspiration and Canonicity of the Bible*, pp. 85–128.

Everett F. Harrison, "Criteria of Biblical Inerrancy," in *Christianity Today*, Jan. 20, 1958, pp. 16 ff.

B. B. Warfield, *Revelation and Inspiration*, pp. 169–226, 395–425.

Edward J. Young, *Thy Word is Truth*. Grand Rapids: Wm. B. Eerdmans Publishing Co., 1957. Pp. 113–185.

16. THE EVIDENCE OF PROPHECY AND MIRACLE

Charles P. McIlvaine, *The Evidences of Christianity*. London: Fischer, Fisher and Jackson, 1833.

Blaise Pascal, *Pensées* (translated by H. F. Stewart). New York: Pantheon Books, 1950.

Bernard Ramm, *Protestant Christian Evidences*. Chicago: Moody Press, 1953 (second ed., 1957).

Alan Richardson, *Christian Apologetics*. New York: Harper & Bros., 1948.

Wilbur M. Smith, *Therefore Stand*. Boston: W. A. Wilde Co., 1945.

17. THE HOLY SPIRIT AND THE SCRIPTURES

Wick Broomall, *The Holy Spirit*. New York: American Tract Society, 1940.

————, *Biblical Criticism*. Grand Rapids: Zondervan Publishing House, 1957.

Carl F. H. Henry, *The Protestant Dilemma*. Grand Rapids: Wm. B. Eerdmans Publishing Co., 1949.

J. K. S. Reid, *The Authority of Scripture*. New York: Harper & Bros., n.d.

Ronald S. Wallace, *Calvin's Doctrine of the Word and Sacrament*. Grand Rapids: Wm. B. Eerdmans Publishing Co., 1957.

J. Gresham Machen, *Christianity and Liberalism*. New York: The Macmillan Company, 1925.

Cornelius Van Til, *The New Modernism*.

18. THE PRINCIPLES OF INTERPRETATION

Louis Berkhof, *Principles of Biblical Interpretation*. Grand Rapids: Baker Book House, 1950.

A. B. Davidson, *Old Testament Prophecy*. Edinburgh: T. & T. Clark, 1903.

Frederic W. Farrar, *History of Interpretation*. London: The Macmillan Co., 1886.

Bernard Ramm, *Protestant Biblical Interpretation*. Chicago: Moody Press, 1953 (second ed., 1957).

19. ARCHAEOLOGICAL CONFIRMATION OF THE OLD TESTAMENT

W. F. Albright, *Recent Discoveries in Bible Lands*. New York: Funk & Wagnalls, 1955.

———, *The Archaeology of Palestine*. London, Baltimore: Penguin Books, 1956.

F. F. Bruce, *Second Thoughts on the Dead Sea Scrolls*. 1957.

W. Millar Burrows, *What Mean These Stones?* New Haven, Conn.: American Schools of Oriental Research, 1941.

G. E. Wright, *Biblical Archaeology*. Philadelphia: Westminster Press, 1957.

20. ARCHAEOLOGICAL CONFIRMATION OF THE NEW TESTAMENT

W. F. Albright, "Recent Discoveries in Palestine and the Gospel of St. John," in *The Background of the New Testament and Its Eschatology* (edited by W. D. Davies and D. Daube; C. H. Dodd *Festschrift*), pp. 153-172. Cambridge University Press, 1956.

E. M. Blaiklock, *Out of the Earth*. Grand Rapids: Wm. B. Eerdmans Publishing Co., 1957.

F. F. Bruce, "Qumran and Early Christianity," in *New Testament Studies* II(1955-56), pp. 176-190.

M. Burrows, *The Dead Sea Scrolls*. New York: The Viking Press, 1955.

A. Deissmann, *Light from the Ancient East* (English translation). London: Hodder & Stoughton, 1927.

J. Finegan, *Light from the Ancient Past*. London: Oxford University Press, 1946. Pp. 209-352.

W. M. Ramsay, *The Bearing of Recent Discovery on the Trustworthiness of the New Testament*. London: Hodder & Stoughton, 1915.

R. Syme, "Galatia and Pamphylia under Augustus: the Governorships of Piso, Quirinius and Silvanus," in *Klio* XXVII, 1934, pp. 122-148.

21. REVERSALS OF OLD TESTAMENT CRITICISM

G. Ch. Aalders, *De huidige stand der Oud-testamentische wetenschap*, 1957.

Herbert F. Hahn, *The Old Testament in Modern Research*. Philadelphia: Muhlenberg, 1956.

Emil G. Kraeling, *The Old Testament Since the Reformation*. New York: Harper & Brothers, 1955.

Hans Joachim Kraus, *Geschichte der historisch-kritischen Erforschung des Alten Testaments*. 1956.

H. H. Rowley (ed.), *Old Testament and Modern Study* (second ed.). Oxford University Press, 1953.

Edward J. Young, *An Introduction to the Old Testament* (second ed.)
Grand Rapids: Wm. B. Eerdmans Publishing Co., 1954.

22. REVERSALS OF NEW TESTAMENT CRITICISM

W. F. Albright, "Recent Discoveries in Palestine and the Gospel of St.
John," in *The Background of the New Testament and Its Eschatology*,
pp. 153–171.

Henry J. Cadbury, *The Book of Acts in History*. London: A. & C. Black,
1956.

William Hendriksen, *New Testament Commentary: I & II Timothy and
Titus*. Grand Rapids: Baker Book House, 1957.

D. E. Nineham (ed.), *Studies in the Gospels*. Oxford: Basil Blackwell,
1955. See particularly A. M. Farrer: "On Dispensing with Q," pp.
55–88.

W. M. Ramsay, *The Bearing of Recent Discovery on the Trutsworthiness of
the New Testament*. 1920, pp. 35–52, 79–89.

———, *Luke, the Physician*. London: Hodder & Stoughton, 1908, pp. 1–68.

———, *Pauline and Other Studies*. New York: A. C. Armstrong & Son,
1906. Pp. 3–23, 191–202, 301–324.

E. K. Simpson, *The Pastoral Epistles*. Grand Rapids: Wm. B. Eerdmans Co.,
1954.

H. B. Swete (ed.), *Cambridge Biblical Essays*. London: Macmillan & Co.,
1909. Cf. especially Allan E. Brooke, "The Historical Value of the
Fourth Gospel," pp. 289–328, and Henry L. Jackson, "The Present
State of the Synoptic Problem," pp. 421–460.

23. AUTHORITY AND THE BIBLE

J. Norval Geldenhuys, *Supreme Authority*. Grand Rapids: Wm. B. Eerdmans Publishing Co., 1953; London: Marshall, Morgan and Scott,
1953.

Carl F. H. Henry, "Revelation and the Bible," in *Christianity Today*, June
9, 1958, pp. 5 ff.

Ned B. Stonehouse, "The Authority of the New Testament" in *The Infallible
Word*.

Edward J. Young, "The Authority of the Old Testament" in *The Infallible Word*.

24. THE UNITY OF THE BIBLE

A. C. Gaebelein, *The Harmony of the Prophetic Word*. New York: Fleming
H. Revell Co., 1905.

Floyd E. Hamilton, *The Basis of Christian Faith*. New York: Harper &
Brothers, 1948.

Francis L. Patton, *Fundamental Christianity*. New York: The Macmillan
Company, 1926.

Arthur T. Pierson, *The Bible and Spiritual Criticism*. New York: The Baker
& Taylor Co., 1905.

Adolph Saphir, *Christ and the Scriptures*. London: Morgan, n.d.

B. B. Warfield, "Inspiration," in *The International Standard Bible Encyclopedia*, Vol. III, pp. 1473–83.

AUTHOR INDEX

SUBJECT INDEX

Acts, date of, 357 f.
Acts and Epistles, harmony of, 248
Apocrypha, 138, 159 ff., 166 ff., 171-185
    attitude of Fathers and Early
        Church, 176 f.
    New Testament attitude, 175
    value of, 185
Archaeology, Old Testament, 301-316,
        339, 347
    New Testament, 319-331
Authority, 7, 84, 94, 99, 103, 134, 157,
    168, 190, 191, 193, 221, 222, 371-386, 390

Belgic Confession, 15
Bible, date of writings, 9, 263
    unity of, 389-401
    witness of, 10, 71, 91 f., 95 ff., 99,
        134, 195, 213, 225, 230, 270 ff.
    witness of (to its own inspiration),
        78, 84 ff., 107-118, 250
Bibliolatry, 96, 232, 400 f.

Canon, 72, 138
    Old Testament, 155-168, 173
    Old Testament, Roman Catholic
        view, 171 f., 190
    New Testament, 189-201
    New Testament, acceptance in
        Early Church, 197 ff.
Canons of Dort, 17
Chronology, problems of, 240 f.
Council of Trent, 14, 19
Criticism, higher, O.T., 335-350
    N.T., 353-367

Dead Sea Scrolls, 142, 315, 319, 329,
        361

Ecumenism, 8
Empiricism, 33, 34, 216
Encounter, 7, 9, 52 f., 71, 96, 100 ff.,
        228
    and language, 64 ff.
Ethical harmony, 249

Faith and reason, 29 ff.
Form Criticism, 242, 339, 355 ff.
Fourth Gospel, problems of, 358 f.
Fundamentalist, 8

General revelation, 9, 13 ff.
    common grace, 20 f.
    conscience, 21
    and faith, 18 ff.
    and guilt, 15 ff., 19
    and the heathen, 20
    and the Law, 20
    natural theology, 15, 17, 30 ff.
    and non-Christian religions, 27
    and special revelation, 21 ff.

History of Religions School, 13, 45, 346

Idealism, 46 ff., 215
Illumination, definition of, 222
Imago Dei, 9, 41
Inerrancy, Preface, 94, 98, 99, 107, 134,
        213 f., 222, 232 f., 237 f., 250
    and scientific criteria, 239
Inspiration, 9
    alien conceptions, 206-216
    Church doctrine of, 90, 205-217
    Patristic period, 207 f.
    Medieval, 209
    Reformation, 210 ff.
    Post-Reformation, 212 ff.
    18th century rationalism, 214 f.
    Church view, 233 f., 237 f.
    degrees of, 222
    degrees excluded, 213
    dictation theory, 95 f., 208 f., 222
    meaning of, 107 f.
    New Testament view, 84 ff.
    plenary, 272 ff.
    Reformation view, 90
    Roman Catholic view, 90
    verbal, 41, 43 ff., 69, 100, 149 f.,
        210, 222 f., 228, 233, 237
Irrationalism, 35, 37 f.

Jesus, use of Scripture, 79 ff.
    view of Scripture, 121-134, 224, 237

Liberalism, 7 ff., 216, 221, 253, 260

Natural theology, 2, 3, 30 ff., 91
Neo-orthodoxy, 7 ff., 35 ff., 49 ff., 53 ff.,
        90, 93 ff., 221, 225, 233
New Covenant, 79 ff.

46889